SAMS
Teach Yourself

Microsoft® Office
Access 2003

in 24 Hours

Alison Balter

SAMS   *800 E. 96th St., Indianapolis, Indiana 46240 USA*

Sams Teach Yourself Microsoft Office Access 2003 in 24 Hours

Copyright © 2004 by Sams Publishing

International Standard Book Number: 0-672-32545-4

Library of Congress Catalog Card Number: 2003093135

Printed in the United States of America

First Printing: August 2003

08 07 06   8 7 6 5 4

Bulk Sales

Sams Publishing offers excellent discounts on this book when ordered in quantity for bulk purchases or special sales. For more information, please contact:

> **U.S. Corporate and Government Sales**
> **1-800-382-3419**
> corpsales@pearsontechgroup.com

For sales outside of the U.S., please contact:

> **International Sales**
> international@pearsoned.com

Trademarks

All terms mentioned in this book that are known to be trademarks or service marks have been appropriately capitalized. Sams Publishing cannot attest to the accuracy of this information. Use of a term in this book should not be regarded as affecting the validity of any trademark or service mark.

Warning and Disclaimer

Every effort has been made to make this book as complete and as accurate as possible, but no warranty or fitness is implied. The information provided is on an "as is" basis. The author and the publisher shall have neither liability nor responsibility to any person or entity with respect to any loss or damages arising from the information contained in this book.

ASSOCIATE PUBLISHER
Michael Stephens

ACQUISITIONS EDITOR
Loretta Yates

DEVELOPMENT EDITOR
Audrey Doyle

MANAGING EDITOR
Charlotte Clapp

PROJECT EDITOR
Elizabeth Finney

COPY EDITOR
Kitty Jarrett

INDEXER
Erika Millen

PROOFREADER
Leslie Joseph

TECHNICAL EDITOR
Greg Perry

TEAM COORDINATOR
Cindy Teeters

MULTIMEDIA DEVELOPER
Dan Scherf

INTERIOR DESIGNER
Gary Adair

COVER DESIGNER
Alan Clements

Contents at a Glance

Contents

Part V Advanced Topics   393

HOUR 18 Sharing Data with Other Applications   395

HOUR 19 Access and the Internet   415

About the Author

Alison Balter is the president of InfoTechnology Partners, Inc., a computer consulting firm based in Camarillo, California. Alison is a highly experienced independent trainer and consultant specializing in Windows applications training and development. During her 19 years in the computer industry, she has trained and consulted with many corporations and government agencies. Since Alison founded InfoTechnology Partners, Inc. (formerly Marina Consulting Group) in 1990, its client base has expanded to include major corporations and government agencies such as Shell Oil, Accenture, Northrop, the U.S. Drug Enforcement Administration, Prudential Insurance, Transamerica Insurance, Fox Broadcasting, the U.S. Navy, and others.

InfoTechnology Partners, Inc., is a Microsoft Certified Partner, and Alison is a Microsoft Certified Professional. Alison was one of the first professionals in the computer industry to become a Microsoft Certified Solutions Developer.

Alison is the author of more than 300 internationally marketed computer training videos, including 18 Access 2000 videos, 35 Access 2002 videos, and 15 Access 2003 videos. These videos are available by contacting Alison's company, InfoTechnology Partners, Inc. Alison travels throughout North America, giving training seminars on Microsoft Access, Visual Studio .NET, Microsoft SQL Server, Visual Basic, and Visual Basic for Applications. She is also featured in several live satellite television broadcasts for National Technological University.

Alison is a regular contributing columnist for *Access/Office/VB Advisor* as well as other computer publications. She is also a regular on the Access, Visual Studio .NET, SQL Server, and Visual Basic national speaker circuits. She was one of four speakers on the Visual Basic 4.0 and 5.0 World Tours seminar series cosponsored by Application Developers Training Company and Microsoft.

Alison is also author of five other books published by Sams Publishing: *Alison Balter's Mastering Access 95 Development*, *Alison Balter's Mastering Access 97 Development*, *Alison Balter's Mastering Access 2000 Development*, *Alison Balter's Mastering Access 2002 Desktop Development*, and *Alison Balter's Mastering Access 2002 Enterprise Development*. Alison is a co-author of three Access books published by Sams Publishing: *Essential Access 95*, *Access 95 Unleashed*, and *Access 97 Unleashed*.

An active participant in many user groups and other organizations, Alison is a past president of the Independent Computer Consultants Association of Los Angeles and of the Los Angeles Clipper Users' Group.

On a personal note, Alison keeps herself busy horseback riding, skiing, ice skating, running, lifting weights, hiking, traveling, and dancing. She most enjoys spending time with her husband, Dan, their daughter, Alexis, their son, Brendan, and their golden retriever, Brandy.

Alison's firm, InfoTechnology Partners, Inc., is available for consulting work and onsite training in Microsoft Access, Visual Studio .NET, Visual Basic, and SQL Server, as well as for Windows Server 2003, Windows 2000, Windows NT, Windows 98, Windows XP, PC networking, and Microsoft Exchange Server. You can contact Alison by email at `Alison@InfoTechnologyPartners.com`, or visit the InfoTechnology Partners Web site, at `www.InfoTechnologyPartners.com`.

Dedication

I dedicate this book to my husband, Dan, my daughter, Alexis, my son, Brendan, my parents, Charlotte and Bob, and my real father, Herman. Dan, you are my partner in life and the wind beneath my wings. You are a true partner in every sense of the word. I am so lucky to be traveling the path of life with such a spectacular person. Alexis, you are the sweet little girl that I always dreamed of. You are everything that I could have ever wanted and so very much more. You make every one of my days a happy one! Brendan, you are the one who keeps me on my toes. There is never a dull moment with you around. I wish I had just a small portion of your energy. I thank you for the endless laughter that you bring to our family and for reminding me about all the important things in life. Mom and Dad, without all that you do to help out with life's chores, the completion of this book could never have been possible. Words cannot express my gratitude!

Herman, I credit my ability to soar in such a technical field to you. I hope that I inherited just a small part of your intelligence, wit, and fortitude. I am sorry that you did not live to see this accomplishment. I hope that you can see my work and that you are proud of it. I also hope that in some way you share in the joy that Dan, Alexis, and Brendan bring to me.

Finally, I want to thank God for giving me the gift of gab, a wonderful career, an incredible husband, two beautiful children, a very special home, and an awesome life. Through Your grace, I am truly blessed.

Acknowledgments

Writing a book is a monumental task. Without the support and understanding of those close to me, my dreams for this book would have never come to fruition. Special thanks go to the following special people who helped to make this book possible:

Dan Balter (my incredible husband), for his ongoing support, love, encouragement, friendship, and, as usual, being patient with me while I wrote this book. Dan, words cannot adequately express the love and appreciation that I feel for all that you are and all that you do for me. You treat me like a princess! Thank you for being the phenomenal person you are. I enjoy sharing not only our career successes, but even more I enjoy sharing the life of our beautiful children, Alexis and Brendan. I look forward to continuing to reach highs we never dreamed of. There is no one I'd rather spend forever with than you.

Alexis Balter (my precious daughter), for giving life a special meaning. Your intelligence, compassion, caring, and perceptiveness are far beyond your years. Alexis, you make all my hard work worth it. No matter how bad my day, when I look at you, sunshine fills my life. You are the most special gift that anyone has ever given me.

Brendan Balter (my adorable son), for showing me the power of persistence. Brendan, you are small, but, boy, are you mighty! I have never seen such tenacity and fortitude in such a little person. Your imagination and creativity are amazing! Thank you for your sweetness, your sensitivity, and your unconditional love. Most of all, thank you for reminding me how important it is to have a sense of humor.

Charlotte and Bob Roman (Mom and Dad), for believing in me and sharing in both the good times and the bad. Mom and Dad, without your special love and support, I never would have become who I am today. Without all your help, I could never get everything done. Words can never express how much I appreciate all that you do!

Al Ludington, for helping me to slow down and experience the shades of gray in the world. You somehow walk the fine line between being there and setting limits, between comforting me and confronting me. Words cannot express how much your unconditional love means to me. Thanks for showing me that a beautiful mind is not such a bad thing after all.

Sue Terry, for being the most wonderful best friend anyone could possibly have. You inspire me with your music, your love, your friendship, and your faith in God. Whenever I am having a bad day, I picture you singing "Dear God" or "Make Me Whole," and suddenly my day gets better. Thank you for the gift of friendship.

Roz, Ron, and Charlie Carriere, for supporting my endeavors and for encouraging me to pursue my writing. It means a lot to know that you guys are proud of me for what I do. I enjoy our times together as a family. Charlie, have a great time at Yale.

Steven Chait, for being a special brother. I want you to know how much you mean to me. When I was a little girl, I was told about your gift to write. You may not know this, but my desire to write started as a little girl, wanting to be like her big brother.

Sonia Aguilar, for being the best nanny that anyone could ever dream of having. You are a person far too special to describe in words. I can't tell you how much it means to know that Alexis and Brendan have someone so loving and caring with whom to spend their days. You are an amazing model of love, kindness, and charity.

Doug and Karen Sylvester, for being wonderful friends. You are loads of fun to be with and are always there when we need you. We are so glad you are such an integral part of our lives.

Anita Srinivasa, for being a wonderful friend, doctor, and confidante. You've been there in both the good times and the bad and have known when to step in and when not to. You are a very special person, and I hope that you are always a part of our lives.

Greggory Peck from Blast Through Learning, for your contribution to my success in this industry. I believe that the opportunities you gave me early on have helped me reach a level in this industry that would have been much more difficult for me to reach on my own.

Edie Swanson, for being a great assistant. Thanks for making my day-to-day work life easier.

Diane Dennis, Shell Forman, Joyce Milner, Bob Hess, Scott Barker, Ron Henderson, Norbert Foigelman, Chris Sabihon, and all the other wonderful friends that I have in my life. Diane, you have been my soul mate in life since we were four! Shell, my special "sister," I am lucky to have such a special friend as you. Joyce, miles can't keep our hearts apart. I only wish that we could see more of each other. Bob, you are always there when we need you, and you somehow manage to keep a smile on your face. Scott, you have always been a great business and personal support. Ron, you started out as a client but have a *very* special place in my heart. Norbert, you are a very special friend to me and to my family. Chris, not only are you a special friend, but you have had an important impact on my spiritual path in life!

Jack Gupton, my friends at the Archdiocese of Los Angeles, Ellen McCrea, Tim Wade, Peter Hapke, Bruce Doering, Glenn Berger, Steve Flint, Chuck Hinkle, and all the other special clients and work associates that I have in my life. Although all of you started out as work associates, I feel that our relationship goes much deeper than that. I am *very* lucky to have people in my work life like you. Thank you all for your patience with my schedule as I wrote this book.

Kim Spilker, Loretta Yates, Audrey Doyle, Elizabeth Finney, Charlotte Clapp, Kitty Jarrett, and Greg Perry for making my experience with Sams a positive one. I know that you all worked very hard to ensure that this book came out on time and with the best quality possible. Without you, this book wouldn't have happened. I have *really* enjoyed working with *all* of you over these past several months. I appreciate your thoughtfulness and your sensitivity to my schedule and commitments outside this book. It is nice to work with people who appreciate me as a person, not just as an author.

We Want to Hear from You!

As the reader of this book, *you* are our most important critic and commentator. We value your opinion and want to know what we're doing right, what we could do better, what areas you'd like to see us publish in, and any other words of wisdom you're willing to pass our way.

As an associate publisher for Sams Publishing, I welcome your comments. You can email or write me directly to let me know what you did or didn't like about this book—as well as what we can do to make our books better.

Please note that I cannot help you with technical problems related to the *topic* of this book. We do have a User Services group, however, where I will forward specific technical questions related to the book.

When you write, please be sure to include this book's title and author as well as your name, email address, and phone number. I will carefully review your comments and share them with the author and editors who worked on the book.

Email: feedback@samspublishing.com

Mail: Michael Stephens
            Associate Publisher
            Sams Publishing
            800 East 96th Street
            Indianapolis, IN 46240 USA

For more information about this book or another Sams title, visit our Web site, at www.samspublishing.com. Type the ISBN (excluding hyphens) or the title of a book in the Search field to find the page you're looking for.

Introduction

Welcome to *Sams Teach Yourself Microsoft Office Access 2003 in 24 Hours*! This book is composed of 24 one-hour lessons designed to teach you the basics of working with the very powerful database product Access.

This book is divided into five parts. Part I is "Introduction to Relational Databases and Access 2003." As its name implies, this part is an overview to both relational databases and Access. In this part you'll learn the types of tasks you can perform in Access. You'll also get a preview of Microsoft Access, and of the various database components.

The hours in Part II, "Working with Existing Databases and Objects," are designed to provide you with all the skills necessary to work with existing databases, tables, queries, forms, and reports. Many people who use Access are not responsible for designing databases or the objects within them. They are simply responsible for entering new data, modifying or viewing existing data, and running queries and reports. Part II provides all the necessary skills to perform these important tasks.

Part III, "Creating Your Own Database and Objects," is for those of you who are ready to roll up your sleeves and get involved in the design of database objects. Part III teaches you how to create databases with and without the use of wizards. You'll learn how to create tables and establish relationships. Then you'll learn the basic skills necessary to build queries, forms, and reports. Finally, you'll learn how to automate databases by using macros.

Part IV, "Power Access Techniques," is for those of you who are power users or wish to get started as developers. In Part IV you'll learn power table techniques, power query techniques, power form techniques, and power report techniques. Armed with these power techniques, you will be ready to take full advantage of all the features that tables, queries, forms, and reports have to offer.

Part V, "Advanced Topics," includes several important additional topics. This part begins by showing you how you can share Access data with other applications, such as Microsoft Excel. You'll then learn how Access integrates with the Internet. Part V then covers special topics such as database administration, database documentation, and database security. If you are interested in application development, you should take a look at Hour 23, "Modules Introduced," which provides an introduction to modules and application development with Access 2003. The final hour covers the process of adding important finishing touches to the databases that you build.

Access is a very fun and exciting database tool to work with. With the keys to deliver all that it offers, you can produce databases that provide much satisfaction and solve important business problems. After you complete this hands-on guide, you, too, can become masterful at this very powerful database tool. This book is dedicated to demonstrating how you can fulfill the promise of making Access 2003 perform up to its lofty capabilities. As you will see, you have the ability to really make Access 2003 shine in the everyday world!

Conventions Used in This Book

The people at Sams Publishing have spent many years developing and publishing computer books designed for ease of use and to contain the most up-to-date information available. With that experience, we've learned what features help you the most. Look for these features throughout the book to help enhance your learning experience and get the most out of Access:

- Screen messages, code listings, and command samples appear in `monospace type`.
- Uniform resource locators (URLs) used to identify pages on the Web and values for HTML attributes also appear in `monospace type`.
- Terms that are defined in the text appear in *italics*. *Italics* are sometimes used for emphasis, too. If a term is defined in a paragraph, a new term icon appears at the beginning of the paragraph.
- In code lines, placeholders for variables are indicated by `italic monospace type`.

Tips give advice on quick or overlooked procedures, including shortcuts.

Notes present useful or interesting information that isn't necessarily essential to the current discussion but might augment your understanding with background material or advice related to the topic.

Cautions warn you about potential problems a procedure might cause, unexpected results, or mistakes that could prove costly.

PART I

Introduction to Relational Databases and Access 2003

HOUR 1

Relational Databases and Office Access 2003 Introduced

In talking to users and developers, I find that Access is a very misunderstood product. Many people think that it is just a toy for managers or secretaries wanting to play with data. Others feel that it is a serious developers' product intended for no one but experienced application developers. This hour dispels the myths of Access. It helps you to decipher what Access is and what it isn't. After reading the text in this hour, you will know when Access is the tool for you and when it makes sense to explore other products.

In this hour you'll learn the following:

- What types of things you can do with Access
- How to start Microsoft Access
- How to open an existing database
- How to work with the Database window
- How to work with the various components of an Access database

What Is a Relational Database?

NEW TERM The term *database* means different things to different people. For many years, in the world of xBase (that is, dBASE, FoxPro, CA-Clipper), *database* was used to describe a collection of fields and records. (Access refers to this type of collection as a *table*.) In a client/server environment, *database* refers to all the data, schema, indexes, rules, triggers, and stored procedures associated with a system. In Access terms, a *database* is a collection of all the tables, queries, forms, data access pages, reports, macros, and modules that compose a complete system. *Relational* refers to the fact that the tables that comprise the database relate to one another.

What Types of Things Can I Do with Microsoft Access?

I often find myself explaining exactly what types of applications you can build with Microsoft Access. Access offers a variety of features for different database needs. You can use it to develop six general types of applications:

- Personal applications
- Small-business applications
- Departmental applications
- Corporationwide applications
- Front-end applications for enterprisewide client/server databases
- Intranet/Internet applications

Access as a Development Platform for Personal Applications

At a basic level, you can use Access to develop simple personal database-management systems. I know people who automate everything from their wine collections to their home finances. The one thing to be careful of is that Access is deceptively easy to use. Its wonderful built-in wizards make Access look like a product that anyone can use. After answering a series of questions, you have finished application switchboards that allow you to easily navigate around the application, data-entry screens, and reports, as well as the underlying tables that support them. In fact, when Microsoft first released Access, many people asked if I was concerned that my business as a computer programmer and trainer would diminish because Access seemed to let absolutely anyone write a database application. Although it's true that you can produce the simplest of Access applications without any thought for design and without any customization, most applications require at least some design and customization.

If you're an end user and don't want to spend too much time learning the intricacies of Access, you'll be satisfied with Access as long as you're happy with a wizard-generated personal application. After reading this text, you can make minor modifications, and no problems should occur. It's when you want to substantially customize a personal application without the proper knowledge base that problems can happen.

Access as a Development Platform for Small-Business Applications

Access is an excellent platform for developing an application that can run a small business. Its wizards let you quickly and easily build the application's foundation. The ability to build code modules allows power users and developers to create code libraries of reusable functions, and the ability to add code behind forms and reports allows them to create powerful custom forms and reports.

The main limitation of using Access for developing a custom small-business application is the time and money involved in the development process. Many people use Access wizards to begin the development process but find they need to customize their applications in ways they can't accomplish on their own. Small-business owners often experience this problem on an even greater scale than personal users. The demands of a small-business application are usually much higher than those of a personal application. Many doctors, attorneys, and other professionals have called me in after they reached a dead end in the development process. They're always dismayed at how much money it will cost to make their application usable. An example is a doctor who built a series of forms and reports to automate her office. All went well until it came time to produce patient billings, enter payments, and product receivable reports. Although at first glance these processes seem simple, upon further examination, the doctor realized that the wizard-produced reports and forms did not provide the sophistication necessary for her billing process. Unfortunately, the doctor did not have the time or programming skills to add the necessary features. So, in using Access as a tool to develop small-business applications, it is important that you be realistic about the time and money involved in developing anything but the simplest of applications.

Access as a Development Platform for Departmental Applications

Access is perfect for developing applications for departments in large corporations. Most departments in large corporations have the development budgets to produce well-designed applications.

Fortunately, most departments also usually have a PC guru who is more than happy to help design forms and reports. This gives the department a sense of ownership because it has contributed to the development of its application. If complex form or report design or coding is necessary, large corporations usually have on-site resources available that can provide the necessary assistance. If the support is not available within the corporation, most corporations are willing to outsource to obtain the necessary expertise.

Access as a Development Platform for Corporationwide Applications

Although Access might be best suited for departmental applications, you can also use it to produce applications that you distribute throughout an organization. How successful this endeavor is depends on the corporation. There's a limit to the number of users who can concurrently share an Access application while maintaining acceptable performance, and there's also a limit to the number of records that each table can contain without a significant performance drop. These numbers vary depending on factors such as the following:

- How much traffic already exists on the network.
- How much RAM and how many processors the server has.
- How the server is already being used. For example, are applications such as Microsoft Office being loaded from the server or from local workstations?
- What types of tasks the users of the application are performing. For example, are they querying, entering data, running reports, and so on?
- Where Access and Access applications are run from (the server or the workstation).
- What network operating system is in place.

My general rule of thumb for an Access application that's not client/server based is that poor performance generally results with more than 10–15 concurrent users and more than 100,000 records. Remember that these numbers vary immensely depending on the factors mentioned, as well as on the what you and the users define as acceptable performance. If you go beyond these limits, you should consider using Access as a front end to a client/server database such as Microsoft SQL Server—that is, you can use Access to create forms and reports while storing tables and possibly queries on the database server.

Access as a Front End for Enterprisewide Client/Server Applications

A client/server database, such as Microsoft SQL Server or Oracle, processes queries on the server machine and returns results to the workstation. The server software itself can't display data to the user, so this is where Access comes to the rescue. Acting as a front end, Access can display the data retrieved from the database server in reports, datasheets, or forms. If the user updates the data in an Access form, the workstation sends the update to the back-end database. You can accomplish this process either by linking to these external databases so that they appear to both you and the user as Access tables or by using techniques to access client/server data directly.

Alison Balter's Mastering Access 2002 Enterprise Development, published by Sams, covers the details of developing client/server applications with Microsoft Access.

Access as a Development Platform for Intranet/Internet Applications

NEW TERM By using *data access pages*, intranet and Internet users can update application data from within a browser. *Data access pages* are *Hypertext Markup Language (HTML)* documents that are bound directly to data in a database. Although Access stores data access pages outside a database, you use them just as you do standard Access forms except that Microsoft designed them to run in Microsoft Internet Explorer 5.5 or higher, rather than in Microsoft Access. Data access pages use dynamic HTML in order to accomplish their work. Because they are supported only in Internet Explorer 5.5 or higher, data access pages are much more appropriate as an intranet solution than as an Internet solution.

NEW TERM In addition to using data access pages, you can also publish database objects as either static or dynamic HTML pages. *Static HTML pages* are standard HTML pages that you can view in any browser. You can publish database objects either dynamically to the HTX/IDC file format or to the ASP (Active Server Pages) file format. *Dynamically* means that these pages are published by the Web server each time that they are rendered. The Web server publishes HTX/IDC files dynamically, and these files are therefore browser independent. The Web Server also dynamically publishes ASP files published by Microsoft Access, but the published ASP pages require Internet Explorer 4.0 or higher on the client machine.

Access 2002 introduced the ability to create Extensible Markup Language (XML) data and schema documents from Jet or SQL Server structures and data. You can also import data and data structures into Access from XML documents. You can accomplish this either using code or via the user interface.

Starting Microsoft Access

The first step in getting started with using Access is to launch Microsoft Access. You launch Microsoft Access from the Start menu or from a desktop shortcut.

To start Access from the Start menu, you select Start|Programs|Microsoft Office| Microsoft Office Access 2003. The Access Desktop with the Getting Started window appears (see Figure 1.1). Here you can get help, open an existing database, or create a new database.

FIGURE 1.1

The Getting Started window.

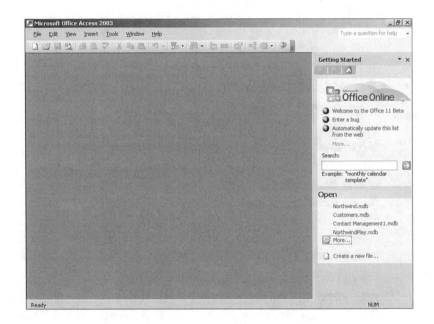

To start Access from a desktop shortcut, with the Windows desktop active, you simply double-click the Desktop shortcut. Access launches.

When you first launch Access, a special window, called the task pane, appears on the right-hand side of the screen. From the task pane, you can easily open a recently used database, create a new database of any type, or navigate to any database stored locally or on a network drive.

Opening an Existing Database

NEW TERM After you have started Access, you can create a new database or open an existing database. A *database* is a single file that contains *objects* such as tables, queries, forms, and reports. A database is stored as a file on your computer or on a network computer. To work with the objects in a database, you must open the database file.

To open an existing database from the Getting Started window, follow these steps:

1. Click More... under the Open options. The Open dialog box appears (see Figure 1.2).

FIGURE 1.2

The Open dialog box.

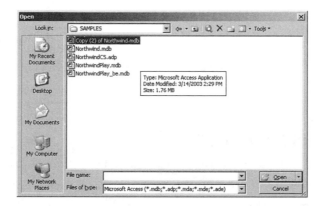

2. If necessary, open the Look In drop-down list box to select another drive or directory.
3. Click to select the filename of the database you want to open.
4. Click Open. Access opens the database.

To open a recently used database from the Getting Started window, follow these steps:

1. Locate the database in the list of files in the Getting Started window.
2. Click the link to the desired database. Access opens the database.

To open an existing database from the File menu, follow these steps:

1. Choose File|Open. The Open dialog box appears (refer to Figure 1.2).
2. If necessary, open the Look In drop-down list box to select another drive or directory.
3. Click to select the filename of the database you want to open.
4. Click Open. Access opens the database.

To open a recently used database from the File menu, follow these steps:

1. Open the File menu.

2. Locate the desired database in the list of recently used files at the bottom of the File menu.

3. Click to select the desired file. Access opens the database.

> You can open only one database at a time. When you open a database, Access automatically closes the currently open database.

> On the Open dialog box, you can click My Recent Documents to open a database that you have recently worked with. You can click Desktop, My Documents, My Computer, or My Network Places to quickly locate documents stored in those special places.

The Access Desktop

The Access Desktop contains a title bar, a menu bar, one or more toolbars, and the Database window (see Figure 1.3).

FIGURE 1.3

The Access Desktop.

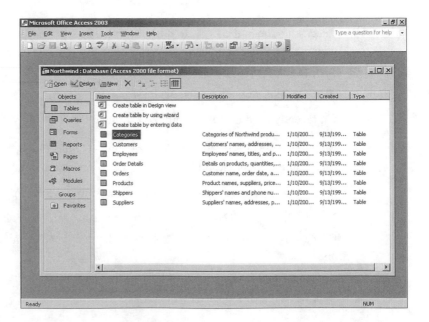

Menu bars and toolbars change, depending on the view you are in at any given time. For example, when you look at a table object, there are tools on the toolbar that are appropriate when working with tables. When you are in Design view for a form, you see tools appropriate for designing a form.

The Database Window

When you open a database, the Database window appears (refer to Figure 1.3). The Database window, which appears within the Access desktop window, allows you to select any of the Objects tabs. In Figure 1.3, for example, the Tables tab is selected. In addition to what its parent window, the Access desktop window, contains, the Database window contains its own buttons and objects. Table 1.1 describes these buttons and objects and what they do. The objects are discussed in more detail in the sections that follow.

TABLE 1.1   The Buttons and Objects in the Database Window

Button/Object	Description
Open	Opens the object you have selected.
Design	Allows you to modify the design of the selected object.
New	Opens a new object based on the type of object selected.
Tables	Lists the tables in the database. Each table contains data about a particular subject.
Queries	Lists the queries in the database. Each query is a stored question about data in the database.
Forms	Lists the forms in the database. Each form allows you to view, add, edit, and delete data.
Reports	Lists the reports for the database. Each report allows you to send table data to the printer or screen in a format that you define.
Pages	Lists the data access pages. This allows viewing of and working with data from the Internet or an intranet.
Macros	Lists the macros created to automate the way you work with data.
Modules	Lists the modules of programming code created for the database.
Groups/Favorites	Allows you to create your own groups of favorite objects that you frequently work with (forms, reports, and so on). An example would be sales reports.

A Preview of the Database Components

As mentioned previously, tables, queries, forms, reports, data access pages, macros, and modules combine to comprise an Access database. Each of these objects has a special function. The following sections take you on a tour of the objects that make up an Access database.

Tables: A Repository for Data

Tables are the starting point for an application. Whether data is stored in an Access database or you are referencing external data by using linked tables, all the other objects in a database either directly or indirectly reference tables.

To view all the tables that are contained in an open database, you click the Tables icon in the Objects list. (Note that you don't see any hidden tables unless you have checked the Hidden Objects check box in the Options dialog box's View page.) If you want to view the data in a table, you double-click the name of the table you want to view. (You can also select the table and then click the Open button.) Access displays the table's data in a datasheet that includes all the table's fields and records (see Figure 1.4). You can modify many of the datasheet's attributes and even search for and filter data from within the datasheet. If the table is related to another table (such as the `Northwind Customers` and `Orders` tables), you can also expand and collapse the subdatasheet to view data stored in child tables. Hour 2, "Tables Introduced," covers these techniques.

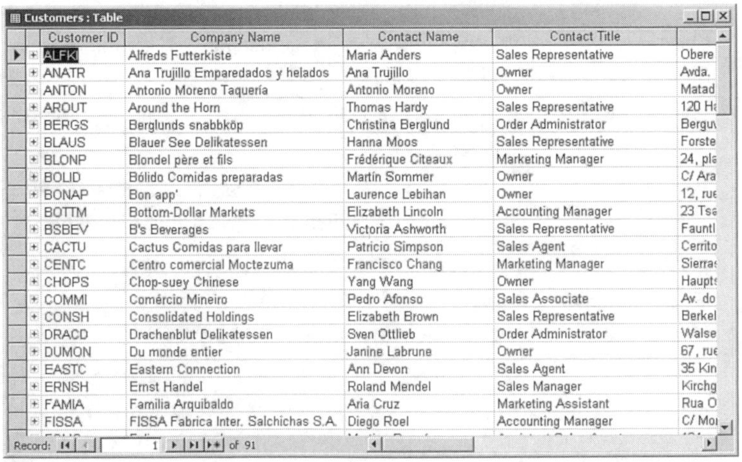
Customers : Table

Customer ID	Company Name	Contact Name	Contact Title	
ALFKI	Alfreds Futterkiste	Maria Anders	Sales Representative	Obere
ANATR	Ana Trujillo Emparedados y helados	Ana Trujillo	Owner	Avda.
ANTON	Antonio Moreno Taquería	Antonio Moreno	Owner	Matad
AROUT	Around the Horn	Thomas Hardy	Sales Representative	120 Ha
BERGS	Berglunds snabbköp	Christina Berglund	Order Administrator	Bergu
BLAUS	Blauer See Delikatessen	Hanna Moos	Sales Representative	Forste
BLONP	Blondel père et fils	Frédérique Citeaux	Marketing Manager	24, pla
BOLID	Bólido Comidas preparadas	Martín Sommer	Owner	C/ Ara
BONAP	Bon app'	Laurence Lebihan	Owner	12, rue
BOTTM	Bottom-Dollar Markets	Elizabeth Lincoln	Accounting Manager	23 Tsa
BSBEV	B's Beverages	Victoria Ashworth	Sales Representative	Fauntl
CACTU	Cactus Comidas para llevar	Patricio Simpson	Sales Agent	Cerrito
CENTC	Centro comercial Moctezuma	Francisco Chang	Marketing Manager	Sierras
CHOPS	Chop-suey Chinese	Yang Wang	Owner	Haupts
COMMI	Comércio Mineiro	Pedro Afonso	Sales Associate	Av. do
CONSH	Consolidated Holdings	Elizabeth Brown	Sales Representative	Berkel
DRACD	Drachenblut Delikatessen	Sven Ottlieb	Order Administrator	Walse
DUMON	Du monde entier	Janine Labrune	Owner	67, rue
EASTC	Eastern Connection	Ann Devon	Sales Agent	35 Kin
ERNSH	Ernst Handel	Roland Mendel	Sales Manager	Kirchg
FAMIA	Familia Arquibaldo	Aria Cruz	Marketing Assistant	Rua O
FISSA	FISSA Fabrica Inter. Salchichas S.A.	Diego Roel	Accounting Manager	C/ Moi

Record: 1 of 91

FIGURE 1.4
Datasheet view of the `Customers` *table in the* `Northwind` *database.*

As an Access power user or developer, you will often want to view the table's design, which is the blueprint or template for the table. To view a table's design (see Figure 1.5), you click the Design icon with the table selected. In Design view, you can view or modify all the field names, data types, and field and table properties. Access gives you the power and flexibility you need to customize the design of tables. Hour 8, "Creating Tables," and Hour 14, "Power Table Techniques," cover these topics.

FIGURE 1.5

The design of the Customers *table.*

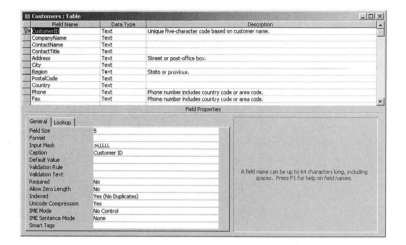

Relationships: Tying the Tables Together

To properly maintain data's integrity and ease the process of working with other objects in a database, you must define relationships among the tables in a database. You accomplish this by using the Relationships window. To view the Relationships window, with the Database window active, you select Tools|Relationships or you click Relationships on the toolbar. In this window, you can view and maintain the relationships in the database (see Figure 1.6). If you or a fellow user or developer have set up some relationships, but you don't see any in the Relationships window, you can select Relationships|Show All to unhide any hidden tables and relationships (you might need to click to expand the menu for this option to appear).

Notice that many of the relationships in Figure 1.6 have join lines between tables and show a number *1* on one side of the join and an infinity symbol on the other. This indicates a one-to-many relationship between the tables. If you double-click a join line, the Edit Relationships dialog box opens (see Figure 1.7). In this dialog box, you can specify the exact nature of the relationship between tables. The relationship between the Customers and Orders tables in Figure 1.7, for example, is a one-to-many relationship with referential integrity enforced. This means that the user cannot add orders for customers who don't exist. Notice in Figure 1.7 that the check box Cascade Update Related

Fields is checked. This means that if the user updates a `CustomerID` field, Access updates all records containing that `CustomerID` value in the `Orders` table. Because Cascade Delete Related Records is not checked in Figure 1.7, the user cannot delete from the `Customers` table customers who have corresponding orders in the `Orders` table.

FIGURE 1.6

The Relationships window, where you view and maintain the relationships in a database.

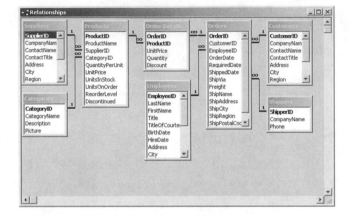

FIGURE 1.7

The Edit Relationships dialog box, which lets you specify the nature of the relationships between tables.

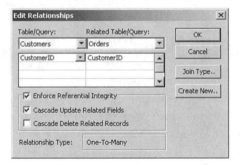

Hour 9, "Creating Relationships," extensively covers the process of defining and maintaining relationships. It also covers the basics of relational database design. For now, you should remember that you should establish relationships both conceptually and literally as early in the design process as possible. Relationships are integral to successfully designing and implementing your application.

Queries: Stored Questions or Actions You Apply to Data

Queries in Access are powerful and multifaceted. A *query* retrieves data from a database based on criteria you specify. An example would be a query that retrieves all employees who live in Florida. Select queries allow you to view, summarize, and perform calculations on the data in tables. Action queries let you add to, update, and delete table data. To run a query, you select Queries from the Objects list and then double-click the query you want to run, or you can click in the list of queries to select the query you want to run and then click Open. When you run a Select query, a datasheet appears, containing all the fields specified in the query and all the records meeting the query's criteria (see Figure 1.8). When you run an Action query, Access runs the specified action, such as making a new table or appending data to an existing table. In general, you can update the data in a query result because the result of a query is actually a dynamic set of records, called a dynaset, that is based on the tables' data. A *dynaset* is a subset of data on which you can base a form or report.

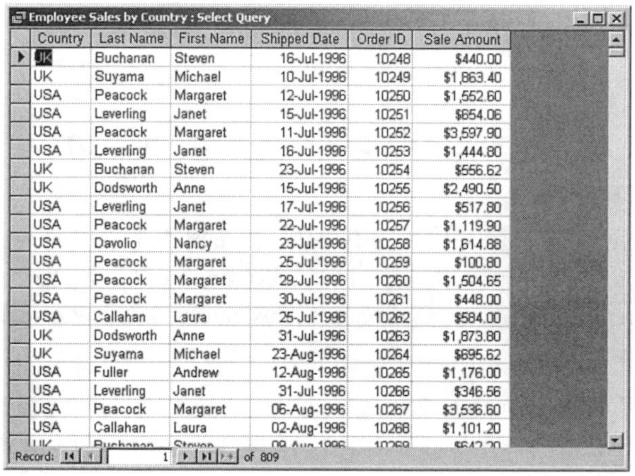

Country	Last Name	First Name	Shipped Date	Order ID	Sale Amount
UK	Buchanan	Steven	16-Jul-1996	10248	$440.00
UK	Suyama	Michael	10-Jul-1996	10249	$1,863.40
USA	Peacock	Margaret	12-Jul-1996	10250	$1,552.60
USA	Leverling	Janet	15-Jul-1996	10251	$654.06
USA	Peacock	Margaret	11-Jul-1996	10252	$3,597.90
USA	Leverling	Janet	16-Jul-1996	10253	$1,444.80
UK	Buchanan	Steven	23-Jul-1996	10254	$556.62
UK	Dodsworth	Anne	15-Jul-1996	10255	$2,490.50
USA	Leverling	Janet	17-Jul-1996	10256	$517.80
USA	Peacock	Margaret	22-Jul-1996	10257	$1,119.90
USA	Davolio	Nancy	23-Jul-1996	10258	$1,614.88
USA	Peacock	Margaret	25-Jul-1996	10259	$100.80
USA	Peacock	Margaret	29-Jul-1996	10260	$1,504.65
USA	Peacock	Margaret	30-Jul-1996	10261	$448.00
USA	Callahan	Laura	25-Jul-1996	10262	$584.00
UK	Dodsworth	Anne	31-Jul-1996	10263	$1,873.80
UK	Suyama	Michael	23-Aug-1996	10264	$695.62
USA	Fuller	Andrew	12-Aug-1996	10265	$1,176.00
USA	Leverling	Janet	31-Jul-1996	10266	$346.56
USA	Peacock	Margaret	06-Aug-1996	10267	$3,536.60
USA	Callahan	Laura	02-Aug-1996	10268	$1,101.20

FIGURE 1.8
The result of running the `Employee Sales by Country` *query.*

NEW TERM When you store a query, Access stores only the query's definition, layout, or formatting properties in the database. Access offers an intuitive, user-friendly tool that helps you design queries: the Query Design window (see Figure 1.9). To open this window, you select Queries from the Objects list in the Database window, choose the query you want to modify, and click Design. The query pictured in Figure 1.9 selects data from `Employees`, `Orders`, and `Order Subtotals` tables. It displays the `Country`, `LastName`, and `FirstName` fields from the `Employees` table, the `ShippedDate` and `OrderID` fields from the `Orders` table, and the `Subtotal` field from the `Order Subtotals` query. The query's output displays only records within a specific `Shipped Date` range. This special type of query is called a *parameter query*. It prompts for criteria at runtime, using the criteria entered by the user to determine which records it includes in the output. Hours 10, "Creating Queries," and 15, "Power Query Techniques," both cover the process of designing queries. Because queries are the foundation for most forms and reports, they are covered throughout this book as they apply to other objects in the database.

FIGURE 1.9

The design of a query that displays data from the Employees *and* Orders *tables and the* Order Subtotals *query.*

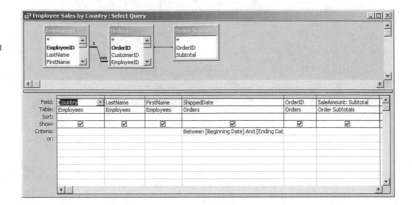

Forms: A Means of Displaying, Modifying, and Adding Data

Although you can enter and modify data in a table's Datasheet view, you can't control the user's actions very well, nor can you do much to facilitate the data-entry process. This is where forms come in. Access forms can have many traits, and they're very flexible and powerful.

To view a form, you select Forms from the Objects list. Then you double-click the form you want to view or click in the list of forms to select the form you want to view and then click Open. Figure 1.10 illustrates a form in Form view. This Customer Orders form is actually three forms in one: one main form and two subforms. The main form displays information from the Customers table, and the subforms display information from the Orders table and the Order Details table (tables that are related to the Customers table). As the user moves from customer to customer, the form displays the orders associated with that customer. When the user clicks to select an order, the form displays the products included on that order.

Like tables and queries, you can also view forms in Design view. The Design view provides tools you can use to edit the layout of a report. To view the design of a form, you select the Forms icon from the Objects list, choose the form whose design you want to modify, and then click Design. Figure 1.11 shows the Customer Orders form in Design view. Notice the two subforms within the main form. Hours 11, "Creating Forms," and 16, "Power Form Techniques," cover forms in more detail.

FIGURE 1.10

The Customer Orders *form, which includes customer, order, and order detail information.*

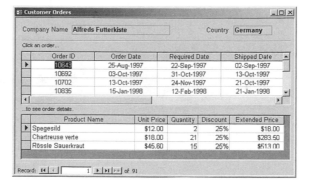

FIGURE 1.11

The design of the Customer Orders *form, showing two subforms.*

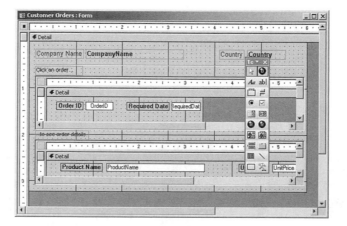

Reports: Turning Data into Information

Forms allow you to enter and edit information, but with reports, you can display information, usually to a printer. Figure 1.12 shows a report in Preview mode. To preview any report, you select Reports from the Objects list. You double-click the report you want to preview or choose the report you want to preview from the list of reports in the Database window, and then you click Preview. Notice the graphic in the report in Figure 1.12, as well as other details, such as the shaded line. Like forms, reports can be elaborate and exciting, and they can contain valuable information.

As you may have guessed, you can view reports in Design view, as shown in Figure 1.13. To view the design of a report, you select Reports from the Objects list, select the report you want to view, and click Design. Figure 1.13 illustrates a report with many sections; in the figure you can see the Page Header, CategoryName Header, Detail section, CategoryName Footer, Page Footer, and Report Footer sections—just a few of the many sections available on a report. Just as a form can contain subforms, a report can contain subreports. Hour 12, "Creating Reports," and Hour 17, "Power Report Techniques," cover the process of designing reports.

FIGURE 1.12

A preview of the Catalog *report.*

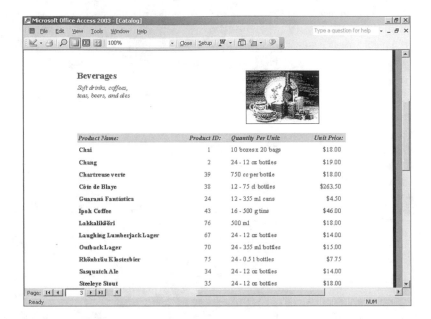

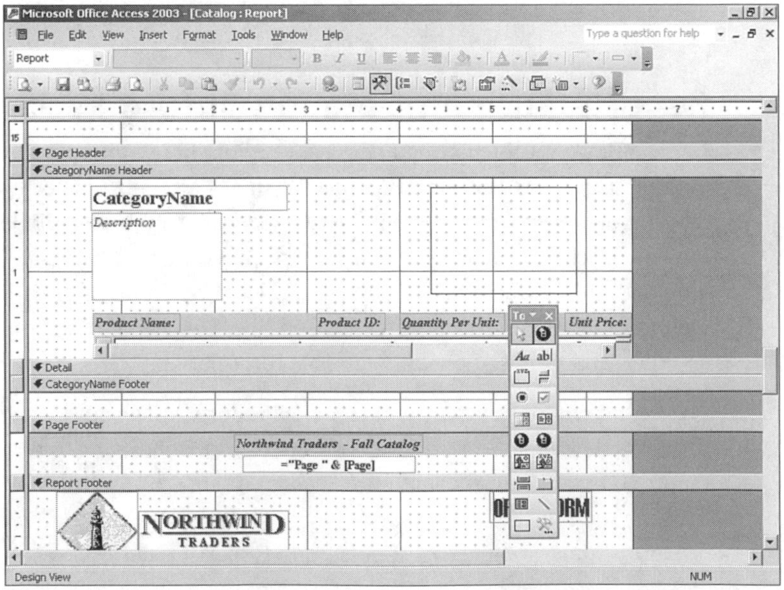

FIGURE 1.13

Design view of the Catalog *report.*

Pages: Forms Viewed in a Browser

Data access pages, discussed earlier in this hour, first appeared in Access 2000. They allow you to view and update the data in a database from within a browser. Although Access stores them outside the Access database file (that is, the .MDB file), you create and maintain them similarly to the way you create and maintain forms. Figure 1.14 shows a data access page viewed within Access. Although Microsoft targets data access pages for use with a browser, you can preview them within the Access application environment.

FIGURE 1.14

An example of a data access page based on the Employees *table.*

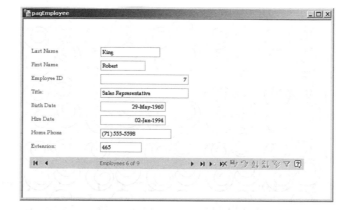

You can also view and modify data access pages in Design view. Figure 1.15 shows a data access page in Design view. As you can see, the Design view of a data access page is similar to that of a form in Design view. This makes working with data access pages, and the deployment of an application over an intranet, very easy.

Access 2002 introduced the ability to save an Access form as a data access page. This feature makes it easy to develop forms used by Access users and browser-based users simultaneously.

FIGURE 1.15

*A data access page
shown in Design view.*

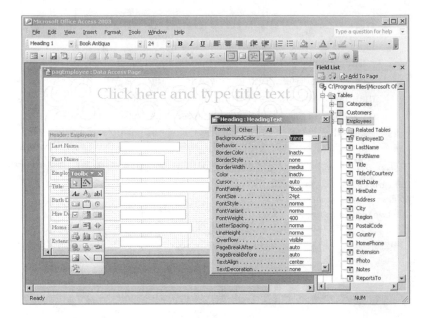

Macros: A Means of Automating a System

Macros in Access aren't like the macros in other Office products. You can't record them, as you can in Microsoft Word or Excel, and Access does not save them as Visual Basic for Applications (VBA) code. With Access macros, you can perform most of the tasks that you can manually perform from the keyboard, menus, and toolbars. Macros allow you to build logic into your application flow.

To run a macro, you select Macros from the Objects list, click the macro you want to run, and then click Run. Access then executes the actions in the macro. To view a macro's design, you select Macros from the Objects list, select the macro you want to modify, and click Design to open the Macro Design window (see Figure 1.16). The macro pictured in Figure 1.16 has four columns. The Macro Name column is where you can specify the name of a subroutine within a macro. The Condition column allows you to specify a condition. The Action column is where you specify an action for the macro. (The action in the macro's Action column won't execute unless the condition for that action evaluates to true.) The Comment column lets you document the macro. In the bottom half of the Macro Design window, you specify the arguments that apply to the selected action. In Figure 1.16, the selected action is MsgBox, which accepts four arguments: Message, Beep, Type, and Title.

FIGURE 1.16

The design of the Customers macro, which contains macro names, conditions, actions, and comments.

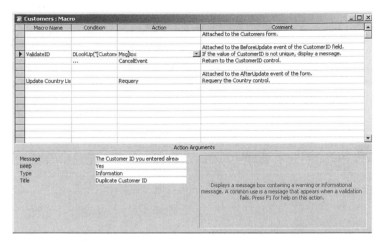

Modules: The Foundation of the Application Development Process

Modules, the foundation of any complex Access application, let you create libraries of functions that you can use throughout an application. You usually include subroutines and functions in the modules that you build. A function always returns a value; a subroutine does not. By using code modules, you can do just about anything with an Access

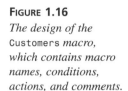

application. Figure 1.17 shows an example of a module. As its title implies, Hour 23, "VBA Introduced," introduces you to the concept of modules. If you want more information on modules after reading this book, see *Alison Balter's Mastering Access Office 2003 Desktop Development*, published by Sams, which provides extensive coverage of modules and Access coding techniques.

FIGURE 1.17

The global code module in Design view, showing the General Declarations section and the IsLoaded *function.*

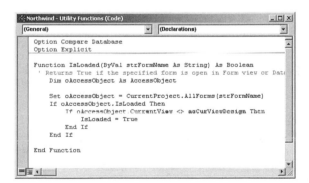

Closing an Access Database

Closing an Access database is quite simple: You just select File|Close. If you have any objects open in Design view, Access prompts you to save those objects. You can also close a database by opening another database or by exiting Access.

Summary

Before you learn about the practical aspects of Access development, you need to understand what Access is and how it fits into the application development world. Access is an extremely powerful product with a wide variety of uses; you can find Access applications on everything from home PCs to the desks of many corporate PC users going against enterprisewide client/server databases.

When you understand what Access is and what it does, you're ready to learn about its many objects. Access applications are made up of tables, queries, forms, reports, data access pages, macros, modules, command bars, ActiveX controls, relationships, and other objects, all of which this book covers. When designed properly, an Access application effectively combines these objects to give the user a powerful, robust, utilitarian application.

Q&A

Q Describe the main limitation associated with using Access to develop small-business applications.

A The main limitation in using Access to develop small-business applications is the time and money involved. It is important that you be realistic about both of these aspects of the application development process.

Q Explain the limitations of Access as an Internet/intranet development tool.

A Internet/intranet applications developed with Microsoft Access must be run on machines with Internet Explorer 5.5 or higher and Microsoft Office installed.

Q Describe what Access stores when you save a query.

A When you save a query, Access stores the definition, layout, and formatting properties—not the result of the query.

Workshop

The Workshop includes quiz questions that are designed to help you test your understanding of the material covered and activities to help put what you've learned to practice. You can find the answers to the questions in the section immediately following the quiz.

Quiz

1. Name the types of applications that you can build in Access.

2. You can modify information while viewing a report (True/False).

3. You can record an Access macro (True/False).

4. Access is a client/server database (True/False).

5. Data access pages are stored outside the database (.MDB) file (True/False).

Quiz Answers

1. With Access you can build personal, small-business, departmental, corporationwide, and Internet/intranet applications, and you can create a front end to a client/server database.

2. False. You cannot modify information while viewing a report. You can only display the information, usually to a printer.

3. False. You cannot record an Access macro. You must either drag and drop objects onto a macro or manually enter macro arguments for each line of the macro.

4. False. Access is a file server database.

5. True.

Activities

Open the Northwind sample database that ships with Access 2003. Open a table in Datasheet view. View it in Design view. Open a query in Datasheet view. View its design. Open a form in Form view. View its design. Run a report. View its design. Open a data access page. View its design. View the design of a macro. View the design of a module.

PART II

Working with Existing Databases and Objects

HOUR 2

Tables Introduced

Tables are the foundation of any Access application. In working with tables, the first thing you'll want to be able to do is open them in Datasheet view and navigate around them. This hour covers all the basics of working with tables in Datasheet view. In this hour you'll learn the following:

- How to view and navigate table data
- How to edit table data
- How to add records to a table
- How to select and delete records
- How to find and replace table data
- How to apply and remove filters
- How to modify the appearance of a datasheet
- How to use the spell check and AutoCorrect features

Viewing and Navigating Table Data

Tables are the basis of everything that you do in Access. Most of the data for a database resides in tables, so if you're creating an employee payroll database, the employee data will be stored in a table, your payroll codes might be stored in a table, and your past payroll records could be stored in a table. A table contains data about a specific topic or subject (for example, customers, orders, or employees). Tables are arranged in rows and columns, similarly to a spreadsheet. The columns represent the fields, and the rows represent the records (see Figure 2.1).

FIGURE 2.1

A table composed of columns and rows associated with customers.

Opening an Access Table

Before you can view the data in a table and work with its records, you must open the table. To open a table in Datasheet view, follow these steps:

1. Select Tables in the list of objects in the Database window.

2. Select the table you want to open and click the Open button in the database window *or* double-click the table you want to open.

Navigating Around a Table

You can move around a table by using the keyboard or mouse. When you are editing or adding records, your hands are on the keyboard and you might find it easiest to move around a table by using the keyboard. However, if you are looking for a specific record, you might find it most convenient to use the mouse.

Table 2.1 shows the keyboard and mouse actions for moving around a table and their resulting effects. As you can see, Microsoft Access provides numerous keyboard and mouse alternatives for moving around a table.

TABLE 2.1   Keyboard and Mouse Actions to Move Around a Table

Keyboard Action	Mouse Action	Effect
Tab or right arrow	Click the right arrow on the bottom scrollbar.	Moves one field to the right of the current field.
Shift+Tab or left arrow	Click the left arrow on the bottom scrollbar.	Moves one field to the left of the current field.
Down arrow	Click the next record button ▶.	Moves down one record.
Up arrow	Click the previous record button ◀.	Moves up one record.
Page Down	(No equivalent mouse action.)	Moves down one screen of records.
Page Up	(No equivalent mouse action.)	Moves up one screen of records.
Home	(No equivalent mouse action.)	Selects the first field of the current record.
End	(No equivalent mouse action.)	Selects the last field of the current record.
Ctrl+Home	Click the first record button ◀◀.	Moves to the first record of the table.
Ctrl+End	Click the last record button ▶▶.	Moves to the last record of the table.
F2	Click and drag within a field.	Selects the text in the field.

The insertion point does not change locations just because you move the mouse; only the mouse pointer moves when you move the mouse. You need to click *within* a field before you begin typing, or the changes occur in the original mouse location.

The Table window includes tools that allow you to scroll through the fields and records, move from record to record, expand and collapse to show and hide related records, and more. Figure 2.2 illustrates these features. Table 2.2 provides a list of these features and provides a description of each.

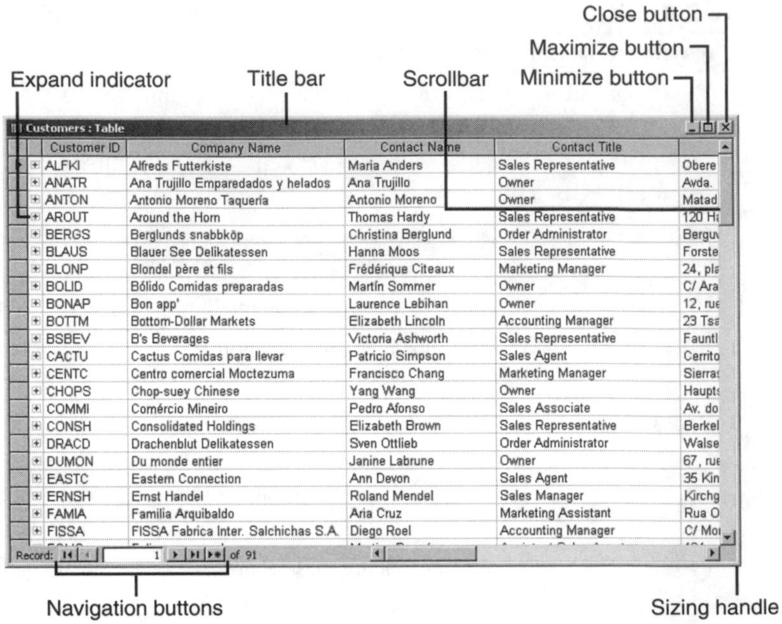

FIGURE 2.2

The Table window.

TABLE 2.2   The Components of the Table Window

Table Component	Description
Title bar	You can move a window by putting the mouse pointer on the title bar, holding down the mouse button, and dragging.
Close button	Clicking the close button closes the table.
Maximize button	You can click the maximize button, which is a square, to maximize the window. The datasheet then fills the applications window.
Minimize button	You can click the minimize button, which looks like an underscore within a square, to minimize the window. The icon appears on the taskbar. You can restore the window by clicking the icon.
Sizing handle	To change the size of the window, you put the pointer on the lower-right corner, hold down the mouse button, and drag. When the window is the size you want, you release the button.
Scrollbar	You can use the scrollbars to move up and down and right and left in the table.
Navigation buttons	These icons allow you to select the first record, last record, next record, or previous record in the table.
Expand indicator	The expand indicator allows you to view the data hierarchy by showing you any subdata records that are linked to the main record.

Closing a Table

When you are finished working with a table, you need to close it. To close a table, you choose File|Close or click the close button in the upper-right corner of the Table window.

> Access often prompts you as you close a table, asking if you want to save changes to the layout of the table. It is important that you understand that Access is *not* asking you if you want to save changes to the data. As you'll learn in a moment, Access saves changes to data the moment you move off a record. When you close a table and Access prompts you, it is asking you if you want to save formatting changes, such as changes to column width, to the look of the datasheet, and so on.

Editing Table Data

You can change the data in a table any time that you are in Datasheet view of a table, the result of a query, or Form view of a form. Access saves changes you make to a record as soon as you move off the record.

Modifying Table Data

One task you might want to perform is to simply modify table data. Here's the process:

1. Select the record you want to change by using any of the techniques listed in Table 2.1.
2. Select the field you want to change by clicking the field or using the arrow keys.
3. Type to make the necessary changes to the data. When you move off the record, Access saves your changes.

Deleting Field Contents

Now that you know how to modify the contents of a field, let's talk about how to delete the contents of a field. The process is simple:

1. Select the field contents you want to delete.
2. Press the Delete key. Access deletes the contents of the field.

It's important to note that Access saves changes to the current record as soon as you move off the current record. If you want to cancel all the changes you made to a record, you simply press the Esc key twice. Access cancels all changes you made to that record.

Undoing Changes

There are different options available when you're undoing changes to a field or to a record. The options differ, depending on whether you are still within a field, have left the field, or have left the record. The sections that follow explore the various options that are available.

Undoing Changes Made to the Current Field

When you are in the process of making changes to a field, you might realize that you really didn't want to make changes to that field or to that record. To undo changes to the current field, you can either click the Undo tool on the toolbar, select Edit|Undo Typing, or press the Esc key once. For example, if you meant to change the contact first name from Alison to Sue but realized that you were accidentally typing Sue in the Customer field, you could press the Esc key once, click the Undo tool on the toolbar, or select Edit| Undo Typing to undo your change.

Undoing Changes After You Move to Another Field

The process of undoing changes after you move to another field is slightly different from the process of undoing changes made to the current field. You can either click the Undo tool on the toolbar, select Edit|Undo Current Field/Record, or press the Esc key once. For example, if you meant to change the contact first name from Alison to Sue but realized that you accidentally typed Sue in the Customer field, and then you moved to another field, you could click the Undo tool on the toolbar, press the Esc key once, or select Edit| Undo Current Field/Record to undo your change.

Undoing Changes After You Save a Record

When you make changes to a field and then move to another record, Access saves all changes to the modified record. As long as you do not begin making changes to another record, you can still undo the changes you made to the most recently modified record. To do this, you can either click the Undo tool on the toolbar, select Edit|Undo Saved Record, or press the Esc key twice. For example, if you meant to change the contact first name from Alison to Sue but realized that you accidentally typed Sue in the Customer field, and you then moved to another record, you could click the Undo tool on the toolbar, select Edit|Undo Saved Record, or press the Esc key twice to undo your change.

If Access is unable to undo a change, the Undo tool appears dimmed.

After you have made changes to a record and then have gone on to make changes to another record, you cannot undo the changes that you made to the first record.

Adding Records to a Table

Access adds records to the end of a table, regardless of how you add them to the table.

To add records, follow these steps:

1. Select the table to which you want to add information.

2. Click the New Record Navigation button at the bottom of the Datasheet window.

3. Add the necessary information to the fields within the record. When you move off the record, Access saves the new record.

There are some tips that you should be aware of because they help you to get data entry done more effectively. The first is Ctrl+". You use it to repeat the data in the field directly above the current field. Another is Edit I Go To I New Record. This is another method that you can use to add records to a table.

It is also important to note that Access always displays one blank record at the end of a table. When you're entering data, pressing the Tab key at the end of a record that you just added allows you to continue to add additional records.

Deleting Records

Before you can delete records, you must select them. The following sections therefore cover the process of selecting records and then the process of deleting records.

Selecting One or More Records

To select one record, you simply click the gray record selector button to the left of the record within the datasheet.

To select multiple records, you click and drag within the record selector area. Access selects the contiguous range of records in the area over which you click and drag. As an alternative, you can click the gray selector button for the first record you want to select, hold down the Shift key, and then click the gray selector button of the last record that you want to select. When you do this, Access selects the entire range of records between them. Figure 2.3 shows the Customers table with three records selected.

If you want to select a single record when the cursor is within the record, you can simply select Edit|Select Record.

FIGURE 2.3

The Customers *table with three records selected.*

	Customer ID	Company Name	Contact Name	Contact Title	
+	ALFKI	Alfreds Futterkiste	Maria Anders	Sales Representative	Obere
+	ANATR	Ana Trujillo Emparedados y helados	Ana Trujillo	Owner	Avda.
+	ANTON	Antonio Moreno Taquería	Antonio Moreno	Owner	Matad
+	AROUT	Around the Horn	Thomas Hardy	Sales Representative	120 Ha
+	BERGS	Berglunds snabbköp	Christina Berglund	Order Administrator	Bergu
+	BLAUS	Blauer See Delikatessen	Hanna Moos	Sales Representative	Forste
+	BLONP	Blondel père et fils	Frédérique Citeaux	Marketing Manager	24, pla
+	BOLID	Bólido Comidas preparadas	Martín Sommer	Owner	C/ Ara
+	BONAP	Bon app'	Laurence Lebihan	Owner	12, rue
+	BOTTM	Bottom-Dollar Markets	Elizabeth Lincoln	Accounting Manager	23 Tsa
+	BSBEV	B's Beverages	Victoria Ashworth	Sales Representative	Fauntl
+	CACTU	Cactus Comidas para llevar	Patricio Simpson	Sales Agent	Cerrito
+	CENTC	Centro comercial Moctezuma	Francisco Chang	Marketing Manager	Sierra:
+	CHOPS	Chop-suey Chinese	Yang Wang	Owner	Haupts
+	COMMI	Comércio Mineiro	Pedro Afonso	Sales Associate	Av. do
+	CONSH	Consolidated Holdings	Elizabeth Brown	Sales Representative	Berkel
+	DRACD	Drachenblut Delikatessen	Sven Ottlieb	Order Administrator	Walse
+	DUMON	Du monde entier	Janine Labrune	Owner	67, rue
+	EASTC	Eastern Connection	Ann Devon	Sales Agent	35 Kin
+	ERNSH	Ernst Handel	Roland Mendel	Sales Manager	Kirchg
+	FAMIA	Familia Arquibaldo	Aria Cruz	Marketing Assistant	Rua O
+	FISSA	FISSA Fabrica Inter. Salchichas S.A.	Diego Roel	Accounting Manager	C/ Mor

Record: I◄ ◄   5 ► ►I ►* of 91

Deleting Records

When you know how to select records, deleting them is quite simple. You just follow these steps:

1. Select the record(s) you want to delete.
2. Press the Delete key. The dialog box in Figure 2.4 appears, asking if you're sure you want to delete the record(s).
3. Click the Yes button. Access deletes the records.

FIGURE 2.4

Access asks if you want to delete the selected record.

The process of deleting a record is not so simple if you have established referential integrity between the tables in a database and the row that you are attempting to delete has child rows. Hour 9, "Creating Relationships," covers relationships and referential integrity. For now, you can think about the fact that customers generally have orders associated with them, and those orders have order detail records associated with them. The relationship between the Customers table and the Orders table prohibits the user from deleting customers who have orders. Here's how you delete a customer who has orders:

1. Select the record(s) you want to delete.
2. Press the Delete key. The dialog box in Figure 2.5 appears, telling you that the records cannot be deleted because the table includes related records.
3. Click OK to close the dialog box.

FIGURE 2.5

Access notifying you that you cannot delete the selected records.

Access provides a *referential integrity* option with which you can cascade a deletion down to the *child table* (a table related to a parent table, such as orders related to customers). This means, for example, that if you attempt to delete an order, Access deletes the associated order detail records. If you establish referential integrity with the cascade delete option, the deletion process works like this:

1. Select the record(s) you want to delete.
2. Press the Delete key. The dialog box in Figure 2.6 appears, asking if you're sure you want to delete the records.
3. Click Yes to complete the deletion process.

FIGURE 2.6

Access asking if you want to delete the parent row and the associated child records.

After you have selected records, they appear in black and you can copy them, delete them, or modify them as a group. Remember that deleting records is a permanent process. You cannot undo record deletion.

Finding and Replacing Records

When you are working with records in a large data table, you often need a way to locate specific records quickly. By using the Find feature, you can easily move to specific records within a table. After you have found records, you can also replace the text within them.

Finding a Record That Meets Specific Criteria

The Find feature allows you to search in a datasheet for records that meet specific criteria. Here's how it works:

1. Select the field containing the criteria for which you are searching.

2. Click the Find button on the toolbar. The Find and Replace dialog box appears (see Figure 2.7).

FIGURE 2.7

The Find tab of the Find and Replace dialog box, which you can use to search for values in a datasheet.

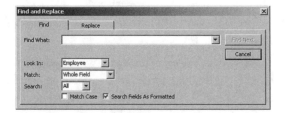

3. Type the criteria in the Find What text box.

4. Use the Look In drop-down list box to designate whether you want to search only the current field or all fields in the table.

5. Use the Match drop-down list box to designate whether you want to match any part of the field you are searching, the whole field you are searching, or the start of the field you are searching. For example, if you type Federal in the Find What text box and you select Whole Field in the Match drop-down list box, you find only entries where Ship Via is set to Federal. If you select Any Part of Field, you find Federal Shipping, Federal Express, United Federal Shipping, and so on. If you select Start of Field, you find Federal Shipping and Federal Express, but you do not find United Federal Shipping.

6. Use the Search drop-down list box to designate whether you want to search only up from the current cursor position, only down, or in all directions.

7. Use the Match Case check box to indicate whether you want the search to be case-sensitive.

8. Use the Search Fields as Formatted check box to indicate whether you want to find data only based on the display format (for example, 17-Jul-96 for a date).

9. Click the Find Next button to find the next record that meets the designated criteria.

10. To continue searching after you close the dialog box, use the Shift+F4 keystroke combination.

Replacing Data in a Table

There may be times when you want to update records that meet specific criteria. You can use the Replace feature to automatically insert new information into the specified fields. Here's the process:

1. Click within the field that contains the criteria you are searching for.

2. Click the Find button on the toolbar. The Find and Replace dialog box appears.

3. Select the Replace tab (see Figure 2.8).

FIGURE **2.8**

The Replace tab of the Find and Replace dialog, with which you can replace table data.

4. Type the criteria in the Find What text box.

5. Type the new information (the replacement value) in the Replace With text box.

6. Choose values for the Look In drop-down list box, Match drop-down list box, Search drop-down list box, Match Case check box, and Search Fields as Formatted check box, as described in the "Finding a Record That Meets Specific Criteria" section of this hour.

7. Click the Find Next button. Access locates the first record that meets the criteria designated in the Find What text box.

8. Click the Replace button. Access replaces the text for the record and finds the next occurrence of the text in the Find What text box.

9. Repeat step 8 to find all occurrences of the value in the Find What text box and replace them. As an alternative, you can click the Replace All button to replace all occurrences at once.

You should use Replace All with quite a bit of caution. Remember that the changes you make are *permanent*. Although Replace All is a viable option, when you use it you need to make sure you have a recent backup and that you are quite certain of what you are doing. In fact, I usually do a few replaces to make sure that I see what Access is doing *before* I click Replace All.

10. Click Cancel when you're done.

If you are searching a very large table, Access can find a specific value in a field fastest if the field you are searching on is the primary key or an indexed field. Hours 8, "Creating Tables," and 14 "Power Table Techniques," cover primary keys and indexes.

NEW TERM   With either Find or Replace, you can use several wildcard characters. A *wildcard character* is a character you use in place of an unknown character. Table 2.3 describes the wildcard characters.

TABLE 2.3 Wildcard Characters You Can Use When Searching

Wildcard Character	Description
*	Acts as a placeholder for multiple characters.
?	Acts as a placeholder for a single character.
#	Acts as a placeholder for a single number.

Filtering Table Data

In a table you can apply filters to fields to limit what records you view. This is very helpful if you want to view just the data associated with a subset of the records. For example, you might want to view just the data associated with sales managers.

Filtering by Selection

The Filter by Selection feature allows you to select text and then filter the data in the table to that selected text. To use the Filter by Selection feature, follow these steps:

1. Open a table in Datasheet view.

2. Select the record and field in the table that contain the value on which you want to filter.

 3. Click the Filter by Selection button. The data is filtered to only the specified rows. For example, in Figure 2.9, the data shows only orders associated with Steven Buchanan.

FIGURE 2.9

Data filtered to show orders for Steven Buchanan.

	Order ID	Customer	Employee	Order Date	Required Date	Shipped Date
	10248	Wilman Kala	Buchanan, Steven	04-Jul-1996	01-Aug-1996	16-Jul-1996	Fe
	10254	Chop-suey Chinese	Buchanan, Steven	11-Jul-1996	08-Aug-1996	23-Jul-1996	Un
	10269	White Clover Markets	Buchanan, Steven	31-Jul-1996	14-Aug-1996	09-Aug-1996	Sp
	10297	Blondel père et fils	Buchanan, Steven	04-Sep-1996	16-Oct-1996	10-Sep-1996	Un
	10320	Wartian Herkku	Buchanan, Steven	03-Oct-1996	17-Oct-1996	18-Oct-1996	Fe
	10333	Wartian Herkku	Buchanan, Steven	18-Oct-1996	15-Nov-1996	25-Oct-1996	Fe
	10358	La maison d'Asie	Buchanan, Steven	20-Nov-1996	18-Dec-1996	27-Nov-1996	Sp
	10359	Seven Seas Imports	Buchanan, Steven	21-Nov-1996	19-Dec-1996	26-Nov-1996	Fe
	10372	Queen Cozinha	Buchanan, Steven	04-Dec-1996	01-Jan-1997	09-Dec-1996	Un
	10378	Folk och fä HB	Buchanan, Steven	10-Dec-1996	07-Jan-1997	19-Dec-1996	Fe
	10397	Princesa Isabel Vinhos	Buchanan, Steven	27-Dec-1996	24-Jan-1997	02-Jan-1997	Sp
	10463	Suprêmes délices	Buchanan, Steven	04-Mar-1997	01-Apr-1997	06-Mar-1997	Fe
	10474	Pericles Comidas clásicas	Buchanan, Steven	13-Mar-1997	10-Apr-1997	21-Mar-1997	Un
	10477	Princesa Isabel Vinhos	Buchanan, Steven	17-Mar-1997	14-Apr-1997	25-Mar-1997	Un
	10529	Maison Dewey	Buchanan, Steven	07-May-1997	04-Jun-1997	09-May-1997	Un
	10549	QUICK-Stop	Buchanan, Steven	27-May-1997	10-Jun-1997	30-May-1997	Sp
	10569	Rattlesnake Canyon Grocery	Buchanan, Steven	16-Jun-1997	14-Jul-1997	11-Jul-1997	Sp
	10575	Morgenstern Gesundkost	Buchanan, Steven	20-Jun-1997	04-Jul-1997	30-Jun-1997	Sp
	10607	Save-a-lot Markets	Buchanan, Steven	22-Jul-1997	19-Aug-1997	25-Jul-1997	Sp
	10648	Ricardo Adocicados	Buchanan, Steven	28-Aug-1997	09-Oct-1997	09-Sep-1997	Un
	10649	Maison Dewey	Buchanan, Steven	28-Aug-1997	25-Sep-1997	29-Aug-1997	Un
	10650	Familia Arquibaldo	Buchanan, Steven	29-Aug-1997	26-Sep-1997	03-Sep-1997	Fe

Record: 1 of 42 (Filtered)

Removing Filters

After you have applied filters, you might want to remove them so that you can once again view all rows or apply a different filter. The process is very simple. You simply click the Remove Filter button on the toolbar.

Modifying the Appearance of a Datasheet

You can customize how data in a datasheet appears to make the data easier to work with. Changes made to the appearance of the Datasheet view affect only the display of the data, not the underlying structure of the table.

Changing the Appearance of Text

One of the things that you can change about a datasheet is the appearance of its text. Here's the process:

1. Choose Format|Font. The Font dialog box appears (see Figure 2.10).

FIGURE 2.10

The Font dialog box, which you can use to customize the datasheet font.

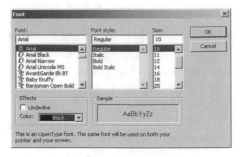

2. Select the desired font, color, font size, and so on.

3. Click OK when you're finished. Access applies the selections to the entire datasheet.

Changing Column Widths

In addition to customizing the datasheet font, you can modify the width of the columns within a datasheet. This is how you do it:

1. Move the mouse within the right column separator in the column heading until you get a double-headed arrow.

2. Drag to the right or left to increase or decrease the size of the column.

3. Release the mouse when the column reaches the desired size.

Changing Row Height

Whereas the process of changing a column width changes the width of the selected column(s), the process of changing the row height affects all rows in the table. To change the row height, follow these steps:

1. Place the mouse pointer at the lower row border in the record selector area until the mouse pointer turns into a double-headed arrow.

2. Drag up or down to increase or decrease the height of the row.

3. Release the mouse when the row reaches the desired height. Notice that in Figure 2.11 the row height has been increased.

Freezing Columns

There are times when you want to ensure that specific columns remain visible, even when you scroll to view other columns in the table. For example, you might want the

CustomerID and CompanyName columns to remain visible, even when you scroll to the right to view other fields. Freezing table columns solves this problem. Here's how it works:

1. Click the column selectors of the columns you want to freeze to select the desired columns.

2. Choose Format|Freeze Columns. Notice that a dark line appears between those columns and the other columns (see Figure 2.12).

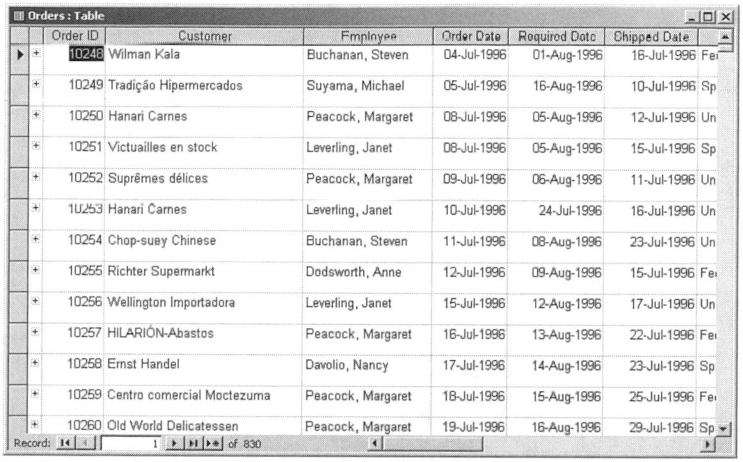

FIGURE 2.11

Increasing the row height, which affects all rows in a datasheet.

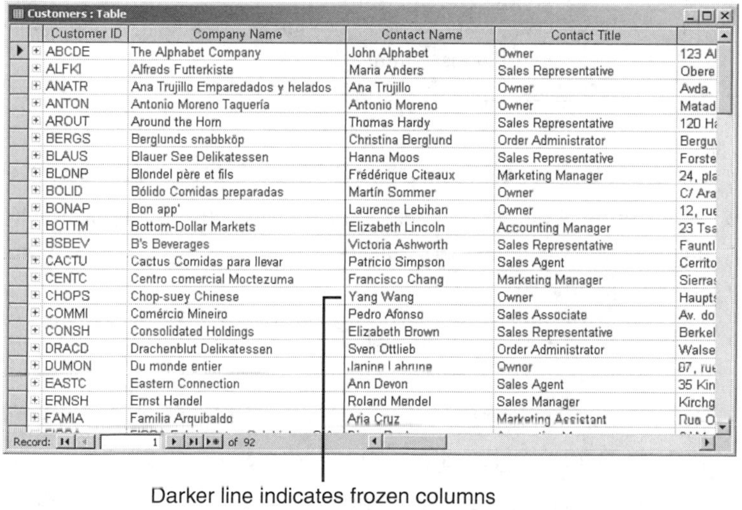

		Order ID	Customer	Employee	Order Date	Required Date	Shipped Date	
▶	+	10248	Wilman Kala	Buchanan, Steven	04-Jul-1996	01-Aug-1996	16-Jul-1996	Fer
	+	10249	Tradição Hipermercados	Suyama, Michael	05-Jul-1996	16-Aug-1996	10-Jul-1996	Sp
	+	10250	Hanari Carnes	Peacock, Margaret	08-Jul-1996	05-Aug-1996	12-Jul-1996	Un
	+	10251	Victuailles en stock	Leverling, Janet	08-Jul-1996	05-Aug-1996	15-Jul-1996	Sp
	+	10252	Suprêmes délices	Peacock, Margaret	09-Jul-1996	06-Aug-1996	11-Jul-1996	Un
	+	10253	Hanari Carnes	Leverling, Janet	10-Jul-1996	24-Jul-1996	16-Jul-1996	Un
	+	10254	Chop-suey Chinese	Buchanan, Steven	11-Jul-1996	08-Aug-1996	23-Jul-1996	Un
	+	10255	Richter Supermarkt	Dodsworth, Anne	12-Jul-1996	09-Aug-1996	15-Jul-1996	Fer
	+	10256	Wellington Importadora	Leverling, Janet	15-Jul-1996	12-Aug-1996	17-Jul-1996	Un
	+	10257	HILARIÓN-Abastos	Peacock, Margaret	16-Jul-1996	13-Aug-1996	22-Jul-1996	Fer
	+	10258	Ernst Handel	Davolio, Nancy	17-Jul-1996	14-Aug-1996	23-Jul-1996	Sp
	+	10259	Centro comercial Moctezuma	Peacock, Margaret	18-Jul-1996	15-Aug-1996	25-Jul-1996	Fer
	+	10260	Old World Delicatessen	Peacock, Margaret	19-Jul-1996	16-Aug-1996	29-Jul-1996	Sp

Record: 1 of 830

FIGURE 2.12

The column separator, which is a dark line between the frozen columns and the other columns.

		Customer ID	Company Name	Contact Name	Contact Title	
▶	+	ABCDE	The Alphabet Company	John Alphabet	Owner	123 Al
	+	ALFKI	Alfreds Futterkiste	Maria Anders	Sales Representative	Obere
	+	ANATR	Ana Trujillo Emparedados y helados	Ana Trujillo	Owner	Avda.
	+	ANTON	Antonio Moreno Taquería	Antonio Moreno	Owner	Matad
	+	AROUT	Around the Horn	Thomas Hardy	Sales Representative	120 Ha
	+	BERGS	Berglunds snabbköp	Christina Berglund	Order Administrator	Berguv
	+	BLAUS	Blauer See Delikatessen	Hanna Moos	Sales Representative	Forste
	+	BLONP	Blondel père et fils	Frédérique Citeaux	Marketing Manager	24, pla
	+	BOLID	Bólido Comidas preparadas	Martín Sommer	Owner	C/ Ara
	+	BONAP	Bon app'	Laurence Lebihan	Owner	12, rue
	+	BOTTM	Bottom-Dollar Markets	Elizabeth Lincoln	Accounting Manager	23 Tsa
	+	BSBEV	B's Beverages	Victoria Ashworth	Sales Representative	Fauntl
	+	CACTU	Cactus Comidas para llevar	Patricio Simpson	Sales Agent	Cerrito
	+	CENTC	Centro comercial Moctezuma	Francisco Chang	Marketing Manager	Sierras
	+	CHOPS	Chop-suey Chinese	Yang Wang	Owner	Haupts
	+	COMMI	Comércio Mineiro	Pedro Afonso	Sales Associate	Av. do
	+	CONSH	Consolidated Holdings	Elizabeth Brown	Sales Representative	Berkel
	+	DRACD	Drachenblut Delikatessen	Sven Ottlieb	Order Administrator	Walse
	+	DUMON	Du monde entier	Janine Labrune	Owner	67, rue
	+	EASTC	Eastern Connection	Ann Devon	Sales Agent	35 Kin
	+	ERNSH	Ernst Handel	Roland Mendel	Sales Manager	Kirchg
	+	FAMIA	Familia Arquibaldo	Aria Cruz	Marketing Assistant	Rua O

Record: 1 of 92

Darker line indicates frozen columns

3. Using the scrollbar at the bottom of the page, scroll to the right. Notice that the frozen columns remain onscreen as you view columns to the right (see Figure 2.13).

FIGURE 2.13

The CustomerID *and* CompanyName *columns, which remain onscreen at all times.*

Customer ID	Company Name	Postal Code	Country	Phone	Fax
ABCDE	The Alphabet Company				
ALFKI	Alfreds Futterkiste	12209	Germany	030-0074321	030-0076545
ANATR	Ana Trujillo Emparedados y helados	05021	Mexico	(5) 555-4729	(5) 555-3745
ANTON	Antonio Moreno Taquería	05023	Mexico	(5) 555-3932	
AROUT	Around the Horn	WA1 1DP	UK	(171) 555-7788	(171) 555-6750
BERGS	Berglunds snabbköp	S-958 22	Sweden	0921-12 34 65	0921-12 34 67
BLAUS	Blauer See Delikatessen	68306	Germany	0621-08460	0621-08924
BLONP	Blondel père et fils	67000	France	88.60.15.31	88.60.15.32
BOLID	Bólido Comidas preparadas	28023	Spain	(91) 555 22 82	(91) 555 91 99
BONAP	Bon app'	13008	France	91.24.45.40	91.24.45.41
BOTTM	Bottom-Dollar Markets	T2F 8M4	Canada	(604) 555-4729	(604) 555-3745
BSBEV	B's Beverages	EC2 5NT	UK	(171) 555-1212	
CACTU	Cactus Comidas para llevar	1010	Argentina	(1) 135-5555	(1) 135-4892
CENTC	Centro comercial Moctezuma	05022	Mexico	(5) 555-3392	(5) 555-7293
CHOPS	Chop-suey Chinese	3012	Switzerland	0452-076545	
COMMI	Comércio Mineiro	05432-043	Brazil	(11) 555-7647	
CONSH	Consolidated Holdings	WX1 6LT	UK	(171) 555-2282	(171) 555-9199
DRACD	Drachenblut Delikatessen	52066	Germany	0241-039123	0241-059428
DUMON	Du monde entier	44000	France	40.67.88.88	40.67.89.89
EASTC	Eastern Connection	WX3 6FW	UK	(171) 555-0297	(171) 555-3373
ERNSH	Ernst Handel	8010	Austria	7675-3425	7675-3426
FAMIA	Familia Arquibaldo	05442-030	Brazil	(11) 555-9857	

Record: ◄◄ ◄ 1 ► ►► ►* of 92

> There are some tips and tricks that you should know in working with columns (not just frozen columns). You can double-click the column field name border to autofit the column size. To unfreeze columns, you can choose Format | Unfreeze All Columns. Finally, to select more than one column, you can click the field selector for the first column and drag to select contiguous columns.

Modifying the Appearance of a Datasheet

So far in this hour, you've learned how to modify the appearance of the text within a datasheet, but you have not learned how to modify the appearance of the datasheet itself. Here's the process:

1. Choose Format | Datasheet. The Datasheet Formatting dialog box appears (see Figure 2.14).

2. Select the desired option from the Cell Effect group box: Flat, Raised, or Sunken.

3. Indicate whether you want to include horizontal and/or vertical gridlines.

4. Designate the background color and gridline color for the grid.

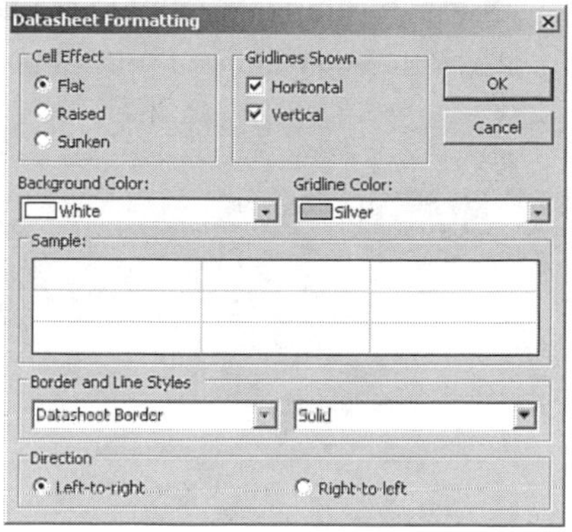

FIGURE 2.14

The Datasheet Formatting dialog box, which you can use to modify the appearance of a datasheet.

2

5. Specify the border as Datasheet Border, Horizontal Gridline, Vertical Gridline, or Column Header Underline. Specify the line style as Transparent Border, Solid, Dashes, Short Dashes, Dots, Sparse Dots, Dash-Dot, Dash-Dot-Dot, or Double Solid.

6. Indicate whether the text should appear from left-to-right or right-to-left within the grid.

7. Click OK to close the dialog box and apply the changes.

Hiding and Unhiding Columns

Sometimes it is not necessary to view certain columns in a datasheet. Fortunately, you can hide and unhide columns as necessary.

To hide columns, follow these steps:

1. Select the column(s) to be hidden.

2. Choose Format|Hide Columns. The selected columns disappear.

Although you might not need to see the data in a column for some time, you might need to see it at a later time. To unhide columns, follow these steps:

1. Choose Format|Unhide Columns. The Unhide Columns dialog box appears (see Figure 2.15).

2. Click to select the columns you want to redisplay.

3. Click Close to close the dialog box and apply the changes.

Expanding to Show the Subdatasheet Data

There may be times when you want to show all the subdatasheet data for all the records in a datasheet. Fortunately, you do not need to click to expand the datasheet for each row individually! You simply choose Format|Subdatasheet|Expand All. All subdatasheets appears (see Figure 2.16). To collapse them again, you select Format|Subdatasheet| Collapse All.

FIGURE 2.15

The Unhide Columns dialog box, which you can use to selectively unhide columns.

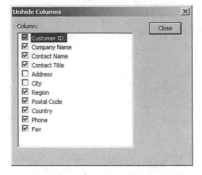

FIGURE 2.16

The Customers *table after the subdatasheets are expanded.*

Correcting Errors by Using Spell Check and AutoCorrect

Using spell check and AutoCorrect to correct data entry errors improves the accuracy of the data in tables. You generally do not want to use spell check for data that contains names and addresses because that type of data contains many entries that are not in the dictionary.

Using the Spell Check Feature

The spell check feature in Microsoft Access is shared with the rest of Microsoft Office. So if you are familiar with spell check in a product such as Microsoft Word, this section should be easy for you. Here's how you run spell check:

1. Select the columns of data that you want to check.

2. Choose Tools|Spelling or click the Spelling tool on the toolbar.

3. If the spell checker locates a spelling error, the Spelling dialog box appears (see Figure 2.17). After you select the appropriate option for an error, the spell checker locates the next error. This process continues until the spell checker finds no additional errors. At that time, a dialog box appears, indicating that the spell check process is complete.

FIGURE 2.17

The Access spell checker, which is shared with the rest of Microsoft Office.

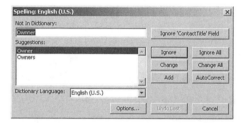

Using AutoCorrect

Like the spell checker, AutoCorrect is a feature that Access shares with the rest of Microsoft Office. It is a feature that is designed to automatically correct common spelling errors as you type. In addition to catching those "common" errors, you can add your own common misspellings to AutoCorrect so that AutoCorrect will immediately correct your common mistakes in the future. Here's how you use AutoCorrect:

1. Type a commonly misspelled word (for example, recieve).

2. Press the spacebar. AutoCorrect changes the spelling to *receive*.

AutoCorrect corrects commonly misspelled words. You can add your own AutoCorrect information by choosing Tools|AutoCorrect and filling in the Replace and With text boxes. Any words you add to AutoCorrect are available in other Microsoft Office applications.

Summary

As you have seen in this hour, there's quite a bit you can accomplish with tables, without ever exploring the other database objects. In this hour you have learned how to view and navigate table data. You have learned how to add, edit, and delete records. You have also learned how to find and replace, as well as how to filter table data. You have learned about the many ways you can customize the look and feel of a datasheet, and you have learned how the Microsoft Access spell checker and AutoCorrect features work.

Q&A

Q Why might Access prohibit you from deleting a record?

A If you attempt to delete a record that has child records and you have established referential integrity between the parent table and the child table, Access prohibits you from deleting the parent record. For example, if you attempt to delete a customer, that customer has orders associated with him or her, and you have established referential integrity between the Customers table and the Orders table, Access prohibits you from deleting the customer.

Q What wildcard characters can you use when searching? Explain the differences between them.

A The three wildcard characters you can use when searching are *, #, and ?. You use * to search for any character or characters. For example, st* searches for anything that begins with St. You use ? to search for any single character. For example, st? searches for anything that begins with St and is followed by any single character. Finally, you use # to search for any single number. For example, st# searches for anything that begins with St and is followed by any single number.

Q Explain how the spell check and AutoCorrect features in Access relate to the rest of Microsoft Office.

A Access shares spell check and AutoCorrect with the rest of Microsoft Office. This means that when you add a word to spell check or AutoCorrect from within Access, it appears for the rest of Office and vice versa. Furthermore these tools function in Access the same way they function in the rest of Office.

Q Explain the various levels of the Undo feature.

A You can undo changes while you are still within a field, after you move off a field, or after you move off a record. To undo changes while you are still within a field, you press Esc once or select Edit|Undo Typing. To undo changes after you move off a field, you press Esc once or select Edit|Undo Current Field/Record. To undo changes after you have saved a record, you press Esc twice or select Edit|Undo Saved Record.

Workshop

The Workshop includes quiz questions that are designed to help you test your understanding of the material covered and activities to help put what you've learned to practice. You can find the answers to the questions in the section immediately following the quiz.

Quiz

1. Name two ways that you can move to the last record in a table.

2. How do you undo all changes made to the last record modified?

3. How can you improve the speed of searches performed with Find or Find and Replace?

4. Changing the appearance of a datasheet affects the underlying structure of the table (True/False).

5. All rows in a table must be the same height (True/False).

Quiz Answers

1. You can press Ctrl+End or click the last record button.

2. Press the Esc key twice or select Edit|Undo Saved Record.

3. You can add indexes to the fields you are searching on.

4. False. The underlying structure of a table is unaffected by changes you make to the appearance of the datasheet.

5. True.

Activities

Open a table in Datasheet view. Use the techniques that you have learned in this hour to navigate around the datasheet. Practice modifying the table data and undoing your changes. Practice adding and deleting records. Find records that meet specific criteria. Then practice replacing data that meets specific criteria. Use the Filter by Selection tool to view just data that meets specific criteria. Remove the filter. Finally, practice modifying the appearance of the datasheet. Change the appearance of the text. Change the column widths and the row height, and then practice freezing and hiding columns.

HOUR 3

Queries Introduced

Queries are stored questions about data. They are an extremely powerful aspect of Microsoft Access. By using queries, you can retrieve just the data you want, how you want it, whenever you want it. In this hour you'll learn the following:

- What a query is and when you should use one
- How to open a query in Datasheet view
- How to open a query in Design view
- How to run a query
- How to add fields to a query, change the sort order of a query, and modify a query's criteria
- How to save a query
- How to print query results
- How to close a query

What Is a Query and When Should You Use One?

NEW TERM   A *Select query* is a stored question about the data stored in a database's tables. Select queries are the foundation of much of what you do in Access. They underlie most forms and reports, and they allow you to view the data you want, when you want. You use a simple Select query to define the tables and fields whose data you want to view and also to specify the criteria that limits the data the query's output displays. A Select query is a query of a table or tables that just displays data; the query doesn't modify data in any way. An example is a query that allows you to view customers who have placed orders in the past month. You can use more advanced Select queries to summarize data, supply the results of calculations, or cross-tabulate data. You can use *Action queries* to add, edit, or delete data from tables, based on selected criteria, but this hour covers Select queries. Hour 15, "Power Query Techniques," covers other types of queries, including Action queries.

Opening a Query in Datasheet View

When you're working with an existing query, you need to be able to open it in Datasheet view. Here are the steps in involved:

1. Select Queries in the list of objects in the Database window.
2. Click to select the query that you want to run, and then select Open on the Database window toolbar or double-click the query to run it. The result of the query appears in Datasheet view (see Figure 3.1).

FIGURE 3.1

The Current Product List *query in Datasheet view.*

Opening a Query in Design View

A query has an underlying design, which you can think of as the *blueprint* for the query. This blueprint—not the result of running the query—is what Access stores in the database when you save a query. The following sections explore the various methods that you can use to view a query in Design view.

Viewing the Design of a Query from the Database Window

It is not necessary to first run a query to view its design. You can go directly into Design view of a query from the Database window. Here's how:

1. Select the query whose design you want to view.

2. Click the Design tool on the Database window toolbar. The query appears in Design view (see Figure 3.2).

FIGURE 3.2

The Current Product List query in Design view.

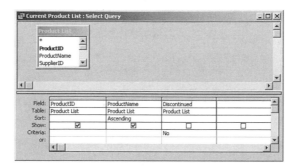

Viewing the Design of a Query While in Datasheet View

It is easy to toggle back and forth between Datasheet view and Design view. You accomplish it by using the View tool on the Query Design and Query Datasheet toolbars. Notice in Figure 3.3 that the View tool allows you to toggle between the various views available for a query. This makes it very easy for you to switch from Design view to Datasheet view and back as needed.

FIGURE 3.3

The View tool, which allows you to toggle between views.

Running a Query

There are several different ways that you can cause a query to run. In fact, you have seen two of them already. Here's a list of some of the techniques you can use to run a query:

- Select a query and then select Open from the Database window.
- Right-click a query in the Database window and then select Open.

- While in the Design view of a query, use the View tool to select Datasheet view.
- While in the Design view of a query, right-click the gray area of the query grid and select Datasheet View (see Figure 3.4).

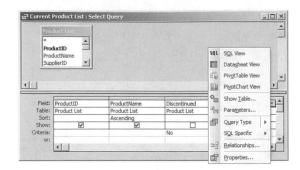

- Click the Run button (which looks like an exclamation point) on the Query Design toolbar (see Figure 3.5).

I challenge you to find even more ways that you can run a query.

Run Button on Query Design Tool Bar

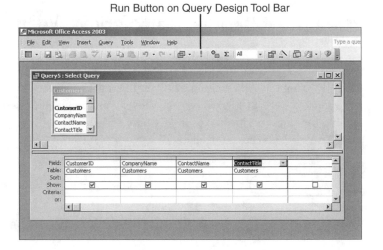

Adding and Removing Fields

When viewing a query in Design view, you might decide to modify the fields that you want to include in the query's output. In other words, you might want to add fields to or remove fields from the query grid. You would do this if you had an existing query and you realized that it was missing fields, if you had a new query and were adding fields for the first time, or if you were working with an existing query and realized that you no longer wanted to include a field in the query.

Adding a Field Between Other Fields

There are times when you need to insert a field between two existing fields. For example, your query might already contain the city and zip code, and you have decided to add a state field and place it between the city and the zip code fields. To do so, you simply drag the field from the field list to the grid and drop it where you want it to appear. The fields already included in the query then move over to the right.

Adding a Field to the End of the Query Grid

Sometimes you want to add a field to the end of the list of existing fields. Fortunately, the process is extremely easy. You simply double-click in the field list on the field that you want to add. Access adds the field at the end of the existing field list. This is the technique that I use to add fields to a new query as I build it. I generally double-click each field that I want to add to the query. Access simply adds each field to the query grid in the order in which I select the fields.

Adding a Group of Contiguous Fields to the Query Grid

It would be very tedious if you had to add each field, one field at a time, in order to add a contiguous group of fields from the field list to the query grid. Fortunately, Access allows you to add the fields as a group. The process is simple:

1. Click the first field that you want to add to the query.
2. Scroll through the field list until you can see the last field that you want to add to the query.
3. Hold down the Shift key as you click the last field that you want to add to the query.
4. Drag the fields as a group to the query grid. The fields are placed on the query grid at the position where you dropped them.

This is a great technique to use when you are lucky and several of the fields you want to include in the query appear together in the field list.

Adding a Group of Noncontiguous Fields to the Query Grid

The process for adding a noncontiguous group of fields from the field list to the query grid is much simpler than adding the fields one at a time. You would add a noncontiguous list of fields when there are several fields that you want to add to the query, but they do not appear together in the field list. Here's what you do:

1. Click the first field that you want to add.

2. Hold down the Ctrl key as you click each additional field that you want to add.

3. Drag the fields to the query grid by clicking any of the selected fields and dragging to the query grid. Access adds the selected fields to the query grid at the position at which you drop them.

Modifying the Sort Order of a Query

You might want to modify the sort order designated by the designer of a query. As described in the following sections, you can sort on a single field or you can sort on multiple fields and you can sort in ascending order or you can sort in descending order. For example, you might want to sort in ascending order by company name in a company table but in descending order by sales amount in a sales table so that the highest sales amount appears first. An example where you might want to sort on multiple fields would be employee last name combined with employee first name.

Sorting on a Single Field

Sorting on a single field is a very simple process. It works like this:

1. Open the desired query in Design view.

2. Click in the Sort row of the field you want to sort by.

3. Click the drop-down arrow button to display the choices for the sort order (see Figure 3.6).

4. Select the sort order:

   • **Ascending**—A to Z or 0 to 9

   • **Descending**—Z to A or 9 to 0

   • **Not Sorted**—No sorting

5. Click the Run button. The data appears in the designated sort order.

FIGURE 3.6

Selecting the sort order of a query.

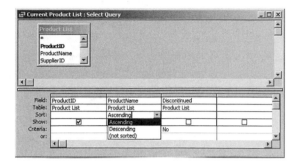

Sorting on More Than One Field

The process for sorting on more than one field is slightly more complicated than the process of sorting on one field. It works like this:

1. Repeat steps 1–4 in the previous section, "Sorting on a Single Field," for the first field that you want to sort by.
2. Click in the Sort row of the second field that you want to sort by.
3. Click the drop-down arrow button to display the choices for sort order.
4. Select the sort order.
5. Click the Run button.

Moving a Field on the Query Grid

Access sorts the data in the query grid from left to right, meaning that if the first name field appears on the query grid before the last name field (see Figure 3.7), the data appears in order by first name and then within first name by last name (see Figure 3.8). Because you probably want the data in order by last name and then by first name, you need to move the Last Name field so that it appears before the First Name field. This is the process:

The gray selector bar

FIGURE 3.7

The query grid with the First Name field before the Last Name field.

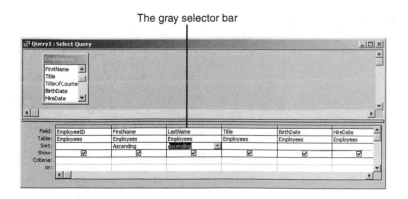

FIGURE 3.8

Datasheet view with the First Name *field before the* Last Name *field.*

1. Click the gray selector bar that contains the field name. This selects the entire column.

2. Drag the field to the new location. Access moves the field (in this case, the Last Name field is moved before the First Name field).

The resulting query grid is shown in Figure 3.9. The resulting output is shown in Figure 3.10.

FIGURE 3.9

The query grid with the Last Name *field before the* First Name *field.*

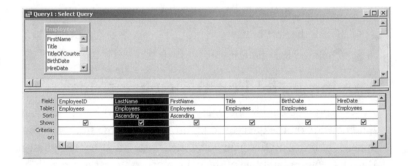

FIGURE 3.10

Datasheet view with the Last Name *field before the* First Name *field.*

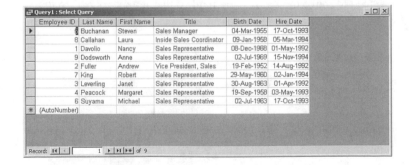

Working with Simple Criteria

You can limit the records that you see in the result of a query by adding criteria to the query. For example, you might want to see just the customers in California, or you might want to view just the orders with sales over $500. You could also view sales that occurred within a specific date range. By using criteria, you can easily accomplish any of these tasks, and many, many more.

Using an Exact Match Query

An exact match query locates data only when there is an exact match with the criteria that you enter. Here's how you run an exact match query:

1. Open the desired query in Design view.

2. Select the cell on the Criteria row below the field for which you want to add the condition.

3. Type the criteria you want to apply for that field. For example, type **Sales Representative** in the Title field (see Figure 3.11).

FIGURE 3.11

Entering simple criteria.

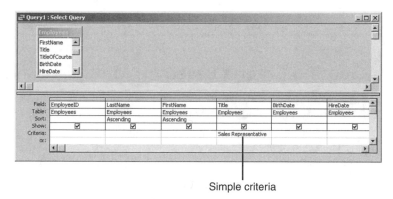

Simple criteria

4. Click the Run button. The results of this query are shown in Figure 3.12.

Although Access is not case-sensitive, and you can therefore enter criteria in either upper- or lowercase, the criteria you enter must follow specific rules. These rules vary depending on the type of field the criteria apply to (see Table 3.1).

FIGURE 3.12

Records with Sales
Representative *in the*
Title *field.*

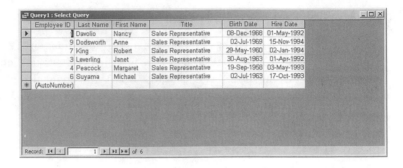

TABLE 3.1   Rules for Criteria, Based on Type of Field

Type of Field	Description
Text	After you type the text, Access puts quotes around the text entered.
Number/Currency	You type the digits, without commas or dollar signs but with decimals, if applicable.
Date/Time	You enter any date or time format.
Counter	You type the digits.
Yes/No	For a yes, you type **yes** or **true**. For no, you type **no** or **false**.

Creating Criteria Based on Multiple Conditions

NEW TERM   There may be times when you want to create a query that contains two or more conditions. You would do this, for example, if you only wanted records in the state of California that had sales within a certain date range to appear in the output. The *And condition* is used to indicate that *both* of two conditions must be met in order for the row to be included in the resulting recordset. You can use the And condition in the same field or on multiple fields.

Using the And Condition on Multiple Fields

By placing criteria for multiple fields on the *same* line of the query grid, you create an And condition. This means that *both* conditions must be true in order for the records to appear in the result. An example of an And condition on two fields would be State Field = 'TX' And Credit limit >=5000. Here's how you create an And condition:

1. Open the desired query in Design view.

2. Select the cell on the Criteria row below the field that contains the first condition you want to enter.

3. Type the first criterion you want to enter. For example, you can type **Sales Manager** as the criterion for Contact Title.

4. Select the cell on the Criteria row below the field that contains the second condition you want to apply.

5. Type the second criterion you want to apply. Figure 3.13 shows USA as the criterion for Country.

FIGURE 3.13

The design of a query with criteria for Contact Title *and* State.

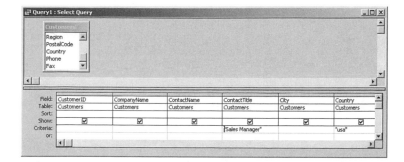

6. Click the Run button to run the query. Only rows that meet both conditions appear in the query result (see Figure 3.14).

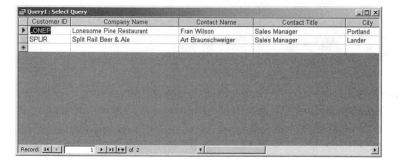

Using the And Condition in a Single Field

There are only a few situations in which you would use an And condition in a single field. This is because in most situations, using the And condition in a single field would yield a recordset with no results. For example, the criteria State = TX And State = CA would yield no results because the state cannot be equal to both values at the same time. On the other hand, HireDate > 7/1/2001 And HireDate < 6/30/2002 would return all employees hired in that date range. Here's how you would enter this sort of criteria:

1. Open the desired query in Design view.

2. Select the cell on the Criteria row below the field that contains the condition you want to add.

3. Type the first criterion you want to add (for example, HireDate > 7/1/2001).

4. Type the keyword **And**.

5. Type the second criterion (for example, **HireDate < 6/30/2002**).

6. Click the Run button. Access runs the query.

> You need to make sure when you are adding the criteria to each field that you remain on the same row of the query grid.

Using Wildcards in a Query

You can use wildcards to select records that follow a pattern. However, you can use the wildcard characters only in Text or Date/Time fields. You use the * to substitute for multiple characters and the ? to substitute for single characters. To practice using wildcards in a query, follow these steps:

1. Open the desired query in Design view.

2. Select the cell on the Criteria row below the field that contains the condition.

3. Type the criteria, using a wildcard in the desired expression. In Figure 3.15 the expression Like Sales* is entered for the Contact Title field. This expression returns all rows where the Contact Title begins with Sales.

FIGURE 3.15

An example that contains Sales* *as the criterion for* Contact Title.

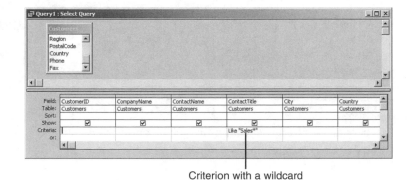

Criterion with a wildcard

4. Click the Run button. The result of the query, shown in Figure 3.16, indicates all the records where Contact Title begins with Sales.

Table 3.2 provides examples of how to use wildcards.

FIGURE 3.16

The result of running a query with criterion that contains the wild-card *.

Customer ID	Company Name	Contact Name	Contact Title	City
ALFKI	Alfreds Futterkiste	Maria Anders	Sales Representative	Berlin
AROUT	Around the Horn	Thomas Hardy	Sales Representative	London
BLAUS	Blauer See Delikatessen	Hanna Moos	Sales Representative	Mannheim
BSBEV	B's Beverages	Victoria Ashworth	Sales Representative	London
CACTU	Cactus Comidas para llevar	Patricio Simpson	Sales Agent	Buenos A
COMMI	Comércio Mineiro	Pedro Afonso	Sales Associate	São Paul
CONSH	Consolidated Holdings	Elizabeth Brown	Sales Representative	London
EASTC	Eastern Connection	Ann Devon	Sales Agent	London
ERNSH	Ernst Handel	Roland Mendel	Sales Manager	Graz
FRANS	Franchi S.p.A.	Paolo Accorti	Sales Representative	Torino
FURIB	Furia Bacalhau e Frutos do Mar	Lino Rodriguez	Sales Manager	Lisboa
GODOS	Godos Cocina Típica	José Pedro Freyre	Sales Manager	Sevilla
GOURL	Gourmet Lanchonetes	André Fonseca	Sales Associate	Campina
HILAA	HILARIÓN-Abastos	Carlos Hernández	Sales Representative	San Crist

Record: 1 of 40

TABLE 3.2 Examples of Using Wildcards

Expression	Results
Sm?th	Finds *Smith* or *Smyth*.
L*ng	Finds any record that starts with *L* and ends in *ng*.
*th	Finds any record that ends in *th* (for example, 158th or Garth).
on	Finds any record that has *on* anywhere in the field.
*/2000	Finds all dates in *2000*.
6/*/2000	Finds all dates in *June 2000*.

Access displays the word *Like* in the criteria cell before a wildcard criterion. It is not necessary to type the word *Like* in the criterion cell before the criterion.

Using Comparison Operators in a Query

Sometimes you want to select records in a table that fall within a range of values. You can use comparison operators (=, <, >, <=, and >=) to create criteria based on the comparison of the value contained in a field to a value that you specify in your criteria. Each record is evaluated, and only records that meet the condition are included in the recordset. To practice using comparison operators in queries, follow these steps:

1. Open the desired query in Design view.
2. Select the cell on the Criteria row below the field for which you want to apply the condition.
3. Type a comparison operator and the criterion you want the query to apply (for example, >100).
4. Click the Run button. The result of the query appears, in Datasheet view.

Table 3.3 gives an example of comparison operators used for a field called Sales. It shows the operators, provides an example of each, and discusses the records that Access would include in the output.

TABLE 3.3   Comparison Operators Used to Compare Against a Field Called Sales

Operator	Indicates	Example	Includes Records Where
>	Greater than	>7500	sales are over 7500
>=	Greater than or equal to	>=7500	sales are 7500 or more
<	Less than	<7500	sales are under 7500
<=	Less than or equal to	<=7500	sales are 7500 or less
<>	Does not equal	<>7500	sales are not 7500
Between	Range of values	Between 5000 And 7500	sales are between 5000 and 7500

You can use the word Not in place of the <> symbols.

Using the Or Condition on a Single Field

NEW TERM   The *Or condition* states that *either* condition of two conditions should be met in order for the record to appear in the result set. You can use the Or condition on a single field or on more than one field. To practice using an Or condition on a single field, follow these steps:

1. Open the desired query in Design view.
2. Select the cell on the Criteria row below the field that contains the condition.
3. Type the first criterion you want the query to apply. For example, you could type **Sales Manager** as a criterion for the Contact Title field.
4. Select the cell below the current cell (this is the Or row).
5. Type the second criterion you want the query to apply. For example, you could type **Sales Agent** as the criterion for the Contact Title field (see Figure 3.17).
6. Click the Run button. The result of this query is shown in Figure 3.18. Notice that the result contains all the sales managers, sales agents, sales representatives, and owners.

FIGURE 3.17

Using an Or *condition on the* Contact Title *field.*

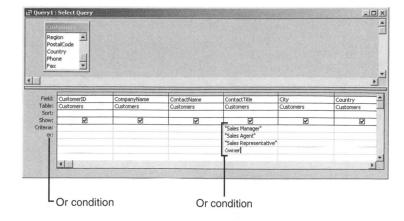

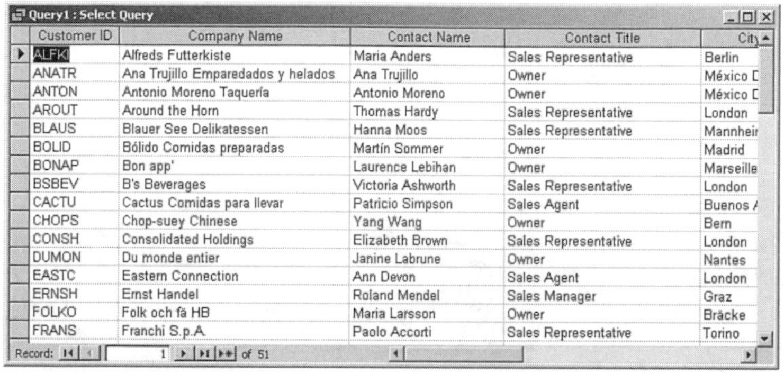

Or condition   Or condition

FIGURE 3.18

The result of a query that contains all the records that contain Sales Manager, Sales Agent, Sales Representative, *or* Owner *in the* Contact Title *field.*

Using the Or Condition on Multiple Fields

An alternative to using the Or condition on a single field is to use the Or condition to create criteria on multiple fields. An example would be City equals London or Contact Title equals Sales Agent. These criteria would return all companies in London, regardless of the contact title, and all sales agents, regardless of the city. Here's how you use the Or condition on multiple fields:

1. Open the desired query in Design view.
2. Select the cell on the Criteria row below the field for which you want to apply the first condition.
3. Type the first criterion you want the query to apply (from the criterion mentioned in the introduction to these steps).
4. Select the cell in the Or row below the second field for which you want to apply the criterion.

5. Type the second criterion you want the query to apply (see Figure 3.19).

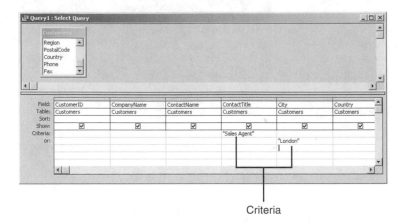

Criteria

6. Click the Run button. The result of this query is shown in Figure 3.20. Notice that the output contains all rows where City is London or Contact Title is Sales Agent.

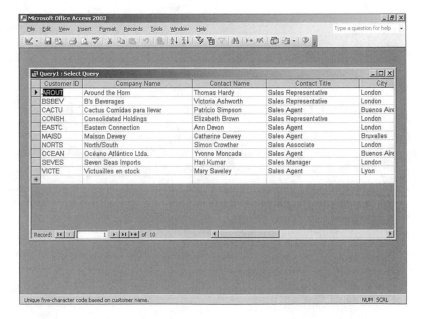

When you use two fields in an Or condition, you need to make sure the criteria are listed on two separate lines. If you don't, they will combine as an And condition.

You need to use the Or condition to find dates or numbers that fall outside a range (for example, before 6/1/96 or after 1/1/97).

You can use the word In and list the multiple criteria, separated by commas, in parentheses (for example, In ('USA', 'France', 'Canada')).

Modifying the Datasheet View of a Query

Just as you can modify the Datasheet view of a table, you can modify the Datasheet view of a query. You can change things such as the font, the column order, the column widths, and the attributes of the datasheet itself (such as background color). When you close the query, if you have made no changes to the design of the query but you have made changes to the layout of the datasheet, Access prompts you with the dialog box displayed in Figure 3.21. In this dialog box, Access asks if you want to change the layout changes that you made. If you click Yes, Access remembers the layout changes. If you click No, Access reverts to the layout that appeared when you first viewed the query.

FIGURE 3.21
Saving the layout of a query.

Saving a Query

To save a query, you click the Save button on the toolbar. The Save As dialog box appears (see Figure 3.22). After you provide a name and click OK, Access saves the Structured Query Language (SQL) statement underlying the query. It does not save the result of the query.

The industry standard for naming queries is to prefix the name with qry.

FIGURE **3.22**

The Save As dia-
log box.

Printing Query Results

It is easy to print query results. Although not as elegant as a printed report, printed query results are often sufficient to meet people's needs. Here's how you print query results:

1. Run the query whose results you want to print.
2. Click the Print icon on the toolbar to invoke the Print dialog box or click the Print Preview icon to preview the query before you send it to a printer (see Figure 3.23). If you go to the Print Preview window, modify the print setup as well as other print settings and then click the Print icon.

FIGURE **3.23**

The Print Preview
option, which allows
you to preview query
results.

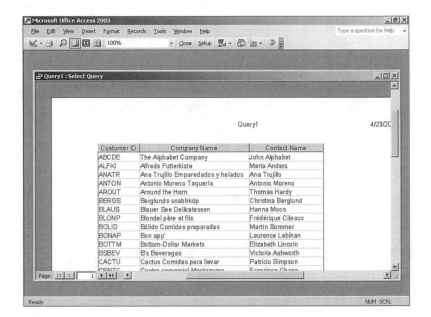

Closing a Query

You close a query by using the close button (the ×) in the upper-right corner of the Query Design window. How Access responds depends on the following three conditions:

- Whether you previously named and saved the query
- Whether you made design changes to the query
- Whether you made changes to the layout of the query while you were in Data-sheet view

If you did not previously name and save the query, Access prompts you with the Save As dialog box when you attempt to close the query. If you previously named and saved the query but did not make any design or layout changes to the query, Access provides no prompts. If you made design changes or design and layout changes, Access asks if you want to save those design changes. If you made *only* layout changes, Access asks if you want to save the layout changes.

Task: Working with Queries

To Do ▼

To practice working with queries you're going to create two queries. You will base the first query on the Customers table. The query will ultimately return only salespeople in the United States and then customers in the region BC. The second query will be based on the Orders table. It will locate all orders placed within a specific date range:

1. Open the Customers table in the Northwind database that ships with Microsoft Access. View the records in this table.

2. Create a query in Design view, using the Customers table. Add all the fields to the query grid.

3. Sort the records in ascending order on the ContactTitle and CompanyName fields. Run the query.

4. Select only the records for customers in the United States. Run the query.

5. Add to the query criteria to show only the customers whose ContactTitle begins with Sales.

6. Remove the criteria for ContactTitle and Country and then change the criteria to display only the customers in the BC region.

7. Close and save the query, giving the query a name. Hours Query1

8. Create a query based on the Orders table.

▲ 9. Display all orders where the OrderDate is between 7/1/1997 and 8/31/1997. Sort the results by the OrderDate.

Summary

In this hour you have learned how to work with existing queries. You have learned why queries are important and you have learned about the ins and outs of working in both

Datasheet view and Design view. You now know the basics of adding fields and applying sorting and simple criteria.

Q&A

Q Explain the difference between the And and Or query conditions.

A With the And condition, both of the specified conditions must be true in order for the row to appear in the query result. With the Or condition, only one of the specified conditions must be true in order for the row to appear in the query result.

Q Explain the difference between ? and * in query criteria.

A ? acts as a wildcard for a single character, whereas * acts as a wildcard for multiple characters.

Q Explain the difference between a Select query and an Action query.

A A Select query retrieves data, whereas an Action query inserts, updates, or deletes data (that is, modifies data in some way).

Q Explain the difference between saving a query and saving the layout of a query.

A Saving a query saves the SQL underlying the query. Saving the layout of a query saves the visual appearance of the datasheet.

Workshop

The Workshop includes quiz questions that are designed to help you test your understanding of the material covered and activities to help put what you've learned to practice. You can find the answers to the questions in the section immediately following the quiz.

Quiz

1. When you're sorting by more than one field, the order in which the fields appear on the query grid is important (True/False).

2. Access is case-sensitive, so you must be careful to enter criteria in the correct case (True/False).

3. Placing criteria on one line of the query grid creates an And condition (True/False).

4. What does the query expression 2/*/2003 return? All Feb 03

5. What type of condition do you create by placing criteria on different lines of the query grid? OR

Quiz Answers

1. True.

2. False. Access is not case-sensitive.

3. True.

4. All entries in February 2003.

5. You get an Or condition.

Activities

Open an existing query. Add some fields to it. Change the sort order. Change the criteria. Run the query several times and see how the results change as you change the sort order and the criteria. Modify the appearance of the datasheet. Save the query and then print the query results. Close the query and then reopen it. Run the query and notice that the changes you made to the datasheet are saved with the query.

3

Hour 4

Forms Introduced

Forms allow you to display data in an aesthetically pleasing way. They also provide an excellent mechanism for data entry. In this hour you'll learn the following:

- What types of forms are available
- How to open a form
- How to work with data from within a form
- How to find and replace table data in a form
- How to sort and filter form data
- How to view the design of a form
- How to close a form
- How to use the AutoForm feature and Form Wizard to create new forms
- How to use conditional formatting to enhance forms

Uses for Forms

Developers often think that forms exist solely for the purpose of data entry. To the contrary, forms serve many different purposes in Access 2003:

- **Data entry**—They can be used for displaying and editing data.
- **Application flow**—They can be used for navigating through an application.

- **Custom dialog boxes**—They can be used to provide messages to users.
- **Printing information**—They can be used to provide hard copies of data-entry information.

Probably the most common use of an Access form is as a vehicle for displaying and editing existing data or for adding new data. Fortunately, Access offers many features that allow you to build forms that ease data entry for users. Access also makes it easy for you to design forms that let users view and modify data, view data but not modify it, or add new records only. Much of what you can do with forms you can also accomplish from Datasheet view. You will find that forms are much easier to look at and work with than Datasheet view. They also provide additional protection against data entry errors.

Although not everyone immediately thinks of an Access form as a means of navigating through an application, forms are quite strong in this area. Figure 4.1 shows a form created with the Switchboard Manager in Access 2003; Figure 4.2 shows a "homegrown" switchboard form. Although the Switchboard Manager makes designing a switchboard form very simple, any type of switchboard is easy to develop. You can be creative with switchboard forms by designing forms that are both utilitarian and exciting. Switchboard forms are covered in detail in Hour 24, "Finishing Touches."

FIGURE 4.1

A form created with the Switchboard Manager.

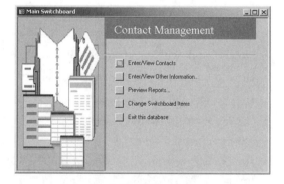

FIGURE 4.2

A custom switchboard with ToolTips and bitmaps.

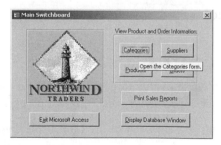

You can use Access to create custom dialog boxes that display information or retrieve information from users. The custom dialog box shown in Figure 4.3 gets the information needed to run a report. The user must fill in the required information before he or she can proceed.

FIGURE 4.3

A custom dialog box that lets the user specify information to run a report.

Another strength of Access is its capability to produce professional-looking printed forms. With many other products, it's difficult to print a data-entry form; sometimes the entire form needs to be re-created as a report. In Access, printing a form is simply a matter of clicking a button that has a little code written behind it. You have the option of creating a report that displays the information the user is entering or of printing the form itself.

Access offers many styles of forms. You can display the data in a form one record at a time, or you can let the user view several records at once. You can display forms *modally*, meaning that the user must respond to and close the form before continuing, or you can display forms so that the user can move through open forms at will. The important thing to remember is that there are many uses for and styles of forms. You will learn about them throughout this hour, in Hour 11, "Creating Forms," and in Hour 16, "Power Form Techniques." As you read the text in this hour, remember that your forms are limited only by your imagination.

Opening a Form

Before you can work with a form, you must first open it. Here are the steps involved:

1. Click Forms in the list of objects.

2. Click to select the form you want to open.

3. Click the Open button on the Database window toolbar. Access opens the selected form.

Working with Data in a Form

After you have opened a form, you probably want to work with the data you have bound it to. You most likely want to move from record to record, edit data, add new records, delete records, and copy records. The process of editing data includes learning important techniques such as how to select records, delete field contents, undo changes, and search and replace. The following sections cover all these techniques.

Moving from Record to Record in a Form

The Navigation Bar appears at the bottom of the Form window (see Figure 4.4). It allows you to move from record to record. The First Record navigation tool moves you to the first record, the Previous Record navigation tool moves you to the previous record, and the Record Number navigation tool allows you to quickly move to a desired record. To the right of the Record Number tool are the Next Record tool, the Last Record tool, and the New Record tool.

FIGURE 4.4

The Navigation Bar.

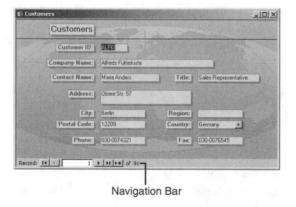

Navigation Bar

You can also you use keystrokes to move from record to record. Pressing Page Down moves you forward through the records, one record at a time. Pressing Page Up moves you backward through the records, one record at a time. Pressing Ctrl+End moves you to the last record, and pressing Ctrl+Home moves you to the first record. Finally, Ctrl+ moves you to a new record.

Editing the Data Underlying a Form

You can modify the table data from within a form. For example, you might want to change a customer's company name or address. Here's the process:

1. Select the record you want to change by using any of the techniques covered in the previous section of this hour, "Moving from Record to Record in a Form."

2. Select the field you want to change by clicking the field or using the directional keys.

3. Type to make the necessary changes to the data.

Deleting Field Contents Within a Form

Now that you know how to modify the contents of a field, let's talk about how to delete the contents of a field. In following along with this section, make sure that you understand that you are not deleting records, you are simply deleting the contents of an individual field *within* a record. You would do this, for example, if you entered a region for a company and then realized that the company was located in a country that did not have regions. The process is simple:

1. Select the field contents you want to delete.

2. Press the Delete key.

A couple items are important to note. First, if you press the Esc key twice, Access cancels all changes you made to that record. Second, it is important to recognize that Access saves the record you are working with as soon as you move off it onto another record.

4

Undoing Changes Made Within a Form

There are many times when you need to undo changes that you made to a control or to a record. An example is when you started making changes to the incorrect control—or even to the incorrect record. Undo comes to the rescue! You have several different options for how to do this, depending on whether you are still within a control, have left the control, or have left the record. You can use the Undo feature only to undo the last change made to a control or changes made to the most recently modified record.

Undoing Changes Made to the Current Control

When you are in the process of making changes to a control, you might realize that you really didn't want to make changes to that control or to that record. To undo changes to the current control, you can either click the Undo tool on the toolbar, select Edit|Undo Typing, or press the Esc key once.

Undoing Changes After You Move to Another Control

The process of undoing changes after you move to another control is slightly different from the process of undoing changes made to the current control. You can either click the Undo tool on the toolbar, select Edit|Undo Current Field/Record, or press the Esc key once.

Undoing Changes After You Save the Record

When you make changes to a control and then move to another record, Access saves all changes to the modified record. As long as you do not begin making changes to another record, you can still undo the changes you made to the most recently modified record. To do this, you can either click the Undo tool on the toolbar, select Edit|Undo Saved Record, or press the Esc key twice.

If Access is unable to undo a change, the Undo tool appears dimmed.

If you have made changes to a record and then have gone on to make changes to another record, you cannot undo the changes that you made to the first record.

Using a Form to Add New Records to a Table

Access adds records to the end of a table, regardless of how you add them to the table. To use a form to add new records to a table, follow these steps:

1. Click the New Record tool on the Navigation Bar at the bottom of the form.
2. Type the data for the new record (see Figure 4.5).
3. Press Tab to go to the next control.
4. Repeat steps 2 and 3 to enter all the data for the record.
5. Press Tab to move to another new record. Access saves the record.

There are some important things you should be aware of when adding new records. First, you can add records to a table by choosing Edit|Go To|New Record. Second, Access always displays one blank record at the end of a table. This blank record is ready to act as the new record. Finally, you can press the Tab key to add a record when you are on the last field of the last record in the table.

FIGURE **4.5**

Adding a new record.

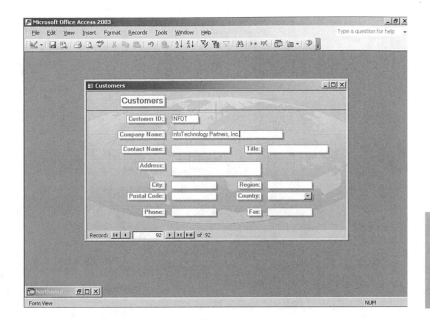

Using a Form to Delete Records from a Table

Before you can delete records, you must first select them. I therefore cover the process of selecting records before I cover the process of deleting records.

Selecting One or More Records

To select a record, you simply click the gray record selector button to the left of a record within a form (see Figure 4.6). Access selects the record.

NEW TERM To select multiple records (when the form is in Continuous Forms view or Datasheet view), you click and drag within the record selector area. *Continuous Forms view* allows you to view multiple rows of data in a form at a time. Access selects the contiguous range of records in the area over which you click and drag. As an alternative, you can click the selector button for the first record you want to select,

4

hold down the Shift key, and then click the selector button of the last record that you want to select. Access selects the entire range of records between the two selector buttons. Figure 4.7 shows the Orders table, with three records selected.

The gray selector button

FIGURE 4.6

The gray selector button.

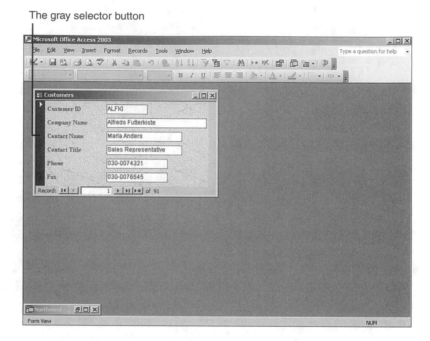

If you want to select a single record when the cursor is within the record, you can simply select Edit|Select Record.

FIGURE 4.7

The Orders *table, with three records selected.*

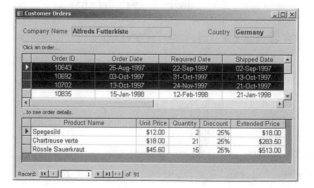

Deleting Records from Within a Form

When you know how to select records, deleting them is quite simple. The process is almost identical to that of deleting records in a datasheet:

1. Select the record you want to delete.

2. Press the Delete key. A dialog box appears, asking if you're sure you want to delete the record(s) (see Figure 4.8).

3. Click the Yes button.

FIGURE 4.8

A dialog box that asks if you want to delete the selected records.

The process of deleting a record is not so simple if you have established referential integrity between the tables in a database and the row that you are attempting to delete has child rows. Hour 9, "Creating Relationships," covers relationships and referential integrity. For now, you can think about the fact that customers generally have orders associated with them, and those orders have order detail records associated with them. The relationship between the Customers table and the Orders table prohibits the user from deleting customers who have orders. Here's how you delete a customer who has orders:

1. Select the record(s) you want to delete.

2. Press the Delete key. A dialog box appears, saying that the record cannot be deleted or changed because the table includes related records (see Figure 4.9).

3. Click OK to close the dialog box.

FIGURE 4.9

Access notifying you that you cannot delete the selected records.

Access provides a referential integrity option with which you can cascade a deletion down to the child table. This means, for example, that if you attempt to delete an order,

Access deletes the associated order detail records. If you establish referential integrity with the cascade delete option, the deletion process works like this:

1. Select the record(s) you want to delete.

2. Press the Delete key. A dialog box appears, asking whether you are sure you want to delete the record(s) (see Figure 4.10).

3. Click Yes to complete the deletion process.

FIGURE 4.10

Access asking if you want to delete the parent row and the associated child records.

After you have selected records, they appear in black and you can copy them, delete them, or modify them as a group. It is important to be aware that deleting records is a permanent process. You cannot undo a deletion.

Copying Records Within a Form

At times you may want to copy an entire record. This generally occurs because you are creating a new record and the new record is very similar to an existing record. For example, you might have two contacts at the same company who share similar information. You can copy the existing record and then make the necessary changes to the new record. Here's the process:

1. Select the record you want to copy. You can select the record by clicking the gray record selector or by selecting Edit | Select Record.

2. Select Edit | Copy.

3. Select Edit | Paste Append. Access copies the original record and places you in the new record (the copy).

Copying a record often results in what is called a *referential integrity error*. This occurs, for example, when copying a record would cause a duplicate primary key (that is, unique record identifier). In such a situation, you see an error message such as that displayed in Figure 4.11. You can either change the data in the field or fields that constitute the duplicate key, or you can press the Esc key to cancel the process of appending the new row. For example, in the example shown in Figure 4.11, you can modify the category name.

FIGURE **4.11**

*A referential integrity
error that appears
when copying a
record.*

Finding a Record That Meets Specific Criteria

If you are editing records in a form, you need to find specific records quickly. The same
procedure used in Datasheet view helps you to quickly locate data in a form:

1. Select the field that contains the criteria for which you are searching (in this case,
   ShipCity).

2. Click the Find button on the toolbar. The Find and Replace dialog box appears (see
   Figure 4.12).

FIGURE **4.12**

*The Find tab of the
Find and Replace dia-
log box, where you
search for values in a
datasheet.*

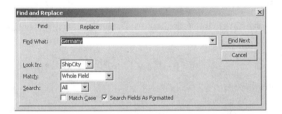

4

3. Type the criteria in the Find What text box. For this example, type **Madrid**.

4. Use the Look In drop-down list box to designate whether to search only the current
   field or all fields in the table. For this example, designate that you want to search
   only the current field.

5. Use the Match drop-down list box to designate whether to match any part of the
   field you are searching, the whole field you are searching, or the start of the field
   you are searching. For example, if you type the word **Federal** in the Find What
   text box and you select Whole Field in the Match drop-down list box, you find
   only entries where Ship Via is set to Federal. If you select Any Part of Field, you
   find Federal Shipping, Federal Express, United Federal Shipping, and so on. If you
   select Start of Field, you find Federal Shipping and Federal Express, but you do
   not find United Federal Shipping. For this example, designate that you want to
   match the whole field.

6. Use the Search drop-down list box to designate whether to search only up from the
   current cursor position, only down, or in all directions. For this example, designate
   that you want to search in all directions.

7. Use the Match Case check box to indicate whether you want the search to be case-sensitive.

8. Use the Search Fields as Formatted check box to indicate whether you want to find data only based on the display format (for example, 17-Jul-96 for a date).

9. Click the Find Next button to find the next record that meets the designated criteria.

10. To continue searching after you close the dialog box, use the Shift+F4 keystroke combination or the Find Again menu option.

Replacing Data in the Table Underlying a Form

There may be times when you want to update records that meet specific criteria. You might want to do this, for example, if a company changes its name or if you realize that you have improperly entered an employee's Social Security number. The Replace feature automatically inserts new information into the specified fields. Here's the process:

1. Click within the field that contains the criteria you are searching for (ShipCity, for this example).

2. Click the Find button on the toolbar. The Find and Replace dialog box appears.

3. Select the Replace tab (see Figure 4.13).

FIGURE 4.13

The Replace tab of the Find and Replace dialog box, where you can replace table data.

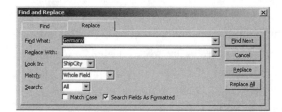

4. Type the criteria in the Find What text box. Type **Madrid** for this example.

5. Type the new information (the replacement value) in the Replace With text box. Type **GreatCity** for this example.

6. Choose values for the Look In drop-down list box, Match drop-down list box, Search drop-down list box, Match Case check box, and Search Fields as Formatted check box, as described in the "Finding a Record That Meets Specific Criteria" section of this hour.

7. Click the Find Next button. Access locates the first record that meets the criteria designated in the Find What text box.

8. Click the Replace button.

9. Repeat steps 7 and 8 to find all occurrences of the value in the Find What text box and replace them. As an alternative, you can click the Replace All button to replace all occurrences at once.

> You should use Replace All with quite a bit of caution. Remember that the changes you make are *permanent*. Although Replace All is a viable option, when you use it, you need to make sure you have a recent backup and that you are quite certain of what you are doing. In fact, I usually do a few replaces to make sure that I see what Access is doing *before* I click Replace All.

10. Click Cancel when you're done.

> If you are searching a very large table, Access can find a specific value in a field fastest if the field you are searching on is the primary key or an indexed field. Hours 8, "Creating Tables," and 14 "Power Table Techniques," cover primary keys and indexes.

4

When using either Find or Replace, you can use several wildcard characters. A *wildcard character* is a character you use in place of an unknown character. Table 4.1 describes the wildcard characters.

TABLE 4.1   Wildcard Characters You Can Use When Searching

Wildcard Character	Description
*	Acts as a placeholder for multiple characters.
?	Acts as a placeholder for a single character.
#	Acts as a placeholder for a single number.

Sorting Records

You can change the order of records by using sort buttons. You use this feature when you want to view your records in a particular order. For example, you might want to first view the records in order by company name, and later view them in order by most recent order date. The wonderful thing is that with this easy-to-use feature, changing the sort order involves a simple mouse click.

To sort on a field, follow these steps:

1. Click anywhere within the field.

2. Click the Sort Ascending button or click the Sort Descending button. Access reorders the form data based on the designated column.

> Another way to do this is to right-click a field and then choose Sort Ascending or Sort Descending.

Filtering the Data Underlying a Form

From the Form view, you can apply a filter to view a select group of records. You do this when you want to focus on a select group of records. For example, you might just want to work with the records in the Customers table for which the contact title is owner. You can use the Filter by Form feature to accomplish this task. When you learn how to use the Filter by Form feature, you need to know how to remove filters and how to work with multiple filter criteria.

Using the Filter by Form Feature

The Filter by Form feature is a wonderful feature that is built into Access 2003. It allows you to easily implement filtering while viewing data within a form. Here's how you use it:

1. Open the form whose data you want to filter.

2. Choose Records|Filter|Filter by Form. The Filter by Form feature appears.

3. Click in the field whose data you want to use as the filter criteria.

4. Select the field data to filter on from the drop-down list (see Figure 4.14).

5. Choose Filter|Apply Filter/Sort or click the Apply Filter tool on the toolbar. Access filters the data to just the designated rows.

Removing a Filter

To remove a filter, you simply choose Records|Remove Filter/Sort or click the Remove Filter toolbar button. Access then displays all the records in the record source underlying the form.

The Filter by form feature

FIGURE 4.14
The Filter by Form feature.

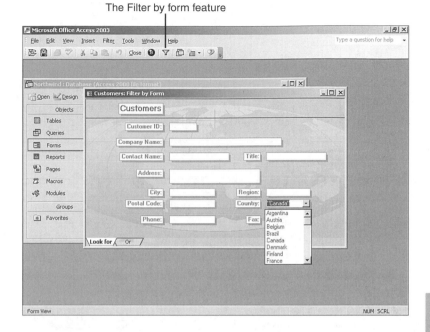

Using Multiple Filter Criteria

So far in this hour you have learned how to apply a single filter criterion for a single field. The following steps describe how to apply multiple filter criteria for multiple fields or multiple filter criteria for a single field. The process is similar to that of applying a single filter criterion for a single field:

1. Open the form whose data you want to filter.

2. Choose Records|Filter|Filter by Form. The Filter by Form feature appears.

3. Click in the first field you want to filter by.

4. Select the field data to filter on from the drop-down list that automatically appears when you click the Filter by Form tool and then click in a text box.

5. Select the Or tab.

6. Click in the next field you want to filter by. A drop-down list appears for that field.

7. Select the field data to filter on from the drop-down list.

8. Repeat steps 5 through 7 to apply as many additional filter options as desired.

9. Choose Filter|Apply Filter/Sort after you have applied all the desired filters. Access applies the designated filter.

You can filter by right-clicking a field and selecting Filter by Selection.

When creating multiple filters by using the Or tab, the records that meet either condition appear in the output.

Viewing the Design of a Form

You can use the View tool on the toolbar to toggle back and forth between Design view and Form view. Figure 4.15 shows a form in Design view. When you are in Design view, you can modify the underlying blueprint of the form. You can move and size controls, and you can add and remove controls. In fact, you can change the entire look, feel, and functionality of the form. Hours 11 and 16 cover form design techniques.

FIGURE 4.15

A form in Design view.

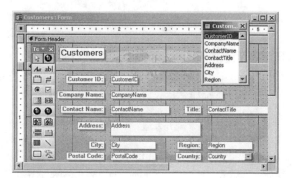

Closing a Form

To close a form, you click the close button (×) in the upper-right corner of the form. If you try to close a form without having made any *design changes*—that is, changes that you make to the design of the form—Access does not prompt you to save. This is because Access saves all data changes as you move from row to row. If you close a form and save design changes, those changes are permanent for all users of the form.

Using the AutoForm Feature

You can quickly build forms by using the AutoForm feature. The AutoForm feature gives you absolutely no control over how a form appears, but it provides you with an instantaneous means of data entry.

Creating a Form by Using the AutoForm Feature

Creating a form by using the AutoForm feature is amazingly easy. Here's how it works:

1. Select the table or query on which you want to base the new form. Select the Customers table for this example.

2. Select AutoForm from the New Object drop-down list box (see Figure 4.16). Access creates a form based on the selected table or query (see Figure 4.17).

FIGURE **4.16**

Selecting AutoForm from the New Object drop-down list box.

FIGURE **4.17**

Access creating a form based on the selected table or query.

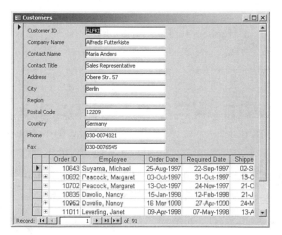

4

Saving a Form

Although Access automatically saves all the data changes that you make to a form, it is up to you to save all the design changes that you make to the form. As you work with the design of a form, you should periodically click the Save tool on the toolbar to save changes. When you close the form, Access prompts you to once again save your changes. Here's the process:

1. Choose File|Close. A dialog box appears, asking if you want to save your changes.
2. Click the Yes button.
3. If you have not yet named the form, Access prompts you with the Save As dialog box, asking you to provide a name for the form.
4. Enter a form name and click OK.

> Naming standards suggest that you use the `frm` prefix to name a form.

> The name of a form can be up to 64 characters and can contain text, numbers, and spaces.

> Subdata datasheets are available within forms, just as they are in datasheets.

Using the Form Wizard to Build a Form

Using the Form Wizard gives you more flexibility than using the AutoForm feature to create forms. It also requires more knowledge on your part. Here's how you use it:

1. Click Forms in the list of objects in the Database window.
2. Double-click the Create Form by Using Wizard option.
3. Select the table or query on which you want to base the form (see Figure 4.18).

FIGURE 4.18
Selecting a table or query.

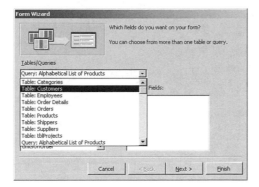

4. Select the fields you want to include on the form (see Figure 4.19).

FIGURE 4.19
Selecting fields.

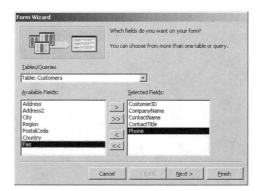

5. Click Next. Select a layout for the form (see Figure 4.20).

FIGURE 4.20
Selecting a layout.

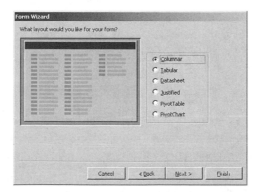

6. Click Next. Select a style for the form (see Figure 4.21).

FIGURE 4.21
Selecting a style.

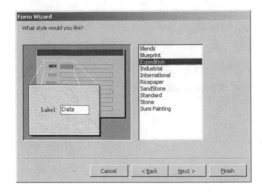

7. Click Next. Provide a title for the form (see Figure 4.22).

FIGURE 4.22
Providing a title.

8. Click Finish.

If you create a form by clicking the New button on the Database toolbar, you have choices about what kind of form you want to create:

*   The Columnar option places the fields on the left side of the screen.
*   The Tabular option displays the records in columns from left to right across the form.
*   The Datasheet option displays the records in Datasheet view.
*   Using the AutoForm feature lets Access design the form for you.
*   The Chart Wizard assists you in creating a form that contains a graph.
*   The Pivot Table Wizard assists you in creating a form that contains an embedded Excel PivotTable.

Using the Conditional Formatting Feature of a Form

At some point you might need to have a control stand out if it meets certain criteria. You can add formatting to the control to set what condition should be met in order for a particular type of formatting to appear in the record. An example would be for the inventory amount to appear in red if the inventory amount is less than the reorder amount. Here's how you use this Conditional Formatting feature:

1. Open the form that you want to format in Design view.

2. Click in the control that will contain the conditional formatting.

3. Choose Format|Conditional Formatting. The Conditional Formatting dialog box appears (see Figure 4.23).

FIGURE 4.23

The Conditional Formatting dialog box.

4. Select the condition (equal to, greater than, and so on).

5. Type the appropriate criteria.

6. Select the desired formatting.

7. Click OK. Access applies the conditional formatting expression.

You can click the Add button to specify a second condition for a field.

Task: Creating, Filtering, and Saving Forms

To practice many of the skills you've learned in this hour, you can create a new form that you can use to add data to the Customers table. You can then use the Filter by Form feature to find all records with Owner in the ContactTitle field.

▼   1. Open the Northwind database that ships with Access.

        2. Create a new form for the Customers table by using the wizard. Here are the selections that you should make when creating the new form:
            • Add all the fields to the form.
            • Choose a columnar layout.
            • Choose a style you like.
            • Title the form Customer Data Entry Form.

        3. Add a new record to the table, using the following information:

Client ID	Company Name	Contact Name	Contact Title	Address	City	Phone
XOXOX	Fireworks Galore	Alexis Balter	Head Honcho	74 July Street	Red	805/777-4747

        4. Use the Filter by Form feature to find all records with Owner in the ContactTitle field.

        5. Remove the filter.

▲   6. Close the form.

Summary

As you have seen in this hour, there's quite a bit you can accomplish with forms. In this hour you have learned how to view and navigate table data via a form. You have learned how to add, edit, and delete records via a form. You have also learned how to find and replace, as well as how to filter table data by using the Filter by Form feature. You have learned how to view the design of a form and how to close and save a form. You have also learned how to use the AutoForm feature and the Form Wizard to create new forms. In this hour you have also learned how to use the very powerful Conditional Formatting feature to add conditional formatting to the forms that you build.

Q&A

Q Name four uses of forms.

A Forms can be used for data entry, as switchboards, as dialog boxes, and as printed forms.

Q Explain the difference between AutoForm and the Form Wizard.

A With AutoForm, you make no decisions. Access creates the form with no input from you. The process is very easy for you, but you have no control over the outcome. With the Form Wizard, you must make some decisions. Compared to using AutoForm, using the Form Wizard requires more knowledge and training on your part, but it gives you more control over the outcome.

Q Explain the use of the Conditional Formatting feature.

A As its name implies, the Conditional Formatting feature allows you to conditionally format data. For example, if the sales amount is greater than a specified amount, you could display it in one color, and if it is less than or equal to that amount, you could display it in another color. As the user browses the form, the sales amounts stand out as appropriate.

Workshop

The Workshop includes quiz questions that are designed to help you test your understanding of the material covered and activities to help put what you've learned to practice. You can find the answers to the questions in the section immediately following the quiz.

Quiz

1. Name the menu selection that allows you to copy a record and add it as the last record in the form.
2. Name the feature that allows you to easily filter form data.
3. You must save changes to data while working with a form (True/False).
4. You must save changes to the design of a form (True/False).
5. Name the quickest way to create a new form.

Quiz Answers

1. Edit|Copy, Edit|Paste Append.
2. Filter by Form.
3. False. Access saves data changes as you move to another row.
4. True.
5. Using the AutoForm feature.

Activities

Practice using a form to add, edit, and delete records. Practice searching and replacing. Practice sorting and filtering. View the design of the form. Use both the AutoForm feature and the Form Wizard to create new forms. Finally, practice using the Conditional Formatting feature to conditionally format data.

HOUR 5

Reports Introduced

Reports provide printed output of the data in a database. They are generally a major objective of any database application that you develop. In this hour you'll learn the following:

- How to open and view a report
- How to navigate around a report
- How to print a report
- How to use the AutoReport feature and the Report Wizard to create new reports
- How to view the design of a report
- How to close a report
- How to print database objects

To learn how to modify the design of a report, you should take a look at Hour 12, "Creating Reports," and Hour 17, "Power Report Techniques."

Opening and Viewing a Report

Microsoft Access provides an excellent means of working with existing reports. You can either send a report directly to the printer, or you can first preview a report that you want to work with. Let's begin by taking a look at the process of previewing a report:

1. Click the Reports list of objects in the Database window (see Figure 5.1).

Preview button

FIGURE 5.1

The Reports list of objects.

Reports list —

2. Double-click the report you want to open or single-click the report and then click the Preview button on the Database toolbar. The report appears in Preview mode (also called Print Preview mode).

Moving from Page to Page

A report is a way to present the data from a table or query in a formatted document. Although you can print datasheets, reports control how you present and summarize the data. When you open a report, you can use the navigation buttons to easily move from page to page. You accomplish this by using the page navigation buttons at the bottom of the report window (see Figure 5.2). By using these buttons, you can easily navigate to the first page of the report, the previous page, the next page, or the last page of the report. By typing a number into the text box on the navigation bar, you can easily navigate to any page in the report.

Zooming In and Out

When previewing reports, you can change the amount of text (and the size of the text) that you see onscreen in a report. You do this by zooming in and out of the report page. There are two different techniques that you can use to set the zoom level. Here's the first technique:

1. Place the mouse pointer over the report so that it appears as a magnifying glass.

2. Click the mouse. The page zooms in.

3. Click the mouse again. The page zooms out.

FIGURE 5.2

Report navigation buttons.

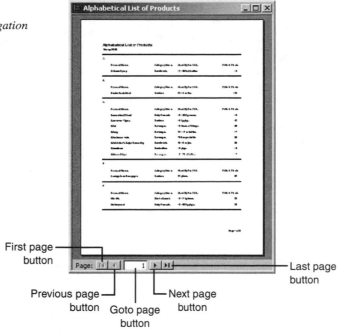

First page button

Previous page button

Goto page button

Next page button

Last page button

Here's the second technique:

1. Click the Zoom drop-down list box (see Figure 5.3).

2. Select a size. The report zooms to the designated level.

The Fit option within the Zoom drop-down list box fits the report within the available screen real estate of the report window.

5

Viewing Multiple Pages

While you're previewing an Access report, you can preview more than one page at a time. To view two pages, you click the Two Pages button on the Print Preview toolbar. To view multiple pages, you click the Multiple Pages button and select how many pages you want to view (see Figure 5.4).

FIGURE 5.3

The Zoom drop-down list box, which allows you to select a zoom level.

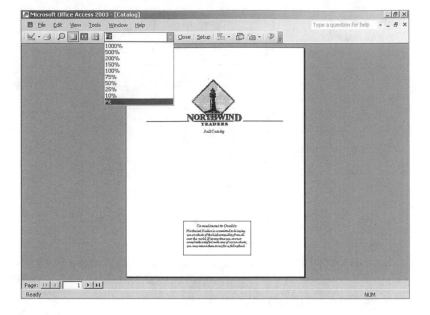

FIGURE 5.4

Selecting how many pages you want to view.

Printing a Report

Before you print a report, you can change the report margins, orientation, paper size, and several other important options. You accomplish this by using the Page Setup feature. Here's how it works:

1. While previewing the report, click the Setup button on the Preview toolbar. The Page Setup dialog box appears (see Figure 5.5).

2. The Margins tab allows you to modify the margins. The Page tab allows you to customize important settings such as the orientation, paper size and source, and printer you wish to use. The Columns tab allows you to designate column size and other information applicable for multicolumn reports. Select the desired options.

3. Click OK to accept your changes.

FIGURE 5.5

The Page Setup dialog box, where you select report settings.

Sending Reports to a Printer

You can print the reports you create by using the Print dialog box that you access by selecting File|Print or using the Print button from the Standard toolbar. You can also print a report while you are in Print Preview mode. To print a report by using the File menu, follow these steps:

1. Click Reports in the list of objects in the Database window.
2. Click to select the report you want to print.
2. Choose File|Print.
3. Complete the dialog box, entering information such as the number of copies you want to print, the printer you wish to print to, and so on.
4. Click OK to complete the process.

The process of printing a report by using the Print button from the Standard toolbar works like this:

1. Click Reports in the list of objects in the Database window.
2. Click to select the report you want to print.
3. Click the Print tool on the Standard toolbar. Access immediately sends the report to the printer without invoking the Print dialog box or asking for further confirmation.

You can also print a report while you are in Print Preview mode. You simply click the Print button on the Print Preview toolbar. As when you use the Print button on the Standard toolbar, Access immediately sends the report to the printer.

5

The AutoReport Feature and the Report Wizard

To help you create reports, Access provides the Report Wizard. The Report Wizard asks questions about the report and then creates the report based on your answers. In Access you can also use the AutoReport feature to create a report.

Using the AutoReport Feature

NEW TERM   Using the *AutoReport feature* is the quickest and easiest way to create a report. Access creates a report via the AutoReport feature without asking you any questions. Although you can create this type of report effortlessly, as you will see, it is not very flexible in that it does not ask you *any* questions. Here's how it works:

1. Select Tables or Queries in the list of objects in the Database window.

2. Select the table or query on which you want to base the report.

3. Click the New Object button drop-down arrow (see Figure 5.6).

4. Select AutoReport. Access creates a report based on the selected table or query.

FIGURE 5.6

The New Object drop-down arrow, which allows you to create a report with the AutoReport feature.

Creating a Report by Using the Report Wizard

Although the AutoReport feature is great at producing a quick report, it does not offer much in terms of flexibility. The Report Wizard asks a series of questions and then better customizes the report to your needs. Let's take a look at how it works:

1. Select Reports in the list of objects in the Database window.

2. Click Create Report by Using Wizard.

3. In the first step of the wizard, select the table or query on which you want to base the report.

4. Select the fields you want to include in the report (see Figure 5.7). You can add any type of field to a report. You can also add as many fields or as few fields as you'd like. In fact, you can even include fields from more than one table! Click Next.

FIGURE 5.7

Step 1: Selecting the fields you want to include in a report.

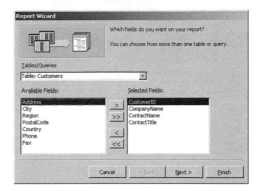

5. In the second step, the wizard prompts you to select any fields that you want to group by (see Figure 5.8). Click Next.

FIGURE 5.8

Step 2: Selecting the fields that you want to group by.

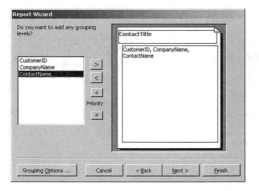

6. In the third step of the wizard, select the desired sort order (see Figure 5.9). You can select either ascending or descending. In Figure 5.9, ascending is selected. Click Next.

7. In the fourth step of the wizard, select the desired layout for the report (see Figure 5.10). The layout you select is a matter of personal preference, as well as which layout will work best with the data selected for the report. Click Next.

8. The fifth step of the wizard prompts you to select the desired style for the report (see Figure 5.11). The style you select is mostly a matter of personal preference.

After you complete the wizard, you can modify the selected style to, for example, format the report header differently from the rest of the report. Click Next.

FIGURE 5.9

Step 3: Selecting a sort order for a report.

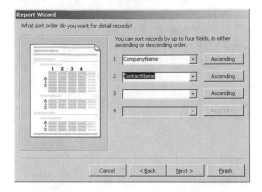

FIGURE 5.10

Step 4: Selecting a layout for a report.

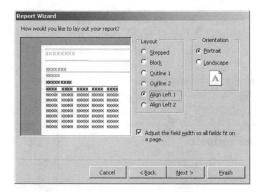

FIGURE 5.11

Step 5: Selecting a style for a report.

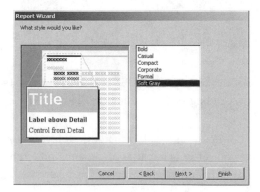

9. The sixth step of the wizard prompts you to type the report title.
10. Click the Finish button. Access creates the report and places you in Preview mode.

As you can see, the Report Wizard offers quite a bit more flexibility than the AutoReport feature. By using the Report Wizard, you can designate the fields you want to include on a report, the data groupings you want to add to a report, the sort order for a report, the layout for a report, and a style for a report. I find that the Report Wizard can generally do most of the work for me, and then I can add finishing touches.

Viewing the Design of a Report

Reports created with the AutoReport feature are limiting because they are very generic. But after you create such a rather-dull, generic report by using the AutReport feature, you can make modifications by using the Design view. Access does the basics, and then you add bells and whistles to make the report more individual and better suited to your specific application. Furthermore, although the Report Wizard gives you many choices, you still might want to customize many of the options that it sets.

After you have created a report by using the AutoReport feature or the Report Wizard, you will probably want to customize the report. You must switch to Design view of the report to accomplish this task. While previewing the report, you simply click the View tool on the Print Preview toolbar (see Figure 5.12) to switch to Design view. The report is shown in Design view in Figure 5.13. You can easily toggle between Design view and Preview mode, to view the report and then modify its design.

FIGURE 5.12
The View tool, which switches you to Design view.

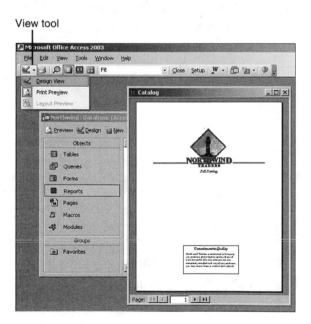

5

FIGURE 5.13
The report in Design view.

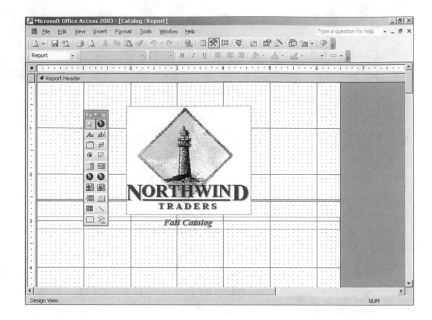

Closing a Report

When you are finished working with a report, you need to close it. Access first prompts you and asks you if you want to save changes to the report. You should click Yes. If you have not yet provided a name for the report, Access prompts you to name the report.

Naming standards suggest that you use the `rpt` prefix to name a report (for example, `rptCustomers`).

Printing Database Objects

Sometimes it is unnecessary to go through the process of building a report. It might be sufficient, for example, to simply print the datasheet that shows the result of running a query. Access allows you to print table datasheets, query results, and forms. The following sections cover the process of printing each of these objects.

Printing Table Datasheets

You can easily print a table datasheet. Here's how:

1. Select Tables in the list of database objects.
2. Double-click the table whose data you want to print.

3. Click the Print Preview button to preview the data before you print it or click Print to send the data directly to a printer. As an alternative, if you want to modify print settings, you can select File|Print. The Print dialog box appears (see Figure 5.14). Modify any print settings and click OK to proceed.

FIGURE 5.14

The Print dialog box, which allows you to modify print settings.

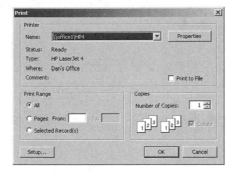

 While in Print Preview mode, you can change the page setup options by choosing File|Page Setup. Access does not save these changes when you close Print Preview.

Printing Queries

You can print the datasheet that is the result of running a query by following these steps:

1. Click Queries in the list of objects in the Database window.

2. Double-click the query whose result set you want to print.

3. Click the Print Preview button to preview the data before you print it or click Print to send the data directly to a printer. As an alternative, if you want to modify print settings, you can select File|Print. The Print dialog box appears. Modify any print settings and click OK to proceed.

Printing Forms

When you print a form, you print the data and the layout of the form. Here's how you do it:

1. Select Form in the list of database objects.

2. Double-click the form you want to print.

3. Click the Print Preview button to preview the data before you print it (see Figure 5.15) or click Print to send the form directly to a printer. As an alternative, if you

5

want to modify print settings, you can select File|Print. The Print dialog box appears. Modify any print settings and click OK to proceed.

FIGURE 5.15
Previewing a form before you print it.

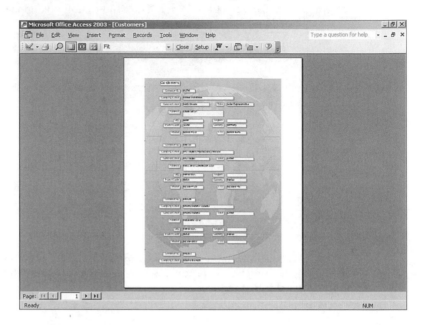

Task: Working with Reports

It's important that you be able to create a report by using the Report Wizard and that you be able to modify and print that report. This task walks you through that process:

1. Create a new report based on the Customers table in the Northwind sample database that comes with Access. Use the Report Wizard to do so. The process involves adding the appropriate fields and groupings, selecting a sort order, and selecting a layout and style. The following are the specifics:

    • Add all the fields to the report.

    • Group on the Country field.

    • Sort on the City field.

    • Choose the layout and style you like.

    • Title the report Customers by Country.

2. Preview the report.

3. Close the report.

4. Open the report you just saved.

▼ 5. Print the report.

▲ 6. Close the report. Close the database.

Task: Printing Database Objects

To Do

It is important that you be comfortable printing database objects. This task walks you through that process:

1. Open the NORTHWIND database that ships with Access.

2. Preview and then print the Customers table.

3. Preview and then print the Sales by Category query.

4. Preview and then print the Product List form.

▲ 5. Print the Sales by Category report from the Database window.

Summary

Reports are a vital part of any Access application. In this hour you have learned the basics of working with reports. You have learned how to open a report and navigate around it while in Print Preview mode. You have also learned how to create very simple reports by using both the AutoReport feature and the Report Wizard. You have learned how to view the design of a report. In this hour you have also learned about closing a report and printing other database objects, such as tables, queries, and forms.

Q&A

Q Explain the difference between the AutoReport feature and the Report Wizard.

A With AutoReport you make no decisions. Access creates a report with no input from you. The process is very easy for you, but you have no control over the outcome. With the Report Wizard, you must make some decisions. The process requires more knowledge and training on your part, but you have more control over the outcome.

Q Explain the difference between Print and Print Preview.

A Print immediately sends the output to a printer. Print Preview allows you to view the output onscreen before you send it to a printer.

Q Explain why you might want to print other database objects.

A Sometimes it is unnecessary to go through the process of building a report. It might be sufficient, for example, to simply print the datasheet that shows the result of running a query.

5

Workshop

The Workshop includes quiz questions that are designed to help you test your under-standing of the material covered and activities to help put what you've learned to prac-tice. You can find the answers to the questions in the section immediately following the quiz.

Quiz

1. How do you change printer options?
2. How many zoom levels can you get by simply clicking a report while previewing it?
3. Name some things you can change in the Page Setup dialog box.
4. You must close a report after previewing it before you can view its design (True/False).
5. Name the quickest way to create a new report.

Quiz Answers

1. Select File|Print from the Database window or while previewing the report.
2. Two.
3. Margins, orientation, paper size, printer used, and column size.
4. False. You can toggle to Design view.
5. By using the AutoReport feature.

Activities

Practice opening an existing report. Practice moving from page to page, zooming in and out, and viewing multiple pages. View the design of the report. Use both the AutoReport feature and the Report Wizard to create new reports. Finally, practice printing a table, a query result, a form, and a report.

PART III

Creating Your Own Database and Objects

HOUR 6

Using Wizards to Create a Database

Access provides many wizards that facilitate the process of creating a database and the objects within it. These wizards can provide everything that you need. Sometimes, however, you might run the wizards and then have to modify the design of the objects that the wizards create, or you might find it easier to build the objects from scratch. This hour focuses on the wizards, and in later hours, you'll learn how to modify the objects that the wizards create and build the objects from scratch.

In this hour you'll learn the following:

- How to use the Database Wizard to create a new database
- How to create an empty database from scratch
- How to use wizards to create queries, forms, and reports

Using a Database Template to Create a Database

You can use the Database Wizard to create a new database based on a template (a Customer database, for example). You can select options provided by the wizard to make the database suit your specific needs. After you have completed the process of running the wizard, you can then modify the design of any of the objects that the wizard creates.

To create a new database by using the Database Wizard, follow these steps:

1. With the Database window active, select File|New. The New File panel appears on the right-hand side of the screen.
2. Select On my computer from the list of options that appears below Templates on the right-hand side of the screen (see Figure 6.1). The Templates dialog box appears.

FIGURE 6.1

Selecting On my computer from the list of options under Templates.

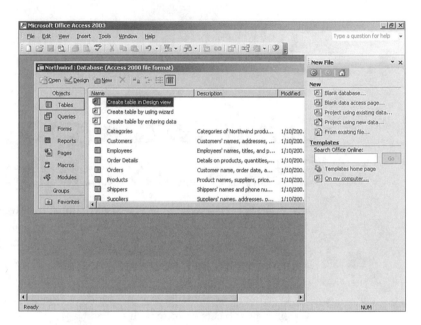

3. Select the Databases tab in the Templates dialog box (see Figure 6.2).

FIGURE 6.2

Database templates you can use to get started.

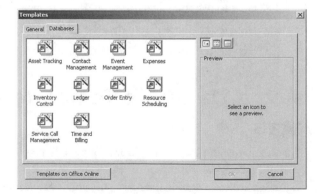

4. Double-click the desired template (for example, Contact Management).

5. Type the filename and location for the new database.

6. Click the OK button. The Database Wizard appears.

7. Click Next. The wizard prompts you with a list of selected tables and fields (see Figure 6.3).

FIGURE 6.3

A list of suggested tables and fields.

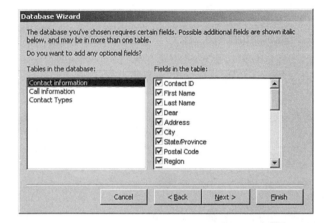

8. Scroll down to view the list of optional fields for each table (see Figure 6.4).

FIGURE 6.4

A list of optional fields to include in tables.

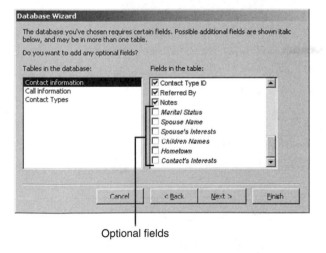

Optional fields

9. Click to include the desired optional fields.

10. Click Next to continue.

11. Select a style for the forms and click Next.

12. Select a style for the reports and click Next.

13. Select a title for the database and, if you want to, select a picture that Access should include on reports. Click Next.

14. Click Finish to complete the process. The resulting application switchboard should look like the one shown in Figure 6.5.

NEW TERM The Database Wizard creates a *switchboard* that allows you to very easily add data to tables, view the data entered, and run reports. After you run the wizard, you can add new objects to the database and customize the existing objects to your liking.

FIGURE 6.5
The application switchboard.

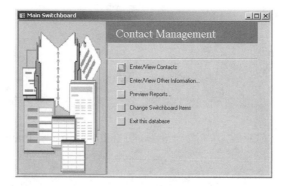

15. Press F11, and the Database window appears.

16. Click Tables in the list of objects. Notice what tables the wizard has added to the database (see Figure 6.6).

FIGURE 6.6
Tables added to the database.

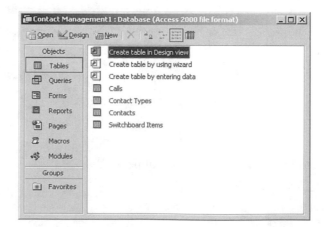

17. Click the various object categories (tables, queries, and so on) to view the other types of objects that the Database Wizard created.

Creating a Database from Scratch

When none of the available databases that the wizard creates gives you what you need, you need to create a database on your own. To create a new database from scratch, follow these steps:

1. Choose File|New.
2. Select Blank Database from the list of options on the right-hand side of the screen.
3. Select a drive and/or folder where you will place the database.
4. Type a filename for the database.
5. Click the OK button.

Access creates an empty database file. You can add the necessary tables, queries, forms, reports, data access pages, macros, and modules that comprise a functional application.

> Database filenames must follow these rules:
>
> - Database names can contain up to 255 characters.
> - Database names can contain spaces, but you should avoid special characters such as asterisks.
> - Access assigns the extension .MDB to a databases that you create.

Building a Table by Using a Wizard

The Table Wizard can assist you with the process of building basic tables. It provides you with the table structures necessary to collect data for many common personal and business systems.

To build a table by using the Table Wizard, follow these steps:

1. Select the Tables icon from the list of objects in the Database window.
2. Double-click the Create Table by Using Wizard icon. The Table Wizard appears (see Figure 6.7).
3. The first step in the Table Wizard lets you choose specific fields from one of many predefined tables. The tables are categorized as business and personal. If you select

6

the Business option, you see a set of business-related tables; if you select Personal, you see a set of tables for Personal topics.

FIGURE 6.7
The Table Wizard.

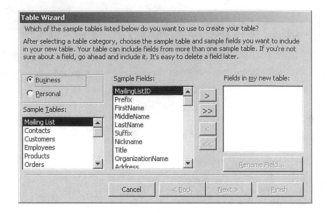

4. After you have selected a type of table, you can specify which fields you want to include in the table. To do this, double-click the field you want or click the right-arrow button. In Figure 6.8, the EmployeeID, FirstName, LastName, Title, Extension, DateHired, and Salary fields are selected from the table called Employees.

FIGURE 6.8
Designating which fields you want to include in a table.

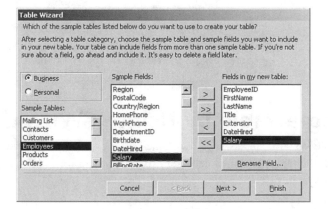

5. After you have selected the table and fields you want, click Next to open the dialog box shown in Figure 6.9. In this step of the Table Wizard, you name the table and indicate whether you want Access to set the primary key for you. (Primary keys are covered in more detail in Hour 8, "Creating Tables.") It's always a good idea for a table to have a primary key, which is used to uniquely identify each record. If you don't tell Access to set a primary key, you'll have the opportunity

later to designate a unique field as the primary key. If you haven't entered a unique identifier (that is, some field that differentiates each record from the next) for the table, select Yes. Access then adds an AutoNumber field to the table and designates it as the primary key.

FIGURE **6.9**

Naming the new table and indicating whether you want Access to set the primary key.

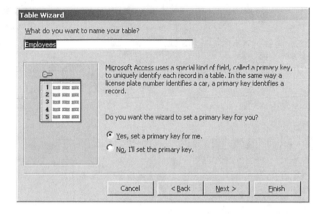

The industry standard is to begin table names with the tag tbl. For example, you should name the Employees table tblEmployees to make it easily recognizable as a table.

6. **NEW TERM**   In the next step of the Table Wizard (see Figure 6.10), Access tries to identify relationships between the new table and existing tables (if there are any existing tables). The process of establishing relationships is an important part of Access development. Relationships allow you to normalize a database and to "flatten out" the data structure at runtime. *To normalize* means to test tables against a series of rules to ensure that the application runs as efficiently as possible. Relationships also help you ensure the integrity of an application's data. For example, you can define a relationship so that it's impossible to enter orders for customers who don't exist. Although Access automatically identifies relationships if it can, you can modify or add relationships by clicking the Relationships button. When you're satisfied with the relationships that you have established, click Next.

7. The final dialog box of the Table Wizard, shown in Figure 6.11, allows you to indicate whether you want to modify the design of the table, enter data into the table, or let Access automatically build both the table and a data-entry form for you. Click Finish to complete the process. Access creates the table with the options that you specified.

6

FIGURE 6.10

*Designating relation-
ships between the new
table and any existing
tables.*

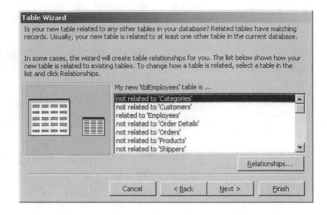

FIGURE 6.11

*Specifying what you
want the wizard to do
when it has finished
processing.*

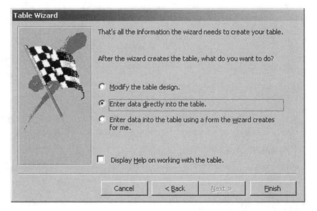

Building a Query by Using a Wizard

Just as the Table Wizard facilitates the process of creating tables, the Simple Query
Wizard helps you to build basic queries. Here's how you use it:

1. Select the Queries icon from the list of objects in the Database window.

2. Double-click the Create Query by Using a Wizard icon. The Simple Query Wizard
   appears (see Figure 6.12).

3. From the Tables/Queries drop-down list box, select the table or query on which
   you want to base the query. Then select the fields that you want to include in the

query. In the example in Figure 6.13, the Customers table from the Northwind data-base is selected, and the CustomerID, CompanyName, ContactName, ContactTitle, Country, and Phone fields are selected from the table.

FIGURE 6.12

The Simple Query Wizard.

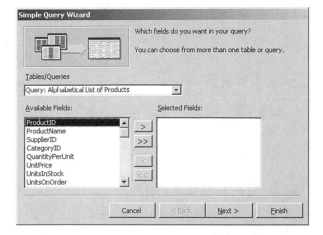

FIGURE 6.13

Choosing the table and fields for the output of the query.

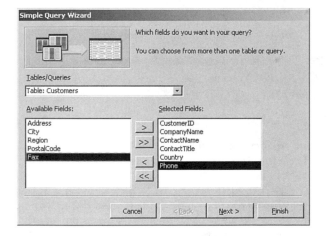

4. Click Next to continue with the wizard. The second and final step of the Simple Query Wizard prompts you to name the query and allows you to either immediately run the query or modify the design of the query (see Figure 6.14).

5. Click Finish to complete the process.

6

FIGURE 6.14

Naming a query and opening it to view its design.

Building a Form by Using a Wizard

Just as the wizards we've looked at so far in this hour can give you a jump start when creating tables and queries, the Form Wizard can give you the help you need to get started with building forms.

To create a form with the Form Wizard, follow these steps:

1. Select the Create Form by Using a Wizard icon with the Forms icon selected from the Objects list. You can also select Form Wizard from the New Form dialog box and click OK.

> Another way to start the Form Wizard is to click the Tables or Queries icon in the Objects list and then select the table or query you want the form to be based on. From the New Object drop-down list box on the toolbar, you select Form; this opens the New Form dialog box. Then you select Form Wizard. You don't have to use the Tables/Queries drop-down list box to select a table or query because Access automatically selects the table or query you selected before invoking the wizard.

2. The Form Wizard prompts you for the name of the table or query you want to use as the form's foundation (see Figure 6.15). Whether you're creating a form with the Form Wizard or from Design view, it's generally best to base a form on a query or on an embedded Structured Query Language (SQL) statement (that is, a query stored as part of a form). Doing so offers better performance than basing a form on

a table (unless a form requires all fields and all records), allows for more flexibility, and lets you create a form based on data from several tables. Figure 6.15 shows the Tables/Queries drop-down list box, in which all the queries and tables are listed, followed by all the queries.

FIGURE 6.15

A list of tables and queries available for use in the Form Wizard.

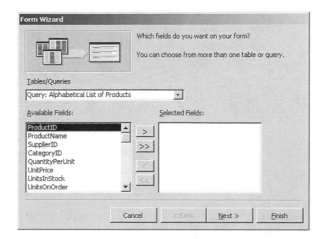

3. After you select a particular table or query, Access displays its fields in the Available Fields list box (see Figure 6.16). To select the fields to include on the form, double-click the name of the field or click on the field, and then click the right-arrow button. In the example shown in Figure 6.16, several fields from the Alphabetical List of Products query in the Northwind sample database are selected. Select the fields you want and then click Next.

FIGURE 6.16

Selected fields from the Alphabetical List of Products *query.*

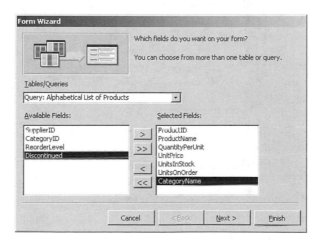

6

4. The second step of the Form Wizard allows you to specify the layout for the form you're designing. You can select from Columnar, Tabular, Datasheet, Justified, PivotTable, and PivotChart layouts (see Figure 6.17); the most common choice is Columnar. Select a form layout and then click Next.

FIGURE 6.17

Specifying a layout for the form you are creating.

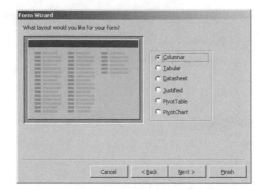

5. In the third step of the Form Wizard, you can select a style for a form from several predefined styles (see Figure 6.18). Although you can use Design view to modify all the properties set by the wizard after the wizard creates the form, to save time, it's best to select the appropriate style while you're running the wizard. Select a style for your form and then click Next.

FIGURE 6.18

Selecting a form style.

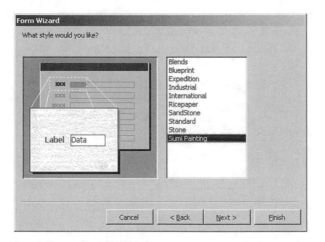

6. In the final step of the Form Wizard, supply a title for the form. (If you just accept the default, the form will have the same name as the underlying table or query, which could be confusing.) Unfortunately, the form's title becomes the name of the

form as well. For this reason, you should type the text you want to use as the name of the form. If you want to follow standard naming conventions, you should begin the name of the form with the tag `frm`. Later, if you want to change the title of the form, you can do so in Design view. This last step of the Form Wizard also lets you specify whether you want to view the results of your work or open the form in Design view. It's usually best to view the results and then modify the form's design after you have taken a peek at what the Form Wizard has done. Click Finish. Figure 6.19 shows an example of a completed form.

FIGURE 6.19

A form created by the Form Wizard.

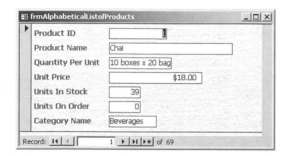

Building a Report by Using a Wizard

The final wizard that we're going to take a look at in this hour is the Report Wizard. No matter how experienced you are as an Access user or developer, the Report Wizard can save you much time and effort. For instance, the Report Wizard can lay out controls and create summary calculations much more quickly than I can in Design view.

To create a report with the Report Wizard, follow these steps:

1. Click Reports in the Objects list and then double-click the Create Report by Using a Wizard icon. This launches the Report Wizard.

Another way to start the Report Wizard is to select Tables or Queries from the Objects list in the Database container and then click the table or query that you want the report to be based on. From the New Object drop-down list box on the toolbar, you select Report. In the New Report dialog box, you select Report Wizard. You don't have to use the Tables/Queries drop-down list box to select a table or query because the one you selected before invoking the wizard is automatically selected for you.

6

2. In the first step of the wizard, you select the table or query that will supply data to the report. I prefer to base reports on queries or on embedded SQL statements. This generally improves performance because it returns the smallest dataset possible. Basing reports on queries also enhances your ability to produce reports based on varying criteria. After you select a table or query, you can select the fields you want to include on the report. Access displays the fields included in the selected table or query in the Available Fields list box. To add fields to the report, double-click the name of the field you want to add or click the field name and then click the right-arrow button. In the example in Figure 6.20, several fields from the Alphabetical List of Products query in the Northwind database are selected. When you are done selecting a table or query and the fields you want to include on the report, click Next.

FIGURE 6.20

Making table/query and field selections.

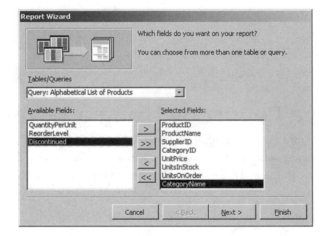

3. If you based your report on data from more than one table or on a query that retrieves data from multiple tables, the Report Wizard shows a dialog box that lets you determine how to view the data. For example, in Figure 6.21, the Report Wizard prompts you to select whether to view the data by category or by product. If this dialog box appears, make a selection and click Next.

4. Access prompts you to add group levels (see Figure 6.22), which add report groupings, to the report. Add group levels if you need to visually separate groups of data or include summary calculations (subtotals) in a report. Notice that in Figure 6.22 the CategoryName grouping appears. This is because I opted to view the data by category in the previous step of the wizard. If a report doesn't require additional groupings, click Next.

FIGURE 6.21

Selecting how you want to view data.

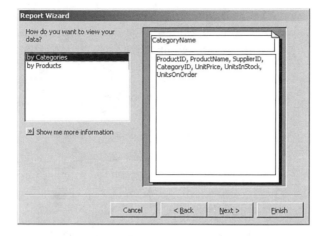

FIGURE 6.22

Adding group levels to a report.

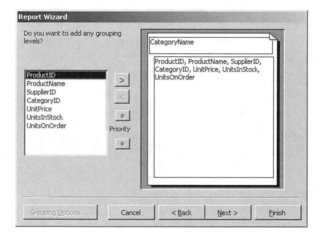

5. In the next step of the Report Wizard, you choose sorting levels for the report. Because the order of a query underlying a report is overridden by any sort order designated in the report, it's a good idea to designate a sort order for the report. You can add up to four sorting levels by using the Report Wizard. In the example shown in Figure 6.23, the report is sorted by the SupplierID and then the ProductID fields. Notice the Ascending buttons to the right of the drop-down list boxes. If you click the buttons, they toggle to read Descending, causing the data to sort in descending order. After you select the fields you want to sort on, click Next.

6. In the next step of the Report Wizard, you decide on the report's layout and orientation (see Figure 6.24). The layout options vary depending on what selections you have made in the wizard's previous steps. The orientation can be Portrait or

6

Landscape. This step of the Report Wizard also allows you to specify whether you want Access to adjust the width of each field so that all the fields fit on each page. Supply Access with this information and then click Next.

FIGURE 6.23

Determining the sorting of report data.

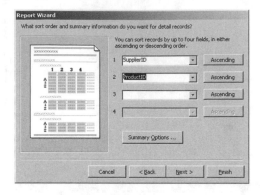

FIGURE 6.24

Selecting the appropriate layout and orientation for a report.

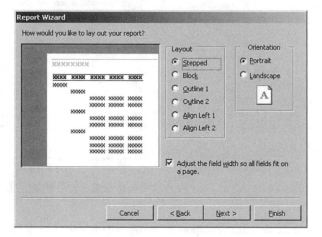

7. In the Report Wizard's next step, you choose a style for the report (see Figure 6.25). The choices are Bold, Casual, Compact, Corporate, Formal, and Soft Gray. You can preview each look before you make a decision by simply clicking the style. Later on, you can modify any of the style attributes that the Report Wizard applies, as well as other report attributes that the wizard defines. You accomplish this in Design view any time after the wizard produces the report. After you select a style, click Next.

8. The final step of the Report Wizard prompts you for the report's title. Access uses this title as both the name and the caption for the report. (You can supply a stan-

dard Access report name and modify the caption after the Report Wizard has finished its process.) You're then given the opportunity to preview the report or modify the report's design. If you opt to modify the report's design, Access places you
in Design view rather than in Print Preview view (see Figure 6.26). You can then
preview the report at any time (see Figure 6.27). You can optionally mark the check
box Display Help on Working with the Report to have Access display the Help
window and list the associated report topics.

FIGURE 6.25

Selecting a style for a report.

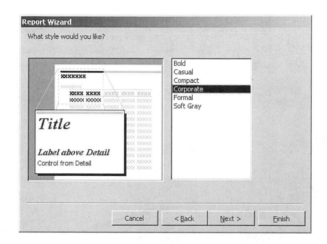

FIGURE 6.26

Design view of a completed report.

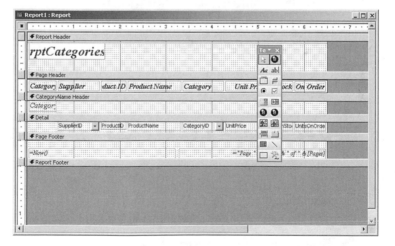

6

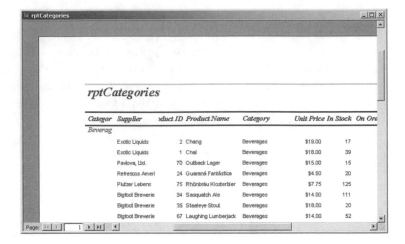

FIGURE 6.27

Print Preview view of a completed report.

Summary

Microsoft provides a number of wizards that make it easy to create databases, tables, queries, forms, and reports. Using the Database Wizard, you can build an entire application. The Table Wizard, Simply Query Wizard, Form Wizard, and Report Wizard allow you to build single tables, queries, forms, and reports, respectively. Regardless of what wizard you use, you can easily modify the objects that the wizard creates. The hours that follow cover the techniques you use to accomplish this.

Q&A

Q **Discuss some pros and cons of using the Database Wizard to create a database.**

A The Database Wizard saves you a lot of time in creating a simple application. If it produces an application with the look, feel, and features that you need, you are finished. The problem is that the customizations that might be necessary in the wizard-generated application often require more work than would have been required if you had built the application from scratch in the first place. You must evaluate which situation applies to you.

Q **Describe the applications that the Database Wizard creates.**

A The Database Wizard creates an application switchboard, data entry forms, and the reports that are necessary to view the data entered into the forms.

Q What limitations do you notice regarding the Simple Query Wizard?

A With the Simple Query Wizard, you cannot set sort order or specify criteria.

Workshop

The Workshop includes quiz questions that are designed to help you test your under-standing of the material covered and activities to help put what you've learned to prac-tice. You can find the answers to the questions in the section immediately following the quiz.

Quiz

1. How many characters can a database name contain?
2. What is the industrywide naming convention for forms?
3. What are the two categories of tables that the Table Wizard provides?
4. The sort order of the query underlying a report determines the sort order of the report (True/False).
5. It is generally more efficient to base a form or report on a query than on a table (True/False).

Quiz Answers

1. 255.
2. Beginning the form name with the tag `frm`.
3. Business and Personal.
4. False. The sort order designated in the report overrides the sort order designated in the underlying query.
5. True.

Activities

Practice using the Database Wizard, Table Wizard, Simple Query Wizard, Form Wizard, and Report Wizard. Build a `Customer` table and an `Order` table. Add records to each. Practice using the Simple Query Wizard to build queries that retrieve specific records from the tables. Use the Form Wizard to build data entry forms for each table. Finally, use the Report Wizard to build reports that show the data entered into each table.

6

HOUR 7

Designing Databases

Many developers believe that because Access is a rapid application development environment, there's absolutely no need for system analysis or design when creating an application. I couldn't disagree more. Access applications are deceptively easy to create. Without proper planning, they can become disasters. In this hour you'll learn about the following:

- Analyzing the tasks you are automating
- The data analysis and design phase of the development process
- Prototyping and why it is important
- The steps in the testing process
- Successfully implementing an application
- The maintenance phase of an application

Task Analysis

NEW TERM   The first step in the development process is *task analysis*, which involves considering each and every process that occurs during the user's workday—a cumbersome but necessary task. When I first started working for a large corporation as a mainframe programmer, I was required to carefully follow a task-analysis checklist. I had to find out what each user of the system did to complete his or her daily tasks, document each procedure, determine the flow of each task to the next, relate each task of each user to his or her other tasks as well as to the tasks of every other user of the system, and tie each task to corporate objectives. In this day and age of rapid application development and changing technology, task analysis in the development process seems to have gone out the window. I maintain that if you don't take the required care to complete this process, you will have to rewrite large parts of the application.

Data Analysis and Design

After you have analyzed and documented all the tasks involved in a system, you're ready to work on the data analysis and design phase of an application. In this phase, you must identify each piece of information needed to complete each task. You must assign these data elements to subjects, and each subject will become a separate table in the database. For example, a subject might be a client; every data element relating to that client—the name, address, phone number, credit limit, and any other pertinent information—would become fields within the client table.

You should determine the following for each data element:

- The appropriate data type
- The required size
- Validation rules

You should also determine whether you will allow the user to update each data element and whether the user will enter each update or the system will calculate it. Then you can figure out whether you have properly normalized the table structures.

Database Terms Introduced

In the preceding hours we have briefly mentioned some terms that are integrally important now that you will be designing your own objects. The following are the most important of these terms and what they mean:

- **Column or field**—A single piece of information about an object (for example, a company name).
- **Row or record**—A collection of information about a single entity (for example, all the information about a customer).
- **Table**—A collection of all the data for a specific type of entity (for example, all the information for all the customers stored in a database). It is important that each table contain information about only a single entity. In other words, you would not store information about an order in the Customers table.

- **Primary key field**—A field or a combination of fields in a table that uniquely identifies each row in the table (for example, the CustomerID).
- **Natural key field**—A primary key field that is naturally part of the data contained within the table (for example, a Social Security number). Generally it is better to use a contrived key field, such as an AutoNumber field, than a natural key field as the primary key field.
- **Composite key field**—A primary key field comprising more than one field in a table (for example, LastName and FirstName fields). It is preferable to create a primary key based on an AutoNumber field than to use a composite key field.
- **Relationship**—Two tables in a database sharing a common key value. An example is a relationship between the Customers table and the Orders table: The CustomerID field in the Customers table is related to the CustomerID field in the Orders table.
- **Foreign key field**—A field on the many side of the relationship in a one-to-many relationship. Whereas the table on the one side of the relationship is related by the primary key field, the table on the many side of the relationship is related by the foreign key field. For example, one customer has multiple orders, so whereas the CustomerID field is the primary key field in the Customers table, it is the foreign key field in the Orders table.

Normalization Introduced

NEW TERM *Normalization* is a fancy term for the process of testing a table design against a series of rules to ensure that the application will operate as efficiently as possible. These rules are based on set theory and were originally proposed by Dr. E. F. Codd. Although you could spend years studying normalization, its main objective is to create an application that runs efficiently with as little data manipulation and coding as possible. Hour 9, "Creating Relationships," covers normalization and database design in detail. For now, here are six of the basic normalization rules:

- **NEW TERM** Fields should be *atomic*—that is, each piece of data should be broken down as much as possible. For example, rather than create a field called Name, you should create two fields: one for the first name and another for the last name. This method makes the data much easier to work with. If you need to sort or search by first name separately from the last name, for example, you can do so without any extra effort.
- Each record should contain a unique identifier so that you have a way of safely identifying the record. For example, if you're changing customer information, you can make sure you're changing the information associated with the correct customer. This unique identifier is called the *primary key*.

7

- **NEW TERM** The *primary key* is a field (or fields) that uniquely identifies the record. Sometimes you can assign a natural primary key. For example, a Social Security number in an employees table should serve to uniquely identify each employee to the system. At other times, you might need to create a primary key. Because two customers could have the same name, for example, a customer name might not uniquely identify the customer to the system. It might be necessary to create a field that would contain a unique identifier for each customer, such as a customer ID.

- A primary key should be short, stable, and simple. *Short* means it should be small in size (not a 50-character field). *Stable* means the primary key should be a field whose value rarely, if ever, changes. For example, whereas a customer ID would rarely change, a company name is rather likely to change. *Simple* means it should be easy for a user to work with.

- Every field in a table should supply additional information about the record that the primary key serves to identify. For example, every field in a customers table should describe the customer who has a particular customer ID.

- Information in a table shouldn't appear in more than one place. For example, a particular customer name shouldn't appear in more than one record.

Let's look at an example. The datasheet shown in Figure 7.1 is an example of a table that hasn't been normalized. Notice that the CustInfo field is repeated for each order, so if the customer address changes, it has to be changed in every order assigned to that customer. In other words, the CustInfo field is not atomic. If you want to sort by city, you're out of luck because the city is in the middle of the CustInfo field. If the name of an inventory item changes, you need to make the change in every record where that inventory item was ordered. Probably the biggest limitation of this example involves items ordered. With this design, you must create four fields for each item the customer orders: name, supplier, quantity, and price. This design would make it extremely difficult to build sales reports and other reports your users need to effectively run the business.

Figure 7.2 shows the same data shown in Figure 7.1, but in this case the data is normalized. Notice that the data is broken out into several different tables: tblCustomers, tblOrders, tblOrderDetails, and tblSuppliers. The tblCustomers table contains data that relates only to a specific customer. Each record is uniquely identified by a contrived CustID field, which is used to relate the orders table, tblOrders, to tblCustomers. The tblOrders table contains only information that applies to the entire order, rather than to a particular item that the customer ordered. The tblOrders table contains the CustID of the customer who placed the order and the date of the order, and it is related to the tblOrderDetails table based on the OrderID. The tblOrderDetails table holds information about each item ordered for a particular OrderID. There's no limit to the potential number of items that the user can place on an order. The user can add as many items to the order as needed, simply by adding more records to the tblOrderDetails table. Finally, the supplier information appears in a separate table, tblSuppliers, so that if any of the supplier information changes, the user has to change it in only one place.

FIGURE 7.1

A table that hasn't been normalized.

Order#	CustInfo	OrderTotal	OrderDate	Item1Name	Item1Supplier	Item1Quantity	Item1Price
1	12 Any Street Anywhere, CA	$350.00	5/1/2001	Widget	Good Supplier	5	$1.50
2	12 Any Street Anywhere, CA	$0.00		Gadget	Bad Supplier	2	$2.25
3	12 Any Street Anywhere, CA	$0.00		Nut	Okay Supplier	7	$7.70
4	12 Any Street Anywhere, CA	$0.00		Bolt	Another Supplier	9	$3.00
5	45 Any Street Somewhere,	$0.00		Pencil	Good Supplier	2	$1.50
6	45 Any Street Somewhere,	$0.00		Eraser	Someone	4	$2.20
(AutoNumber)		$0.00				0	$0.00

Record: 7 of 7

FIGURE 7.2

Data normalized into four separate tables.

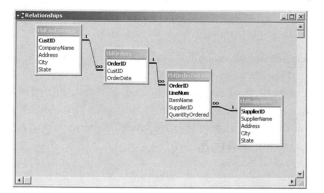

Prototyping

Although the task analysis and data analysis phases of application development haven't changed much since the days of mainframes, the prototyping phase has changed. In working with mainframes or DOS-based languages, it was important to develop detailed specifications for each screen and report. I remember requiring users to sign off on every screen and report. Even a change such as moving a field on a screen required a change order and approval for additional hours. After the user signed off on the screen and report

7

specifications, the programmers would spend days working arduously to develop each screen and report. They would return to the user after many months, only to hear that everything was wrong. This meant back to the drawing board for the developer and many additional hours before the user could once again review the application.

The process is quite different now. As soon as you have outlined the tasks and the data analysis is complete, you can design the tables and establish relationships among them. The form and report prototype process can then begin. Rather than the developer going off for weeks or months before having further interaction with the user, the developer needs only a few days, using the Access wizards to quickly develop form and report prototypes. They can then present these to the users, get users' feedback, and continue to refine the application. Application development today is an iterative process.

Testing

As far as testing goes, you just can't do enough. I recommend that if an application is going to be run in Windows 98, Windows NT, Windows 2000, and Windows XP, you test in all these environments. I also suggest that you test an application extensively on the lowest-common-denominator piece of hardware so you can ensure that it will work on all the machines in the environment; an application might run great on your machine but show unacceptable performance on a user's slower machine.

It usually helps to test your application both in pieces and as an integrated application. Recruit several people to test your application and make sure they range from the most savvy of users to the least computer-adept person you can find. These different types of users will probably find completely different sets of problems. Most importantly, make sure you're not the only tester of your application because you're the least likely person to find errors in your own programs.

Implementation

After you have tested an application, it is finally ready to go out into the world—at least you hope it is! At this point, you need to distribute the application to a subset of users and make sure they know they're performing the test implementation. You should make them feel honored to participate as the first users of the system but warn them that problems might occur, and it's their responsibility to make you aware of them. If you distribute your application on a wide-scale basis and it doesn't operate exactly as it should, it will be difficult to regain the confidence of your users. That's why it is so important to roll out your application slowly.

Maintenance

Because Access is a rapid application development environment, the maintenance period tends to be much more extended than that for a mainframe or DOS-based application. Users are much more demanding; the more you give them, the more they want. For a consultant, this is great. You just don't want to get into a fixed-bid situation: Because the scope of the application changes, you could very well end up on the losing end of that deal.

There are three categories of maintenance activities: bug fixes, specification changes, and frills. You need to handle bug fixes as quickly as possible. The implications of specification changes need to be clearly explained to the user, including the time and cost involved in making the requested changes. As far as frills go, you should try to involve the users as much as possible in adding frills by teaching them how to enhance forms and reports and by making the application as flexible and user defined as possible. Of course, the final objective of any application is a happy group of productive users.

Summary

Many people dismiss database design as an unnecessary part of the development process. I couldn't disagree more. It is only with the strong foundation of a proper design document that the application design process can be successful. The steps in the design process include task analysis, data analysis and design, prototyping, testing, implementation, and maintenance. This hour briefly discusses each of those phases and gives you a solid idea of what each entails.

Q&A

Q Summarize the task analysis process.

A The task analysis process requires you to consider every process that occurs during the user's workday.

Q During the data analysis and design phase, what must you determine for each data element?

A You must determine the appropriate data type, the required size for the data, and any required validation rules.

Q Define *field*.

A A field is a single piece of information about an object.

7

Q Define *record*.

A A record is a collection of information about a single entity.

Workshop

The Workshop includes quiz questions that are designed to help you test your understanding of the material covered and activities to help put what you've learned to practice. You can find the answers to the questions in the section immediately following the quiz.

Quiz

1. A composite key is always made up of more than one field (True/False).

2. Name three rules for creating a primary key.

3. An AutoNumber field is an example of a natural key (True/False).

4. Atomic means that information should appear in only one place (True/False).

5. When you are ready to implement an application, you should distribute the application to all your users.

Quiz Answers

1. True.

2. You should make a primary key short, stable, simple.

3. False. An AutoNumber field is a contrived key.

4. False. Atomic means that each piece of data should be broken down as much as possible.

5. False. When you are ready to implement an application, you should first distribute the application to a small group of users.

Activities

Practice applying the techniques that you learned in this hour to some task that you or a co-worker must perform at your office. Come up with the table structures necessary to support the development process. As you proceed through the hours that follow, continue to build this test application and try to find problems with the table design you have selected.

HOUR 8

Creating Tables

It is useful to think of the process of table design as being similar to the process of building a foundation for a house. Just as a house with a faulty foundation will fall over, an application with a poor table design will be difficult to build, maintain, and use. This hour covers all the ins and outs of table design in Access 2003. After this hour, you will be ready to build the other components of an application, knowing that the tables you design provide the application with a strong foundation. In this hour you'll learn the following:

- How to build a new table
- How to select the appropriate field type for data
- How to add a primary key to a table

Building a New Table

There are several ways to add a new table to an Access 2003 database: You can use a wizard to help you with the design process, design the table from scratch, build the table from a *datasheet* (a spreadsheet-like format), import the table from another source, or link to an external table. This hour discusses the processes of building a table from a datasheet and designing a table from scratch; Hour 6, "Using Wizards to Create a Database," covers the process of using a wizard to help with the design process, and Hour 18, "Sharing Data with Other Applications," covers the processes of importing and linking.

Regardless of which method you choose, you should start building a new table by selecting the Tables icon from the list of objects in the Database window. The icons that appear allow you to create a table in Design view, create a table using a wizard, and create a table by entering data (see Figure 8.1).

FIGURE **8.1**

Creating a new table.

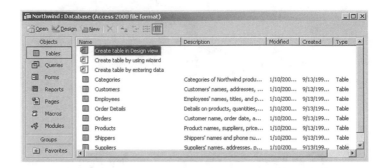

Access 2003 natively supports the Access 2000 file format so that you can read and write to Access 2000 files under Access 2003 without converting the file format. Access 2003 gives you the option of choosing which file format to use as a default. From the menu bar, you click Tools Options and select the Advanced tab. Then you select either Access 2000 or Access 2002-2003 as the default file format that you prefer from the drop-down list box.

Building a Table from a Datasheet

Building a table from a datasheet might seem simple, but it isn't always the best way to build a table because it's easy to introduce severe design flaws into a table. Microsoft added this method of building tables as an "enhancement" to Access—and it is primarily for spreadsheet users getting their feet wet in the database world. I suggest you use one of the other methods to design tables. If you decide to use the datasheet method, though, follow these steps:

1. Select the Tables icon from the list of objects in the Database window.

2. Click the New button. The New Table dialog box appears.

3. Select Datasheet View from the New Table dialog box. A window similar to that shown in Figure 8.2 appears.

4. Rename each column by double-clicking the column heading (for example, Field1) you want to change or by right-clicking the column and selecting Rename Column from the context menu. Type a name for the field and then press Enter.

FIGURE 8.2

Building a table from a datasheet.

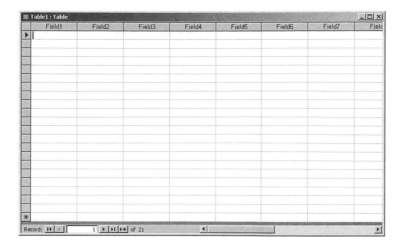

5. Enter data into the datasheet. Be sure to enter the data in a consistent format. For example, if a table includes a column for employee hire dates, make sure all entries in that column are valid dates and that you enter all dates in the same format (see Figure 8.3). Access uses the contents of each column to determine the data type for each field, so inconsistent data entry confuses Access and causes unpredictable results.

FIGURE 8.3

Data determining the new table's structure.

EmployeeID	FirstName	LastName	HireDate	Salary	Field6	Field7	Field
1	Dan	Balter	3/25/93	75000			
2	Alison	Balter	4/1/90	80000			
3	Sue	Terry	4/15/94	95000			
4	Shell	Forman	5/1/95	82000			
5	Anita	Srinivasa	7/2/99	125000			

6. After you have added all the columns and data you want, click the Save button on the toolbar. Access prompts you for a table name and asks whether you want to add a primary key.

7. Access assigns data types to each field based on the data you have entered. When Access is done with this, click the View button on the toolbar to look at the design of the resulting table.

8. Add a description to each field to help make the table self-documenting. Your table design should look something like Figure 8.4.

FIGURE 8.4

*The table design after
a table is built with the
datasheet method.*

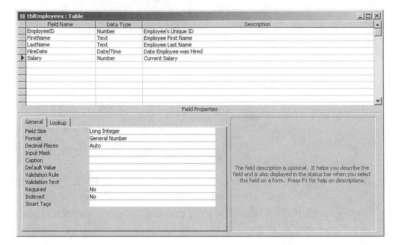

It is very important that you be cognizant of the type of data in each column. For example, if you accidentally place a letter in a number field, Access considers the entire column a text field. It is therefore important that you recognize that although this might be the easiest method of creating a table, you should use it with extreme caution.

Adding descriptions to table, query, form, report, macro, and module objects goes a long way toward making an application self-documenting. Such documentation helps you, or anyone who modifies an application, perform any required maintenance on the application's objects. Hour 21, "Database Documentation," covers documenting databases.

If you forget a field and need to insert it later, you can right-click the column heading to the right of where you want to insert the new column and then select Insert Column from the context menu. Access inserts a column that you can rename by double-clicking the column heading.

Designing a Table from Scratch

Designing tables from scratch offers flexibility and encourages good design principles. It is almost always the best choice when you're creating a custom business solution. Although it requires some knowledge of database and table design, it gives you much more control and precision than designing a table from Datasheet view. It allows you to select each field name and field type and to define field properties. To design a table from scratch, you select Tables from the list of objects and double-click the Create Table in Design View icon. The Table Design view window, pictured in Figure 8.5, appears.

FIGURE 8.5

Entering field names, data types, and descriptions for all the fields in a table.

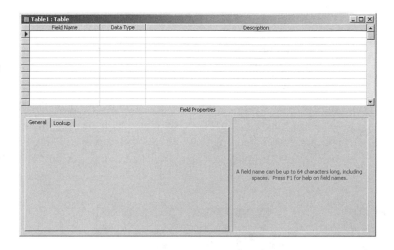

When the Table Design view window appears, follow these steps to design a table:

1. Define each field in the table by typing its name in the Field Name column.

> If you prefer, you can click the Build button on the toolbar (the button with the ellipsis [...]) to open the Field Builder dialog box, shown in Figure 8.6. The Field Builder lets you select from predefined fields that have predefined properties. Of course, you can modify the properties at any time.

2. Tab to the Data Type column. Select the default field type, which is Text, or use the drop-down combo box to select another field type. You can find details on which field type is appropriate for data in the "Selecting the Appropriate Field Type for Data" section, later in this hour. Note that if you use the Field Builder, it sets a data type value for you that you can modify.

FIGURE 8.6

The Field Builder dia-log box.

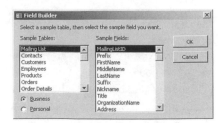

3. Tab to the Description column and enter a description for the data. What you type in this column appears on the status bar when the user is entering data into the field. This column is also great for documenting what data is actually stored in the field.

4. Continue entering fields. If you need to insert a field between two existing fields, click the Insert Rows button on the toolbar. Access inserts the new field above the field you were on. To delete a field, select it and click the Delete Rows button.

5. To save your work, click the Save tool on the toolbar. The Save As dialog box, shown in Figure 8.7, appears. Enter a table name and click OK. A dialog box appears, recommending that you establish a primary key. Every table should have a primary key. Primary keys are discussed in the section "The All-Important Primary Key," later in this hour.

FIGURE 8.7

The Save As dialog box.

Access supplies default names for the tables that you create (for example, Table1, Table2). I suggest that you supply more descriptive names. I gener-ally follow the industrywide naming convention of prefixing all my table names with tbl.

Field names can be up to 64 characters long. For practical reasons, you should try to limit them to 10–15 characters, which is enough to describe the field without making the name difficult to type.

Field names can include any combination of letters, numbers, spaces, and other charac-ters, excluding periods, exclamation points, accents, and brackets. I recommend that you stick to letters. Spaces in field names can be inconvenient when you're building queries, modules, and other database objects. You shouldn't be concerned that users will see the field names without the spaces. The Caption property of a field, discussed in Hour 14, "Power Table Techniques," allows you to designate the text that Access displays for users.

A field name can't begin with leading spaces. As mentioned previously, field names shouldn't contain any spaces, so the rule to not begin a field name with spaces shouldn't be a problem. Field names also cannot include ASCII control characters (ASCII values 0–31).

You should try not to duplicate property names, keywords, function names, or the names of other Access objects when naming fields (for example, naming a field Date). Although the code might work in some circumstances, you might get unpredictable results in others.

To make a potential move to the client/server platform as painless as possible, you should be aware that not all field types are supported by every back-end database. Furthermore, most back-end databases impose stricter limits than Access does on the length of field names and the characters that are valid in field names. To reduce the number of problems you'll encounter if you migrate tables to a back-end database server, you should consider these issues when you're naming the fields in Access tables.

Selecting the Appropriate Field Type for Data

The data type you select for each field can greatly affect the performance and functionality of an application. Several factors can influence your choice of data type for each field in a table:

- The type of data that's stored in the field
- Whether the field's contents need to be included in calculations
- Whether you need to sort the data in the field
- The way you want to sort the data in the field
- How important storage space is to you

The type of data you need to store in a field has the biggest influence on which data type you select. For example, if you need to store numbers that begin with leading zeros, you can't select a Number field because leading zeros entered into a Number field are ignored. This rule affects data such as zip codes (some of which begin with leading zeros) and department codes.

If it is unimportant that leading zeros be stored in a field and you simply need them to appear on forms and reports, you can accomplish this by using the Format property of the field. Hour 14 covers the Format property.

If the contents of a field need to be included in calculations, you must select a Number or Currency data type. You can't perform calculations on the contents of fields defined with the other data types. The only exception to this rule is Date data type fields, which you can include in date/time calculations.

You must also consider whether you will sort or index the data in a field. You can't sort the data in OLE Object and Hyperlink fields, so you shouldn't select these field types if you must sort or index the data in the field. Furthermore, you must think about the *way* you want to sort the data. For example, in a Text field, a set of numbers would be sorted in the order of the numbers' leftmost character, then the second character from the left, and so on (that is, 1, 10, 100, 2, 20, 200) because data in the Text field is sorted as characters rather than numbers. On the other hand, in a Number or Currency field, the numbers would be sorted in ascending value order (that is, 1, 2, 10, 20, 100, 200). You might think you would never want data sorted in a character sequence, but sometimes it makes sense to sort certain information, such as department codes, in this fashion. Access 2003 gives you the ability to sort or group based on a Memo field, but it performs the sorting or grouping only based on the first 255 characters. Finally, you should consider how important disk space is to you. Each field type takes up a different amount of storage space on a hard disk, and this could be a factor when you're selecting a data type for a field.

Nine field types are available in Access: Text, Memo, Number, Date/Time, Currency, AutoNumber (known as Counter in Access 2.0), Yes/No, OLE Object, and Hyperlink. Table 8.1 briefly describes the appropriate uses for each field type and the amount of storage space each type needs.

TABLE 8.1 Appropriate Uses and Storage Space for Access Field Types

Field Type	Appropriate Uses	Storage Space
Text	Data containing text, a combination of text and numbers, or numbers that don't need to be included in calculations. Examples are names, addresses, department codes, and phone numbers.	Based on what's actually stored in the field; ranges from 0 to 255 bytes
Memo	Long text and numeric strings. Examples are notes and descriptions.	Ranges from 0 to 65,536 bytes.

continues

TABLE 8.1   continued

Field Type	Appropriate Uses	Storage Space
Number	Data that's included in calculations (excluding money). Examples are ages, codes (such as employee IDs), and payment methods.	1, 2, 4, or 8 bytes, depending on the field size selected (or 16 bytes for Replication ID).
Date/Time	Dates and times. Examples are date ordered and birth date.	8 bytes.
Currency	Currency values. Examples are amount due and price.	8 bytes.
AutoNumber	Unique sequential or random numbers. Examples are invoice numbers and project numbers.	4 bytes (16 bytes for replication ID).
Yes/No	Fields that contain one of two values (for example, yes/no, true/false). Sample uses are indicating bills paid and tenure status.	1 bit.
OLE Object	Objects such as Word documents or Excel spreadsheets. Examples are employee reviews and budgets.	0 bytes to 1GB, depending on what's stored within the field.
Hyperlink	Text or a combination of text and numbers, stored as text and used as a hyperlink for a Web address (uniform resource locator [URL]) or a universal naming convention (UNC) path. Examples are Webpages and network files.	0 to 2,048 bytes for each of the three parts that compose the address (up to 64,000 characters total).

Although Microsoft loosely considers the Lookup Wizard a field type, it is really not its own field type. You use it to create a field that allows the user to select a value from another table or from a list of values via a combo box that the wizard helps define for you. The Lookup Wizard requires that same storage size as the primary key for the lookup field. The Lookup Wizard is covered in more detail in Hour 14.

The Hyperlink field type contains a hyperlink object. The hyperlink object consists of three parts. The first part is called the *display text*; it's the text that appears in the field or control. The second part is the actual *file path* (UNC path) or *page* (URL) the field is referring to. The third part is the *sub-address*, a location within the file or page.

The most difficult part of selecting a field type is knowing which type is best in each situation. The following detailed descriptions of each field type and when you should use them should help you with this process.

Text Fields: The Most Common Field Type

Most fields are Text fields. Many developers don't realize that it's best to use Text fields for any numbers that are not used in calculations. Examples of such numbers are phone numbers, part numbers, and zip codes. Although the default size for a Text field is 50 characters, you can store up to 255 characters in a Text field. Because Access allocates disk space dynamically, a large field size doesn't use hard disk space, but you can improve performance if you allocate the smallest field size possible. You can control the maximum number of characters allowed in a Text field by using the FieldSize property.

Memo Fields: For Long Notes and Comments

A Memo field can store up to 65,536 characters of text, meaning that it can hold up to 16 pages of text for each record. Memo fields are excellent for any type of notes you want to store with table data. Remember that in Access 2003 you can sort by a Memo field.

Number Fields: For When You Need to Calculate

You use Number fields to store data that you must include in calculations. If currency amounts are included in calculations or if calculations require the highest degree of accuracy, you should use a Currency field rather than a Number field.

The Number field is actually several types of fields in one because Access 2003 offers seven sizes of numeric fields. Byte can store integers from 0 to 255, Integer can hold whole numbers from −32768 to 32767, and Long Integer can hold whole numbers ranging from less than −two billion to just over two billion. Although all three of these sizes offer excellent performance, each type requires an increasingly large amount of storage space. Two of the other numeric field sizes, Single and Double, offer floating decimal points and, therefore, much slower performance than Integer and Long Integer. Single can hold fractional numbers to 7 significant digits; Double extends the precision to 14 significant digits. Decimal, a numeric data type that was introduced with Access 2002, allows storage of very large numbers and provides decimal precision up to 28 digits! The final size, Replication ID, supplies a unique identifier required by the data synchronization process.

Date/Time Fields: For Tracking When Things Happened

You use the Date/Time field type to store valid dates and times. Date/Time fields allow you to perform date calculations and make sure dates and times are always sorted properly.

Access actually stores the date or time internally as an 8-byte floating-point number. Access represents time as a fraction of a day.

Any date and time settings you establish in the Windows Control Panel are reflected in your data. For example, if you modify Short Date Style in Regional Settings within the Control Panel, your forms, reports, and datasheets will immediately reflect those changes.

Currency Fields: For Storing Money

The Currency field is a number field that is used when currency values are being stored in a table. A Currency field prevents the computer from rounding off data during calculations. It holds 15 digits of whole dollars, plus accuracy to one-hundredth of a cent. Although very accurate, this type of field is quite slow to process.

Any changes to the currency format made in the Windows Control Panel are reflected in your data. Of course, Access doesn't automatically perform any actual conversion of currency amounts. As with dates, if you modify the currency symbol in Regional Settings within the Control Panel, your forms, reports, and datasheets will immediately reflect those changes.

AutoNumber Fields: For Unique Record Identifiers

The AutoNumber field in Access 2003 is equivalent to the Counter field in Access 2.0. Access automatically generates AutoNumber field values when the user adds a record. In Access 2.0, counter values have to be sequential. The AutoNumber field type in Access 2003 can be either sequential or random. The random assignment is useful when several users are adding records offline because it's unlikely that Access will assign the same random value to two records. A special type of AutoNumber field is a Replication ID. This randomly produced, unique number helps with the replication process by generating unique identifiers used to synchronize database replicas.

You should note a few important points about sequential AutoNumber fields. If a user deletes a record from a table, its unique number is lost forever. Likewise, if a user is adding a record but cancels the action, the unique counter value for that record is lost forever. If this behavior is unacceptable, you can generate your own counter values.

Yes/No Fields: For When One of Two Answers Is Correct

You should use Yes/No fields to store a logical true or false. What Access actually stores in the field is -1 for yes, 0 for no, or Null for no specific choice. The display format for the field determines what the user actually sees (normally Yes/No, True/False, On/Off, or a third option—Null—if you set the TripleState property of the associated control on a form to True). Yes/No fields work efficiently for any data that can have only a true or false value. Not only do they limit the user to valid choices, but they also take up only 1 bit of storage space.

OLE Object Fields: For Storing Just About Anything

OLE Object fields are designed to hold data from any OLE server application that is registered in Windows, including spreadsheets, word processing documents, sound, and video. There are many business uses for OLE Object fields, such as storing resumes, employee reviews, budgets, or videos. However, in many cases, it is more efficient to use a Hyperlink field to store a link to the document rather than store the document itself in an OLE Object field.

Hyperlink Fields: For Linking to the Internet

Hyperlink fields are used to store uniform resource locator addresses, which are links to Web pages on the Internet or on an intranet, or UNC paths, which are links to a file location path. The Hyperlink field type is broken into three parts:

- What the user sees
- The URL or UNC
- A subaddress, such as a range name or bookmark

After the user places an entry in a Hyperlink field, the entry serves as a direct link to the file or page it refers to.

The All-Important Primary Key

NEW TERM   A *primary key* is a field or a combination of fields in a table that uniquely identifies each row in the table (for example, CustomerID). The most important index in a table is called the *primary key index*; it ensures uniqueness of the fields that make up the index and also gives the table a default order. You must set a primary key for the fields on the one side of a one-to-many relationship. To create a primary key index, you select the field(s) you want to establish as the primary key and then click the Primary Key button on the toolbar.

Hour 9, "Creating Your Own Relationships," discusses the details of relationships. In Hour 9, you will also learn about the types of relationships such as one-to-many relationships.

Figure 8.8 shows the `tblCustomer` table with a primary key index based on the `CustomerID` field. Notice that the index name of the field designated as the primary key of the table is called `PrimaryKey`. Note that the `Primary` and `Unique` properties for this index are both set to `Yes` (true).

FIGURE 8.8

A primary key index based on the `CustomerID` *field.*

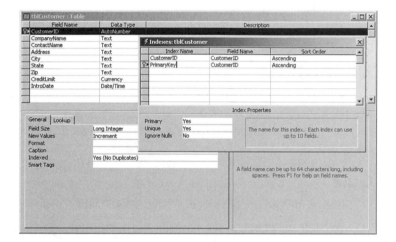

Summary

Tables are the foundation for an application. A poorly designed table structure can render an otherwise well-designed application useless. This hour begins by walking through several methods for creating tables. It then discusses theoretical issues, such as selecting the correct field type. Finally, it talks about primary keys.

Q&A

Q Name five ways to add a table to an Access database.

A You can create a table from a datasheet, you can build it from scratch, you can use a wizard to build it, you can import it, or you can link to it.

Q What is the main problem with building a table from a datasheet?

A It is easy to build design flaws into a table when you use this method of table design and Access does not maintain the consistency in your data.

Q What are the five factors that influence what data type you select for a field?

A You must consider the type of data that you will store in a field, whether you need to include the field's contents in calculations, whether you need to sort the data in the field, how you must sort the data in the field, and how important storage space is to you.

Q What is the purpose of the primary key index of a table?

A It ensures uniqueness of the fields that make up the primary key and it determines the default order for the table.

Workshop

The Workshop includes quiz questions that are designed to help you test your understanding of the material covered and activities to help put what you've learned to practice. You can find the answers to the questions in the section immediately following the quiz.

Quiz

1. Name the two file formats that Access 2003 natively supports.

2. What is the industrywide accepted prefix for naming tables?

3. Name the three types of fields that support calculations.

4. What two types of fields *don't* support sorting?

5. How many parts make up a `Hyperlink` field?

Quiz Answers

1. Access 2000 and Access 2002-2003.

2. `tbl`.

3. `Number`, `Currency`, and `Date`.

4. `OLE Object` and `Hyperlink`.

5. Three: what the user sees, the URL or UNC, and a subaddress.

Activities

Build a table. Add to the table fields with various types. Give the table a primary key. Save and name the table.

Hour 9

Creating Relationships

NEW TERM   A *relationship* exists between two tables when one or more key fields from one table are matched to one or more key fields in another table. The fields in both tables usually have the same name, data type, and size. Relationships are a necessary by-product of the data normalization process. *Data normalization*, introduced in Hour 7, "Designing Databases," is the process of eliminating duplicate information from a system by splitting information into several tables, each containing a unique value (that is, a primary key). Although data normalization brings many benefits, it means you need to relate an application's tables to each other so that users can view the data in the system as a single entity. After you define relationships between tables, you can build queries, forms, reports, and data access pages that combine information from multiple tables. In this way, you can reap all the benefits of data normalization while ensuring that a system provides users with all the information they need. Referential integrity is another very important topic covered in this hour. *Referential integrity* consists of a series of rules that the Jet Engine applies to ensure that Jet properly maintains relationships between tables. In this hour you'll learn about the following:

- Relational database design principles
- The types of relationships available
- Establishing relationships
- Establishing referential integrity

Introduction to Relational Database Design

Many people believe Access is such a simple product to use that database design is something they don't need to worry about. I couldn't disagree more! Just as a poorly planned vacation will generally not be very much fun, a database with poorly designed tables and relationships will fail to meet the needs of its users.

The History of Relational Database Design

New Term Dr. E. F. Codd first introduced formal relational database design in 1969 while he was at IBM. *Relational theory*, which is based on set theory and predicate logic, applies to both databases and database applications. Codd developed 12 rules that determine how well an application and its data adhere to the relational model. Since Codd first conceived these 12 rules, the number of rules has expanded into the hundreds.

You should be happy to learn that, although Microsoft Access is not a perfect application development environment, it measures up quite well as a relational database system.

Goals of Relational Database Design

The number-one goal of relational database design is to, as closely as possible, develop a database that models some real-world system. This involves breaking the real-world system into tables and fields and determining how the tables relate to each other. Although on the surface this might appear to be a trivial task, it can be an extremely cumbersome process to translate a real-world system into tables and fields.

A properly designed database has many benefits. The processes of adding, editing, deleting, and retrieving table data are greatly facilitated in a properly designed database. In addition, reports are easy to build. Most importantly, the database is easy to modify and maintain.

Rules of Relational Database Design

To adhere to the relational model, you must follow certain rules. These rules determine what you store in a table and how you relate the tables. These are the rules:

- The rules of tables
- The rules of uniqueness and keys
- The rules of foreign keys and domains

The Rules of Tables

NEW TERM Each table in a system must store data about a single entity. An *entity* usually represents a real-life object or event. Examples of objects are customers, employees, and inventory items. Examples of events include orders, appointments, and doctor visits.

The Rules of Uniqueness and Keys

NEW TERM Tables are composed of rows and columns. To adhere to the relational model, each table must contain a unique identifier. Without a unique identifier, it is programmatically impossible to uniquely address a row. You guarantee uniqueness in a table by designating a *primary key*, which is a single column or a set of columns that uniquely identifies a row in a table.

NEW TERM Each column or set of columns in a table that contains unique values is considered a *candidate key*. One candidate key becomes the *primary key*. The remaining candidate keys become *alternate keys*. A primary key made up of one column is considered a *simple key*. A primary key composed of multiple columns is considered a *composite key*.

It is generally a good idea to choose a primary key that is

- Minimal (has as few columns as possible)
- Stable (rarely changes)
- Simple (is familiar to the user)

Following these rules greatly improves the performance and maintainability of a database application, particularly if it deals with large volumes of data.

NEW TERM Consider the example of an employee table. An employee table is generally composed of employee-related fields such as Social Security number, first name, last name, hire date, salary, and so on. The combination of the first name and the last name fields could be considered a primary key. This might work until the company hires two employees who have the same name. Although the first and last names could be combined with additional fields (for example, hire date) to constitute uniqueness, that would violate the rule of keeping the primary key minimal. Furthermore, an employee might get married, and her last name might change. This violates the rule of keeping a primary key stable. Therefore, using a name as the primary key violates the principle of stability. The Social Security number might be a valid choice for primary key, but a foreign employee might not have a Social Security number. This is a case in which a derived, rather than a natural, primary key is appropriate. A *derived key* is an artificial key that you create. A *natural key* is one that is already part of the database.

In examples such as this, I suggest adding EmployeeID as an AutoNumber field. Although the field would violate the rule of simplicity (because an employee number is meaningless to the user), it is both small and stable. Because it is numeric, it is also efficient to process. In fact, I use AutoNumber fields as primary keys for most of the tables that I build.

The Rules of Foreign Keys and Domains

A *foreign key* in one table is the field that relates to the primary key in a second table. For example, the CustomerID field may be the primary key in a Customers table and the foreign key in an Orders table.

NEW TERM   A *domain* is a pool of values from which columns are drawn. A simple example of a domain is the specific data range of employee hire dates. In the case of the Orders table, the domain of the CustomerID column is the range of values for the CustomerID in the Customers table.

Normalization and Normal Forms

NEW TERM   Some of the most difficult decisions that you face as a developer are what tables to create and what fields to place in each table, as well as how to relate the tables that you create. As you learned in Hour 7, *Normalization* is the process of applying a series of rules to ensure that a database achieves optimal structure. *Normal forms* are a progression of these rules. Each successive normal form achieves a better database design than the previous form. Although there are several levels of normal forms, it is generally sufficient to apply only the first three levels of normal forms. The following sections describe the first three levels of normal forms.

First Normal Form

NEW TERM   To achieve first normal form, all columns in a table must be *atomic*. This means, for example, that you cannot store first name and last name in the same field. The reason for this rule is that data becomes very difficult to manipulate and retrieve if you store multiple values in a single field. Let's use the full name as an example. It would be impossible to sort by first name or last name independently if you stored both values in the same field. Furthermore, you or the user would have to perform extra work to extract just the first name or just the last name from the field.

Another requirement for first normal form is that the table must not contain repeating values. An example of repeating values is a scenario in which Item1, Quantity1, Item2, Quantity2, Item3, and Quantity3 fields are all found within the Orders table (see Figure 9.1). This design introduces several problems. What if the user wants to add a fourth item to the order? Furthermore, finding the total ordered for a product requires searching several columns. In fact, all numeric and statistical calculations on the table are extremely cumbersome. Repeating groups make it difficult to summarize and manipulate table data. The alternative, shown in Figure 9.2, achieves first normal form. Notice that each item ordered is located in a separate row. All fields are atomic, and the table contains no repeating groups.

FIGURE 9.1
A table that contains repeating groups.

tblOrdersBefore1NF : Table

OrderID	CustomerID	OrderDate	Item1	Quantity1	Item2	Quantity2	Item3	Quantity3
1	1	5/1/2001	Widget	2	Hammer	5	Diskette	7
2	2	5/1/2001	Horn	4	Car	8	Computer	2
3	1	5/7/2001	Calendar	8	Painting	2	Book	4
4	3	5/18/2001	Boat	2	Leaf	3	Hat	8
(AutoNumber)	0			0		0		0

Record: 1 of 4

FIGURE 9.2
A table that achieves first normal form.

tblOrders1NF : Table

OrderID	OrderItemID	CustomerID	OrderDate	Item	Quantity
1	1	1	5/1/2001	Widget	2
1	2	1	5/1/2001	Horn	4
1	3	1	5/1/2001	Calendar	8
2	1	2	5/18/2001	Boat	2
2	2	2	5/18/2001	Car	1
3	1	1	6/2/2001	Horse	2
3	2	1	6/2/2001	Computer	5
3	3	1	6/2/2001	Chair	6
4	1	3	7/4/2001	Book	2
4	2	3	7/4/2001	Chair	3
4	3	3	7/4/2001	Widget	2
4	4	3	7/4/2001	Painting	3
0	0	0			0

Record: 1 of 12

Second Normal Form

NEW TERM For a table to achieve second normal form, all non-key columns must be fully dependent on the primary key. In other words, each table must store data about only one subject. For example, the table shown in Figure 9.2 includes information about the order (`OrderID`, `CustomerID`, and `OrderDate`) and information about the items the customer is ordering (`Item` and `Quantity`). To achieve second normal form, you must break this data into two tables—an order table and an order detail table. The process of breaking the data into two tables is called *decomposition*. Decomposition is considered to be *non-loss* decomposition because no data is lost during the decomposition process. After you separate the data into two tables, you can easily bring the data back together by joining the two tables via a query. Figure 9.3 shows the data separated into two tables. These two tables achieve second normal form because the fields in each table pertain to the primary key of the table.

Third Normal Form

To attain third normal form, a table must meet all the requirements for first and second normal forms, and all non-key columns must be mutually independent. This means that you must eliminate any calculations, and you must break out the data into lookup tables. Lookup tables include tables such as inventory tables, course tables, state tables, and any other table where you look up a set of values from which you select the entry that you store in the foreign key field. For example, from the Customer table, you look up within the set of states in the state table to select the state associated with the customer.

FIGURE 9.3

Tables that achieve second normal form.

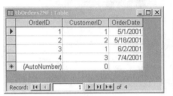

An example of a calculation stored in a table is the product of price multiplied by quantity. Instead of storing the result of this calculation in the table, you would generate the calculation in a query or in the control source of a control on a form or a report.

The example in Figure 9.3 does not achieve third normal form because the description of the inventory items is stored in the Order Details table. If the description changes, all rows with that inventory item need to be modified. The Order Details table, shown in Figure 9.4, shows the item descriptions broken into an Inventory table. This design achieves third normal form. We have moved the description of the inventory items to the Inventory table, and ItemID is stored in the Order Details table. All fields are mutually independent. You can modify the description of an inventory item in one place.

Denormalization: Purposely Violating the Rules

NEW TERM   Although a developer's goal is normalization, there are many times when it makes sense to deviate from normal forms. This process is called *denormalization*. The primary reason for applying denormalization is to enhance performance.

An example of when denormalization might be the preferred tact could involve an open invoices table and a summarized accounting table. It might be impractical to calculate summarized accounting information for a customer when you need it. Instead, you can maintain the summary calculations in a summarized accounting table so that you can easily retrieve them as needed. Although the upside of this scenario is improved performance, the downside is that you must update the summary table whenever you make changes to the open invoices. This imposes a definite trade-off between performance and maintainability. You must decide whether the trade-off is worth it.

FIGURE 9.4

A table (on the right) that achieves third normal form.

9

If you decide to denormalize, you should document your decision. You should make sure that you make the necessary application adjustments to ensure that you properly maintain the denormalized fields. Finally, you need to test to ensure that the denormalization process actually improves performance.

Integrity Rules

Although integrity rules are not part of normal forms, they are definitely part of the database design process. Integrity rules are broken into two categories: overall integrity rules and database-specific integrity rules.

Overall Integrity Rules

NEW TERM The two types of overall integrity rules are referential integrity rules and entity integrity rules. *Referential integrity rules* dictate that a database does not contain any orphan foreign key values. This means that

- Child rows cannot be added for parent rows that do not exist. In other words, an order cannot be added for a nonexistent customer.

- A primary key value cannot be modified if the value is used as a foreign key in a child table. This means that a CustomerID in the Customers table cannot be changed if the Orders table contains rows with that CustomerID.

- A parent row cannot be deleted if child rows have that foreign key value. For example, a customer cannot be deleted if the customer has orders in the Orders table.

Entity integrity dictates that the primary key value cannot be Null. This rule applies not only to single-column primary keys, but also to multicolumn primary keys. In fact, in a multicolumn primary key, no field in the primary key can be Null. This makes sense because if any part of the primary key can be Null, the primary key can no longer act as a unique identifier for the row. Fortunately, the Jet Engine does not allow a field in a primary key to be Null.

Database-Specific Integrity Rules

Database-specific integrity rules are not applicable to all databases, but are, instead, dictated by business rules that apply to a specific application. Database-specific rules are as important as overall integrity rules. They ensure that the user enters only valid data into a database. An example of a database-specific integrity rule is requiring the delivery date for an order to fall after the order date.

The Types of Relationships

Three types of relationships can exist between tables in a database: one-to-many, one-to-one, and many-to-many. Setting up the proper type of relationship between two tables in a database is imperative. The right type of relationship between two tables ensures

- Data integrity
- Optimal performance
- Ease of use in designing system objects

The reasons behind these benefits are covered throughout this hour. Before you can understand the benefits of relationships, though, you must understand the types of relationships available.

One-to-Many Relationships

NEW TERM   A one-to-many relationship is by far the most common type of relationship. In a *one-to-many relationship*, a record in one table can have many related records in another table. A common example is a relationship set up between a Customers table and an Orders table. For each customer in the Customers table, you want to have more than one order in the Orders table. On the other hand, each order in the Orders table can belong to only one customer. The Customers table is on the "one" side of the relationship, and the Orders table is on the "many" side. In order for you to implement this relationship, the field joining the two tables on the "one" side of the relationship must be unique.

In the Customers and Orders tables example, the CustomerID field that joins the two tables must be unique within the Customers table. If more than one customer in the Customers table has the same customer ID, it is not clear which customer belongs to an order in the Orders table. For this reason, the field that joins the two tables on the "one" side of the one-to-many relationship must be a primary key or have a unique index. In almost all cases, the field relating the two tables is the primary key of the table on the "one" side of the relationship. The field relating the two tables on the "many" side of the relationship is the foreign key.

One-to-One Relationships

NEW TERM In a *one-to-one relationship*, each record in the table on the "one" side of the relationship can have only one matching record in the table on the "many" side of the relationship. This relationship is not common and is used only in special circumstances. Usually, if you have set up a one-to-one relationship, you should have combined the fields from both tables into one table. The following are the most common reasons to create a one-to-one relationship:

- The number of fields required for a table exceeds the number of fields allowed in an Access table.

- Certain fields that are included in a table need to be much more secure than other fields in the same table.

- Several fields in a table are required for only a subset of records in the table.

The maximum number of fields allowed in an Access table is 255. There are very few reasons a table should ever have more than 255 fields. In fact, before you even get close to 255 fields, you should take a close look at the design of the system. On the rare occasion when having more than 255 fields is appropriate, you can simulate a single table by moving some of the fields to a second table and creating a one-to-one relationship between the two tables.

NEW TERM The second reason to separate into two tables data that logically would belong in the same table involves security. An example is a table that contains employee information. Certain information, such as employee name, address, city, state, zip code, home phone, and office extension, might need to be accessed by many users of the system. Other fields, including the hire date, salary, birth date, and salary level, might be highly confidential. Field-level security is not available in Access. You can simulate field-level security by using a special attribute of queries called *Run with Owner's Permissions*. The alternative to this method is to place the fields that all users can access in one table and the highly confidential fields in another. You give only a special Admin user (that is, a user with special security privileges—not one actually named Admin) access to the table that contains the confidential fields.

The last situation in which you would want to define one-to-one relationships is when you will use certain fields in a table for only a relatively small subset of records. An example is an Employees table and a Vesting table. Certain fields are required only for employees who are vested. If only a small percentage of a company's employees are vested, it is not efficient, in terms of performance or disk space, to place all the fields containing information about vesting in the Employees table. This is especially true if the vesting information requires a large number of fields. By breaking the information into two tables and creating a one-to-one relationship between the tables, you can reduce disk-space requirements and improve performance. This improvement is particularly pronounced if the Employees table is large.

Many-to-Many Relationships

NEW TERM   In a *many-to-many relationship*, records in two tables have matching records. You cannot directly define a many-to-many relationship in Access; you must develop this type of relationship by adding a table called a *junction table*. You relate the junction table to each of the two tables in one-to-many relationships. For example, with an Orders table and a Products table, each order will probably contain multiple products, and each product is likely to be found on many different orders. The solution is to create a third table, called OrderDetails. You relate the OrderDetails table to the Orders table in a one-to-many relationship based on the OrderID field. You relate it to the Products table in a one-to-many relationship based on the ProductID field.

Establishing Relationships in Access

You use the Relationships window to establish relationships between Access tables, as shown in Figure 9.5. To open the Relationships window, you click Relationships on the toolbar with the Database window active or you choose Tools|Relationships. If you have not established any relationships, the Show Table dialog box appears. The Show Table dialog box allows you to add tables to the Relationships window.

FIGURE 9.5

The Relationships window, which enables you to view, add, modify, and remove relationships between tables.

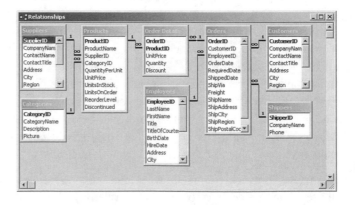

By looking at the Relationships window, you can see the types of relationships for each table. All the one-to-many and one-to-one relationships defined in a database are represented with join lines. If you enforce referential integrity between the tables involved in a one-to-many relationship, the join line between the tables appears with the number *1* on the "one" side of the relationship and with a link symbol (∞) on the "many" side of the relationship. A one-to-one relationship appears with a *1* on each end of the join line.

Establishing a Relationship Between Two Tables

To establish a relationship between two tables, you follow these steps:

1. Open the Relationships window.

2. If this is the first time that you've opened the Relationships window of a particular database, the Show Table dialog box appears. Select each table you want to relate and click Add.

3. If you have already established relationships in the current database, the Relationships window appears. If the tables you want to include in the relationship do not appear, click the Show Table button on the toolbar or choose Relationships| Show Table. To add the desired tables to the Relationships window, select a table and then click Add. Repeat this process for each table you want to add. To select multiple tables at once, press Shift while clicking to select contiguous tables or press Ctrl while clicking to select noncontiguous tables; then click Add. Click Close when you are finished.

4. Click and drag the field from one table to the matching field in the other table. The Edit Relationships dialog box appears.

5. Determine whether you want to establish referential integrity and whether you want to cascade update related fields or cascade delete related records by enabling the appropriate check boxes (see Figure 9.6). These topics are covered later in this hour, in the section "Establishing Referential Integrity."

FIGURE 9.6

The Edit Relationships dialog box, which enables you to view and modify the relationships between the tables in a database.

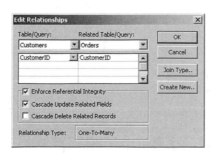

6. Click OK. The dialog box closes, and you return to the Relationships window.

Following Guidelines for Establishing Relationships

You must remember a few important things when establishing relationships. If you are not aware of these important gotchas, you could find yourself in some pretty hairy situations:

- It is important to understand the correlation between the Relationships window and the actual relationships established within a database. The Relationships window lets you view and modify the existing relationships. When you establish relationships, Access creates the relationship the moment you click OK. You can delete the tables from the Relationships window (by selecting them and pressing Delete), but the relationships still exist. (The "Modifying an Existing Relationship" section of this hour covers the process of permanently removing relationships.) The Relationships window provides a visual blueprint of the relationships that are established. If you modify the layout of the window by moving around tables, adding tables to the window, or removing tables from the window, Access prompts you to save the layout after you close the Relationships window. Access is not asking whether you want to save the relationships you have established; it is simply asking whether you want to save the visual layout of the window.

- When you're adding tables to the Relationships window by using the Show Tables dialog box, it is easy to accidentally add a table to the window many times. This is because the tables you are adding can hide behind the Show Tables dialog box, or they can appear below the portion of the Relationships window that you are viewing. If this occurs, you see multiple occurrences of the same table when you close the Show Tables dialog box. Access gives each occurrence of the table a different alias, and you must remove the extra occurrences.

- You can add queries to the Relationships window by using the Show Tables dialog box. Although this method is rarely used, it might be useful if you regularly include the same queries within other queries and want to permanently establish relationships between them.

- If you remove tables from the Relationships window (remember that this does not delete the relationships) and you want to once again show all relationships that exist in the database, you can click Show All Relationships on the toolbar or choose Relationships|Show All. All existing relationships are then shown.

- To delete a relationship, you can click the join line and press Delete.

Modifying an Existing Relationship

Modifying an existing relationship is easy. Access gives you the capability to delete an existing relationship or to simply modify the nature of the relationship.

To permanently remove a relationship between two tables, you follow these steps:

1. With the Database window active, click Relationships on the toolbar.

2. Click the line joining the two tables whose relationship you want to delete.

3. Press Delete. Access prompts you to verify your actions. Click Yes.

You often need to modify the nature of a relationship rather than remove it. To modify a relationship, you follow these steps:

1. With the Database window active, click Relationships on the toolbar.

2. Double-click the line joining the two tables whose relationship you want to modify.

3. Make the required changes.

4. Click OK. All the normal rules regarding the establishment of relationships apply.

9

Task: Establishing Relationships

▲ To Do

Relationships are an extremely important aspect of any database that you build. Let's practice the process of creating a brand-new database. We'll add tables and then establish relationships between them. To begin, you create a new database and add a table called tblCustomers, another called tblOrders, and a third called tblOrderDetails. The tables should have the following fields:

```
tblCustomers:  CustomerID,  CompanyName,  Address,  City,  State,  ZipCode

tblOrders:  OrderID,  CustomerID,  OrderDate,  ShipVIA

tblOrderDetails:  OrderID,  LineNumber,  ItemID,  Quantity,  Price
```

After you've built the necessary tables, you're ready to establish the relationships between them. First you need to set some important properties of the fields that you just added. Then you'll be ready to establish the actual relationships between the tables. Here's how this works:

1. In the tblCustomers table, make the CustomerID field a Text field. Designate the CustomerID field as the primary key. Set the size of the field to 5. Make all other fields Text fields and leave their default property values.

2. In the tblOrders table, set OrderID to the AutoNumber field type. Make OrderID the primary key field. Make the CustomerID field a Text field with the field size of 5. Set the field type of the OrderDate field to Date and the field type of the ShipVIA field to Number, with a size of Long Integer.

3. In the tblOrderDetails table, set the field type of the OrderID field to Number and make sure that the size is Long Integer. Set the field type of the LineNumber field to

▼

▼   Number, with a size of Long Integer. Base the primary key of the table on the combination of the OrderID and LineNumber fields. Set the field type of the ItemID and Quantity fields to Number, with a size of Long Integer, and set the field type of the Price field to Currency.

4. Open the Relationships window. With the tblCustomers table in the Show Table dialog box selected, hold down the Shift key and click to select the tblOrders table. Click Add. All three tables appear in the Relationships window. Click Close. Click and drag from the CustomerID field in the tblCustomers table to the CustomerID field in the tblOrders table. After the Edit Relationships dialog box appears, click OK. Repeat the process, clicking and dragging the OrderID field from the tblOrders table
▲   to the OrderID field in the tblOrderDetails table.

Establishing Referential Integrity

As you can see, establishing a relationship is quite easy. Establishing the right kind of relationship is a little more difficult. When you attempt to establish a relationship between two tables, Access makes some decisions based on a few predefined factors:

- Access establishes a one-to-many relationship if one of the related fields is a primary key or has a unique index.

- Access establishes a one-to-one relationship if both of the related fields are primary keys or have unique indexes.

- Access creates an indeterminate relationship if neither of the related fields is a primary key and neither has a unique index. You cannot establish referential integrity in this case.

As discussed earlier in this hour, *referential integrity* consists of a series of rules that the Jet Engine applies to ensure that Jet properly maintains the relationships between tables. At the most basic level, referential integrity rules prevent the creation of orphan records in the table on the "many" side of the one-to-many relationship. After you establish a relationship between a Customers table and an Orders table, for example, all orders in the Orders table must be related to a particular customer in the Customers table. Before you can establish referential integrity between two tables, the following conditions must be met:

- The matching field on the "one" side of the relationship must be a primary key field or must have a unique index.

- The matching fields must have the same data types. (For linking purposes, AutoNumber fields match Long Integer fields.) With the exception of Text fields, the matching fields also must have the same size. Number fields on both sides of the relationship must have the same size (for example, Long Integer).

- Both tables must be part of the same Access database.

- Both tables must be stored in the proprietary Access file (.MDB) format. (They cannot be external tables from other sources.)

- The database that contains the two tables must be open.

- Existing data within the two tables cannot violate any referential integrity rules. All orders in the Orders table must relate to existing customers in the Customers table, for example.

Although Text fields involved in a relationship do not have to be the same size, it is prudent to make them the same size. Otherwise, you degrade performance as well as risk the chance of unpredictable results when you create queries based on the two tables.

After you establish referential integrity between two tables, the Jet Engine applies the following rules:

- You cannot enter in the foreign key of the related table a value that does not exist in the primary key of the primary table. For example, you cannot enter in the CustomerID field of the Orders table a value that does not exist in the CustomerID field of the Customers table.

- You cannot delete a record from the primary table if corresponding records exist in the related table. For example, you cannot delete a customer from the Customers table if related records (for example, records with the same value in the CustomerID field) exist in the Orders table.

- You cannot change the value of a primary key on the "one" side of a relationship if corresponding records exist in the related table. For example, you cannot change the value in the CustomerID field of the Customers table if corresponding orders exist in the Orders table.

If you attempt to violate any of these three rules and you have enforced referential integrity between the tables, Access displays an appropriate error message, as shown in Figure 9.7.

The Jet Engine's default behavior is to prohibit the deletion of parent records that have associated child records and to prohibit the change of a primary key value of a parent record when that parent has associated child records. You can override these restrictions by using the Cascade Update Related Fields and Cascade Delete Related Records check boxes that are available in the Relationships dialog box when you establish or modify a relationship.

The Cascade Update Related Fields Option

The Cascade Update Related Fields option is available only if you have established referential integrity between tables. When this option is selected, the user can change the primary key value of the record on the "one" side of the relationship. When the user attempts to modify the field joining the two tables on the "one" side of the relationship, the Jet Engine cascades the change down to the foreign key field on the "many" side of the relationship. This is useful if the primary key field is modifiable. For example, a purchase number on a purchase order master record might be updateable. If the user modifies the purchase order number of the parent record, you would want to cascade the change to the associated detail records in the purchase order detail table.

> There is no need to select the Cascade Update Related Fields option when the related field on the "one" side of the relationship is an AutoNumber field. You can never modify an AutoNumber field. The Cascade Update Related Fields option has no effect on AutoNumber fields. In fact, this is why, in the preceding Task, you make the CustomerID a Text field. It provides an example that you can later use with a cascade update.

It is very easy to accidentally introduce a loophole into a system. If you create a one-to-many relationship between two tables but forget to set the Required property of the foreign key field to Yes, you allow the addition of orphan records. Figure 9.8 illustrates this point. In this example, I added an order to tblOrders without entering a customer ID. This record is an orphan record because no records in tblCustomers have CustomerID set to Null. To eliminate the problem, you set the Required property of the foreign key field to Yes.

Null

FIGURE 9.8
An orphan record with Null *in the foreign key field.*

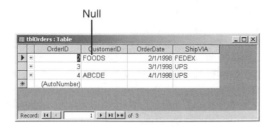

The Cascade Delete Related Records Option

The Cascade Delete Related Records option is available only if you have established referential integrity between tables. When this option is selected, the user can delete a record on the "one" side of a one-to-many relationship, even if related records exist in the table on the "many" side of the relationship. A user can delete a customer even if the customer has existing orders, for example. The Jet Engine maintains referential integrity between the tables because it automatically deletes all related records in the child table.

If you attempt to delete a record from the table on the "one" side of a one-to-many relationship and no related records exist in the table on the "many" side of the relationship, you get the usual warning message, as shown in Figure 9.9. On the other hand, if you attempt to delete a record from the table on the "one" side of a one-to-many relationship and related records exist in the child table, Access warns you that you are about to delete the record from the parent table as well as any related records in the child table (see Figure 9.10).

FIGURE 9.9
A message that appears after the user attempts to delete a parent record that does not has related child records.

FIGURE 9.10
A message that appears after the user attempts to delete a parent record that has related child records.

The Cascade Delete Related Records option is not always appropriate. It is an excellent feature, but you should use it prudently. Although it is usually appropriate to cascade delete from an Orders table to an Order Details table, for example, it generally is not appropriate to cascade delete from a Customers table to an Orders table. This is because you generally do not want to delete all your order history from the Orders table if for some reason you want to delete a customer. Deleting the order history causes important information, such as the profit and loss history, to change. It is therefore appropriate to prohibit this type of deletion and handle the customer in some other way, such as marking him or her as inactive or archiving his or her data. On the other hand, if you delete an order because the customer cancelled it, you probably want to remove the corresponding order detail information as well. In this case, the Cascade Delete Related Records option is appropriate. You need to make the most prudent decision in each situation, based on business needs. You need to carefully consider the implications of each option before you make a decision.

Task: Working with Referential Integrity

In this task you enforce referential integrity between the tblCustomers table and the tblOrders table you created earlier in this hour. It illustrates how enforcing referential integrity between the tables affects the process of adding and deleting records. You need to follow these steps:

1. Open the Relationships window. Double-click the join line between tblCustomers and tblOrders. Enable the Enforce Referential Integrity check box. Click OK. Repeat this process for the relationship between tblOrders and tblOrderDetails.

2. Go into tblCustomer and add a couple records. Take note of the customer IDs. Go into tblOrders. Add a couple records, taking care to assign customer IDs of customers that exist in the tblCustomers table. Now try to add an order for a customer whose customer ID does not exist in tblCustomers. You should get an error message.

3. Attempt to delete from tblCustomers a customer who does not have any orders. You should get a warning message, but Access should allow you to complete the process. Now try to delete a customer who does have orders. The Jet Engine should prohibit you from deleting the customer. Attempt to change the customer ID of a customer who has orders. You should not be able to do this.

Task: Working with Cascade Update Related Fields and Cascade Delete Related Records

To Do ▼

With the Cascade Update Related Fields feature enabled, you are able to update the primary key value of a record that has associated child records. With the Cascade Delete Related Records feature enabled, you can delete a parent record that has associated child records. To see how to use Cascade Update Related Fields and Cascade Delete Related Records, follow these steps:

9

1. Modify the relationship between the `tblCustomers` and `tblOrders` tables you created earlier in this hour. Open the Relationships window. Double-click the join line between `tblCustomers` and `tblOrders`. Enable the Cascade Update Related Fields check box. Modify the relationship between `tblOrders` and `tblOrderDetails`. Enable the Cascade Delete Related Records check box. There is no need to enable Cascade Update Related Fields because the `OrderID` field in `tblOrders` is an `AutoNumber` field.

2. Attempt to delete a customer who has orders. The Jet Engine should prohibit you from doing this because Cascade Delete Related Records is not enabled. In `tblCustomers`, change the customer ID of a customer who has orders. The Jet Engine should allow this change. Take a look at `tblOrders`. The Jet Engine should have updated the customer ID of all corresponding records in the table to reflect the change in the parent record.

3. Add some order details to `tblOrderDetails`. Try to delete any order that has details within `tblOrderDetails`. You should receive a warning, but the Jet Engine should allow you to complete the process.

▲

The Benefits of Relationships

The primary benefit of relationships is the data integrity they provide. Without the establishment of relationships, users are free to add records to child tables without regard to entering required parent information. After you establish referential integrity, you can enable Cascade Update Related Fields or Cascade Delete Related Records, as appropriate, which saves you quite a bit of code in maintaining the integrity of the data in the system. Most relational database management systems require that you write the code to delete related records when the user deletes a parent record or to update the foreign key in related records when the user modifies the primary key of the parent. When you enable the Cascade Update Related Fields and Cascade Delete Related Fields check boxes, you are sheltered from having to write a single line of code to perform these tasks when they are appropriate.

Access automatically carries relationships into your queries. This means that each time you build a new query, Access automatically establishes the relationships between the tables within the query, based on the relationships that are set up in the Relationships window. Furthermore, each time you build a form or report, Access uses relationships between the tables included on the form or report to assist with the design process. Whether you delete or update data by using a datasheet or a form, all referential integrity rules automatically apply, even if you establish the relationship after you build the form.

Summary

Relationships enable you to normalize a database. By using relationships, you can divide data into separate tables and then once again combine the data at runtime. This hour begins by explaining relational database design principles. It describes the types of relationships that you can define. It also covers the details of establishing and modifying relationships between tables and describes all the important aspects of establishing relationships.

The capability to easily establish and maintain referential integrity between tables is an important strength of Microsoft Access. This hour describes the referential integrity options and highlights when each option is appropriate. Finally, this hour summarizes the benefits of relationships.

Q&A

Q Name three benefits of relationships.

A The right type of relationship ensures data integrity, optimal performance, and ease of use in designing system objects.

Q Explain the concept of a foreign key.

A A foreign key in one table is the field that relates to the primary key in a second table. For example, whereas CustomerID is the primary key in the Customers table, it may be the foreign key in the Orders table.

Q Explain referential integrity.

A With referential integrity, a database cannot contain any orphan foreign key values. This means that you cannot add child rows for parents that don't exist, you cannot modify the parent key value if that parent has children (unless the Cascade Update Related Fields option is selected), and you cannot delete parents that have children (unless the Cascade Delete Related Fields option is selected).

Q **Explain the Cascade Update Related Fields option and the Cascade Delete Related Fields option.**

A With the Cascade Update Related Fields option enabled, if the user tries to update the primary key of a parent record that has children, Access updates the foreign key of each of the child rows. With the Cascade Delete Related Fields option enabled, if the user tries to delete a parent record that has children, Access attempts to delete all the associated children rows.

Workshop

The Workshop includes quiz questions that are designed to help you test your understanding of the material covered and activities to help put what you've learned to practice. You can find the answers to the questions in the section immediately following the quiz.

Quiz

1. Name three types of relationships.
2. Name the types of relationship that you cannot directly create in Access.
3. Name the three attributes that constitute a good primary key.
4. Denormalization slows down performance (True/False).
5. The Relationships window always reflects the relationships that are in place in a database (True/False).

Quiz Answers

1. One-to-many, one-to-one, and many-to-many.
2. Many-to-many.
3. Minimal, stable, and simple.
4. False. The primary reason for denormalization is generally to improve performance.
5. False. The Relationships window provides a visual layout of the relationships that are included within the window. This may or may not represent all the relationships in the database.

Activities

Build three related tables. Don't forget to set their primary keys. Establish relationships between them. Set referential integrity. Attempt to add, remove, and modify data. Practice using the Cascade Update Related Fields and Cascade Delete Related Fields options. See how this affects the process of inserting, updating, and deleting data.

Creating Queries

Although tables act as the ultimate foundation for any application you build, queries are very important as well. Most of the forms and reports that act as the user interface for an application are based on queries. Having an understanding of queries—what they are and when and how to use them—is imperative for your success as an Access application developer. In this hour you'll learn the following:

- The basics of working with queries
- How to build queries
- How to add tables and fields to the queries you create
- How to sort query output
- How to limit the data that appears in the query output
- Tips and tricks related to working with queries

Query Basics

Creating a basic query is easy because Microsoft has provided a user-friendly, drag-and-drop interface. There are two ways to start a new query in Access 2003. The first way is to select the Queries icon from the Objects list in the Database window; then double-click the Create query in Design View icon or the Create query by using wizard icon (see Figure 10.1). The second method is to select the Queries icon from the Objects list in the Database window and then click the New command button on the Database window toolbar. The New Query dialog box appears (see Figure 10.2). This dialog box lets you select whether to build the query from scratch or use one of the wizards to help you. The Simple Query Wizard walks you through the steps of creating a basic query. The other wizards help you create three specific types of queries: Crosstab, Find Duplicates, and Find Unmatched queries.

FIGURE 10.1

Selecting the Queries icon from the Objects list.

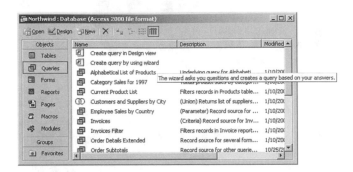

FIGURE 10.2

The New Query dialog box.

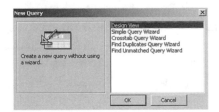

Adding Tables to Queries

If you choose to use Design view rather than one of the wizards, the Show Table dialog box appears (see Figure 10.3). In this dialog box, you can select the tables or queries that supply data to a query. Access doesn't care whether you select tables or queries as the foundation for queries. You can select a table or query by double-clicking the name of the table or query you want to add or by right-clicking the table and then selecting Add from the context menu. You can select multiple tables or queries by holding down the Shift key while you select a contiguous range of tables or the Ctrl key while you select noncontiguous tables. After you have selected the tables or queries you want, you click Add and then click Close. This brings you to the Query Design window, shown in Figure 10.4.

FIGURE 10.3
The Show Table dialog box.

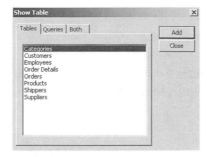

FIGURE 10.4
The Query Design window.

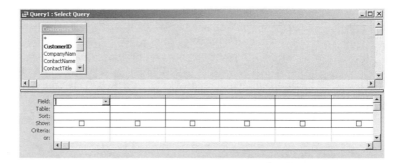

10

An alternate way to add a table is to first select Tables from the Objects list in the Database window and then select the table on which you want to base the query. With the table selected, you select New Query from the New Object drop-down list box on the toolbar or choose Insert | Query. The New Query dialog box appears. This is an efficient method of starting a new query based on only one table because the Show Table dialog box never appears.

Adding Fields to Queries

After you add tables to a query, you can select the fields you want to include in the query. The query shown in Figure 10.4 is based on the Customers table from the Northwind database that ships with Microsoft Access. Notice that the query window is divided into two sections: The top half of the window shows the tables or queries that underlie the query you're designing, and the bottom half shows any fields that you will include in the query output. You can add a field to the query design grid on the bottom half of the query window in several ways:

- You can double-click the name of the field you want to add.

- You can click and drag a single field from the table in the top half of the query window to the query design grid below.

- You can select multiple fields at the same time by using the Shift key (for a contiguous range of fields) or the Ctrl key (for a noncontiguous range). You can double-click the title bar of the field list to select all fields and then click and drag any one of the selected fields to the query design grid.

You can double-click the asterisk in the field list to include all fields within the table in the query result. Although this is very handy in that changes to the table structure magically affect the query's output, this "trick" is dangerous. When you select the asterisk, you include all table fields in the query result, whether you need them or not. This can cause major performance problems in a local area network (LAN), wide area network (WAN), or client/server application.

The easiest way to run a query is to click the Run button on the toolbar. (It looks like an exclamation point.) You can click the Query View button to run a query, but this method works only for Select queries, not for Action queries. The Query View button has a special meaning for Action queries (explained in Hour 15, "Power Query Techniques"). Clicking Run is preferable because when you do that, you don't have to worry about what type of query you're running. After you run a Select query, you should see what looks like a datasheet that contains only the fields you selected. To return to the query's design, you click the Query View button.

Access 2002 introduced shortcut keys that allow you to easily toggle between the various query views: Ctrl+>, Ctrl+period, Ctrl+<, and Ctrl+comma. Ctrl+> and Ctrl+period take you to the next view; Ctrl+< and Ctrl+comma take you to the previous view.

Removing a Field from the Query Design Grid

To remove a field from the query design grid, follow these steps:

1. Find the field you want to remove.

2. Click the column selector (that is, the small horizontal gray button) immediately above the name of the field. The entire column of the query design grid should become black (see Figure 10.5).

FIGURE 10.5

Removing a field from the query design grid.

Column Selectors

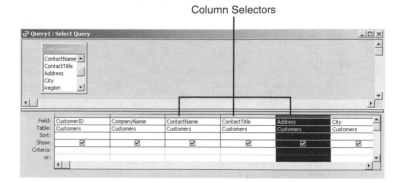

3. Press the Delete key or select Delete from the Edit menu. Access removes the field from the query.

Inserting a Field After a Query Is Built

The process for inserting a field after you have built a query depends on where you want to insert the new field. If you want to insert it after the existing fields, it's easiest to double-click the name of the field you want to add. If you prefer to insert the new field between two existing fields, it's best to click and drag the field you want to add and drop it onto the field you want to appear to the right of the inserted field.

Moving a Field to a Different Location on the Query Design Grid

Although the user can move a column while in a query's Datasheet view, sometimes you want to permanently alter the position of a field in the query output. You can do this as a convenience to the user or, more importantly, to use the query as a foundation for forms and reports. The order of the fields in the query becomes the default order of the fields on any forms and reports you build by using any of the wizards. You can save yourself quite a bit of time by ordering queries effectively.

To move a single column, follow these steps:

1. Select a column while in the query's Design view by clicking its column selector.

2. Click the selected column a second time, and then drag it to a new location on the query design grid.

10

Follow these steps to move more than one column at a time:

1. Drag across the column selectors of the columns you want to move.

2. Click any of the selected columns a second time, and then drag them to a new location on the query design grid.

Moving a column in Datasheet view doesn't modify the query's underlying design. If you move a column in Datasheet view, subsequent reordering in Design view isn't reflected in Datasheet view. In other words, Design view and Datasheet view are no longer synchronized, and you must reorder both manually. This actually serves as an advantage in most cases. As you will learn later in this hour, if you want to sort by the Country field and then by the CompanyName field, the Country field must appear to the left of the CompanyName field in the design of the query. If you want the CompanyName field to appear to the left of the Country field in the query's result, you must make that change in Datasheet view. The fact that Access maintains the order of the columns separately in both views allows you to easily accomplish both objectives.

Saving and Naming Queries

To save a query at any time, you can click the Save button on the toolbar. If the query is a new one, Access prompts you to name the query.

Access supplies default names for the queries that you create (for example, Query1, Query2). I suggest that you supply a more descriptive name. A query name should begin with qry so that you can easily recognize and identify it as a query.

It's important to understand that when you save a query, you're saving only the query's definition, not the actual query result.

Task: Creating a Simple Query

▼ To Do ▼

To practice the skills you've learned so far, in this task you create a simple query. You should use the Northwind database so that you have a good source of existing data as the foundation for the query. Here's the process:

1. Open the Northwind database that comes with Access. If you want to prevent the Startup form from appearing, hold down the Shift key as you open the database.

2. Select Queries in the list of objects and then click the New icon on the Database toolbar.

3. Select Design View in the New Query dialog box.

4. Add the Customers table to the query.

5. Click the CustomerID field.

6. Hold down the Shift key and click the ContactTitle field. This should select the CustomerID, CompanyName, ContactName, and ContactTitle fields.

7. Scroll down the list of fields by using the vertical scrollbar until the Region field is visible.

8. Hold down the Ctrl key and click the Region field.

9. With the Ctrl key still held down, click the Phone field. You should now have selected all six fields.

10. Click and drag any of the selected fields from the table on the top half of the query window to the query design grid on the bottom. All six fields should appear in the query design grid. You might need to use the horizontal scrollbar to view some of the fields on the right.

11. Assume that you have decided to remove the Region field from the query design grid. Use the horizontal scrollbar to see the Region field on the query design grid.

12. Click the column selector immediately above the Region field. The entire column of the query design grid should become black, and the cursor should turn into a downward-pointing arrow.

13. Press the Delete key to remove the Region field from the query design grid.

14. To insert the Country field between the ContactTitle and Phone fields, click and drag the Country field from the table until it's on top of the Phone field. Then drop the Country field. The field is inserted in the correct place. To run the query, click Run on the toolbar.

15. Move the ContactName and ContactTitle fields so that they appear before the CompanyName field. Do this by clicking and dragging from ContactName's column selector to ContactTitle's column selector. Both columns should be selected. Click again on the column selector for either column and then click and drag until the thick black line jumps to the left of the CompanyName field.

16. Return to the Design View of the query. To save your work, click Save on the toolbar. When you're prompted for a name, call the query qryCustomers.

10

Ordering Query Results

When you run a new query, the query output appears in no particular order. Generally, however, you want to order query output. You can do this by using the Sort row of the query design grid.

To order the results of a query, follow these steps:

1. In Design view, click within the query design grid in the Sort cell of the column you want to sort (see Figure 10.6).

FIGURE 10.6

Changing the order of query results.

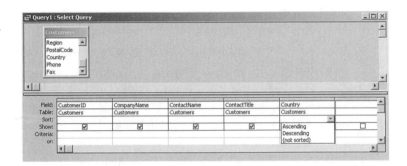

2. Use the drop-down combo box to select an ascending or descending sort. Ascending or Descending appears in the sort cell for the field, as appropriate.

Sorting by More Than One Field

You might often want to sort query output by more than one field. The columns you want to sort must be placed in order, from left to right, on the query design grid, with the column you want to act as the primary sort on the far left and the secondary, tertiary, and any additional sorts following to the right. If you want the columns to appear in a different order in the query output, you must move them manually in Datasheet view after you run the query.

Task: Ordering Query Results

To sort query results in ascending order by the ContactTitle field, follow these steps:

1. In Design view, click the Sort row of the query design grid for the ContactTitle field.

2. From the Sort drop-down combo box, select Ascending.

3. Run the query and view the results. The records should now be ordered based on the ContactTitle field.

▲ To Do ▼

▼   4. If you want to return to Design view of the query, click View on the toolbar.

      5. Sort the query output by the Country field and, within individual country groupings, by the ContactTitle field. Because sorting always occurs from left to right, you must place the Country field before the ContactTitle field. Select the Country field from the query design grid by clicking the thin gray button above the Country column.

      6. After you have selected the Country field, move the mouse back to the thin gray button and click and drag to the left of the ContactTitle field. A thick gray line should appear to the left of the ContactTitle field.

      7. Release the mouse button.

      8. Change the sort order of the Country field to Ascending.

▲   9. Run the query. The records should be in order by country and, within the country grouping, by contact title.

Refining a Query by Using Criteria

So far in this hour, you have learned how to select the fields you want and how to indicate the sort order for query output. One of the important features of queries is the ability to limit output by using selection criteria. Access allows you to combine criteria by using several operators to limit the criteria for multiple fields. Table 10.1 covers the operators and their meanings.

TABLE 10.1   Access Operators

Operator	Meaning	Example	Result of Example
=	Equal to	="Sales"	Finds only records with "Sales" as the field value.
<	Less than	<100	Finds all records with values less than 100 in that field.
<=	Less than or equal to	<=100	Finds all records with or equal to values less than or equal to 100 in that field.
>	Greater than or equal to	>100	Finds all records with values greater than 100 in that field.
>=	Greater than	>=100	Finds all records with or equal to values greater than or equal to 100 in that field.
<>	Not equal to	<>"Sales"	Finds all records with values other than Sales in the field.

TABLE 10.1 continued

Operator	Meaning	Example	Result of Example
And	Both conditions must be true	Created by adding criteria on the same line of the query design grid to more thanone field	Finds all records where the conditions in both fields are true.
Or	Either condition can be true	"CA" or "NY" or "UT"	Finds all records with the value "CA", "NY", or "UT" in the field.
Like	Compares a string expression to a pattern	Like "Sales*"	Finds all records with the value "Sales" at the beginning of the field (the asterisk is a wildcard character).
Between	Finds a range of values	Between 5 and 10	Finds all records with the values 5–10 (inclusive) in the field.
In	Same as Or	In("CA", "NY","UT")	Finds all records with the value "CA", "NY", or "UT" in the field.
Not	Same as <>	Not "Sales"	Finds all records with values other than Sales in the field.
Is Null	Finds nulls	Is Null	Finds all records where no data has been entered in the field.
Is Not Null	Finds all records that are not null	Is Not Null	Finds all records where data has been entered into thefield.

Criteria entered for two fields on a single line of the query design grid are considered an And condition, which means that both conditions need to be true for the record to appear in the query output. Entries made on separate lines of the query design grid are considered an Or condition, which means that either condition can be true for Access to include the record in the query output. Take a look at the example in Figure 10.7; this query would output all records in which the ContactTitle field begins with either Marketing or Owner, regardless of the customer ID. It outputs the records in which the ContactTitle field begins with Sales only for the customers whose IDs begin with the letters *M* through *R*, inclusive. Notice that the word Sales is immediately followed by the asterisk. This means that salesman would be included in the output. On the other hand, Marketing and Owner are both followed by spaces. That means that only entries that begin with Marketing or Owner followed by a space are included in the output.

FIGURE 10.7

Adding And *and* Or *conditions to a query.*

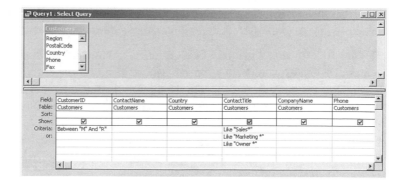

Working with Dates in Criteria

Access gives you significant power for adding date functions and expressions to query criteria. Using these criteria, you can find all records in a certain month, on a specific weekday, or between two dates. Table 10.2 lists the Data criteria expressions and examples.

10

TABLE 10.2   Date Criteria Expressions

Expression	Meaning	Example	Result
Date()	Current date	Date()	Records the current date within a field.
Day(Date)	The day of a date	Day([OrderDate])=1	Records the order date on the first day of the month.
Month(Date)	The month of a date	Month([OrderDate])=1	Records the order date in January.
Year(Date)	The year of a date	Year([OrderDate])=1991	Records the order date in 1991.
Weekday(Date)	The weekday of a date	Weekday([OrderDate])=2	Records the order date on a Monday.
Between Date And Date	A range of dates	Between #1/1/95# and #12/31/95#	Finds all records in 1995.
DatePart (Interval, Date)	A specific part of a date	DatePart ("q",[OrderDate])=2	Finds all records in the second quarter.

The Weekday(Date, [FirstDayOfWeek]) function works based on your locale and how your system defines the first day of the week. Weekday() used without the optional

FirstDayOfWeek argument defaults to vbSunday as the first day. A value of 0 defaults FirstDayOfWeek to the system definition. Other values can be set also.

Figure 10.8 illustrates the use of a date function. Notice that DatePart("q",[OrderDate]) is entered as the expression, and the value 2 is entered for the criterion. Year([OrderDate])] is entered as another expression, with the number 1995 as the criterion. Therefore, this query outputs all records in which the order date is in the second quarter of 1995.

FIGURE 10.8

Using the DatePart() *and* Year() *functions in a query.*

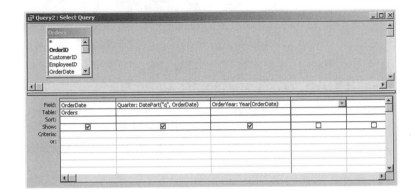

Task: Adding Criteria to a Query

Design a query to find all the sales agents in Brazil or France. The criteria you build should look like those in Figure 10.9. The steps provide criteria for the contact title and country fields.

1. The criterion for the Country field should be "Brazil" Or "France" because you want both Brazil and France to appear in the query output. The criterion for the ContactTitle field should be "Sales Agent". Because you should enter the criteria for both the Country and ContactTitle fields on the same line of the query design grid, both must be true for the record to appear in the query output. In other words, the customer must be in either Brazil or France and must also be a sales agent.

2. Modify the query so that you can output all the customers for whom the contact title begins with Sales.

3. Try changing the criteria for the ContactTitle field to Sales. Notice that no records appear in the query output because no contact titles are just Sales. You must enter "Like Sales*" for the criteria. Now you get Sales Agent, Sales Associate, Sales Manager, and so on. You still don't see Assistant Sales Agent because their titles don't begin with Sales.

4. Try changing the criteria to "Like *Sales*". Now all Assistant Sales Agent appear. This is because the wildcard, the asterisk, appears *both* before and after Sales. This

▼ means that Access returns anything containing the word `Sales` anywhere within it. For full coverage of the asterisk wildcard, see Hour 3, "Queries Introduced."

FIGURE 10.9

The criterion to select sales agents whose country is either Brazil or France.

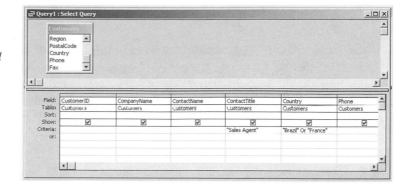

▲

Updating Query Results

If you haven't realized it yet, you can usually update the results of a query. This means that if you modify the data in the query output, Access permanently modifies the data in the tables underlying the query.

To see how this works, follow these steps:

1. Build a query based on the `Customers` table.

2. Add the `CustomerID`, `CompanyName`, `Address`, `City`, and `Region` fields to the query design grid and then run the query.

3. Change the address of a particular customer and make a note of the customer ID of the customer whose address you changed. Make sure you move off the record so that Access writes the change to disk.

4. Close the query, open the actual table in Datasheet view, and find the record whose address you modified. The change you made was written to the original table; this is because a query result is a dynamic set of records that maintains a link to the original data. This happens whether you're on a standalone machine or on a network.

It's essential that you understand how Access updates query results; otherwise, you might mistakenly update table data without realizing you've done so. Updating multitable queries is covered later in this hour, in the sections "Pitfalls of Multitable Queries" and "AutoLookup in Multitable Queries."

Building Queries Based on Multiple Tables

If you have properly normalized your table data, you probably want to bring the data from your tables back together by using queries. Fortunately, you can do this quite easily by using Access queries.

The query in Figure 10.10 joins the Customers, Orders, and Order Details tables, pulling fields from each. Notice in the figure that I have selected the CustomerID and CompanyName fields from the Customers table, the OrderID and OrderDate fields from the Orders table, and the UnitPrice and Quantity fields from the Order Details table. After you run this query, you should see the results shown in Figure 10.11. Notice that you get a record in the query's result for every record in the Order Details table. In other words, there are 2,155 records in the Order Details table, and that's how many records appear in the query output. By creating a multitable query, you can look at data from related tables, along with the data from the Order Details table.

Hour 9 discusses how setting up the right type of relationship ensures ease of use in designing system objects. By setting up relationships between tables in a database, Access knows how to properly join them in the queries that you build.

FIGURE 10.10

A query joining the Customers, Orders, *and* Order Details *tables.*

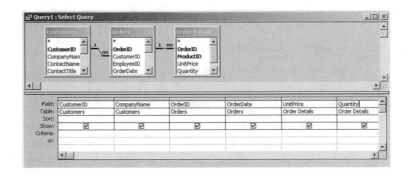

To remove a table from a query, you click anywhere on the table in the top half of the query design grid and then press the Delete key. You can add tables to the query at any time by clicking the Show Table button on the toolbar. If you prefer, you can select the Database window and then click and drag tables directly from the Database window to the top half of the query design grid.

FIGURE 10.11
The results of querying multiple tables.

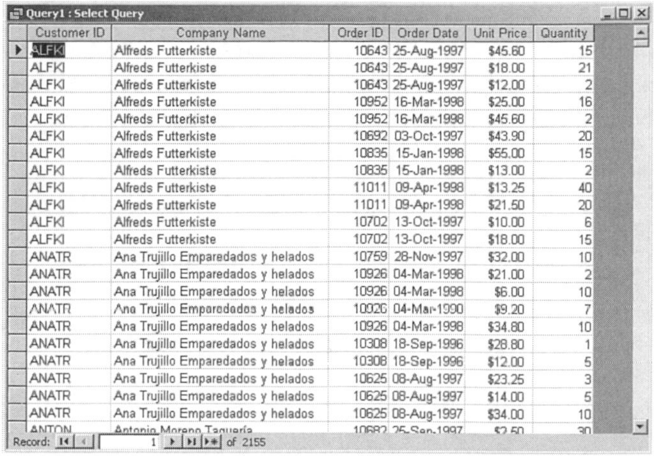

Query1 : Select Query

Customer ID	Company Name	Order ID	Order Date	Unit Price	Quantity
ALFKI	Alfreds Futterkiste	10643	25-Aug-1997	$45.60	15
ALFKI	Alfreds Futterkiste	10643	25-Aug-1997	$18.00	21
ALFKI	Alfreds Futterkiste	10643	25-Aug-1997	$12.00	2
ALFKI	Alfreds Futterkiste	10952	16-Mar-1998	$25.00	16
ALFKI	Alfreds Futterkiste	10952	16-Mar-1998	$45.60	2
ALFKI	Alfreds Futterkiste	10692	03-Oct-1997	$43.90	20
ALFKI	Alfreds Futterkiste	10835	15-Jan-1998	$55.00	15
ALFKI	Alfreds Futterkiste	10835	15-Jan-1998	$13.00	2
ALFKI	Alfreds Futterkiste	11011	09-Apr-1998	$13.25	40
ALFKI	Alfreds Futterkiste	11011	09-Apr-1998	$21.50	20
ALFKI	Alfreds Futterkiste	10702	13-Oct-1997	$10.00	6
ALFKI	Alfreds Futterkiste	10702	13-Oct-1997	$18.00	15
ANATR	Ana Trujillo Emparedados y helados	10759	28-Nov-1997	$32.00	10
ANATR	Ana Trujillo Emparedados y helados	10926	04-Mar-1998	$21.00	2
ANATR	Ana Trujillo Emparedados y helados	10926	04-Mar-1998	$6.00	10
ANATR	Ana Trujillo Emparedados y helados	10926	04-Mar-1998	$9.20	7
ANATR	Ana Trujillo Emparedados y helados	10926	04-Mar-1998	$34.80	10
ANATR	Ana Trujillo Emparedados y helados	10308	18-Sep-1996	$28.80	1
ANATR	Ana Trujillo Emparedados y helados	10308	18-Sep-1996	$12.00	5
ANATR	Ana Trujillo Emparedados y helados	10625	08-Aug-1997	$23.25	3
ANATR	Ana Trujillo Emparedados y helados	10625	08-Aug-1997	$14.00	5
ANATR	Ana Trujillo Emparedados y helados	10625	08-Aug-1997	$34.00	10
ANTON	Antonio Moreno Taquería	10682	25-Sep-1997	$2.50	30

Record: 1 of 2155

Pitfalls of Multitable Queries

You should be aware of some pitfalls of multitable queries: They involve updating as well as which records you see in the query output.

It's important to remember that you cannot update certain fields in a multitable query. You cannot update the join fields on the "one" side of a one-to-many relationship (unless you've activated the Cascade Update Referential Integrity feature). You also can't update the join field on the "many" side of a relationship after you've updated data on the "one" side. More importantly, which fields you *can* update, and the consequences of updating them, might surprise you. If you update the fields on the "one" side of a one-to-many relationship, you must be aware of that change's impact. You're actually updating that record in the original table on the "one" side of the relationship, and several records on the "many" side of the relationship may be affected.

For example, Figure 10.12 shows the result of a query based on the `Customers`, `Orders`, and `Order Details` tables. I have changed `Alfreds Futterkiste` to `Waldo Futterkiste` on a specific record of the query output. You might expect this change to affect only that specific order detail item. However, pressing the down-arrow key to move off the record shows that all records associated with Alfreds Futterkiste are changed (See Figure 10.13). This happens because all the orders for Alfreds Futterkiste were actually getting their information from one record in the `Customers` table—the record for customer ID `ALFKI`—and that is the record I modified while viewing the query result.

The second pitfall of multitable queries has to do with figuring out which records result from a multitable query. So far, you have learned how to build only inner joins. Hour 15 covers join types in detail, but for now, you need to understand that the query output contains only customers who have orders and orders that have order details. This means that not all the customers or orders might be listed. In Hour 15, you'll learn how to build queries in which you can list all customers, regardless of whether they have orders. You'll also learn how to list only the customers that do not have orders.

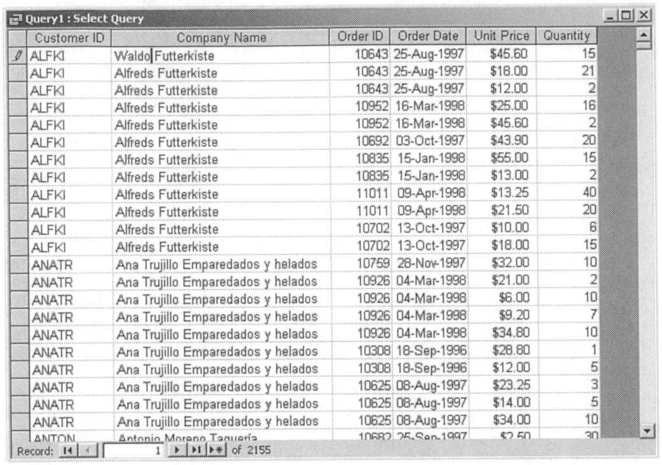

FIGURE **10.12**

Changing a record on the "one" side of a one-to-many relationship.

FIGURE **10.13**

The result of changing a record on the "one" side of a one-to-many relationship.

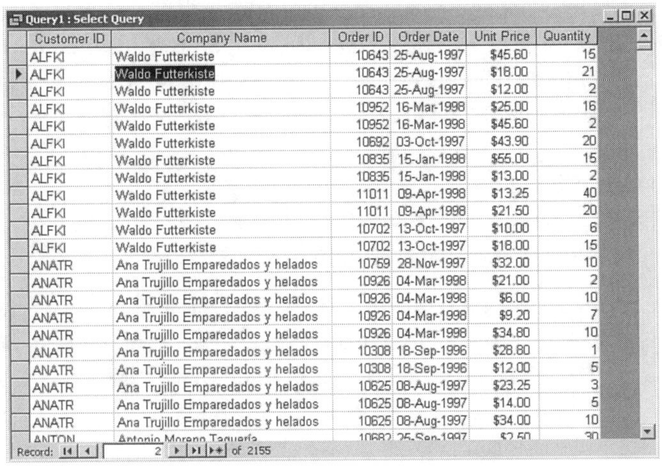

AutoLookup in Multitable Queries

The AutoLookup feature is automatically available in Access. As you fill in key values on the "many" side of a one-to-many relationship in a multitable query, Access automatically looks up the non-key values in the parent table. Most database developers refer to this as *enforced referential integrity*. A foreign key must first exist on the "one" side of the query to be entered successfully on the "many" side. As you can imagine, you don't want to be able to add to a database an order for a nonexistent customer.

For example, I have based the query in Figure 10.14 on the Customers and Orders tables. The fields included in the query are CustomerID from the Orders table; CompanyName, Address, and City from the Customers table; and OrderID and OrderDate from the Orders table. If you change the CustomerID field associated with an order, Access looks up the CompanyName, Address, and City fields from the Customers table and immediately displays them in the query result.

FIGURE 10.14

Using AutoLookup in a query with multiple tables.

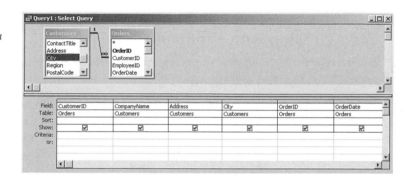

10

Notice in Figure 10.15 how the information for Alfreds Futterkiste is displayed in the query result. Figure 10.16 shows that the CompanyName and Address fields change automatically when the CustomerID field is changed to Around the Horn. Don't be confused by the combo box used to select the customer ID. The presence of the combo box within the query is a result of Access's Lookup feature, covered in Hour 14, "Power Table Techniques." The customer ID associated with a particular order is actually being modified in the query. If you add a new record to the query, Access fills in the customer information as soon as you select the customer ID associated with the order.

FIGURE 10.15

A query result before another customer ID is selected.

Customer	Company Name	Address	
Alfreds Futterkiste	Alfreds Futterkiste	Obere Str. 57	B(
Alfreds Futterkiste	Alfreds Futterkiste	Obere Str. 57	B(
Alfreds Futterkiste	Alfreds Futterkiste	Obere Str. 57	B(
Alfreds Futterkiste	Alfreds Futterkiste	Obere Str. 57	B(
Alfreds Futterkiste	Alfreds Futterkiste	Obere Str. 57	B(
Alfreds Futterkiste	Alfreds Futterkiste	Obere Str. 57	B(
Ana Trujillo Emparedados y hela	Ana Trujillo Emparedados y helados	Avda. de la Constitución 2222	M
Ana Trujillo Emparedados y hela	Ana Trujillo Emparedados y helados	Avda. de la Constitución 2222	M
Ana Trujillo Emparedados y hela	Ana Trujillo Emparedados y helados	Avda. de la Constitución 2222	M
Ana Trujillo Emparedados y hela	Ana Trujillo Emparedados y helados	Avda. de la Constitución 2222	M
Antonio Moreno Taquería	Antonio Moreno Taquería	Mataderos 2312	M
Antonio Moreno Taquería	Antonio Moreno Taquería	Mataderos 2312	M
Antonio Moreno Taquería	Antonio Moreno Taquería	Mataderos 2312	M
Antonio Moreno Taquería	Antonio Moreno Taquería	Mataderos 2312	M
Antonio Moreno Taquería	Antonio Moreno Taquería	Mataderos 2312	M

Record: 14 ◄ 1 ► ►1 ►* of 830

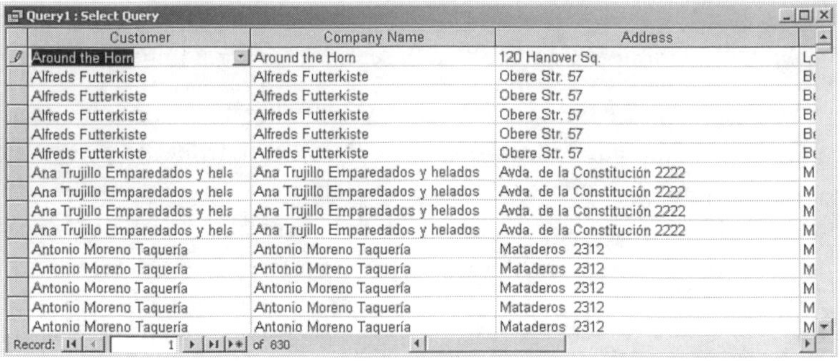

FIGURE 10.16

The result of an auto-lookup after the customer ID is changed.

Task: Working with Multitable Queries

Build a query that combines information from the Customers, Orders, and Order Details tables. To do this, follow these steps:

1. Select the Query tab from the Database window.

2. Click New.

3. Select Design View.

4. From the Show Table dialog box, select Customers, Orders, and Order Details by holding down the Ctrl key and clicking each table name. Then select Add.

5. Click Close.

6. Some of the tables included in the query might be hiding below the visible area of the window. If this is the case, scroll down with the vertical scrollbar to view any tables that aren't visible. Notice the join lines between the tables; they're based on the relationships set up in the Relationships window.

7. Select the following fields from each table:

   Customers: Country, City

   Orders: Order Date

   Order Details: UnitPrice, Quantity

8. Sort by Country field and then City field. The finished query design should look like the one in Figure 10.17.

9. Run the query. Data from all three tables should be included in the query output (see Figure 10.18).

10. Try changing the data in the City field for one of the records in the query result. Notice that Access appears to modify the data for the record (as well as several other records). This happens because the City field actually represents data from the "one" side of the one-to-many relationship. In other words, when you're view-

▼   ing the Country and City fields for several records in the query output, the data for
the fields might originate from one record. The same goes for the Order Date field
because it's also on the "one" side of a one-to-many relationship.

FIGURE 10.17

A sample query design.

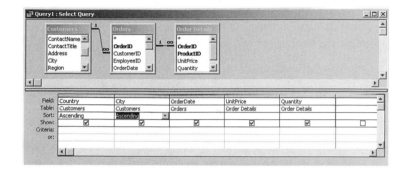

FIGURE 10.18

The Query output.

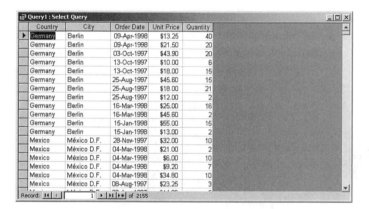

11. Practice modifying the data in the query result, and then return to the original table
▲   and notice which data has changed.

Creating Calculated Fields

One of the rules of data normalization is that you shouldn't include the results of calculations in a database. You can output the results of calculations by building those calculations into queries, and you can display the results of the calculations on forms and
reports by making the query the foundation for a form or report. You can also add to
forms and reports controls that contain the calculations you want. In certain cases, this
can improve performance.

The columns of a query result can hold the result of any valid expression. This makes queries extremely powerful. For example, you could enter the following expression:

```
Left([FirstName],1) & "." & Left([LastName],1) & "."
```

This expression would give you the first character of the first name, followed by a period, the first character of the last name, and another period. An even simpler expression would be this one:

```
[UnitPrice]*[Quantity]
```

This calculation would simply multiply the UnitPrice field by the Quantity field. In both cases, Access would automatically name the resulting expression. For example, Figure 10.19 shows the calculation that results from concatenating the first and last initials. Notice in the figure that Access gives the expression a name (often referred to as an *alias*). To give the expression a name, such as Initials, you must enter it as follows:

```
Initials:Left([FirstName],1) & "." & Left([LastName],1) & "."
```

The text preceding the colon is the name of the expression—in this case, Initials. If you don't explicitly give an expression a name, the name defaults to Expr1.

FIGURE 10.19

The result of using the expression Initials:Left([First Name],1) & "." & Left([LastName],1) & "." *in a query.*

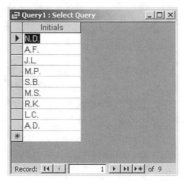

You can enter any valid expression in the Field row of the query design grid. Notice that Access automatically surrounds field names that are included in an expression with square brackets, unless the field name has spaces. If the field name includes any spaces, you must enclose the field name in brackets; otherwise, the query won't run properly. This is just one of the many reasons field and table names shouldn't contain spaces.

Task: Adding a Calculation to a Query

Follow these steps to add a calculation that shows the unit price multiplied by the quantity:

1. Scroll to the right on the query design grid until you can see a blank column.

2. Click the Field row for the new column.

3. Type TotalPrice:UnitPrice*Quantity. If you want to see more easily what you're typing, press Shift+F2 (Zoom). The Zoom dialog box, shown in Figure 10.20, appears.

FIGURE 10.20

Expanding a field by using the Zoom function (Shift+F2).

4. Click OK to close the Zoom window.

5. Run the query. The total sales amount should appear in the far-right column of the query output. The query output should look as shown in Figure 10.21.

FIGURE 10.21

The result of a total price calculation.

Getting Help from the Expression Builder

The Expression Builder is a helpful tool for building expressions in queries as well as in many other situations in Access. To invoke the Expression Builder, you click the Field cell of the query design grid and then click Build on the toolbar. The Expression Builder appears (see Figure 10.22). Notice that the Expression Builder is divided into three columns. The left-hand column shows the objects in the database. After you select an element in the left column, select the elements you want to paste from the middle and right columns.

FIGURE 10.22

The Expression Builder.

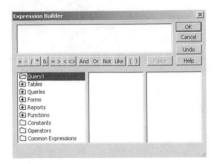

The example in Figure 10.23 shows Functions selected in the left column. Within Functions, both user-defined and built-in functions are listed; here, the Functions object is expanded with Built-In Functions selected. In the center column, Date/Time is selected. After you select Date/Time, all the built-in date and time functions appear in the right column. If you double-click a particular function—in this case, the DatePart function—Access places the function and its parameters in the text box at the top of the Expression Builder window. Notice that the DatePart function has four parameters: Interval, Date, FirstWeekday, and FirstWeek. If you know what needs to go into each of these parameters, you can simply replace the parameter placeholders with your own values. If you need more information, you can invoke Help on the selected function to learn more about the required parameters. Figure 10.24 shows two parameters filled in: the interval and the name of the field being evaluated. After you click OK, Access places the expression in the Field cell of the query.

FIGURE 10.23

The Expression Builder with the DatePart function selected and pasted in the expression box.

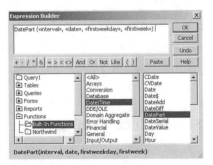

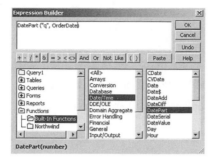

FIGURE 10.24
A function pasted by the Expression Builder, with the parameters updated with appropriate values.

Summary

This hour covers the foundations of perhaps the most important function of a database: getting data from the database and into a usable form. You have learned about the Select query used to retrieve data from a table, how to retrieve data from multiple tables, and how to use functions in queries to make them more powerful by synthesizing data. In Hour 15 you will extend your abilities with Action queries, Parameter queries, and queries that use other join types.

Q&A

Q Why would you want to build multitable queries?

A If you have properly separated data to normalize it (for example, into customers, orders, and order details), you might want to bring the data back together by using queries. To do this, you'd need to use multitable queries.

Q Why are you able to update query results?

A A query result is a dynamic set of records that maintains a link to the original data. When you update a query result, you update the original data.

Q What are the two ways you can run a query? Explain the difference between them.

A You can click the Run button or you can click the Query View button. Whereas the Run button runs any type of query, the Query View button runs only Select queries.

Workshop

The Workshop includes quiz questions that are designed to help you test your understanding of the material covered and activities to help put what you've learned to practice. You can find the answers to the questions in the section immediately following the quiz.

Quiz

1. When sorting a query, the field order on the query grid is important (True/False).

2. You can always update a query result (True/False).

3. What expression would you use to find all records with sales at the beginning of the field?

4. What expression would you use to find all records with the values 5 through 10, inclusive, in a field?

5. What expression would you use to find all records in NV, CA, and UT?

Quiz Answers

1. True.

2. False. In certain conditions, fields, or possibly the entire query result, may not be updateable.

3. `Like Sales*`.

4. `Between 5 and 10`.

5. `"NV" or "CA" or "UT"`. You could also use `In("NV", "CA", "UT")`.

Activities

Practice building several single-table and multitable queries, using your own data. Practice sorting the query results as well as entering various criteria. Also practice updating the query results. Finally, practice using the Expression Builder to build some date/time expressions.

Hour **11**

Creating Forms

NEW TERM   Most Access applications are centered on forms. *Forms* are used to collect and display information, navigate about an application, and more. This hour covers all the basics of creating and working with forms. It begins by looking at the various uses of forms. Then it delves into many important form and control properties. In this hour you'll learn the following:

- How to create a form in Design view
- How to work with the Form Design window
- How to select the correct control for the job
- How to work with important controls such as combo boxes
- How to use many important form properties

Creating a Form in Design View

Although the form wizards are both powerful and useful, in many cases it's best to build a form from scratch, especially if you're building a form that's not bound to data. To create a form without using a wizard, follow these steps:

1. Click Forms in the Objects list.
2. Double-click the Create Form in Design View icon or click New on the Database window toolbar to open the New Form dialog box and select Design View (the default choice).

3. If you clicked New to open the New Form dialog box and your form will be bound to data, use the drop-down list in the New Form dialog box to select the table or query that will serve as the form's foundation (see Figure 11.1).

4. Click OK. The Form Design window appears (see Figure 11.2).

FIGURE 11.1

Selecting a table or query to underlie a form.

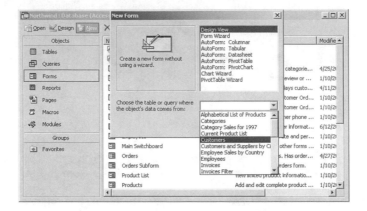

FIGURE 11.2

The Form Design window.

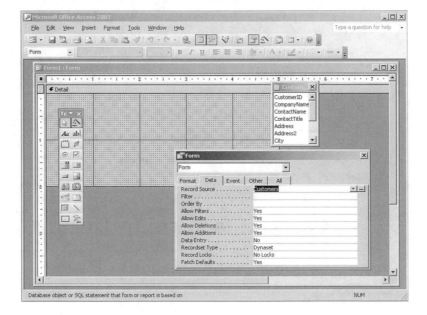

The easiest way to create a new form is by using a wizard. Hour 6, "Using Wizards to Create a Database," covers the process of creating a form with a wizard.

Working with the Form Design Window

You use the Form Design window to build and customize a form. Using this window, you can add objects to a form and customize them by using the many properties available in the Properties window. Microsoft has supplied many form and control properties. After gaining a command of these properties, you can customize the look and feel of your forms.

Understanding and Working with the Form Design Tools

A developer needs the right tools for the job. Fortunately, Microsoft provides tools that help you build exciting and utilitarian forms. The Form Design window includes a toolbar, a toolbox, and the actual form you're designing. Other tools are available to help you with the design process, including the Field List and Properties windows.

By default, two toolbars appear when you're in a form's Design view: the Form Design toolbar and the Formatting toolbar. The Form Design toolbar has buttons you use to save, print, copy, cut, paste, and perform other standard Windows tasks within a form. It also includes buttons that allow you to toggle the different design windows (such as the toolbox). Additional tools in the Form Design toolbar include the Format Painter tool and the Build tool. The Format Painter tool allows you to copy all formatting from one control to one or more additional controls. You can use the Build tool to open the Choose Builder dialog box, where you can invoke the Expression, Macro, and Code builders. The Formatting toolbar contains tools for graphically modifying a form's properties and objects. You can modify the font, font size, and color of selected objects on the form. With the Formatting toolbar, you can also add bold, underline, and italic; change the alignment; and add special effects to the selected objects.

Toggling the Tools to Get What You Want

Many windows are available to help you with the design process when you're in a form's Design view. If you don't have a high-resolution monitor (1,024×768), you'll probably find it annoying to have all the windows open at once. In fact, with all the windows open at once on a low-resolution monitor, a form is likely to get buried underneath all the windows. This is why Microsoft has made each window open and close in a toggle-switch–like fashion. The Form Design toolbar has tools for the Field List, Toolbox, and Properties windows, and each of these toolbar buttons is a toggle. Clicking once on the button opens the appropriate window; clicking a second time closes it.

Figure 11.3 shows a form with the Field List, Toolbox, and Properties windows open. Although you can size each of these windows however you like (and you can dock the toolbox to a window edge), the design environment in this low-resolution display is rather cluttered with all these windows open. One of the tricks in working with Access is

11

to know when it's appropriate to have each set of tools available. The goal is to have the right windows open at the right time as often as possible.

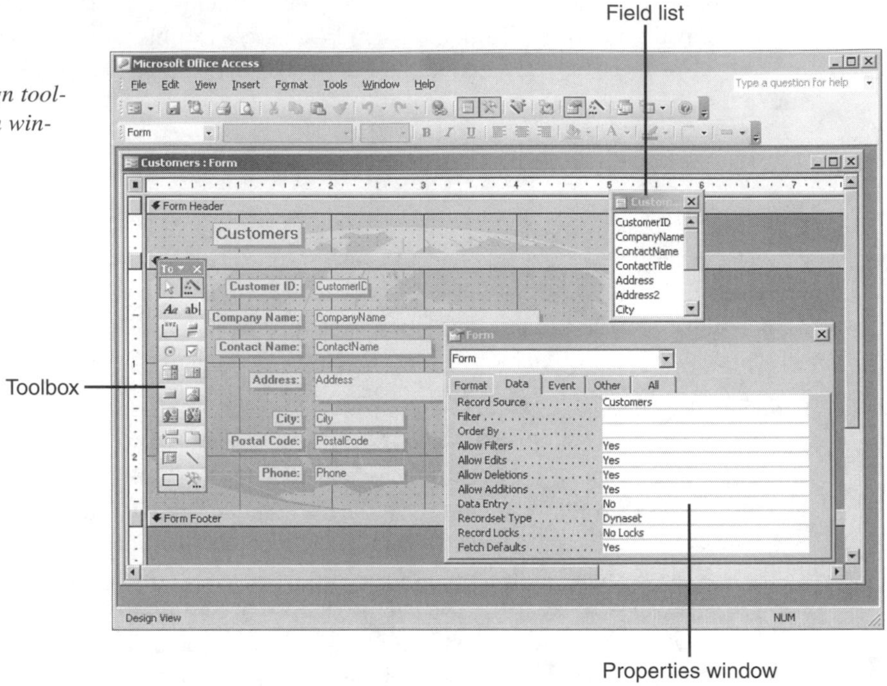

FIGURE 11.3

The Form Design tool-bar with Design windows visible.

Field list

Toolbox

Properties window

You can close the Field List, Toolbox, and Properties windows by using the toolbar buttons. In addition, you can close them by using the Close button on each window, or you can toggle them by using the View menu.

Access 2002 and Access 2003 offer some handy shortcut keystrokes for working with forms and form properties. In Design view, the F4 key displays the property sheet. When you're working with a property sheet in Design view, pressing Shift+F7 shifts the focus to the Form Design window while maintaining the focus on the selected control. You can toggle among all available views for a form (that is, Design, Datasheet, Form, PivotTable, and PivotChart) by pressing Ctrl+> or Ctrl+. (period). You can toggle among the different views in the reverse order using Ctrl+< or Ctrl+, (comma). Access also supports these shortcut keys for toggling between the views that are available for tables, queries, reports, pages, views, and stored procedures.

Adding Fields to a Form

New Term You can use the Field List window to easily add fields to a form. The Field List window contains all the fields that are part of the form's record source. The *record source* for a form is the table, query, or embedded Structured Query Language (SQL) statement that produces the data for the form. For example, in Figure 11.4, the form's record source is the Customers table. The fields listed in the Field List window are the fields that make up the Customers table. To add fields to a form, follow these two steps:

Figure 11.4

A form based on the Customers *table.*

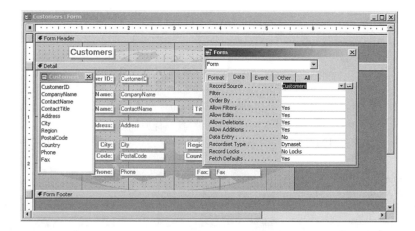

11

1. Make sure the Field List window is visible. If it isn't, click the Field List button on the toolbar.

2. Locate the field you want to add to the form; then click and drag the field from the field list to the place on the form where you want it to appear. The location you select becomes the upper-left corner of the text box, and the attached label appears to the left of where you dropped the control.

New Term A *control* is an object that you add to a form or report. Types of controls include text boxes, combo boxes, list boxes, and check boxes.

To add multiple fields to a form at the same time, follow these steps:

1. Select several fields from the field list.

2. Hold down the Ctrl key to select noncontiguous (not together) fields or the Shift key to select contiguous (together) fields. For example, if you hold down the Ctrl key and click three noncontiguous fields, each of these three fields is selected. If you click a field, hold down the Shift key, and click another field, all fields between the two selected fields are selected. If you want to select all the fields in a list, you double-click the field list title bar and then click and drag any one of the selected fields to the form; all the fields are then added to the form at once.

Selecting, Moving, Aligning, and Sizing Form Objects

You must know several important tricks of the trade for selecting, moving, aligning, and sizing form objects. These tips will save you hours of frustration and wasted time.

Selecting Form Objects

The easiest way to select a single object on a form is to click it. After you have selected the object, you can move it, size it, or change any of its properties. Selecting multiple objects is a bit trickier, but you can accomplish it in several ways. Different methods are more efficient in different situations.

It's important to understand which objects you've actually selected. Figure 11.5 shows a form with four selected objects. The CustomerID text box, the Company Name label, and the Address label and Address text box are all selected; however, the Customer ID label and CompanyName text box aren't selected. If you look closely at the figure, you can see that the selected objects are completely surrounded by selection handles. The Customer ID label and CompanyName text box each has just a single selection handle because each is attached to an object that is selected. If you changed any properties of the selected objects, the Customer ID label and CompanyName text box would be unaffected.

FIGURE 11.5

Selecting objects on a form.

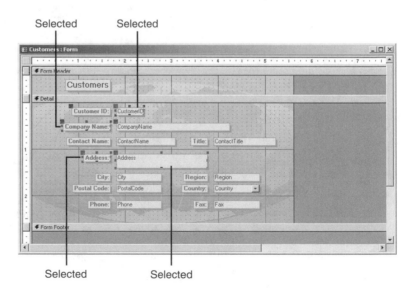

One way to select multiple objects is to hold down the Shift key and click each object you want to select. Access surrounds each selected object with selection handles, indicating that you have selected it.

You can also select objects by lassoing them. Objects to be lassoed must be adjacent to one another on the form. To lasso objects, you place the mouse pointer on a blank area of the form (that is, not over any objects) and then click and drag the mouse pointer around the objects you want to select. You can see a thin line around the objects the mouse pointer is encircling. When you let go of the mouse button, any objects that were within the lasso, including those only partially surrounded, are selected. If you want to deselect any of the selected objects to exclude them, you hold down the Shift key and click the object(s) you want to deselect.

One of my favorite ways to select multiple objects is to use the horizontal and vertical rulers that appear at the edges of the Form Design window. You click and drag within the ruler, and as you do this, two horizontal lines appear, indicating which objects are selected. As you click and drag across the horizontal ruler, two vertical lines appear, indicating the selection area. When you let go of the mouse button, any objects within the lines are selected. As with the process of lassoing, to remove any objects from the selection, you hold down the Shift key and click the object(s) you want to deselect.

> You can use the Ctrl+A keystroke combination to select all controls on a form. After you have selected them, you can move them, size them, or change any of their other properties as a unit.

Moving Things Around

To move a single control with its attached label, you don't need to select it first. You place the mouse over the object and click and drag. An outline appears, indicating the object's new location. When the object reaches the position you want, you release the mouse. The attached label automatically moves with its corresponding control.

To move more than one object at a time, you must first select the objects you want to move. You select the objects by using one of the methods outlined in the previous section. When you place the mouse over any of the selected objects and click and drag, an outline appears, indicating the proposed new position for the objects. You release the mouse when you have reached the position you want for the objects.

Sometimes you want to move a control independently of its attached label, and this requires a special technique. If you click a control, such as a text box, as you move the mouse over the border of the control, a hand icon with five fingers pointing upward appears. If you click and drag, both the control and the attached label move as a unit, and the relationship between them is maintained. Figure 11.6 shows the label and text box before they've been moved as a unit. Figure 11.7 shows them after they've been moved as a unit. If you place the mouse pointer over the larger handle in the upper-left corner of the object, the mouse pointer appears as a hand with only the index finger pointing upward. If you click and drag here, the control moves independently of its attached label, and the relationship between the objects changes. Figure 11.8 depicts objects after they've been moved independently.

FIGURE 11.6

Objects before being moved.

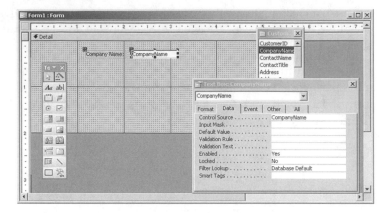

FIGURE 11.7

Objects after being moved as a unit.

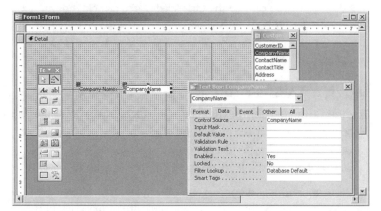

Aligning Objects to One Another

Access makes it easy to align objects. Figure 11.9 shows several objects that aren't aligned. Notice that the attached labels of three of the objects are selected. If you align the attached labels, the controls (in this case, text boxes) remain in their original positions. If you select the text boxes as well, the text boxes try to align with the attached labels. Because Access doesn't allow the objects to overlap, the text boxes end up immediately next to their attached labels. To left-align any objects (even objects of different types), you select the objects you want to align and then choose Format|Align|Left, or you can right-click one of the objects and select Align|Left. Access aligns the selected objects (see Figure 11.10). You can align the left, right, top, or bottom edges of any objects on a form.

FIGURE 11.8
Objects after being moved independently.

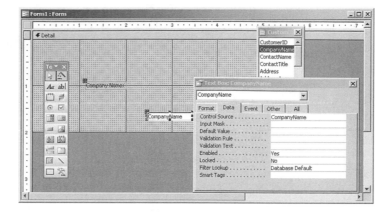

Labels not aligned

FIGURE 11.9
A form before objects are aligned.

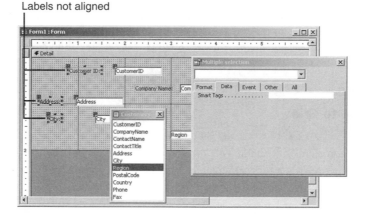

11

You shouldn't confuse the Format|Align feature with the Align tools (that is, Align Left, Center, and Align Right) on the Formatting toolbar. Whereas the Format, Align feature aligns objects one to the other, the Align tools on the Formatting toolbar justify the text inside an object.

Labels aligned

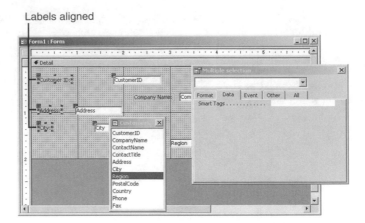

 It is helpful to add to the toolbar the design tools that you commonly use.
For example, you can easily add the Format | Align options to the toolbar. To
modify the toolbar, you select Tools | Customize. Then you click to display the
appropriate toolbar on the Toolbars tab. The alignment tools appear in the
Form/Report Design category. You need to drag and drop the desired tools
from the Commands list onto the appropriate toolbar.

Snap to Grid

The Snap to Grid feature determines whether objects snap to the gridlines on a form as
you move and size them. This feature is found under the Format menu. If you turn off
this feature (it's a toggle), you can move and size objects without regard for the gridlines.

 I prefer to leave the Snap to Grid feature on at all times. You can use a special trick to temporarily deactivate the feature when needed: You hold down
the Ctrl key as you click and drag to move objects, and Access ignores the Snap
to Grid feature.

Sizing Controls

Just as there are several ways to move objects, there are several options for sizing
objects. When you select an object, you can use each handle, except for the handle in the
upper-left corner of the object, to size the object. The handles at the top and bottom of
the object allow you to change the object's height, and the handles at the left and right of

the object let you change the object's width. You can use the handles in the upper-right, lower-right, and lower-left corners of the object to change the width and height of the object simultaneously. To size an object, you place the mouse pointer over a sizing handle, click, and drag. You can select several objects and size them all at once. Each of the selected objects increases or decreases in size by the same percentage; their relative sizes stay intact. You use the upper-left handle to move an object independently of its attached label. This means, for example, that you can place the label associated with a text box above the text box rather than to its left.

Access offers several powerful methods of sizing multiple objects, which you access by selecting Format|Size:

- **To Fit**—Sizes the selected objects to fit the text within them.
- **To Grid**—Sizes the selected objects to the nearest gridlines.
- **To Tallest**—Sizes the selected objects to the height of the tallest object in the selection.
- **To Shortest**—Sizes the selected objects to the height of the shortest object in the selection.
- **To Widest**—Sizes the selected objects to the width of the widest object in the selection.
- **To Narrowest**—Sizes the selected objects to the width of the narrowest object in the selection.

Probably the most confusing of the options is Format|Size|To Fit. This option is somewhat deceiving because it doesn't perfectly size text boxes to the text within them. In today's world of proportional fonts, it isn't possible to perfectly size a text box to the largest possible entry it contains. Generally, however, you can visually size text boxes to a sensible height and width. You use a field's Size property to limit what's typed in the text box. If the entry is too large to fit in the allocated space, the user can scroll to view the additional text. As the following tip indicates, the Format|Size|To Fit option is much more appropriate for labels than it is for text boxes.

To quickly size a label to fit the text within it, you can select the label and then double-click any of its sizing handles, except the sizing handle in the upper-left corner of the label.

Controlling Object Spacing

Access provides excellent tools for spacing the objects on a form an equal distance from one another. Notice in Figure 11.11 that the `CustomerID`, `CompanyName`, `Address`, and `City` text boxes aren't equally spaced vertically from one another. To make the vertical distance between selected objects equal, you choose Format|Vertical Spacing|Make Equal. In Figure 11.12, you can see the result of using this command on the selected objects.

FIGURE **11.11**

A form before vertical spacing is modified.

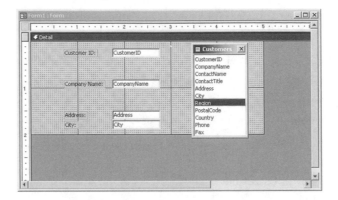

FIGURE **11.12**

A form after vertical spacing is modified.

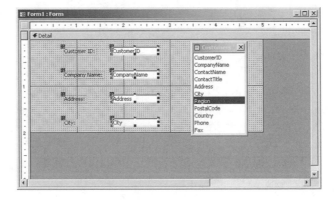

You can make the horizontal distance between objects equal by choosing Format| Horizontal Spacing|Make Equal. Other related commands that are useful are Format| Vertical Spacing|Increase (or Decrease) and Format|Horizontal Spacing|Increase (or Decrease). These commands maintain the relationships between objects while proportionally increasing or decreasing the distances between them.

Modifying Object Tab Order

Access bases the tab order for the objects on a form on the order in which you add the objects to the form. However, this order isn't necessarily appropriate for the user. You might need to modify the tab order of the objects on a form yourself. To do so, you select View|Tab Order to open the Tab Order dialog box, shown in Figure 11.13. This dialog box offers two options. First, you can click the Auto Order button to tell Access to set the tab order based on each object's location in a section on the form. Second, if you want to customize the order of the objects, you click and drag the gray buttons to the left of the object names listed under the Custom Order heading to specify the objects' tab order.

You must set the tab order for the objects in each section of a form (that is, header, detail, and footer) separately. To do this, you select the appropriate section from the Tab Order dialog box and then set the order of the objects in the section. If the selected form doesn't have a header or footer, the Form Header and Form Footer sections are unavailable.

FIGURE 11.13
The Tab Order dialog box, where you select the tab order of the objects in each section of a form.

Selecting the Correct Control for the Job

Windows programming in general, and Access programming in particular, isn't limited to just writing code. Your ability to design a user-friendly interface can make or break the success of an application. Access and the Windows programming environment offer a variety of controls, and each one is appropriate in different situations. The following sections discuss each type of control and describe when and how it should be used. Figure 11.14 shows each control. As you go through each section, you can refer to this figure to get an idea of how each control looks and behaves.

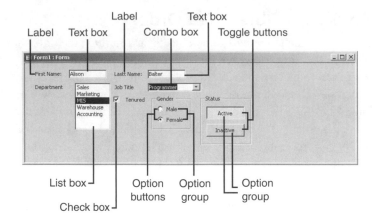

Figure 11.14
*An introduction to the
available controls.*

The `Display Control` property determines the default control type for an object; this default is set in the design of the underlying table.

Labels

You use labels to display information to users. Access automatically adds attached labels to a form when you add other controls, such as text boxes and combo boxes, to the form. You can delete or modify these attached labels as necessary. The default caption of a label is based on the `Caption` property of the field that underlies the control it's attached to. If you enter nothing into a field's `Caption` property, Access uses the field name for the label's caption.

You can use the Label tool, found in the toolbox, to add any text to a form. To do so, you click the Label tool and then click and drag the label to place it on the form. Labels are often used to provide descriptions of forms or to supply instructions to users. You can customize labels by modifying their font, size, color, and so on. Although developers can use Visual Basic for Applications (VBA) code to modify label properties at runtime, users don't have this ability.

Sometimes an attached label gets detached from its associated text box. In this case, the label will no longer move, size, or become selected with the text box that it applies to. To reassociate the label with the text box, you cut the label (by using Ctrl+X), click to select the text box, and then press Ctrl+V to paste.

If you purposely want to disassociate a label from its attached control, you simply cut the label and then paste it back on the form *without* selecting the control that it was attached to. This allows you to perform tasks such as hiding the control without hiding the label.

Text Boxes

You use text boxes to get information from users. *Bound text boxes* display and retrieve field information stored in a table; *unbound text boxes* gather from the user information that's not related to a specific field in a specific record. For example, you can use a text box to gather information about report criteria from a user.

Access automatically adds text boxes to a form when you click and drag a field from the field list to the form. The `Display Control` property for the field must be set to `Text Box`. Another way to add a text box is to select the Text Box tool from the toolbox and then click and drag to place the text box on the form. This process adds an unbound text box to the form. If you want to bind the text box to data, you must set its `Control Source` property.

Combo Boxes

Combo boxes allow users to select from a list of appropriate choices. Access offers several easy ways to add a combo box to a form. If you have set a field's `Display Control` property to `Combo Box`, Access adds a combo box to a form when you add the field to the form. The combo box automatically knows the source of its data as well as all its other important properties.

If a field's `Display Control` property hasn't been set to `Combo Box`, the easiest way to add a combo box to a form is to use the Control Wizards tool. The Control Wizards tool helps you add combo boxes, list boxes, option groups, and subforms to forms. Although you can manually set all the properties set by the Combo Box Wizard, using the wizard saves both time and energy.

If you want Access to launch the Combo Box Wizard when you add a combo box to the form, you need to make sure you click the Control Wizards tool in the toolbox before you add the combo box. Then you select the Combo Box tool in the toolbox and then click and drag to place the combo box on the form. This launches the Combo Box Wizard. As shown in Figure 11.15, the first step of the Combo Box Wizard gives you three choices for the source of the combo box's data. You use the first option if the combo box will select the data that's stored in a field, such as the state associated with a

11

particular customer. I rarely, if ever, use the second option, which requires that you type the values for the combo box. Populating a combo box this way makes it difficult to maintain. Every time you want to add an entry to the combo box, you must modify the application. You use the third option when you want to use the combo box as a tool to search for a specific record. For example, a combo box can be placed in a form's header to display a list of valid customers. After you select a customer, the user is moved to the appropriate record. This option is available only when the form is bound to a record source.

FIGURE 11.15

The first step of the Combo Box Wizard: selecting the source of the data.

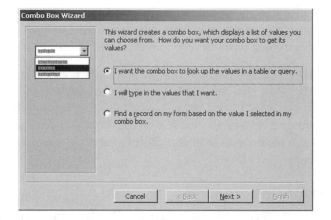

If you select to have the combo box look up the values in a table or query, in the second step of the Combo Box Wizard (shown in Figure 11.16), you select a table or query to populate the combo box and then click Next. In the third step of the wizard (shown in Figure 11.17), you select the fields that appear in the combo box. We'll use the combo box being built in the example to select the customer associated with the current order. Although the CompanyName field will be the only field visible in the combo box, I have selected both CustomerID and CompanyName because CustomerID is a necessary element of the combo box. After the user has selected a company name from the combo box, Access stores the CustomerID associated with the company name in the CustomerID field of the Orders table.

 The fourth step of the wizard allows you to designate the sort order for the data in the combo box (see Figure 11.18). You can opt to sort on as many as four fields.

The fifth step of the wizard lets you specify the width of each field in the combo box. Notice in Figure 11.19 that Access recommends that you hide the key column, CustomerID. The idea is that the user will see the meaningful English description, while Access worries about storing the appropriate key value in the record.

FIGURE 11.16

The second step of the Combo Box Wizard: selecting a table or query.

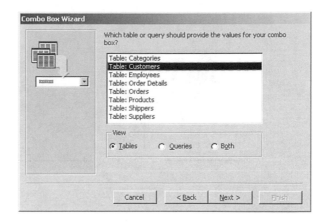

FIGURE 11.17

The third step of the Combo Box Wizard: selecting fields.

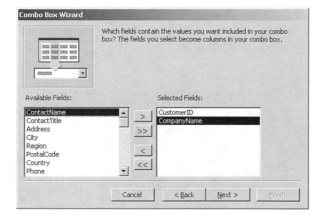

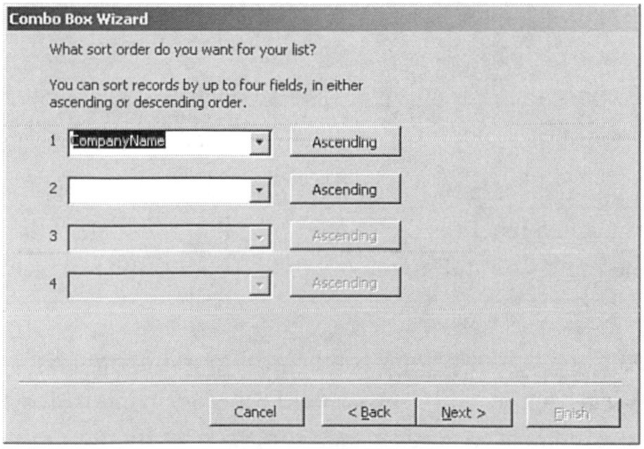

FIGURE 11.18

The fourth step of the Combo Box Wizard: selecting the sort order.

FIGURE 11.19

The fifth step of the Combo Box Wizard: setting column widths.

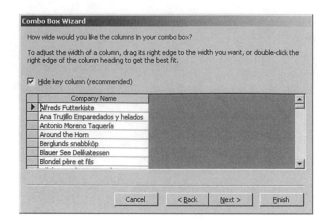

In the wizard's sixth step, you specify whether you want Access to simply remember the selected value or store it in a particular field in a table. In the example shown in Figure 11.20, I have told Access to store the selected combo box value in the CustomerID field of the Orders table.

FIGURE 11.20

The sixth step of the Combo Box Wizard: indicating where the selected value will be stored.

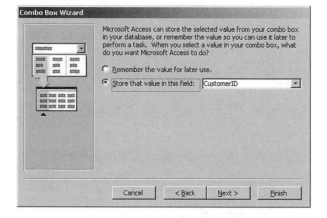

The seventh and final step of the Combo Box Wizard prompts for the text that will become the attached label for the combo box. After you click the Finish button, Access completes the process, building the combo box and filling in all its properties with the appropriate values.

Although the Combo Box Wizard is a helpful tool, it's important that you understand the properties it sets. Figure 11.21 shows the Properties window for a combo box. We're going to take a moment to go over the properties set by the Combo Box Wizard in this example.

The Control Source property indicates the field in which the selected entry is stored. In Figure 11.21, you can see that the selected entry will be stored in the CustomerID field of the Orders table. The Row Source Type property specifies whether the source used to populate the combo box is a table/query, value list, or field list. In the example, the Row Source Type property is set to Table/Query. The Row Source property is the name of the actual table or query used to populate the combo box. In the example, the Row Source property is a SQL SELECT statement that selects the CustomerID and CompanyName from the Customers table. The Column Count property designates how many columns are in the combo box, and the Column Widths property indicates the width of each column. In the example, the width of the first column is zero, which renders the column invisible. Finally, the Bound Column property is used to specify which column in the combo box is being used to store data in the control source. In the example, this is column 1.

FIGURE 11.21

Properties of a combo box, showing that the CustomerID field has been selected as the control source for the Combo3 combo box.

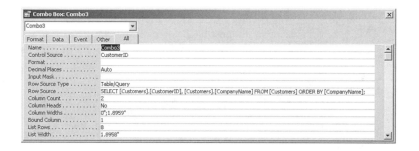

List Boxes

List boxes are similar to combo boxes, but they differ from them in three major ways:

- They consume more screen space.
- They allow the user to select only from the list that's displayed. This means the user can't type new values into a list box (as you can with a combo box).
- They can be configured to let the user select multiple items.

If you set the Display Control property of a field to List Box, Access adds a list box to the form when the field is clicked and dragged from the field list to the form.

The List Box Wizard is almost identical to the Combo Box Wizard. After you run the List Box Wizard, the list box properties affected by the wizard are the same as the combo box properties.

Check Boxes

You use check boxes when you want to limit the user to entering one of two values, such as yes/no, true/false, or on/off. You can add a check box to a form in several ways:

- Set the Display Control property of the underlying field to Check Box and then click and drag the field from the field list to the form.
- Click the Check Box tool in the toolbox; then click and drag a field from the field list to the form. This method adds a check box to the form even if the Display Control property of the underlying field isn't set to Check Box.
- Click the Check Box tool in the toolbox and then click and drag to add a check box to the form. The check box you have added is unbound. To bind the check box to data, you must set the control's Control Source property.

> You use the Triple State property of a check box to add a third value, Null, to the possible choices for the check box value. Null refers to the absence of a value, which is different from the explicit value False.

Option and Toggle Buttons

You can use option buttons and toggle buttons alone or as part of an option group. You can use an option button or toggle button alone to display a true/false value, but this isn't a standard use of an option or toggle button. (Check boxes are standard for this purpose.) As part of an option group, option buttons and toggle buttons force the user to select from a mutually exclusive set of options, such as choosing among American Express, MasterCard, Visa, and Discover for a payment type. This use of option buttons and toggle buttons is covered in the next section, "Option Groups." In summary, although you can use option and toggle buttons outside an option group, you will almost always associate them with an option group.

The difference between option buttons and toggle buttons is in their appearance. Personally, I find toggle buttons confusing to users. I find that option buttons provide a much more intuitive interface (see Figure 11.22).

Option Groups

Option groups allow the user to select from a mutually exclusive set of options. They can include check boxes, toggle buttons, or option buttons, but the most common implementation of an option group is option buttons.

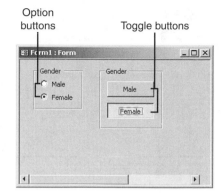

FIGURE 11.22

Option buttons versus toggle buttons.

The easiest way to add an option group to a form is to use the Option Group Wizard. To do so, you select the Control Wizards button in the toolbox, click Option Group in the toolbox, and then click and drag to add the option group to the form. This launches the Option Group Wizard.

The first step of the Option Group Wizard, shown in Figure 11.23, allows you to type the text associated with each item in the option group.

FIGURE 11.23

The first step of the Option Group Wizard: adding text to options.

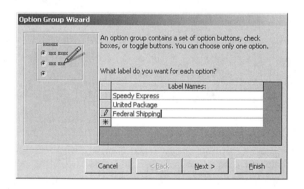

The second step of the wizard gives you the option of selecting a default choice for the option group. This choice goes into effect when the user adds a new record to the table underlying the form.

The third step of the wizard lets you select values associated with each option button (see Figure 11.24). The text displayed with the option button isn't stored in the record; instead, Access stores the underlying numeric value in the record. In Figure 11.24, Access stores the number 2 in the field if the user selects United Package.

FIGURE 11.24

*The third step of the
Option Group Wizard:
selecting values for
options.*

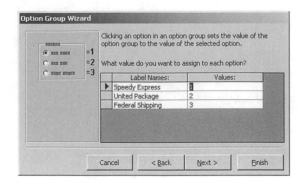

The fourth step of the Option Group Wizard asks whether you want to remember the
option group value for later use or store the value in a field. In Figure 11.25, for example, the option group value is stored in the ShipVia field.

FIGURE 11.25

*The fourth step of the
Option Group Wizard:
tying the group to
data.*

In the fifth step of the wizard, you can select from a variety of styles for the option
group buttons, including option buttons, check boxes, and toggle buttons. You can also
select from etched, flat, raised, shadowed, or sunken effects for the buttons. The wizard
lets you preview each option. The sixth and final step of the wizard allows you to add an
appropriate caption to the option group. The completed group of option buttons created
in this section is shown in Figure 11.26.

It's important to understand that the Option Group Wizard sets properties of the frame,
the option buttons within the frame, and the labels attached to the option buttons. Figure
11.27 shows the properties of the frame. The Option Group Wizard sets the control
source of the frame and the default value of the option group. Each individual option
button is assigned a value, and the caption of the attached label associated with each button is set.

FIGURE **11.26**
The results of running the Option Group Wizard.

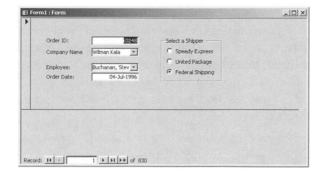

FIGURE **11.27**
An option group frame, showing the properties of the selected button.

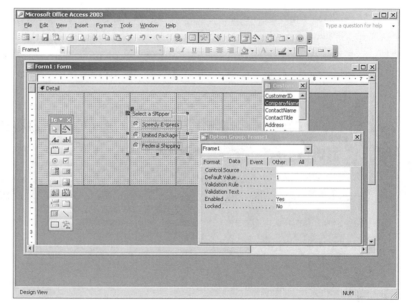

Conditional Formatting

Access 2000 introduced conditional formatting, with which data meeting specified criteria displays differently than does data meeting other criteria. For example, you can use conditional formatting to display sales higher than a certain amount in one color and sales lower than that amount in another color.

To conditionally format data displayed within a control, follow these steps:

1. Select the control you want to conditionally format.

2. Select Format|Conditional Formatting. The Conditional Formatting dialog box appears.

3. Select Field Value Is, Expression Is, or Field Has Focus from the first combo box in the Formatting dialog box. You should select Field Value Is when you want to select from a predefined set of operators such as between, not between, and equal to. You should select Expression when you want to build your own conditional expression, which Access will evaluate at runtime. Finally, you should select Field Has Focus if you want Access to apply the conditional format only when that field has the focus.

4. Select the appropriate operator from the second combo box in the dialog box.

5. Enter the values you are testing for in the text boxes that appear on the right of the dialog box.

6. Select the special formatting (bold, italic, background color, and so on) that you want to apply when the conditional criteria are met.

7. Click Add to add additional formats.

8. Click OK to apply the conditional formatting.

What Form Properties Are Available, and Why Should You Use Them?

Forms have many properties that you can use to affect their look and behavior. The properties are broken down into categories: Format, Data, Event, and Other.

To view a form's properties, you must select the form in one of two ways:

- Click the form selector (the small gray button at the intersection of the horizontal and vertical rulers).
- Choose Edit|Select Form.

It is important that you understand how to work with form properties. The sections that follow begin by focusing on the Properties window. They then hone in on a discussion of important form properties.

Working with the Properties Window

After you have selected a form, you can click the Properties button on the toolbar to view its properties. The Properties window, shown in Figure 11.28, consists of five tabs: Format, Data, Event, Other, and All. Many developers prefer to view all properties at once on the All tab, but a form can have a total of 107 properties! Rather than view all 107 properties at once, you should try viewing the properties by category. The Format category includes all the physical attributes of the form—the ones that affect the form's appearance, such as background color. The Data category includes all the properties of the data that the form is bound to, such as the form's underlying record source. The Event category contains all the Windows events to which a form can respond. For example, you can write code that executes in response to the form being loaded, becoming active, displaying a different record, and so on. The Other category holds a few properties that don't fit into the other three categories.

FIGURE **11.28**

Viewing the Format properties of a form.

Working with the Important Form Properties

As mentioned in the preceding section, a form has 107 properties. Of those 107 properties, 52 are Event properties, and they are covered in most books focused on Access programming. The following sections and Hour 16, "Power Form Techniques," cover the Format, Data, and Other properties of forms.

The Format Properties of a Form

The Format properties of a form affect its physical appearance. A form has 31 Format properties, described in the following sections.

Caption

The `Caption` property sets the text that appears on the form's title bar.

Default View

The Default View property allows you to select from five available options:

- Single Form—Allows only one record to be viewed at a time.
- Continuous Forms—Displays as many records as will fit within the form window at one time, presenting each as the detail section of a single form.
- Datasheet—Displays the records in a spreadsheet-like format, with the rows representing records and the columns representing fields.
- PivotTable—Displays the records in a Microsoft Excel–type PivotTable format.
- PivotChart—Displays the records in a Microsoft Excel–type PivotChart format.

The selected option becomes the default view for the form.

Allow Form View

In versions of Access prior to Access 2002, Access forms have a property called Views Allowed. The Views Allowed property determines whether the user is allowed to switch from Form view to Datasheet view or vice versa. Whereas the Default View property determines the initial default display mode for the form, Views Allowed determines whether the user is permitted to switch out of the default view.

In Access 2002 and Access 2003, Microsoft has separated out each type of view as an additional property for the form. The Allow Form View property specifies whether the user is permitted to switch to the Form view of a form.

Allow Datasheet View

The Allow Datasheet View property determines whether the user is permitted to switch to the Datasheet view of a form.

Allow PivotTable View

The PivotTable View property determines whether the user is allowed to switch to the PivotTable view of a form.

Allow PivotChart View

The Allow PivotChart View property determines whether the user is allowed to switch to the PivotChart view of a form.

Scroll Bars

The Scroll Bars property determines whether scrollbars appear if the controls on a form don't fit within the form's display area. You can select from both vertical and horizontal scrollbars, neither vertical nor horizontal scrollbars, just vertical scrollbars, or just horizontal scrollbars.

Record Selectors

A *record selector* is the gray bar to the left of a record in Form view, or the gray box to the left of each record in Datasheet view. It's used to select a record to be copied or deleted. The Record Selectors property determines whether the record selectors appear. If you give the user a custom menu, you can opt to remove the record selector to make sure the user copies or deletes records using only the features specifically built into the application.

Navigation Buttons

Navigation buttons are the controls that appear at the bottom of aform; they allow the user to move from record to record within a form. The Navigation Buttons property determines whether the navigation buttons are visible. You should set it to No for any dialog box forms, and you might want to set it to No for dataentry forms, too, and add your own toolbar or command buttons to enhance or limit the functionality of the standard buttons. For example, in a client/server environment, you might not want to give users the ability to move to the first or last record because that type of record movement can be inefficient in a client/server architecture.

Dividing Lines

The Dividing Lines property indicates whether you want a line to appear between records when the default view of the form is set to Continuous Forms. It also determines whether Access places dividing lines between the form's sections (that is, header, detail, and footer).

Auto Resize

The Auto Resize property determines whether Access automatically sizes a form to display a complete record.

Auto Center

The Auto Center property specifies whether a form should automatically be centered within the Application window whenever it's opened.

Border Style

The Border Style property is far more powerful than its name implies. The options for the Border Style property are None, Thin, Sizable, and Dialog. The Border Style property is often set to None for splash screens, in which case the form has no border.

11

When the `Border Style` property is set to `Thin`, the border is not resizable and the Size command isn't available in the Control menu. This setting is a good choice for pop-up forms, which remain on top even when other forms are given the focus. The `Sizable` setting is standard for most forms; it includes all the standard options in the Control menu. The `Dialog` setting creates a border that looks like the border created by the `Thin` setting. A form with the `Border Style` property set to `Dialog` can't be maximized, minimized, or resized; when the border style of a form is set to `Dialog`, the Maximize, Minimize, and Resize options aren't available in the form's Control menu. The `Dialog` setting along with the `Pop Up` and `Modal` properties to create custom dialog boxes.

Control Box

The `Control Box` property determines whether a form has a Control menu. You should use this option sparingly. One of your responsibilities as a developer of Access applications is to make applications comply with Windows standards. If you look at the Windows programs you use, you'll find very few forms that do not have Control menu boxes. This should tell you something about how to design applications.

Min Max Buttons

The `Min Max Buttons` property indicates whether the form has minimize and maximize buttons. The available options are `None`, `Min Enabled`, `Max Enabled`, and `Both Enabled`. If you remove one or both of these buttons, the appropriate options also become unavailable in the Control menu. Access ignores the `Min Max` property for forms with the `Border Style` property set to `None` or `Dialog`. Similarly to the `Control Box` property, I rarely use this property. To make applications comply with Windows standards, I set the `Border Style` property and then inherit the standard attributes for each border style.

Close Button

The `Close Button` property determines whether the user can close the form by using the Control menu or double-clicking the Control icon. If you set the value of this property to `No`, you must give the user another way to close the form; otherwise, the user might have to reboot his or her computer to close the application.

Whats This Button

The `Whats This Button` property specifies whether you want the Whats This button to be added to the form's title bar. This feature works only when the form's `Min Max Buttons` property is set to `No`. When the `Whats This Button` property is set to `Yes`, the user can click the Whats This button and then click an object on the form to display Help for that object. If the selected object has no Help associated with it, Help for the form is displayed, and if the form has no Help associated with it, the Microsoft Access Help system is displayed.

Width

The `Width` property is used to specify the form's width. This option is most often set graphically by clicking and dragging to select an appropriate size for the form. You might want to set this property manually when you want forms to be exactly the same size.

Picture, Picture Type, Picture Size Mode, Picture Alignment, and Picture Tiling

The `Picture`, `Picture Type`, `Picture Size Mode`, `Picture Alignment`, and `Picture Tiling` properties let you select and customize the attributes of a bitmap used as the background for a form.

Grid X and Grid Y

You can use the `Grid X` and `Grid Y` properties to modify the spacing of the horizontal and vertical lines that appear in a form in Design view. By setting these properties, you can affect how precisely you place objects on the form when the Snap to Grid feature is active.

Layout for Print

The `Layout for Print` property specifies whether screen or printer fonts are used on a form. If you want to optimize a form for printing rather than display, you should set this property to `Yes`.

SubdatasheetHeight

The `SubdatasheetHeight` property is used to designate the maximum height for a sub-datasheet.

SubdatasheetExpanded

The `SubdatasheetExpanded` property allows you to designate whether a subdatasheet is initially displayed in an expanded format. When this property is set to `False`, the sub-datasheet appears collapsed. When it is set to `True`, the subdatasheet appears in expanded format.

Palette Source

The `Palette Source` property determines the source for selecting colors for a form.

Orientation

The `Orientation` property allows you to take advantage of language-specific versions of Microsoft Access, such as Arabic. This property can be set to support right-to-left display

11

features for language-specific editions of Access, provided that the underlying operating system supports that language and is 32 bit (for example, Windows 2000).

Moveable

The Moveable property determines whether the user can move the form window around the screen by clicking and dragging the form by its title bar.

The Data Properties of a Form

You use the Data properties of a form to control the source for the form's data, what sort of actions the user can take on the data in the form, and how the data in the form is locked in a multiuser environment. A form has 11 Data properties (8 which are covered here).

Record Source

The Record Source property indicates the table, stored query, or SQL statement on which the form's records are based. After you have selected a record source for a form, the controls on the form can be bound to the fields in the record source.

> The Field List window is unavailable until you have set the Record Source property of the form.

Filter

You use the Filter property to automatically load a stored filter along with the form. I prefer to base a form on a query that limits the data displayed on the form. You can pass the query parameters at runtime to customize exactly what data Access displays.

Order By

The Order By property specifies in what order the records on a form appear. You can modify this property at runtime.

Allow Filters

The Allow Filters property controls whether you can filter records at runtime. When this option is set to No, all filtering options become disabled to the user.

Allow Edits, Allow Deletions, and Allow Additions

The Allow Edits, Allow Deletions, and Allow Additions properties let you specify whether the user can edit data, delete records, or add records from within a form. These options can't override any permissions that you have set for the form's underlying table or queries. Hour 22, "Security Introduced," covers the basics of security.

Data Entry

The Data Entry property determines whether users can only add records within a form. You should set this property to Yes if you don't want users to view or modify existing records but want them to be able to add new records.

More About Form and Control Properties

Additional interesting form properties, as well as control properties, help you to further customize forms and the controls that you place on them. Hour 16 further delves into form properties and explores the exciting world of control properties.

Summary

Microsoft Access provides rich, powerful tools you can use to build even very sophisticated forms. This hour gives you an overview of what Access forms are capable of. It talks about the various control types and how they are used. It also covers many important form properties, discussing what they are and why they are important. Using the techniques in this hour, you can control both the appearance and functionality of a form and its objects.

Q&A

Q Describe what the Data properties of a form are used for.

A You use the Data properties of a form to control the source of the form's data and to control the actions the user can take on the data in the form.

Q Describe what the Format properties of a form are used for.

A You use the Format properties of a form to control the physical appearance of the form.

Q Explain differences between combo boxes and list boxes.

A List boxes consume more screen space than combo boxes. Combo boxes allow the user to add additional entries (if you set them up that way), whereas list boxes limit the user to the items contained in the list. Finally, you can configure list boxes to allow the user to select multiple items, whereas combo boxes allow the user to select only a single item.

Q **Explain the differences between a text box and a label.**

A Whereas the user can modify the contents of a text box while viewing the form, he or she cannot modify the contents of a label.

Workshop

The Workshop includes quiz questions that are designed to help you test your understanding of the material covered and activities to help put what you've learned to practice. You can find the answers to the questions in the section immediately following the quiz.

Quiz

1. The user can modify the value of a label at runtime (True/False).
2. Option buttons allow the user to select from a mutually exclusive set of options (True/False).
3. What property determines what appears in a form's title bar?
4. What property do you use to designate the table or query that underlies a form?
5. What property do you use when you want users to be able to only add records to a form?

Quiz Answers

1. False. The user cannot modify the value of a label at runtime.
2. True.
3. The `Caption` property determines what appears in a form's title bar.
4. You use the `Record Source` property to designate the table or query that underlies the form.
5. You set the `Data Entry` property to `Yes` when you want users to be able to only add records to a form.

Activities

Build a form in Design view. Practice adding various types of controls to the form. Practice setting various control properties. Take a look at the effects these properties have on the form.

HOUR 12

Creating Reports

Although forms provide an excellent means for data entry, reports are the primary output device in Access. You can preview reports onscreen, output them to a printer, display them in a browser, and more. They are relatively easy to create, and they are extremely powerful. This hour covers the basics of creating and working with reports. After you read the text covered in the hour, you'll be familiar with the types of reports available. You'll be comfortable building reports with and without the wizards, and you'll know how to manipulate the reports that you build. You will understand the report and control properties available, and you'll know when it is appropriate to use each. You'll also be familiar with many important report techniques. In this hour you'll learn about the following:

- The types of reports that are available
- The different bands that make up an Access report
- How to add controls to and manipulate controls on an Access report
- How to use report properties to control the behavior of a report

Types of Reports

The reporting engine of Microsoft Access is very powerful and has a wealth of features. Many types of reports are available in Access 2003:

- Detail reports
- Summary reports

- Reports containing graphics and charts
- Reports containing forms
- Reports containing labels
- Reports including any combination of the preceding

Detail Reports

NEW TERM A *Detail report* supplies an entry for each record included in the report. As you can see in Figure 12.1, there's an entry for each order in the Orders table during the specified period (1998 through 2000). The report's detail is grouped by country and within country by salesperson and gives subtotals by salesperson and country. The bottom of the report has grand totals for all records included in the report. The report is based on a Parameter query that limits the data displayed on the report based on criteria supplied by the user at runtime.

FIGURE 12.1

An example of a Detail report.

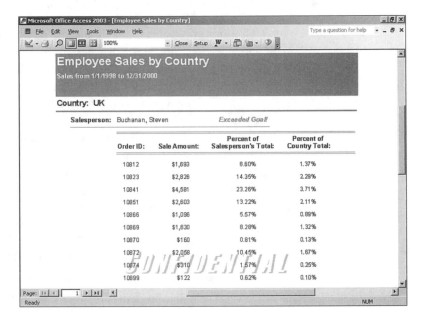

Summary Reports

NEW TERM A *Summary report* provides summary data for all the records included in the report. In Figure 12.2, only total sales by quarter and year are displayed in the report. The underlying detail records that comprise the summary data aren't displayed in the report. The report is based on a query that summarizes the net sales by OrderID. The report itself contains no controls in its Detail section. All controls are placed in report group headers and footers that are grouped on the quarter and year of the ship date. Because no controls are found in the report's Detail section, Access prints summary information only.

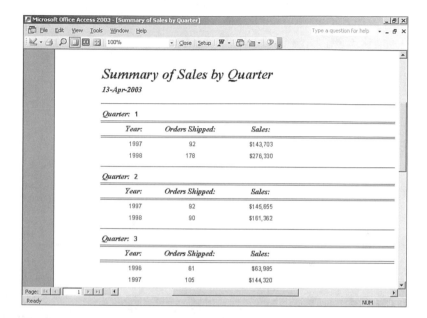

Reports Containing Graphics and Charts

Although the statement "A picture paints a thousand words" is a cliché, it's also quite true: Research has proved that a person retains data much better when it's displayed as pictures rather than numbers. Fortunately, Access makes including graphics and charts in reports quite easy. As shown in Figure 12.3, you can design a report to combine both numbers and charts. The report in Figure 12.3 shows the sales by product, both as numbers and as a bar chart. The main report is grouped by product category and contains a subreport based on a query that summarizes sales by CategoryID, CategoryName, and ProductName for a specific date range. The chart totals product sales by product name, displaying the information graphically. You can include photographs, clip art, hand-drawn graphics, charts, and more within the reports you create.

Reports Containing Forms

Users often need reports that look like printed forms. The Access Report Builder, with its many graphical tools, allows you to quickly produce reports that emulate the most elegant data-entry forms. For example, the report shown in Figure 12.4 produces an invoice for a customer. This report is based on a query that draws information from the

Customers, Orders, Order Details, Products, Employees, and Shippers tables. The report's Filter property (covered in Hour 2) is filled in, limiting the data that appears on the report to the last six records in the Orders table. Using graphics, color, fonts, shading, and other special effects gives the report a professional look.

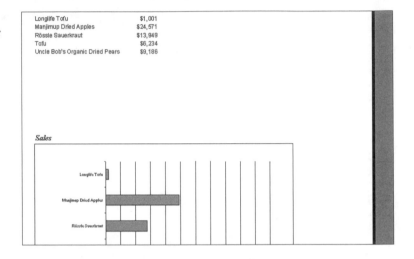

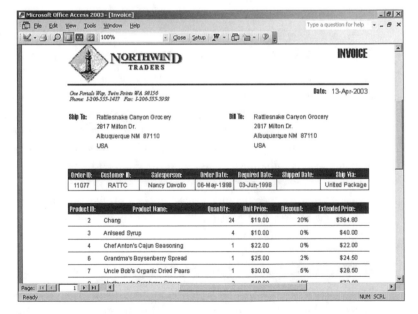

Reports Containing Labels

Creating labels such as mailing labels in Access 2003 is easy when you use the Label Wizard. Labels are simply a special type of report with a page setup that indicates the number of labels across the page and the size of each label. An example of a mailing label report created by using the Label Wizard is shown in Figure 12.5. This report is based on the Customers table but could just as easily be based on a query that limits what mailing labels are produced.

FIGURE 12.5

An example of a report containing mailing labels.

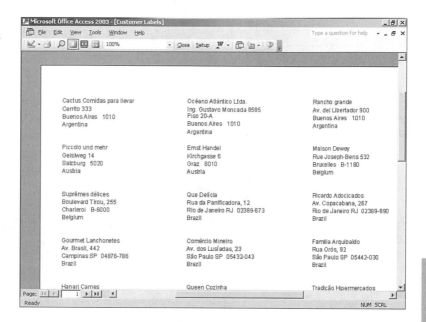

The Anatomy of a Report

Reports can have many parts, referred to as *sections* of the report. A new report is automatically made up of the following three sections, as shown in Figure 12.6:

- Page Header section
- Detail section
- Page Footer section

The Detail section is the main section of the report; it's used to display the detailed data of the table or query underlying the report. Certain reports, such as Summary reports, have nothing in the Detail section. Instead, Summary reports contain data in group headers and footers.

The Page Header section automatically prints at the top of every page of the report. It often includes information such as the report's title. The Page Footer section automatically prints at the bottom of every page of the report and usually contains information such as the page number and date. Each report can have only one page header and one page footer.

FIGURE 12.6

Sections of a report.

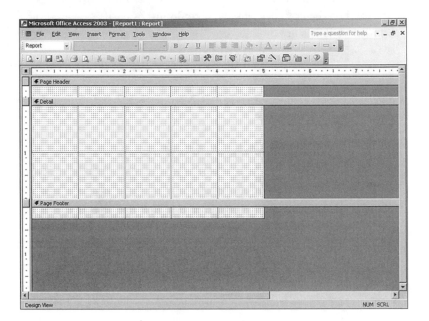

In addition to the three sections that Access automatically adds to every report, a report can have the following sections:

- Report Header section
- Report Footer section
- Group Headers section
- Group Footers section

A report header prints once, at the beginning of the report; the report footer prints once, at the end of the report. Each Access report can have only one report header and one report footer. The report header is often used to create a cover sheet for a report. It can include graphics or other fancy effects to add a professional look to a report. The most common use of the report footer is for grand totals, but it can also include any other summary information for a report.

In addition to report and page headers and footers, an Access report can have up to 10 group headers and footers. Report groupings separate data logically and physically. The group header prints before the detail for the group, and the group footer prints after the detail for the group. For example, you can group customer sales by country and city, printing the name of the country or city for each related group of records. If you total the sales for each country and city, you can place the country and city names in the country and city group headers and the totals in the country and city group footers.

Creating a Report in Design View

Although it is generally most efficient to get started with most reports by using the Report Wizard, you should understand how to create a new report in Design view. To create a report without using a wizard, you click Reports in the Objects list and then double-click the Create Report in Design View icon. The Report Design window appears. You must then set the record source of the report to the table or query on which you want to base the report. Another way to create a report in Design view is to click Reports in the Objects list and then click New to open the New Report dialog box. Then you click Design View and use the drop-down list to select the table or query on which you want to base the report; then you click OK, and the Report Design window appears.

Working with the Report Design Window

You use the Report Design window to build and modify a report. Using this window, you can add objects to a report and modify their properties. Microsoft provides numerous Report, Report Grouping, and Control properties. These are described throughout the remainder of this hour and in Hour 17, "Power Report Techniques." By modifying these properties, you can create reports with diverse looks and functionality.

12

Understanding the Report Design Tools

To help you design reports, several report design tools are available, including the Properties, Toolbox, Field List, and Sorting and Grouping windows. Two toolbars are also available to make developing and customizing reports easier: the Report Design toolbar and the Formatting toolbar. The Report Design toolbar offers tools for saving, previewing, and printing a report and for cutting, copying, and pasting report objects. The Formatting toolbar is specifically designed to help you customize the look of a report. It includes tools for changing the font, font size, alignment, color, shading, and other physical attributes of the report objects.

The Properties, Toolbox, Field List, and Sorting and Grouping windows are all designed as toggles. This means that buttons on the Report Design toolbar alternately hide and show these valuable windows. If you have a high-resolution monitor, you might want to leave the windows open at all times. If you have a low-resolution monitor, you need to get a feel for when it's most effective for each window to be opened or closed.

Adding Fields to a Report

You can most easily add fields to a report by using the Field List window. With the Field List window open, you click and drag a field from the field list onto the appropriate section of the report. You can add several fields at one time, just as you can in forms. You can use the Ctrl key to select noncontiguous fields (that is, fields not proximal to each other) and the Shift key to select contiguous fields (that is, fields immediately proximal to one another), or you can double-click the field list's title bar to select all the fields; then you click and drag them to the report as a unit.

One problem with adding fields to a report is that Access places the fields and the attached labels in the same section of the report. This means that if you click and drag fields from the Field List window to the Detail section of the report, both the fields and the attached labels appear in the Detail section. If you're creating a tabular report, this isn't acceptable, so you must cut the attached labels and paste them into the report's Page Header section. This is one reason you might want to start with the Report Wizard and then use Design view to customize the report to your needs.

Selecting, Moving, Aligning, and Sizing Report Objects

Microsoft Access offers several techniques to help you select, move, align, and size report objects. Different techniques are most effective in different situations. Experience will tell you which technique you should use and when. Selecting, moving, aligning, and sizing report objects are quite similar to performing the same tasks with form objects. The techniques are covered briefly in the following sections; for a more detailed explanation of each technique, refer to Hour 11, "Creating Forms."

Selecting Report Objects

To select a single report object, you click it; selection handles appear around the selected object. After you have selected the object, you can modify any of its attributes (properties), or you can size, move, or align it.

To select multiple objects so that you can manipulate them as a unit, you can use any of the following techniques:

- Hold down the Shift key as you click multiple objects. Each object you click is then added to the selection.
- Place the mouse pointer in a blank area of the report. Click and drag to lasso the objects you want to select. When you let go of the mouse button, any objects completely or even partially within the lasso are selected.

- Click and drag within the horizontal or vertical ruler. As you click and drag, lines appear, indicating the potential selection area. When you release the mouse button, all objects within the lines are selected.

You need to make sure you understand which objects are actually selected; attached labels can cause some confusion. Figure 12.7 shows a report with four objects selected: the Alphabetical List of Products label, the Category Name label, the QuantityPerUnit text box, and the UnitsInStock text box. If you were to modify the properties of the selected objects, they would be the only objects affected.

FIGURE 12.7

Selecting objects in an Access report.

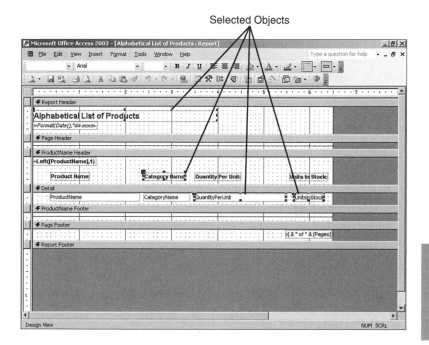

Moving Report Objects

If you want to move a single control along with its attached label, you click the object and drag it to a new location. The object and the attached label move as a unit. To move multiple objects, you use one of the methods described in the previous section to select the objects you want to move. After you have selected the objects, you click and drag any of them; the selected objects and their attached labels move as a unit.

Moving an object without its attached label is a trickier process. When the mouse pointer is placed over the center or border of a selected object (not on a sizing handle), the cursor looks like a hand with all five fingers pointing upward. This indicates that the selected object and its attached label move as a unit, maintaining their relationship to one another. However, if you place the mouse pointer directly over the selection handle in the object's upper-left corner, the cursor looks like a hand with only the index finger pointing upward. This indicates that the object and the attached label move independently of one another so that you can alter the distance between them.

Aligning Objects with One Another

To align objects with one another, you must select them first. To do so, you choose Format|Align and then select Left, Right, Top, Bottom, or To Grid. The selected objects align themselves in relationship to each other.

You need to watch out for a few "gotchas" when you're aligning report objects. If you select several text boxes and their attached labels and align them, Access tries to align the left sides of the text boxes with the left sides of the labels. To prevent this from happening, you have to align the text boxes separately from their attached labels.

During the alignment process, Access never overlaps objects. Therefore, if the objects you're aligning don't fit, Access can't align them. For example, if you try to align the bottoms of several objects horizontally and they don't fit across the report, Access aligns only the objects that fit on the line.

Using Snap to Grid

The Snap to Grid feature is a toggle found under the Format menu. When Snap to Grid is selected, all objects that you're moving or sizing snap to the report's gridlines. To temporarily disable the Snap to Grid feature, you hold down the Ctrl key while sizing or moving an object.

Using Power-Sizing Techniques

Access offers many techniques to help you size report objects. A selected object has eight sizing handles, and you can use any of them, except for the upper-left handle, to size the object. You simply click and drag one of the sizing handles. If you selected multiple object to size at once, Access sizes them by the same percentage.

To size objects, you can also select Format|Size and then To Fit, To Grid, To Tallest, To Shortest, To Widest, or To Narrowest. Hour 11 discusses these options in detail.

Access offers a great trick that can help you size labels to fit. You simply double-click any sizing handle, and Access automatically sizes the object to fit the text within it.

Controlling Object Spacing

Access makes it easy to control object spacing. You can make both the horizontal and vertical distances between selected objects equal. To do so, you select the objects and then choose Format|Horizontal Spacing|Make Equal or Format|Vertical Spacing|Make Equal. You can also maintain the relative relationship between selected objects while increasing or decreasing the space between them. To do this, you choose Format| Horizontal Spacing|Increase/Decrease or Format|Vertical Spacing|Increase/Decrease.

Selecting the Correct Control for the Job

Reports usually contain labels, text boxes, lines, rectangles, image controls, and bound and unbound object frames (see Figure 12.8). The other types of controls (such as combo boxes and list boxes) are generally used for reports that emulate data-entry forms. The different controls that you can place on a report, as well as their uses, are discussed briefly in the following sections.

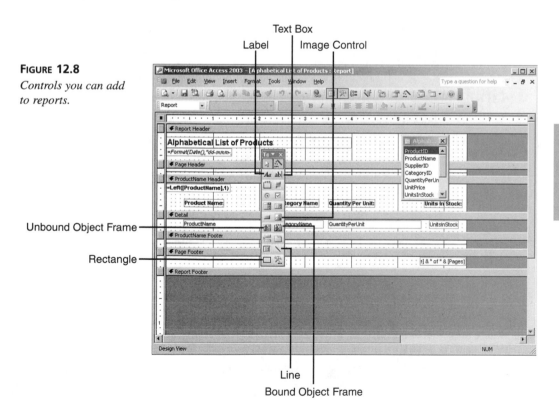

FIGURE 12.8
Controls you can add to reports.

12

Labels

You use labels to display information to users. Labels are commonly used as report headings, column headings, or group headings for a report. Although you can modify the text labels display at runtime by using Visual Basic for Applications (VBA) code, you cannot bind them directly to data.

To add a label to a report, you select the Label tool in the toolbox and then click and drag to place the label on the report.

Text Boxes

You use text boxes to display field information or the result of an expression. You can use them throughout a report's different sections. For example, in a page header, a text box might contain an expression showing the date range that's the criteria for the report. In a group header, a text box might be used to display a heading for the group. The possibilities are endless because a text box can hold any valid expression.

To add a text box to a report, you select the Text Box tool from the toolbox and then you click and drag the text box to place it on the report. You can also add a text box to a report by dragging a field from the field list to a report. This works as long as the field's `Display Control` property is a text box.

Lines

You can use lines to visually separate objects on a report. For example, you can place a line at the bottom of a section or under a subtotal. To add a line to a report, you click the Line tool in the toolbox to select it and then you click and drag to place the line on the report. When a line is added, it has several properties that you can modify to customize its look.

> To make sure that a line you draw is perfectly straight, you can hold down the Shift key while you click and drag to draw the line.

Rectangles

You can use rectangles to visually group items that logically belong together on a report. You can also use them to make certain controls on a report stand out. For example, you can draw rectangles around important subtotal or grand total information that you want to make sure the report's readers notice.

To add a rectangle to a report, you select the Rectangle tool from the toolbox and then click and drag to place the rectangle on the report.

> A rectangle might obscure objects that you have already added to the report. To rectify this problem, you can set the rectangle's Back Style property to Transparent. This setting is fine unless you want the rectangle to have a background color. If you do, you choose Format|Send to Back to layer the objects so that the rectangle lies behind the other objects on the report.

Bound Object Frames

NEW TERM   Bound object frames let you display the data in OLE fields, which contain objects from other applications, such as pictures, spreadsheets, and word processing documents.

To add a bound object frame to a report, you click the Bound Object Frame tool in the toolbox and then click and drag the frame onto the report. You need to then set the Control Source property of the frame to the appropriate field. You can also add a bound object frame to a report by dragging and dropping an OLE field from the field list onto the report.

Unbound Object Frames

You can use unbound object frames to add logos and other pictures to a report. Unlike bound object frames, however, unbound object frames aren't tied to underlying data.

To add an unbound object frame to a report, you click the Unbound Object Frame tool in the toolbox and then click and drag the object frame to place it on the report. An insert object dialog box, shown in Figure 12.9, appears, and you use this dialog box to create a new OLE object or to insert an existing OLE object from a file on disk. If you select the Create from File option, the insert object dialog box changes to look like Figure 12.10. You can click Browse to locate the file you want to include in the report. The insert object dialog box gives you the option of linking to or embedding an OLE object. If you select Link, a reference is created to the OLE object. Access stores only the bitmap of the object in the report, and the report continues to refer to the original file on disk. If you don't select Link, Access copies the object you select and embeds it in the report so that it becomes part of the Access .MDB file; no link to the original object is maintained.

12

FIGURE 12.9

The insert object dialog box, where you insert a new or existing object into an unbound object frame.

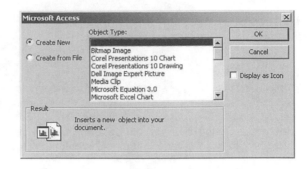

FIGURE 12.10

The insert object dialog box with Create from File selected.

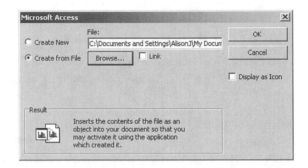

It's usually preferable to use an image control rather than an unbound object frame for static information such as a logo because the image control requires far fewer resources than does an unbound object frame. The next section covers image controls.

Image Controls

Image controls are the best option for displaying static images, such as logos, on a report. An unbound object can be modified after it is placed on a report, but you can't open the object application and modify an image when it's placed on a report. This limitation, however, means far fewer resources are needed with the Image control, so performance improves noticeably. Figure 12.11 shows a report with an image control.

Other Controls

As mentioned earlier in this chapter, it's standard to include mostly labels and text boxes on reports, but you can add other controls, such as combo boxes, when appropriate. To add any other type of control, you click to select the control in the toolbox and then click and drag to place it on the report.

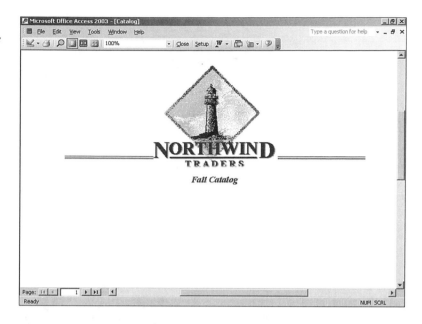

FIGURE 12.11

A report with an image control.

Report Properties and Why to Use Them

You can modify many different properties on reports to change how the report looks and performs. Like form properties, report properties are divided into categories: Format, Data, Event, and Other. To view a report's properties, you first select the report, rather than a section of the report, in one of three ways:

- Click the report selector (see Figure 12.12), which is the small gray button at the intersection of the horizontal and vertical rulers.
- Select Report from the drop-down list box in the Properties window.
- Choose Edit|Select Report.

After you have selected a report, you can view and modify its properties.

Working with the Properties Window

To select a report and open the Properties window at the same time, you double-click the report selector. When you select a report, the Properties window appears, showing all the properties associated with the report. A report has 47 properties available on the property sheet (there are additional properties available only from code), broken down into the appropriate categories in the Properties window. Forty of the properties relate to the report's Format, Data, and the properties on the Other tab; the remaining 7 relate to the events that occur when a report is run. The Format and Data properties are covered in the following sections. Hour 17, "Power Report Techniques," covers the properties on the Other tab. Programming books such as *Alison Balter's Mastering Access 2003 Desktop Development* cover the seven event properties.

Report Selector

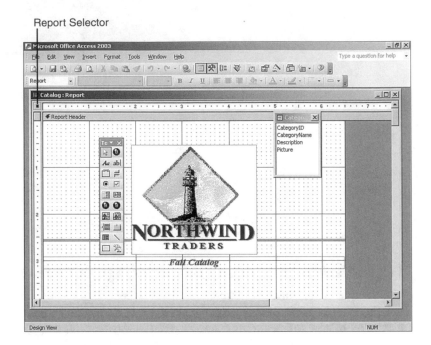

FIGURE 12.12
The report selector.

The Format Properties of a Report

A report has the 23 Format properties described in the following sections for changing the report's physical appearance.

Caption

The Caption property of a report is the text that appears in the Report window's title bar when the user is previewing the report. You can modify it at runtime to customize it for a particular situation.

Auto Resize

The Auto Resize property was introduced with Access 2002. Its setting determines whether a report is resized automatically to display all the data on the report.

Auto Center

You use the Auto Center property, which was introduced with Access 2002, to designate whether you want the Report window to automatically be centered on the screen.

Auto Center property is also new in Access 2002. This property specifies whether a report is centered automatically within the application window whenever it is opened.

Page Header **and** Page Footer

The Page Header and Page Footer properties determine on what pages the Page Header and Page Footer sections appear. The options are All Pages, Not with Rpt Hdr, Not with Rpt Ftr, and Not with Rpt Hdr/Ftr. You might not want the page header or page footer to print on the report header or report footer pages, and these properties give you control over where those sections print.

Grp Keep Together

NEW TERM   In Access, you can keep a group of data together on the same page by using the Grp Keep Together property. The Per Page setting forces the group of data to remain on the same page, and the Per Column setting forces the group of data to remain within a column. A *group of data* refers to all the data within a report grouping (for example, all the customers in a city).

Border Style

The Border Style property was introduced with Access 2002. Like its form counterpart, it is far more powerful than its name implies. The options for the Border Style property are None, Thin, Sizable, and Dialog. If the Border Style property is set to None, the report has no border. If the Border Style property is set to Thin, the border is not resizable; the Size command isn't available in the Control menu. This setting is a good choice for pop-up reports, which remain on top even when other forms or reports are given the focus. Having the Border Style property set to Sizable is standard for most reports. It includes all the standard options in the Control menu. The Dialog setting creates a border that looks like the border created by the Thin setting. The user can't maximize, minimize, or resize a report with the Border Style property set to Dialog. After you set the Border Style property of a report to Dialog, the Maximize, Minimize, and Resize options aren't available in the report's Control menu. Border Style property is new in Access 2002. This setting lets you specify the type of border to be used for the Report window under print preview mode. It also determines whether the Report window is sizable and which border elements are available for the Report window such as the title bar, Close button, the Control menu, and the Minimize and Maximize buttons.

Control Box

The Control Box property, which was introduced with Access 2002, lets you specify whether the Report window under Print Preview mode has the Control menu available. The user activates the Control menu by clicking the icon in the upper-left corner of a

12

window. The Control menu displays options for manipulating the window: Restore, Move, Size, Minimize, Maximize, and Close.

Min Max Buttons

The Min Max Buttons property, which was introduced with Access 2002, lets you specify whether the Minimize and/or Maximize options should be available from the Control menu for the Report window in Print Preview mode. The settings are None, Min Enabled, Max Enabled, and Both Enabled.

Close Button

The Close Button property, which was introduced with Access 2002, specifies whether to enable or disable the Close button on the Print Preview window.

Width

The Width property specifies the width of the report sections.

Picture, Picture Type, Picture Size Mode, Picture Alignment, Picture Tiling, and Picture Pages

The background of a report can be a picture. The Picture, Picture Type, Picture Size Mode, Picture Alignment, Picture Tiling, and Picture Pages properties determine what picture is used as a background for the report and what attributes are applied to it.

Grid X and Grid Y

The Grid X and Grid Y properties determine the density of the gridlines in the Report Design window.

Layout for Print

The Layout for Print property specifies whether screen or printer fonts are used in the report. If you want to optimize reports for preview, you should set this property to No; if you want to optimize reports for the printer, you should set it to Yes. This option is not very important if you select TrueType fonts because TrueType fonts usually print equally well to the screen and the printer.

Palette Source

The Palette Source property determines the source for a report's selectable colors.

Orientation

The Orientation property is used to take advantage of language-specific versions of Microsoft Access, such as Arabic. You can set this property to support right-to-left display features for these language-specific editions of Access, provided that the underlying operating system supports that language and is 32-bit (for example, Windows 2000).

Moveable

The Moveable property determines whether the user can move the Report window around the screen by clicking and dragging the report by its title bar.

The Report's Data Properties

A report has five Data properties, described in the following sections, which are used to supply information about the data underlying a report.

Record Source

The Record Source property specifies the table or query whose data underlies the report. You can modify the record source of a report at runtime. This feature of the Record Source property makes it easy for you to create generic reports that use different record sources in different situations.

Filter

The Filter property allows you to open a report with a specific filter set. I usually prefer to base a report on a query rather than apply a filter to it. At some times, however, it's more appropriate to base the report on a query and then apply and remove a filter as required, based on the report's runtime conditions.

Filter On

The Filter On property determines whether a report filter is applied. If the Filter On property is set to No, the Filter property of the report is ignored.

Order By

The Order By property determines how the records in a report are sorted when the report is opened.

Order By On

The Order By On property determines whether the Order By property of the report is used. If the Order By On property is set to No, the report's Order By property is ignored.

12

Summary

Reports provide valuable information about the data stored in a database. You can build many types of reports in Access 2003, including Detail reports, Summary reports, reports that look like printed forms, and reports that contain graphs and other objects. Access offers many properties for customizing the look and behavior of each report to fit the users' needs. Understanding how to work with each property is integral to the success of the databases that you build. For more information about report design techniques, refer to Hour 17.

Q&A

Q Name the types of reports available in Access, and give a brief description of each.

A Detail report: Supplies an entry for each record included in the report; Summary report: Provides summary data for all the records included in a report; Report with graphics and charts: Combine numbers and charts; Report with forms: Look like printed forms; Report with labels: Produces mailing labels.

Q Name the three sections that Access adds to every new report you create.

A The three sections of a report that Access adds to every new report you create are the Page Header, Detail, and Page Footer sections.

Q Explain the difference between a page header and a report header.

A The report header prints only once, at the very beginning of the report, whereas the page header prints at the top of every page.

Q Describe the design of a Summary report.

A A Summary report contains nothing in its Detail section. All controls are placed in the Group Headers and Group Footers sections as well as in the Report Footer section. Because no controls are found in the Detail section, Access prints summary information only.

Workshop

The Workshop includes quiz questions that are designed to help you test your understanding of the material covered and activities to help put what you've learned to practice. You can find the answers to the questions in the section immediately following the quiz.

Quiz

1. The `Auto Center` property of a report determines whether the controls are centered within the report (True/False).

2. Name the property that determines whether Access applies the report filter designated in the `Filter` property.

3. Name the property that determines how the records in a report are sorted when the report opens.

4. What type of report control is most efficient for storing static images such as logos?

5. Name the report property that determines whether the user can move the Report window while in Print Preview mode.

Quiz Answers

1. False. The `Auto Center` property determines whether Access centers the report window within the screen.

2. The `Filter On` property.

3. The `Order By` property.

4. The `Image` control.

5. The `Moveable` property.

Activities

Practice creating a report in Design view. Designate the record source. Practice adding the types of controls that you learned about in this hour. Set various properties and see how they affect the report output.

12

HOUR 13

Creating Macros

Although you shouldn't use macros to develop complex applications, you can use macros to develop simple applications. It's therefore a good idea for you to have a general understanding of macros and how they work. In fact, there's one task that you can accomplish only by using macros—reassigning a keystroke—so it's important to understand at least the basics of how macros work. Furthermore, using macros can often help you get started with developing complex applications because you can convert the macros that you build to Visual Basic for Applications (VBA) code. This means you can develop part of an application by using macros, convert the macros to VBA code, and then continue developing the application. Although I don't recommend this approach for serious developers, it offers a great jump-start for those new to Access or Windows development in general.

In this hour you'll learn the basics of creating a macro. You'll learn how to run an Access macro, as well as how to modify an existing macro. You'll learn how to document and test a macro. Finally, you'll learn when macros are appropriate and how to create two special types of macros: an AutoExec macro and an AutoKeys macro.

In this hour you will learn the following:

- Why macros are important
- The basics of creating a macro
- How to run an Access macro
- How to create a macro

- How to modify an existing macro
- How to document a macro
- How to test a macro
- When you should use macros and when you shouldn't
- How to convert a macro to VBA code
- How to create an AutoExec macro
- How to create an AutoKeys macro

The Basics of Creating a Macro

To create a macro, you click the Macros tab from the Database window and then click New to open the Macro design window shown in Figure 13.1. In this window, you can build a "program" by adding macro actions, arguments, names, and conditions to the macro.

FIGURE 13.1

The Macro design window, showing the Action and Comment columns.

Macro *actions* are like programming commands or functions; they instruct Access to take a specific action—for example, to open a form. Macro *arguments* are like parameters to a command or function; they give Access specifics on the selected action. For example, if the macro action instructs Access to open a form, the arguments for that action tell Access which form it should open and how it should open it (in Form, Design, or Datasheet view, or using Print Preview).

Macro *names* are like subroutines. You can include several subroutines in one Access macro, and you identify each of these subroutines by its macro name. Macro *conditions* allow you to determine when Access executes a specific macro action. For example, a company might want an inventory reorder form to open if an item is low or out of stock. If the item is fully stocked, perhaps just a detailed description form would display.

Macro Actions

As mentioned earlier, a macro action instructs Access to perform a task. You can add a macro action to the Macro design window in several ways. One method is the following:

1. Click a cell in the Action column.

2. Click to open the drop-down list (see Figure 13.2). A list of all the macro actions appears.

3. Select the action that you want from the list. Access adds it to the macro.

You use this method of selecting a macro action if you aren't sure of the macro action's name and want to browse the available actions.

FIGURE 13.2

The Action drop-down list, showing all the available macro actions.

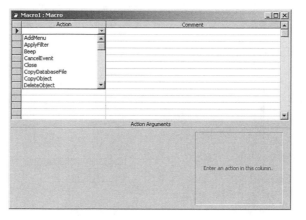

After you have been working with macros for a while, you will know which actions you want to select. Rather than open the drop-down list and scroll through the entire list of actions, you can click a cell in the Action column and then start typing the name of the macro action you want to add. Access fills in the field with the first macro action that begins with the character(s) you type.

You use the OpenTable, OpenQuery, OpenForm, OpenReport, and OpenModule actions to open a table, query, form, report, and module, respectively. You can select these actions and their associated arguments quite easily by using a drag-and-drop technique:

1. Open the Chap13Ex database, which is available at www.samspublishing.com.

2. Select Macros from the list of objects in the Database window.

13

3. Click New to create a new macro. The Macro design window appears.

4. Tile the Database window and the Macro design window on the desktop (see Figure 13.3).

5. Select the appropriate tab from the Database window. For example, if you want to open a form, select the Forms tab.

6. Click and drag the object you want to open to the Macro design window. Access automatically fills in the appropriate action and arguments. Figure 13.4 shows the effects of dragging and dropping the frmClients form onto the Macro design window.

7. Close the Database window and maximize the Macro design window.

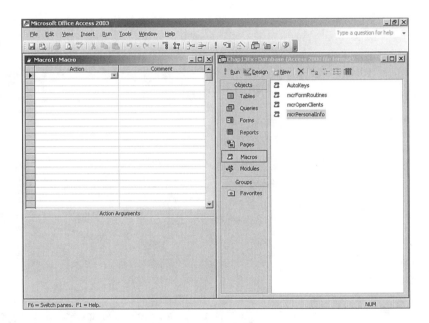

FIGURE **13.3**

The Database window and Macro design window, tiled.

Dragging and dropping a table, query, form, report, or module onto the Macro design window saves you time because Access automatically fills in all the macro action arguments for you. Notice in Figure 13.4 that Access associates six action arguments with the OpenForm action: Form Name, View, Filter Name, Where Condition, Data Mode, and Window Mode. The drag-and-drop process fills in three of the arguments for the OpenForm action: the name of the form (frmClients), the view (Form), and the window mode (Normal). The next section more thoroughly covers macro action arguments.

FIGURE 13.4

The Macro design window after the frmClients *form is dragged and dropped onto it.*

Action arguments —

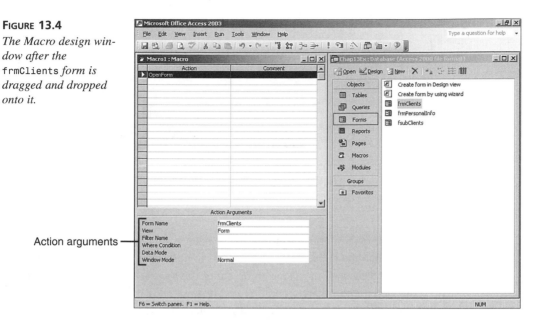

Action Arguments

As mentioned previously, macro action arguments are like command or function parameters: They give Access specific instructions on how to execute the selected macro action. The available arguments differ, depending on what macro action you select. Some macro action arguments force you to select from a drop-down list of appropriate choices; others allow you to enter valid Access expressions. Access automatically fills in macro action arguments when you click and drag a Table, Query, Form, Report, or Module object to the Macro design window. In all other situations, you must supply Access with the arguments required to properly execute a macro action.

To specify a macro action argument, follow these steps:

1. Select a macro action.
2. Press the F6 key to jump down to the first macro action argument for the selected macro action.
3. If the macro action argument needs to be selected from a list of valid choices, click to open the drop-down list of available choices for the first macro action argument associated with the selected macro action. Figure 13.5 shows all the available choices for the Form Name argument associated with the OpenForm action. Because the selected argument is Form Name, Access displays in the drop-down list the names of all the forms included in the database.

13

FIGURE 13.5

*Available choices for
the* OpenForm *argu-
ment.*

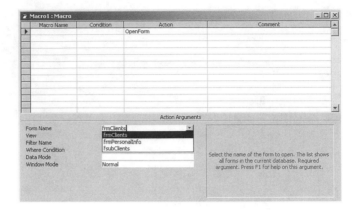

4. If the macro action argument requires you to enter a valid expression, you can type
   the argument into the appropriate text box or get help from the Expression Builder.
   Take a look at the Where Condition argument of the OpenForm action, for example.
   After you click in the Where Condition text box, an ellipsis appears. If you click
   the ellipsis, Access invokes the Expression Builder dialog box. (See Figure 13.6.)

FIGURE 13.6

*Adding complex
expressions to macros.*

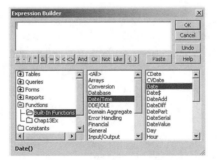

5. To build an appropriate expression, select a database object from the list box on the
   left and then select a specific element from the center and right-hand list boxes.
   Click Paste to paste the element into the text box. In Figure 13.6, the currently
   selected database object is Built-in Functions, and the currently selected elements
   are Date/Time and Date. Click OK to close the Expression Builder. The completed
   expression appears in Figure 13.7.

Remember that each macro action has different macro action arguments. Access requires
some of the arguments associated with a particular macro action, and others are optional.
If you need help with a particular macro action argument, you can click the argument,

and Access gives you a short description of that argument. If you need more help, you can press F1 to see Help for the macro action and all its arguments. (See Figure 13.8.)

FIGURE 13.7

The completed expression for the Where Condition *argument of the* OpenForm *action.*

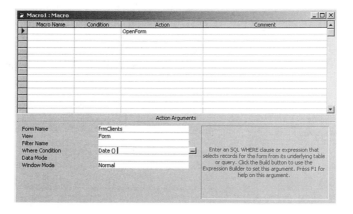

FIGURE 13.8

Help on the OpenForm *action.*

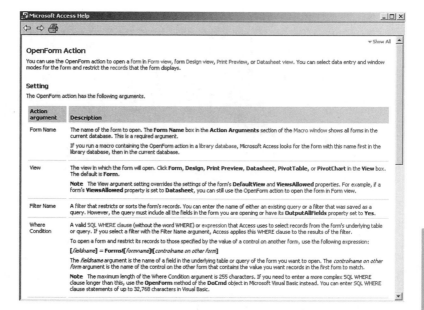

13

Macro Names

As mentioned previously, macro names are like subroutines: They allow you to place more than one routine in a macro. This means you can create many macro routines without having to create several separate macros. You should include macros that perform related functions within one particular macro. For example, you might build a macro that contains all the routines required for form handling and another that has all the routines needed for report handling.

You need to take only two steps to add macro names to a macro:

1. Click the Macro Names button on the Macro Design toolbar or choose View|Macro Names. The Macro Name column appears. (See Figure 13.9.)

Macro names button

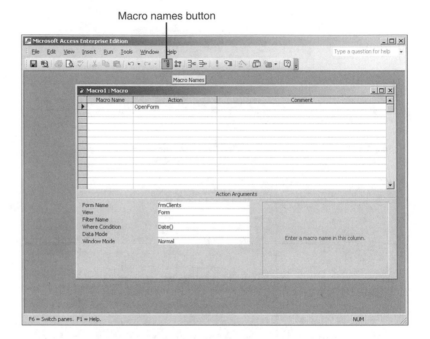

FIGURE **13.9**
Creating subroutines within a macro.

2. Add macro names to each macro subroutine. Figure 13.10 shows a macro with three subroutines: OpenFrmClients, OpenFrmTimeCards, and CloseAnyForm. The OpenFrmClients subroutine opens the frmClients form, showing all the clients added in the past 30 days. The OpenFrmTimeCards subroutine opens the frmTimeCards form, and the CloseAnyForm subroutine displays a message to the user and then closes the active form.

The Macro Name column toggles. You can hide it and show it at will, without losing the information in the column.

FIGURE **13.10**

A macro with three subroutines.

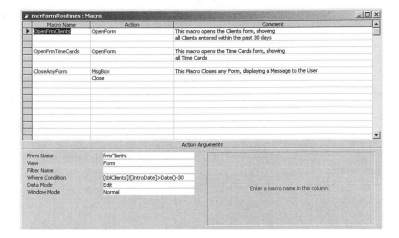

Macro Conditions

At times, you want a macro action to execute only when a certain condition is true. Fortunately, Access allows you to specify the conditions under which a macro action executes:

1. Click the Conditions button on the Macro Design toolbar or choose View|
   Conditions. The Condition column appears. (See Figure 13.11.)

2. Add the conditions you want to each macro action.

The macro pictured in Figure 13.12 evaluates information entered on a form. The CheckBirthDate subroutine evaluates the date entered in the txtBirthDate text box. Here's the expression entered in the first condition:

```
DateDiff("yyyy",[Forms]![frmPersonalInfo]! _
   [txtBirthDate],Date()) Between 25 And 49
```

This expression uses the DateDiff function to determine the difference between the date entered in the txtBirthDate text box and the current date. If the difference between the two dates is between 25 and 49 years, the macro displays a message box indicating that the person is over a quarter century old.

The ellipsis on the second line of the CheckBirthDate subroutine indicates that Access should execute the macro action only if the condition entered on the previous line is true. In this case, if the condition is true, the action terminates the macro.

If the value in the text box doesn't satisfy the first condition, the macro continues evaluating each condition in the subroutine. The CheckBirthDate subroutine displays an age-specific message for each person 25 years of age and older. If the person is younger than

13

25, the text box value does not meet any of the conditions, and the macro does not display a message.

FIGURE 13.11

Designating the condition under which a macro action executes in the Condition column of a macro.

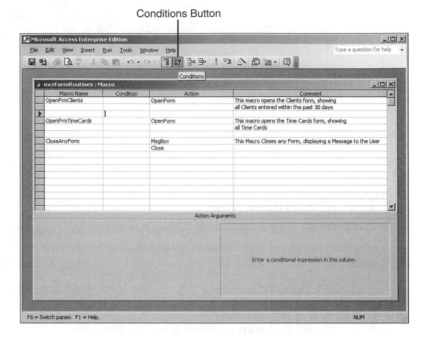

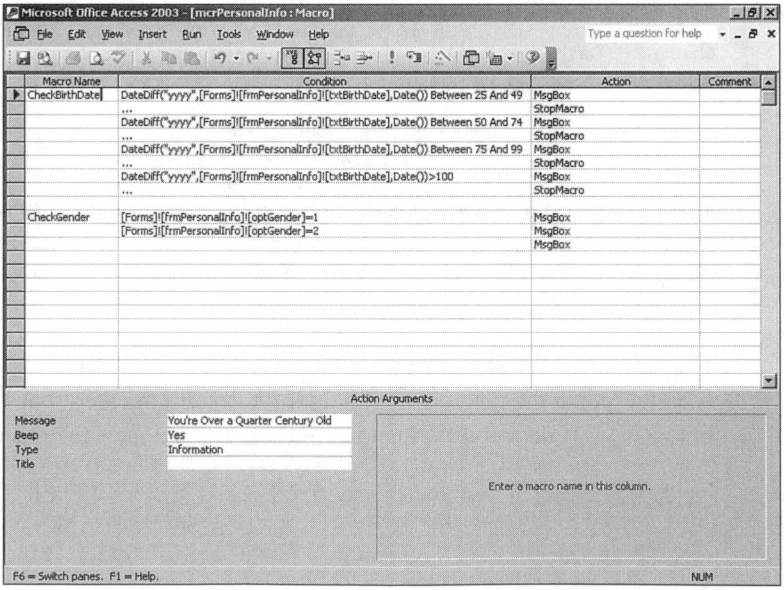

FIGURE 13.12

An example of a macro that contains conditions.

The CheckGender subroutine works a little bit differently. It evaluates the value of the optGender option group. One of the first two lines of the subroutine executes, depending on whether the user selects the first or second option button. The third line of the subroutine executes, regardless of the Option Group value because the macro does not contain an ellipsis on that line of the macro action's Condition column. If you do not enter an ellipsis on any line of the subroutine, the macro action executes unconditionally. If you place an ellipsis before the line, the macro action executes only if the value of OptGender is 2.

Running an Access Macro

You have learned quite a bit about macros, but you have not yet learned how to execute them. The macro execution process varies, depending on what you're trying to do. You can run a macro from the Macro design window, from the Macros tab, from a Form or Report event, or by selecting a menu or toolbar option. The following sections cover the first three methods. Hour 24, "Finishing Touches," covers invoking a macro from a menu or toolbar option.

Running a Macro from the Macro Design Window

You can easily execute a macro from the Macro design window. It's simple to run a macro without subroutines: You just click Run on the Macro Design toolbar or choose Run|Run. Access executes each line of the macro, unless you have placed conditions on specific macro actions. After you click the Run button of the mcrOpenClients macro (shown in Figure 13.13), Access opens the frmClients form.

From Design view of the macro, you can run only the first subroutine in a macro. To run a macro with subroutines, you click Run on the Macro Design toolbar to execute the first subroutine in the macro. As soon as Access encounters the second macro name, it terminates the macro execution. The section "Triggering a Macro from a Form or Report Event," later in this hour, explains how to execute subroutines other than the first one in a macro.

Running a Macro from the Macros Tab

To run a macro from the Macros tab of the Database window, follow these two steps:

1. Click the Macros tab of the Database window.
2. Double-click the name of the macro you want to execute, or click the name of the macro and then click Run.

13

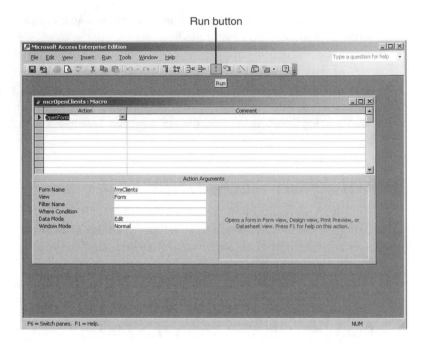

FIGURE 13.13

Running a macro from the Macro design window.

If the macro you execute contains macro names, Access executes only the macro actions within the first subroutine.

Triggering a Macro from a Form or Report Event

You can execute a macro in response to an event. This section explains how to associate a macro with the Click event of a command button.

The form in Figure 13.14 illustrates associating a macro with the Click event of a form's command button. You must take four steps to associate a macro with a Form or Report event:

1. Select the object with which you want to associate the event. In the example, I have selected the cmdCheckGender command button.

2. Open the Properties window and click the Event tab.

3. Click the event you want the macro to execute in response to. In the example, I have selected the Click event of the command button.

4. Use the drop-down list to select the name of the macro you want to execute. If the macro has subroutine macro names, make sure you select the correct macro name

subroutine. In the example, I have selected the macro mcrPersonalInfo and the macro name CheckGender. Notice the period between the name of the macro and the name of the macro name subroutine. You use the period to differentiate the macro group (mcrPersonalInfo, in this case) from the macro name (CheckGender, in this example).

FIGURE 13.14

Associating a macro with a Form or Report event.

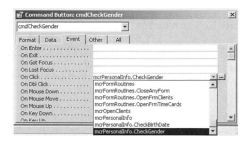

Task: Creating a Macro

To practice the techniques you have learned, build the macro shown in Figure 13.12. This macro includes macro names and conditions. To execute the macro, you build a form and associate the Click events of the command buttons on the form with the macro names of the macros you build. This process helps reinforce all the macro techniques that have been covered thus far in this hour. To create a new macro, follow these steps:

1. Click the Macros tab of the Database window.

2. Click New.

3. Click the Macro Name and Condition buttons on the Macro Design toolbar to show both the Macro Name and Condition columns of the Macro design window.

4. Enter all the macro names, actions, arguments, and conditions shown in Table 13.1.

5. Save the macro and name it **mcrPersonalInfo**.

6. Build a form.

7. Add an option group that has two option buttons. Set one of their Text properties to Male and the other to Female, and then set one of their values to 1 and the other to 2. Name the option group **optGender**.

8. Add a text box for the birth date. Set the Format and Input Mask properties to Short Date. Name the text box **txtBirthDate**.

9. Add two command buttons to the form. Name the first button **cmdCheckGender** and set its Text property to Check Gender, and name the second button **cmdCheckBirthDate** and set its Text property to Check Birth Date. Set the Click event of the first

13

▼ command button to mcrPersonalInfo.CheckGender and the second command button to mcrPersonalInfo.CheckBirthDate.

10. Save the form as **frmPersonalInfo**.

11. Test the macros by clicking each of the command buttons after selecting a gender and entering a birth date.

TABLE 13.1 The mcrPersonalInfo Macro

Macro Name	Macro Condition	Macro Action	Argument	Value
CheckBirthDate	DateDiff("yyyy", [Forms]! [frmPersonalInfo]! [txtBirthDate], Date()) Between 25 And 49	MsgBox	Message	You Are Over a Quarter Century Old
			Type	Information
	..	StopMacro		
	DateDiff("yyyy", [Forms]! [frmPersonalInfo]! [txtBirthDate],Date()) Between 50 And 74	MsgBox	Message	You Are Over a Half Century Old
			Type	Information
	...	StopMacro		
	DateDiff("yyyy",[Forms]! [frmPersonalInfo]! [txtBirthDate],Date()) Between 75 And 99	MsgBox	Message	You Are Over Three Quarters of a Century Old
			Type	Warning
	...	StopMacro		

▼

TABLE 13.1 continued

Macro Name	Macro Condition	Macro Action	Argument	Value
	DateDiff("yyyy",[Forms]!	MsgBox	Message	You Are Over a Century Old!!
	[frmPersonalInfo]! [txtBirthDate], Date())>100			|
			Type	Warning
	...	StopMacro		
CheckGender	[Forms]![frmPersonalInfo]! [optGender]=1	MsgBox	Message	You Are Male
			Type	Information
	[Forms]![frmPersonalInfo]! [optGender]=2	MsgBox	Message	You Are Female
			Type	Information
		MsgBox	Message	Thank You for the Information

Modifying an Existing Macro

You have learned how to create a macro, add macro actions and their associated arguments, create macro subroutines by adding macro names, and conditionally execute the actions in the macro by adding macro conditions. However, after you have created a macro, you might want to modify it. To do so, you must first enter Design view for the macro and then follow these steps:

1. Click the Macros tab of the Database window.
2. Select the macro you want to modify.
3. Click Design.

When the design of the macro appears, you can insert new lines, delete existing lines, move the macro actions around, or copy macro actions to the macro you're modifying or to another macro.

13

Inserting New Macro Actions

To insert a macro action, follow these steps:

1. Click the line above where you want to insert the macro action.

2. Press Insert, click the Insert Rows button on the toolbar, or choose Insert|Rows. Access inserts a new line in the macro at the cursor.

To insert multiple macro actions, follow these steps:

1. Place the cursor on the line above where you want Access to insert the new macro action lines. Click the Macro Action Selector, which is the gray box to the left of the macro's Action column.

2. Click and drag to select the same number of Macro Action Selectors as the number of macro actions you want to insert.

3. Press the Insert key, click the Insert Rows button on the toolbar, or choose Insert| Rows. Access inserts all the new macro lines above the macro actions that you selected.

Deleting Macro Actions

Follow these steps to delete a macro action:

1. Click the Macro Action Selector of the macro action you want to delete.

2. Press the Delete key, click Delete Rows on the toolbar, or choose Edit|Delete Rows.

Follow these steps to delete multiple macro actions (macros):

1. Click and drag to select the Macro Action Selectors of all the macro actions you want to delete. All the macro actions should be highlighted in black. (See Figure 13.15.)

2. Press the Delete key, click Delete Rows, or choose Edit|Delete Rows.

Moving Macro Actions

You can move macro actions in a few ways, including by dragging and dropping and by cutting and pasting.

To move macro actions by dragging and dropping, follow these steps:

1. Click and drag to select the macro action(s) you want to move.

2. Release the mouse button.

These rows will be deleted

FIGURE 13.15

Selecting and deleting macro actions.

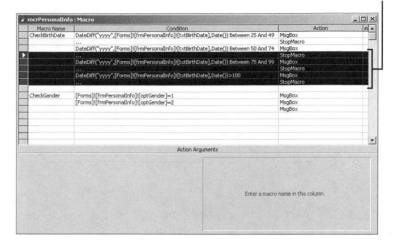

3. Place the mouse cursor over the Macro Action Selector of any of the selected macro actions.

4. Click and drag. A black line appears, indicating where Access will move the selected macro actions.

5. Release the mouse button. Access inserts the macro actions where you release the mouse button.

> If you accidentally drag and drop the selected macro actions to an incorrect place, you can use the Undo button on the Macro Design toolbar or choose Edit I Undo to reverse the action.

To move macro actions by cutting and pasting, follow these steps:

1. Click and drag to select the Macro Action Selectors of the macro actions you want to move.

2. Click Cut on the Macro Design toolbar (or use Ctrl+X).

3. Click the line above where you want Access to insert the cut macro actions. Don't click the Macro Action Selector.

4. Click Paste. Access inserts the macro actions at the cursor.

13

Don't click the Macro Action Selector of the row where you want to insert the cut macro actions, unless you want to overwrite the macro action you have selected. If you don't click to select the Macro Action Selectors, Access inserts the cut lines into the macro, without overwriting any other macro actions; if you click to select Macro Action Selectors, Access overwrites existing macro actions.

Copying Macro Actions

You can copy macro actions within a macro or to another macro.

Follow these steps to copy macro actions within a macro:

1. Click and drag to select the Macro Action Selectors of the macro actions you want to copy.

2. Click Copy on the Macro Design toolbar (or use Ctrl+C).

3. Click the line above where you want to insert the copied macro actions. Don't click any Macro Action Selectors unless you want to overwrite existing macro actions. (See the Caution preceding this section.)

4. Click Paste. Access inserts the macro actions you copied at the cursor.

Follow these steps to copy macro actions to another macro:

1. Click and drag to select the Macro Action Selectors of the macro actions you want to copy.

2. Click Copy on the Macro Design toolbar (or use Ctrl+C).

3. Open the macro that will include the copied actions.

4. Click the line above where you want to insert the copied macro actions.

5. Click Paste. Access inserts the macro actions you copied at the cursor.

Documenting a Macro: Adding Comments

Just as it's useful to document any program, it's useful to document what you're trying to do in a macro. You or others can use these comments when modifying a macro later. Because macro comments print when you print the macro, you can also use macro comments as documentation.

To add a comment to a macro, click the Comment column of the macro and begin to type. Figure 13.16 shows macros with comments. As you can see in Figure 13.17, these comments appear in the printed macro.

FIGURE 13.16

Adding comments to a macro.

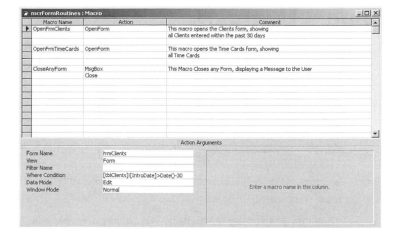

You can add comments to a macro action by placing FALSE in the Condition column of the macro line for which you're creating a comment. This is useful when you're testing or debugging a macro.

FIGURE 13.17

Comments included in a printed macro.

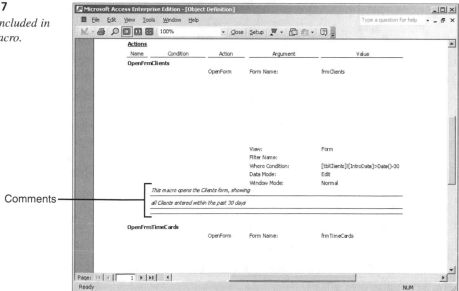

Comments

13

Testing a Macro

Although Access doesn't offer very sophisticated tools for testing and debugging macros, it does give you a method for stepping through each line of a macro:

1. Open the macro in Design view.

2. Click Single Step on the toolbar or select Run|Single Step.

3. To execute the macro, click Run. Access executes the first line of the macro, and the Macro Single Step dialog box appears, showing the macro name, condition, action name, and arguments (see Figure 13.18). In the figure, the macro name is mcrPersonalInfo, the condition evaluates to True, and the action name is MsgBox. The MsgBox arguments are You Are Over a Quarter Century Old, Yes, and Information.

4. To continue stepping through the macro, click the Step button on the Macro Single Step dialog box. If you want to halt the execution of the macro without proceeding, click the Halt button. To continue normal execution of the macro without stepping, click the Continue button.

FIGURE 13.18

Viewing the macro name, condition, action name, and arguments for the current step of a macro.

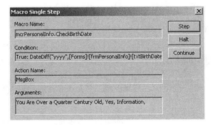

Task: Stepping Through a Macro

It's easiest to learn about stepping through a macro by experiencing it firsthand. Here's what you do:

1. Open (in Design view) the mcrPersonalInfo macro that you created earlier in this hour.

2. Click the Single Step button on the Macro Design toolbar. Run the frmPersonalInfo form, also created earlier in this hour.

3. Select a gender and type in a birth date.

4. Click the Check Gender command button; this should invoke the Macro Single Step dialog box.

5. Step through the macro one step at a time. View the macro name, condition, action name, and arguments for each step.

▼ 6. Change the gender and run the macro again. Carefully observe how this affects the macro's execution.

7. Click the Check Birth Date command button. Step through the macro one step at a time, viewing whether the condition evaluates to True or False.

8. After the macro ends, try entering a different value for the birth date. Step through the macro again and carefully observe whether the condition evaluates to True or False for each step.

As you can see, although Microsoft supplies some tools to help you debug a macro, you will probably agree that they're quite limited. That's one reason most experienced developers prefer to develop applications by using VBA code.

> The Single Step button on the Macro Design toolbar toggles. When you activate Step mode, you activate it for all macros in the current database and all other databases until you either turn the toggle off or exit Access. This can be quite surprising if you don't expect it. You might have invoked Step mode in another database quite a bit earlier in the day, only to remember that you forgot to click the toggle button when you run another macro and that macro unexpectedly goes into Step mode.

▲

When You Should Use Macros and When You Shouldn't

In Access 2003, there's just one task that you can perform only by using macros: reassigning key combinations (using the AutoKeys macro). This hour gives you many other examples of macros, but that's just so you can have a basic understanding of macros and how they work. If you are developing a *large-scale* corporate application, you might consider limiting your use of macros to AutoKeys macros. As you will see later in this section, VBA code is much more appropriate for most of the tasks a large-scale corporate application must perform.

A second common use of macros is as a starting point for an application. Although macros aren't the only choice for this in Access 2003, the AutoExec macro is one of two choices for this task. For more information about the AutoExec macro, see the section "Creating an AutoExec Macro," later in this hour.

However, macros aren't the best tool for creating code that controls industrial-strength applications because they're quite limited in both function and capability. Access macros are limited in the following ways:

13

- You can't include error handling in an Access macro.
- You can't create user-defined functions by using macros.
- Access macros don't allow you to create variables or pass parameters.
- Access macros provide no method of processing table records one at a time.
- When you use Access macros, you can't use object linking and embedding (OLE) automation or dynamic data exchange (DDE) to communicate with other applications.
- It's more difficult to debug Access macros than it is to debug VBA code.
- You can't perform transaction processing when using Access macros.
- You can't call Windows application programming interface (API) functions by using Access macros.
- You can't perform any replication by using Access macros.
- Access macros don't allow you to create database objects at runtime.

Converting a Macro to VBA Code

Now that you have discovered all the limitations of macros, you might be thinking about all the macros you've already written that you wish you had developed by using VBA code. Or, after seeing how easy it is to do certain tasks by using macros, you might be disappointed to learn how limited macros are. Fortunately, with Access 2003 it's easy to convert an Access macro to VBA code, and after you have converted the macro to VBA code, you can modify the code just as you would any VBA module. Follow these steps to convert an Access macro to VBA code:

1. Open the macro you want to convert in Design view.
2. Choose File|Save As. The Save dialog box appears.
3. Select Module from the As drop-down (see Figure 13.19).

FIGURE 13.19

Saving a macro as a VBA module.

4. Click OK. The Convert Macro dialog box, shown in Figure 13.20, appears.

Using the Convert Macro dialog box to indicate whether Access will add error handling and comments to the VBA module.

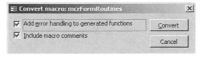

5. Indicate whether you want to add error handling and comments to the generated code and then click Convert.

6. When you get an indication that the conversion is finished, click OK.

7. The converted macro appears under the list of modules, with "Converted Macro:" followed by the name of the macro. Click Design to view the results of the conversion.

Figure 13.21 shows a macro that Access has converted into distinct subroutines—one for each macro name. The macro is complete, with logic, comments, and error handling. Access converts all macro conditions into If...Else...End If statements and all the macro comments into VBA comments. It adds basic error-handling routines to the code.

FIGURE 13.21

A converted macro as a module.

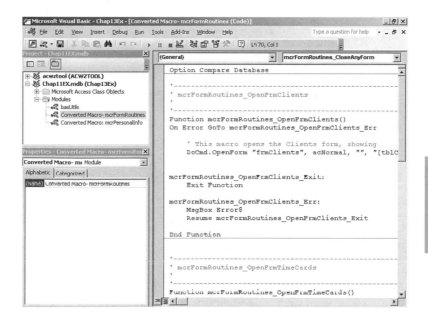

13

When you convert a macro to a VBA module, the original macro remains untouched. Furthermore, all the objects in the application will still call the macro. To effectively use the macro conversion options, you must find all the places where the application calls the macro and replace the macro references with calls to the VBA function.

Creating an `AutoExec` Macro

In versions of Access prior to Access 2003, the only way to have something happen when the user opens a database is to use an `AutoExec` macro. With Access 2003, you can use either an `AutoExec` macro or Startup options to determine what occurs when the user opens a database. Using an `AutoExec` macro to launch the processing of an application is certainly still a viable option.

Creating an `AutoExec` macro is quite simple; `AutoExec` is just a normal macro saved with the name `AutoExec`. An `AutoExec` macro usually performs tasks such as hiding or minimizing the Database window and opening a Startup form or switchboard. The macro shown in Figure 13.22 hides the Database window, displays a welcome message, and opens the `frmClients` form.

FIGURE 13.22

An example of an AutoExec *macro.*

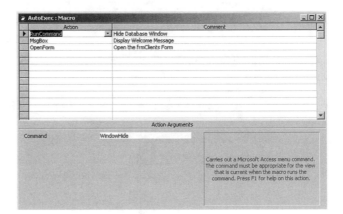

When you're opening a database to make changes or additions to the application, you probably won't want the `AutoExec` macro to execute. To prevent it from executing, you hold down the Shift key as you open the database.

Creating an AutoKeys Macro

An AutoKeys macro allows you to redefine keystrokes within a database. With an AutoKeys macro you can map selected keystrokes to a single command or to a series of commands. Follow these six steps to build an AutoKeys macro:

1. Open a new macro in Design view.

2. Make sure the Macro Name column is visible.

3. Enter a key name in the Macro Name column. Access Help defines the allowable keystroke combinations (see Figure 13.23).

FIGURE 13.23

A list of valid key stroke combinations for the AutoKeys *macro.*

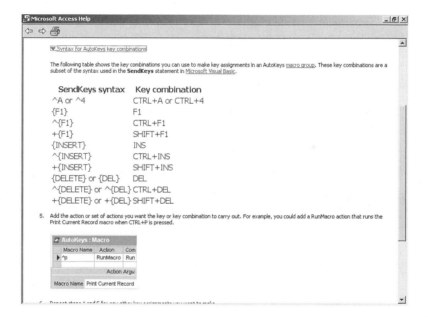

4. From the Action drop-down list box, select the macro action you want to associate with the key name. You can apply conditions and arguments just as you do for a normal macro. You can have Access execute multiple commands in one of three ways: associate multiple macro actions with a key name, perform a RunCode action, or perform a RunMacro action.

5. Continue adding key names and macro actions to the macro as desired. Put one blank line after each key name to improve readability.

6. Save the macro as **AutoKeys**. The moment you save the macro, Access places the key names in effect and remaps the keystrokes. The AutoKeys macro goes into effect automatically each time you open the database.

13

Generally, it's not a good idea to remap common Windows or Access keystrokes. Users become accustomed to certain keystrokes having certain meanings in all Windows applications. If you try to change the definition of a common keystroke, users will become confused and frustrated. That's why it's important to remap only keystroke combinations that are rarely, if ever, used in Windows.

Task: Creating an `AutoExec` Macro

It's time to build an `AutoExec` macro that acts as the launching point for an application. The macro will start the application by hiding the Database window, displaying a message to the user, and opening the `frmClients` form.

Build the macro shown in Figure 13.22, following these steps:

1. Open a new macro in Design view.

2. Set the first action of the macro to `RunCommand`.

3. Set the Command argument to `WindowHide`. This will hide the Database window when the user runs the macro.

4. Set the second action of the macro to `MsgBox`, and set the Message to `Welcome to the Client Billing Application`. Set Beep to `No`, Type to `Information`, and Title to `Welcome`.

5. The final action of the macro opens the `frmClients` form. Set the action to `OpenForm` and set the `FormName` to `frmClients`. Leave the rest of the arguments at their default values.

6. Close and reopen the database. The `AutoExec` macro should automatically execute when you open the database.

7. Close the database and then open it again, holding down the Shift key to prevent the macro from executing.

Summary

Many end users try to develop entire enterprise applications by using macros. Although that is possible, it is *not* appropriate. Macros don't give the developer adequate control, error handling, debugging capabilities, and many other features needed for the successful development of large-scale applications. On the other hand, macros *are* appropriate for small single-user or departmental applications.

Reassigning keystrokes can be done *only* by using macros. Furthermore, using an `AutoExec` macro is one of two ways you can determine what happens when an application loads. If you are performing one of these tasks or are developing a small application, Access macros may be all you need. Otherwise, you should automate an application by using VBA code (which is covered in Hour 23, "VBA Introduced").

Q&A

Q What types of applications most benefit from the use of macros?

A Single-user or small departmental applications most benefit from the use of macros.

Q What are some of the main limitations of macros?

A You cannot include error handling, user-defined functions, variables, parameters, OLE automation, DDE, transaction processing, or Windows API functions within macros. Macros do not allow you to process table records a row at a time or create database objects at runtime. It is also much more difficult to debug macros than it is to debug VBA code.

Q What is the purpose of the Macro Names column of a macro?

A The Macro Names column allows you to place multiple routines in one macro.

Workshop

The Workshop includes quiz questions that are designed to help you test your understanding of the material covered and activities to help put what you've learned to practice. You can find the answers to the questions in the section immediately following the quiz.

Quiz

1. Name the four macro columns.
2. Comments that you add to a macro print when you print the macro (True/False).
3. You turn the Step feature on and off for each macro in a database (True/False).
4. Name the macro that you use to remap keystrokes.
5. Name the macro that you create when you want something to happen as the user opens the database.

Quiz Answers

1. Macro Name, Action, Condition, and Comment.
2. True.

13

3. False. The Step feature applies to all databases that you work with in Access (until you toggle it off).

4. `AutoKeys`.

5. `AutoExec`.

Activities

Practice adding four macros to an application that you build. The macros should include the following:

- An `AutoExec` macro
- An `AutoKeys` macro
- A macro that contains three named macros that open three different forms
- A macro that contains a condition

Build a form with command buttons that execute the named macros and the macro containing the condition.

PART IV

Power Access Techniques

HOUR 14

Power Table Techniques

Working with the design of tables is not as simple as adding a field, naming it, and selecting the field type. You can do a lot more than that to customize what you store in a table and how it behaves. In this hour you'll learn the following:

- How to refine field and table properties
- How to work with the powerful Lookup Wizard
- How to use indexes to improve performance

Working with Field Properties

After you have added fields to a table, you need to customize their properties. Field properties let you control how Access stores data as well as what data the user can enter into a field. The available properties differ depending on which field type you select. You can find a comprehensive list of properties under the Text data type (see Figure 14.1). The following sections describe the various field properties. Notice that the lower portion of the Design view window in Figure 14.1 is the Field Properties pane. This is where you can set properties for the fields in a table.

FIGURE 14.1

Using the Field Properties pane of the Design View window to set the properties of a field.

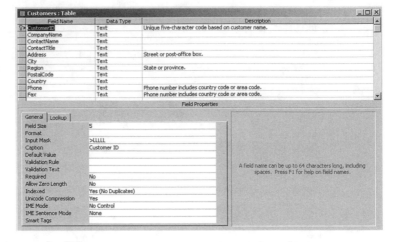

The `Field Size` Property: Limiting What the User Enters into a Field

The `Field Size` property is available for `Text` and `Number` fields only. It's best to set the `Field Size` property to the smallest value possible. For `Number` fields, a small size means lower storage requirements and faster performance. The same is true for `Text` fields. To modify the `Field Size` property, follow these steps:

1. Select the desired field name from the top pane of the Design view window.

2. Click the `Field Size` property text box in the Field Properties pane.

3. Type the desired field size. Figure 14.1 shows 5 as the field size of the `CustomerID` field.

It's important to note that for `Number` fields, you should select the smallest `Field Size` property value that can store the values you will be entering. Limiting the `Field Size` property of `Number` fields saves disk space.

A couple of tips that can save you a lot of time. First, you can move between the two panes of the Design view window by pressing F6. Second, to get help with a field property, you click the property line in the Field Properties pane and press F1.

Task: Working with the `Field Size` Property

It's important that you practice building tables and setting field types. To get the practice that you need, you can build a table with the following fields and types:

```
CompanyID:  AutoNumber

CompanyName:  Text

State:  Text

PhoneNumber:  Text

ContactDate:  Date/Time

CreditLimit: Currency
```

When you've added all the fields and set their types, you're ready to refine them by setting some of their properties. During the remainder of the exercise, you'll set the primary key of the table and the `Field Size` property of the `State` field:

1. Set `CompanyID` as the primary key field.

2. To set the `Field Size` property of the `State` field to two characters, click anywhere in the field and then type **2** for the `Field Size` property.

3. Switch to Datasheet view. Access prompts you to save the table. Name it **tblCustomers**. When you try to enter data into the `State` field, notice that you can enter only two characters.

The `Format` Property: Determining How Access Displays Data

The `Format` property allows you to customize the way Access displays and prints numbers, dates, times, and text. You can select a predefined format or create a custom format.

To select a predefined display format (from Design view), follow these steps:

1. Select the desired field.

2. Click the `Format` property text box in the Field Properties pane.

3. Click the drop-down arrow that appears when you click in the `Format` property.

4. Select the desired format based on the type of field you are formatting.

You create a custom format by using a combination of the special characters, called *placeholders*, listed in Table 14.1.

TABLE 14.1   Placeholders That Allow You to Build a Custom Format

Placeholder	Function
0	Displays a digit if one exists in the position; otherwise, displays a zero. You can use the 0 placeholder to display leading zeros for whole numbers and trailing zeros for decimals.
#	Displays a digit if one exists in the position; otherwise, displays a blank space.
$	Displays a dollar sign in the position.
. % ,	Displays a decimal point, percent sign, or comma at the indicated position.
/	Separates the day, month, and year to format date values.
M	Used as a month placeholder: **m** displays 1, **mm** displays 01, **mmm** displays Jan, **mmmm** displays January.
D	Used as a day placeholder: **d** displays 1, **dd** displays 01, **ddd** displays Mon, **dddd** displays Monday.
Y	Used as a year placeholder: **yy** displays 95, **yyyy** displays 1995.
:	Separates hours and minutes.
h, n, s	Used as time placeholders for **h** hours, **n** minutes, and **s** seconds.
AM/PM	Displays time in 12-hour format, with AM or PM appended.
@	Indicates that a character is required in the position in a text or memo field.
&	Indicates that a character is optional.
>	Changes all the text characters to uppercase.
<	Changes all the text characters to lowercase.

To create a custom display format, follow these steps while in Design view of a form:

1. Select the desired field.
2. Click the Format text box in the Field Properties pane.
3. Type the desired format, using the placeholders listed in Table 14.1.

Field names, as a general rule, should be short and should not contain spaces. You can, however, assign to the field a Caption property that is descriptive of the field's contents. Access displays the Caption property as the field label on forms and reports. For example, you can assign "Fax Number" to the Caption property for a field named FaxNum. The Caption property is discussed in more detail later in this hour.

Task: Working with the `Format` Property

The `Format` property affects the appearance of text. This task lets you practice working with the `Format` property:

1. Set the `Format` property of the `ContactDate` field you created earlier in this hour to **Medium Date**.

2. Switch to Datasheet view and enter some dates in different formats, such as **07/08/05** and **July 8, 2005**.

3. Notice that no matter how you enter the dates, as soon as you tab away from the field, they appear in the format `dd-mmm-yy`, as `08-Jul-05`.

The `Caption` Property: Providing Alternatives to the Field Name

The text you place in the `Caption` property becomes the caption for fields in Datasheet view. Access also uses the contents of the `Caption` property as the caption for the attached label it adds to data-bound controls when you add them to forms and reports. The `Caption` property becomes important whenever you name fields without spaces. Whatever is in the `Caption` property overrides the field name for use in Datasheet view, on forms, and on reports.

> **NEW TERM** A *data-bound control* is a control that is bound to a field in a table or query. The term *attached label* refers to the label that is attached to a data-bound control.

> It's important to set the `Caption` property for fields *before* you build any forms or reports that use those fields. When you produce a form or report, Access looks at the current caption. Access doesn't modify captions for a field on existing forms and reports, so if you add or modify the caption at a later time, the change won't be made.

To set the `Caption` property (from Design view), follow these steps:

1. Select the desired field name from the top pane of the Design view window.

2. Click the `Caption` text box in the Field Properties pane.

3. Type the desired caption.

14

The `Default Value` Property: Saving Data-Entry Time

Assigning a `Default Value` property to a field causes a specified value to be filled in for the field in new records. Setting a commonly used value as the `Default Value` property facilitates the data entry process. When you add data, you can accept the default entry or replace it with another value. For example, if most of your customers are in California, you can assign a default value of `CA`. When you're doing data entry, if the customer is in California, you do not need to change the value for the state. If the customer is in another state, you simply replace `CA` with the appropriate state value.

To set a `Default Value` property (from Design view), follow these steps:

1. Select the desired field from the top pane of the Design view window.

2. Click the `Default Value` property text box in the Field Properties pane.

3. Type the desired value.

> A `Default Value` property can be constant, such as CA for California, or a function that returns a value, such as `Date()`, which displays the current date.

The data users enter in tables must be accurate if the database is to be valuable to you or your organization. You can use the `Validation Rule` property to add data entry rules to the fields in tables. The `Validation Rule` property is covered in more detail later in the hour.

Task: Working with the `Default Value` Property

To Do

The `Default Value` property is a big time-saver. This task gives you practice working with the `Default Value` property:

1. Enter the following default values for the `State`, `ContactDate`, and `CreditLimit` fields you created earlier:

   ```
   State:  CA

   ContactDate:  =Date()

   CreditLimit: 1000
   ```

2. Switch to Datasheet view and add a new record.

3. Notice that default values appear for the `State`, `ContactDate`, and `CreditLimit` fields. You can override these defaults, if you want.

Date() is a built-in Visual Basic for Applications (VBA) function that returns the current date and time. When it is used as a default value for a field, Access enters the current date into the field when the user adds a new row to the table.

The Validation Rule and Validation Text Properties: Controlling What the User Enters in a Field

The Default Value property suggests a value to the user, but the Validation Rule property actually limits what the user can place in the field. Validation rules can't be violated; the database engine strictly enforces them. As with the Default Value property, this property can contain either text or a valid Access expression, but you cannot include user-defined functions in the Validation Rule property. You also can't include references to forms, queries, or tables in the Validation Rule property.

You can use operators to compare two values; the less than (<) and greater than (>) symbols are examples of comparison operators. And, Or, Is, Not, Between, and Like are called *logical operators*. Table 14.2 provides a few examples of validation rules.

TABLE 14.2   Examples of Validation Rules

Validation Rule	Validation Text Examples
>0	Please enter a valid Employee ID Number.
"H" or "S" or "Q"	Only H or S or Q codes will be accepted.
Between Date()-365 and Date()+365	Date cannot be later than one year ago today or more than one year from today.
>0 or is Null	Enter a valid ID number or leave blank if not approved.
Between 0 and 9 or is Null	Rating range is 0 through 9 or is blank.
>Date()	Date must be after today.

Whereas the Validation Rule property limits what the user can enter into the table, the Validation Text property provides the error message that appears when the user violates the validation rule.

If you set the Validation Rule property but do not set the Validation Text property, Access automatically displays a standard error message whenever the user violates the validation rule. To display a custom message, you must enter message text in the Validation Text property.

14

To establish a field-level validation rule (from Design view), follow these steps:

1. Select the desired field name from the top pane of the Design view window.

2. Click the `Validation Rule` property text box in the Field Properties pane.

3. Type the desired validation rule (for example, **Between 0 and 120**).

To add validation text, follow these steps:

1. Click the `Validation Text` property text box in the Field Properties pane.

2. Type the desired text (for example, **Age Must Be Between 0 and 120**).

You can require users of a database to enter a valid value in selected fields when editing or adding records. For example, you can require a user to enter a date for each record in an `Invoice` table.

Task: Working with the `Validation Rule` Property

Add the following validation rules to the `State`, `ContactDate`, and `CreditLimit` fields in a table:

```
State:  In (CA, AZ, NY, MA, UT)

ContactDate:  <= Date()

CreditLimit: Between 0 And 5000
```

Access will place quotation marks around the state abbreviations as soon as you tab away from the property.

Next you need to switch to Datasheet view and test the validation rules that you just created:

1. Switch to Datasheet view. If the table already contains data, when you save your changes, the message shown in Figure 14.2 appears.

> In this example, the expression <= Date() is used to limit the value entered into the field to a date that is on or before the current date. Because the Date() expression always returns the current date, the validation rule applies whether the user is adding a new row or modifying an existing row.

If you select Yes, Access tries to validate all existing data, using the new rules. If it finds any errors, Access notifies you that errors occurred, but it does not tell you which are the offending records (see Figure 14.3). You have to build a query to find

▼ all the records that violate the new rules. If you select No, Access doesn't try to
validate your existing data and does not warn you of any problems.

FIGURE 14.2

*A message box that
asks whether you want
to validate existing
data.*

FIGURE 14.3

*A warning that all data
did not validate suc-
cessfully.*

2. Try to enter an invalid state in the State field; you should see the message box displayed in Figure 14.4. As you can see, this isn't a user-friendly message, which is
why you should create a custom message by using the Validation Text property.

FIGURE 14.4

*The message displayed
when a validation rule
is violated and no vali-
dation text has been
entered.*

▲

The Required Property: Making the User Enter a Value

The Required property is very important: It determines whether you require a user to
enter a value in a field. This property is useful for foreign key fields, when you want to
make sure the user enters data into the field. It's also useful for any field containing
information that's needed for business reasons (company name, for example).

> **NEW TERM** A *foreign key field* is a field that is looked up in another table.
> For example, in the case of a Customers table and an Orders
> table, both might contain a CustomerID field. In the Customers table, the
> CustomerID field is the primary key field. In the Orders table, the CustomerID
> field is the foreign key field because its value is looked up in the Customers
> table.

14

To designate a field as required (from Design view), follow these steps:

1. Select the desired field.

2. Click the `Required` property text box in the Field Properties pane.

3. Type **Yes**.

Task: Working with the `Required` Property

The best way to learn about the `Required` property is to practice using it. The steps that follow provide an example:

1. Set the `Required` property of the `CompanyName` and `PhoneNumber` fields created earlier in this hour to `Yes`.

2. Switch to Datasheet view and try to add a new record, leaving the `CompanyName` and `PhoneNumber` fields blank. Make sure you enter a value for at least one of the other fields in the record. When you try to move off the record, the error message shown in Figure 14.5 appears.

FIGURE 14.5

A message that appears when you leave blank a field that has the Required *property set to* Yes.

The `Allow Zero Length` Property: Accommodating for Situations with Nonexistent Data

You can use the `Allow Zero Length` property to allow a string of no characters. You enter a zero-length string by typing a pair of quotation marks with no space between them (`""`). You use the `Allow Zero Length` property to indicate that you know there is no value for a field.

To allow a zero-length field (from Design view), follow these steps:

1. Select the desired field.

2. Click the `Allow Zero Length` property text box in the Field Properties pane.

3. Select Yes from the drop-down list box.

Task: Working with the `Allow Zero Length` Property

It's easiest to get to know the `Allow Zero Length` property by actually seeing it in action. Let's take a look:

1. Add a new field called `ContactName`.
2. Set the `ContactName` field's `Required` property to `Yes`.
3. Try to add a new record and enter a pair of quotation marks (`""`) in the `ContactName` field. You should not get an error message because in Access 2003, the `Allow Zero Length` property defaults to `Yes`. The zero-length string should appear blank when you move off the field.
4. Return to the Design view of the table.
5. Change the setting for the `Allow Zero Length` property to `No`. Go back to Datasheet view and once again enter a pair of quotation marks in the `ContactName` field. This time you should not be successful—you should get the error message shown in Figure 14.6.

FIGURE 14.6

The result of entering `""` when the `Allow Zero Length` property is set to `No`.

In versions of Access prior to Access 2002, the default setting for the `Allow Zero Length` property is `No`. In Access 2002 and Access 2003, Microsoft has changed this default setting to `Yes`. You need to pay close attention to this new default behavior, especially if you're accustomed to working with prior releases of Access or if you must import Access 2000 databases into Access 2003.

If you want to cancel changes to the current field, you can press Esc once. To abandon all changes to a record, you press Esc twice.

The `Input Mask` Property: Determining What Data Goes into a Field

NEW TERM An *input mask* controls data the user enters into a field. For instance, a short date input mask appears as `--/--/----` when the field is active. You can

14

then simply type 07042005 to display or print 7/4/2005. Based on the input mask, you can ensure that the user enters only valid characters into the field.

Table 14.3 lists some of the placeholders that you can use in character strings for input masks in fields of the Text data type.

TABLE 14.3   Placeholders That Can Be Included in an Input Mask

Placeholder	Description
0	A number (0–9) is required.
9	A number (0–9) is optional.
#	A number (0–9), a space, or a plus or minus sign is optional; a space is used if no number is entered.
L	A letter (A–Z) is required.
?	A letter (A–Z) is not required; a space is used if no letter is entered.
A	A letter (A–Z) or number (0–9) is required.
a	A letter (A–Z) or number (0–9) is optional.
&	Any character or space is required.
C	Any character or space is optional.
>	Any characters to the right are converted to uppercase.
<	All the text characters to the right are changed to lowercase.

To create an input mask (from Design view), follow these steps:

1. Select the desired field.
2. Click the Input Mask property text box.
3. Type the desired format, using the placeholders listed in Table 14.3.

Access includes an Input Mask Wizard that appears when you place the cursor in the Input Mask text box and click the ellipsis (…) button to the right of the text box. The wizard, shown in Figure 14.7, provides common input mask formats from which to choose. To start the Input Mask Wizard, you click the button to the right of the Input Mask property.

The Input Mask Wizard is available only if you selected the Additional Wizards component during Access setup. If you did not select this component and then you try to open the Input Mask Wizard, Access prompts you to install the option on-the-fly the first time you use it.

FIGURE 14.7

*Entering an input mask
with the Input Mask
Wizard.*

For example, the input mask 000-00-0000;;_ (converted to 000\-00\-0000;;_ as soon as you tab away from the property) forces the entry of a valid Social Security number. Everything that precedes the first semicolon designates the actual mask. The zeros force the entry of the digits 0 through 9. The dashes are literals that appear within the control as the user enters data. The character you enter between the first and second semicolon determines whether literal characters (the dashes, in this case) are stored in the field. If you enter a 0 in this position, literal characters are stored in the field; if you enter 1 or leave this position blank, the literal characters aren't stored. The final position (after the second semicolon) indicates what character is displayed to denote the space where the user types the next character (in this case, the underscore).

Here's a more detailed example: In the mask \(999") "000\-0000;;_, the first back-slash causes the character that follows it (the open parenthesis) to be displayed as a literal. The three nines allow the user to enter optional numbers or spaces. Access displays the close parenthesis and space within the quotation marks as literals. The first three zeros require values 0 through 9. The dash that follows the next backslash is displayed as a literal. Four additional numbers are then required. The two semicolons have nothing between them, so the literal characters aren't stored in the field. The second semicolon is followed by an underscore, so an underscore is displayed to indicate the space where the user types the next character. This sounds pretty complicated, but here's how it works. The user types **8054857632**. What appears is (805)485-7632. What is actually stored is 8054857632. Because the input mask contains three 9s for the area code, the area code is not required. The remaining characters are all required numbers.

Task: Working with the Input Mask Property

Use the Input Mask Wizard to add a mask for the PhoneNumber field, which should be set up as a Text field. This involves activating the Input Mask Wizard after you have selected the PhoneNumber field.

1. Click anywhere in the PhoneNumber field and then click the Input Mask property.
2. Click the ellipsis (...) to the right of the Input Mask property.

▼ To Do

14

▼   3. Select Phone Number from the list of available masks and choose not to store the literal characters in the field when the wizard asks How Do You Want to Store the Data?

4. Switch to Datasheet view and enter a phone number. Notice how the cursor skips over the literal characters. Try leaving the area code blank; Access should allow you to do this.

5. Try to enter a letter in any position. Access should prohibit you from doing this.

6. Try to leave any character from the seven-digit phone number blank. Access shouldn't let you do this, either.

When you use an input mask, the user is always in Overtype mode. This behavior is a feature of the product and can't be altered.

▲

The Lookup Wizard

You can select Lookup Wizard as a field's data type. The Lookup Wizard guides you through the steps to create a list of values from which you can choose. You can select the values from a table or a query, or you can create a list of your own values.

To use the Lookup Wizard (from Design View), follow these steps:

1. Select the desired field.

2. Choose Lookup Wizard as the data type (see Figure 14.8).

FIGURE 14.8

Activating the Lookup Wizard.

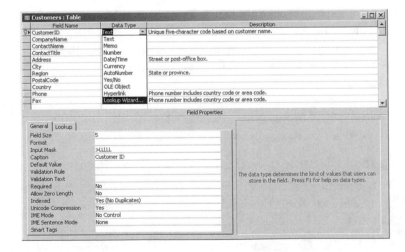

3. Select the desired source of the values and then click Next.

4. Select the table or query to provide the values and then click Next.

5. Double-click the field(s) that contains the desired values and then click Next.

6. Drag the Lookup column to the desired width and then click Next.

7. Type a name for the Lookup column and then click Finish.

There are some things you should be aware of when working with the Lookup Wizard. When you create a form based on a table with a Lookup field, the form automatically displays a combo box (or another designated control) for that field. Also, as you add records to the table that is the source for the lookup values, the new information appears in the list.

Working with Table Properties

In addition to field properties, you can specify properties that apply to a table as a whole. To access the table properties, you click the Properties button on the toolbar while in a table's Design view. The available table properties are shown in Figure 14.9.

FIGURE 14.9

Viewing the available table properties.

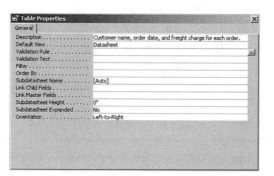

The Description property is used mainly for documentation purposes. The Default View property designates the view in which the table appears when the user first opens it. The Validation Rule property specifies validations that must occur at a record level instead of a field level. For example, credit limits might differ depending on what state a customer is in. In that case, what's entered in one field depends on the value in another field. If you enter a table-level validation rule, it doesn't matter in what order the user

14

enters the data. A table-level validation rule ensures that Access enforces the proper dependency between fields. The validation rule might look something like this:

```
[State] In ("CA","NY") And [CreditLimit]<=2500 Or _
    [State] In ("MA","AZ") And [CreditLimit]<=3500 Or _
    [State] Not In ("CA", "NY", "MA", "AZ")
```

This validation rule requires a credit limit of $2,500 or less for applicants in California and New York and a limit of $3,500 or less for applicants in Massachusetts and Arizona, but it doesn't specify a credit limit for residents of any other states. Table-level validation rules can't be in conflict with field-level validation rules. If they are in conflict, you will not be able to enter data into the table.

The Validation Text property determines what message appears when a user violates the validation rule. If this property is left blank, a default message appears.

The Filter property is used to indicate a subset of records that appears in a datasheet, form, or query. The Order By property is used to specify a default order for the records. The Filter and Order By properties aren't generally applied as properties of a table.

The Subdatasheet Name property identifies the name of a table that is used as a drill-down. If this property is set to [Auto], Access automatically detects the drill-down table, based on relationships established in the database. The Link Child Fields and Link Master Fields properties are implemented to designate the fields that are used to link the current table with the table specified in the Subdatasheet Name property. These properties should be left blank when you select [Auto] for the Subdatasheet Name. You use the Subdatasheet Height property to specify the maximum height of the sub-datasheet and the Subdatasheet Expanded property to designate whether Access automatically displays the subdatasheet in an expanded state.

The Orientation property determines the layout direction for a table when it is displayed. The default setting for USA English is Left-to-Right. The Orientation property is language specific, and the Right-to-Left setting is available only if you are using a language version of Microsoft Access that supports right-to-left language displays. Arabic and Hebrew are examples of right-to-left languages. You must run a 32-bit Microsoft operating system that offers right-to-left support, such as the Arabic version of Windows 2000, to take advantage of this feature in Access. By installing the Microsoft Office Multilanguage Pack and the Microsoft Office Proofing Tools for a specific language, and by enabling the specific right-to-left language under the Microsoft Office language settings, you can also turn on right-to-left support.

Using Indexes to Improve Performance

Indexes improve performance when you're searching, sorting, or grouping on a field or fields. Primary key indexes are used to maintain unique values for records. For example, you can create a single-field index that does not allow a duplicate order number or a multiple-field index that does not allow records with the same first and last names.

To create an index based on a single field (from Design view), follow these steps:

1. Select the field to be indexed.
2. Click the Indexed row of the Field Properties pane.
3. Select the desired index type—No, Yes (Duplicates OK), or Yes (No Duplicates). The Yes (Duplicates OK) option means that you are creating an index and that you will allow duplicates within that field. The Yes (No Duplicates) option means that you are creating an index and you will *not* allow duplicate values within the index. If the index is based on company name and you select Yes (Duplicates OK), you can enter two companies with the same name. If you select Yes (No Duplicates), you cannot enter two companies with the same name.

To create an index based on multiple fields (from Design view), follow these steps:

1. Choose View|Indexes. The Indexes window appears.
2. Type the index name in the Index Name column.
3. From the Field Name column, select the desired fields to include in the index.
4. Select the desired index properties (see Figure 14.10).
5. Click OK to close the Indexes dialog box.

FIGURE 14.10

Creating a multifield index.

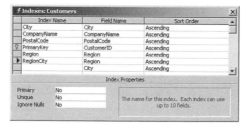

Selecting Yes (No Duplicates) causes duplicate values to not be permitted in the field that is being indexed.

14

Task: Combining Your Skills

It's time to combine your skills. This task takes you through the process of creating a new database and then adding a table to it. It walks you through setting several properties of the table and even adding data to it:

1. Not using a wizard, create a new database called MYDB.

2. Create a new table, called tblEmployees, in Design view. The tblEmployees table should have the structure shown in Table 14.4.

TABLE 14.4   The Structure of the tblEmployees Table

Field Name	Data Type	Size	Description
EmpID	Autonumber	Long Integer	Unique number given each record
LastName	Text	25	Last name of employee
FirstName	Text	15	First name of employee
Address	Text	20	Address of employee
City	Text	15	City of employee
State	Text	2	State of employee
Zip	Text	5	Zip code of employee
Phone	Text	12	Employee phone
DateofHire	Date	N/A	Date of hire
HourlyRate	Currency	N/A	Hourly rate
Pension	Yes/No	N/A	Does employee have a company pension?

3. Set a primary key on the EmpID field.

4. Save the table as tblEmployees.

5. Add to the new table the records shown in Table 14.5.

TABLE 14.5   Records for the tblEmployees Table

Last Name	First Name	Address	City	State	Zip	Phone	Date of Hire	Hourly Rate	Pension
Forman	Shell	123 Main St.	York	PA	17401	717-755-8976	1/1/1995	$125.00	Yes
Terry	Sue	478 Creek View Dr.	Camp Hill	PA	17011	717-737-9087	6/15/2000	$180.00	No

6. Add appropriate captions for the EmpID, LastName, FirstName, DateofHire, and HourlyRate fields.

▼ 7. Format the HourlyRate field as Currency. Provide a default value of $125.00. Add a validation rule to ensure that HourlyRate is between 0 and $250.00. Add appropriate validation text.

8. Format the DateofHire field as Medium Date. Provide a default value of today's date. Add a validation rule to ensure that DateofHire is less than or equal to today's date. Add appropriate validation text.

9. Use the Input Mask Wizard to place a phone number input mask on the Phone field. Depending on the input mask that you select, you can provide a different look and feel for the phone number.

10. Create separate indexes for the FirstName, City, State, HourlyRate, and DateofHire fields.

11. Create a compound index that includes the LastName and FirstName fields. Call
▲ the index FullName.

Summary

Field properties and table properties allow you to refine the behavior of fields in tables. Using field and table properties, you can control not only what data users enter into a field but also how that data appears in Datasheet view and on forms and reports. The Lookup Wizard makes it very easy for you to work with related tables within databases. Finally, the proper use of indexes can greatly improve the performance of the applications that you build. After this hour, you should be ready to use all these powerful features of tables.

Q&A

Q Explain the use of the Caption property.

A Access uses the contents of the Caption property as the column heading in Datasheet view and as the attached label when you add data-bound controls to forms and reports.

Q Explain the benefits of indexes.

A Indexes improve performance when you're searching, sorting, or grouping on a field or fields.

Q Explain the difference between the Format property and the Input Mask property.

A Whereas the Format property determines how data displays, the Input Mask property determines what data the user can enter in a field.

14

Q **Explain the difference between field properties and table properties.**

A Field properties apply to a single field, whereas table properties apply to a table as a whole. By using table properties, for instance, you can compare the contents of one field to the contents of another field.

Workshop

The Workshop includes quiz questions that are designed to help you test your understanding of the material covered and activities to help put what you've learned to practice. You can find the answers to the questions in the section immediately following the quiz.

Quiz

1. The `Field Size` property applies only to `Text` fields (True/False).

2. After you enter a `Validation Rule` property, you must enter the `Validation Text` property (True/False).

3. What property controls how data appears in Datasheet view, on forms, and in reports?

4. What two data types does the Input Mask Wizard apply to?

5. You can base indexes on multiple fields (True/False).

Quiz Answers

1. False. The `Field Size` property applies to `Text` and `Number` fields.

2. False. If you do not enter a `Validation Text` property, Access displays a default message.

3. The `Format` property.

4. `Text` and `Date`.

5. True.

Activities

Build a table. Practice adding field properties and table properties. Use the Lookup Wizard to add some Lookups from one table to another. Finally, add some necessary indexes to the table.

Hour 15

Power Query Techniques

You learned the basics of query design in Hour 10, "Creating Queries," but Access has a wealth of other query capabilities. In addition to the relatively simple Select queries covered in Hour 10, you can create queries that accomplish the following tasks:

- Include calculated fields
- Filter information
- Include parameters that vary at runtime
- Insert, update, and delete table data
- Aggregate table data

This hour covers these topics and some of the more advanced aspects of query design.

Adding Calculated Fields to Select Queries

One of the rules of data normalization is that you should not include the results of calculations in a database. You can output the results of calculations by building those calculations into queries, and you can display the results of the calculations on forms and reports by making the query the foundation for a form or report. You can also add controls to forms and reports that contain the calculations you need. In certain cases, this can improve performance.

You can include in the columns of a query result the result of any valid expression, including the result of a user-defined function. This makes queries extremely powerful. For example, you could enter the following expression:

```
Left([FirstName],1) & "." & Left([LastName],1) & "."
```

This expression would give you the first character of the first name followed by a period, the first character of the last name, and another period. An even simpler expression would be this one:

```
[UnitPrice]*[Quantity]
```

NEW TERM This calculation would simply multiply the UnitPrice field by the Quantity field. In both cases, Access would automatically name the resulting expression. For example, Figure 15.1 shows the calculation that results from concatenating the first and last initials of the employee names in the Employees table of the Northwind database. Notice that in the figure, Access gives the expression a name (often referred to as an *alias*). To give the expression a name, such as Initials, you must enter it as follows:

```
Initials: Left([FirstName],1) & "." & Left([LastName],1) & "."
```

The text preceding the colon is the name of the expression—in this case, Initials. If you don't explicitly give an expression a name, the name defaults to Expr1.

FIGURE 15.1

The result of the expression `Initials:Left([First Name],1) & "." & Left([LastName],1) & "."` *in a query.*

Task: Creating a Calculation Field

Follow these steps to add a calculation that shows unit price multiplied by quantity:

1. Scroll to the right on the query grid until you can see a blank column.

2. Click in the Field row for the new column.

3. Type **TotalPrice:UnitPrice*Quantity**. If you want to see more easily what you're typing, press Shift+F2 to zoom. The Zoom dialog box, shown in Figure 15.2, appears.

FIGURE 15.2

Expanding the field with the Zoom function (Shift+F2).

4. Click OK to close the Zoom dialog box. Access supplies a space after the colon and the square brackets around the field names if you omit them.

5. Run the query. The total sales amount should appear in the far-right column of the query output. The query output should look like that shown in Figure 15.3.

FIGURE 15.3

The result of the total price calculation.

Product	Unit Price	Quantity	TotalPrice
Queso Cabrales	$14.00	12	$168.00
Singaporean Hokkien Fried Mee	$9.80	10	$98.00
Mozzarella di Giovanni	$34.80	5	$174.00
Tofu	$18.60	9	$167.40
Manjimup Dried Apples	$42.40	40	$1,696.00
Jack's New England Clam Chowder	$7.70	10	$77.00
Manjimup Dried Apples	$42.40	35	$1,484.00
Louisiana Fiery Hot Pepper Sauce	$16.80	15	$252.00
Gustaf's Knäckebröd	$16.80	6	$100.80
Ravioli Angelo	$15.60	15	$234.00
Louisiana Fiery Hot Pepper Sauce	$16.80	20	$336.00
Sir Rodney's Marmalade	$64.80	40	$2,592.00
Geitost	$2.00	25	$50.00
Camembert Pierrot	$27.20	40	$1,088.00
Gorgonzola Telino	$10.00	20	$200.00
Chartreuse verte	$14.40	42	$604.80
Maxilaku	$16.00	40	$640.00
Guaraná Fantástica	$3.60	15	$54.00
Pâté chinois	$19.20	21	$403.20
Longlife Tofu	$8.00	21	$168.00
Chang	$15.20	20	$304.00

Record: 1 of 2155

Result of the TotalPrice calculation

You can enter any valid expression in the Field row of a query grid. Notice that Access automatically surrounds field names included in an expression with square brackets. This happens automatically unless a field name has spaces. If a field name includes any spaces, you must enclose the field name in brackets; otherwise, the query won't run properly. This is just one of the many reasons you should *not* include spaces in field and table names.

Getting Help from the Expression Builder

The Expression Builder is a helpful tool for building expressions in queries, as well as in many other situations in Access. To invoke the Expression Builder, you click in the Field cell of the query grid and then click Build on the toolbar. The Expression Builder appears (see Figure 15.4). Notice that Access divides the Expression Builder into three columns. The first column shows the objects in the database. After you select an element in the left column, you can select the elements you want to paste from the middle and right columns.

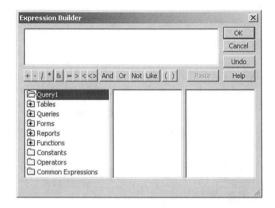

The example in Figure 15.5 shows functions selected in the left column. Under Functions, Access lists both user-defined functions and Built-in Functions; here, I have expanded Functions and selected Built-In Functions. In the center column, I have selected Date/Time. After I selected Date/Time, all the built-in date and time functions appeared in the right column. If you double-click a particular function—in this case, the DatePart function—Access places the function and its parameters in the text box at the top of the Expression Builder window. Notice that the DatePart function has four parameters: interval, date, firstweekday, and firstweek. If you know what needs to go into each of these parameters, you can simply replace the parameter placeholders with your own values. If you need more information, you can invoke Help on the selected function and learn more about the required parameters. In Figure 15.6, I have filled in two parameters: the interval and the name of the field I want Access to evaluate. After I click OK, Access places the expression in the Field cell of the query.

FIGURE 15.5

The Expression Builder with the DatePart *function selected and pasted in the expression box.*

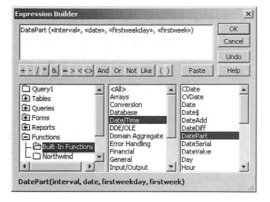

FIGURE 15.6

The Expression Builder, after two parameters are filled in.

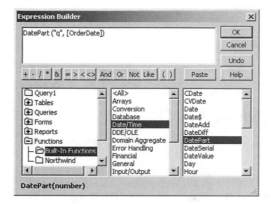

Applying Advanced Filters

Using advanced filters, you can further refine the data that appears in a query result. Here are the steps involved:

1. Open (in Datasheet view) the query or table whose data you want to filter.

2. Select Records|Filter|Advanced Filter/Sort. The filter design grid appears.

3. Add to the design grid the fields on which you want to filter.

4. For each field on the grid, enter the value or expression that you want to use as a filter in the Criteria cell for the fields you have included.

5. Click Apply Filter or select Filter|Apply Filter/Sort. Access applies the filter that you created.

15

Creating and Running Parameter Queries

You might not always know the parameters for the query output when you're designing a query—and your application's users also might not know the parameters. *Parameter queries* let you specify specific criteria at runtime so that you don't have to modify the query each time you want to change the criteria.

For example, imagine you have a query, like the one shown in Figure 15.7, for which you want users to specify the date range they want to view each time they run the query. You have entered the following clause as the criterion for the `OrderDate` field:

```
Between [Enter Starting Date] And [Enter Ending Date]
```

IGURE 15.7

A Parameter query that prompts for a starting date and an ending date.

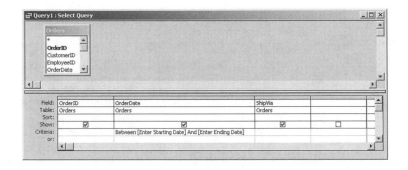

This criterion causes two dialog boxes to appear when the user runs the query. The first one, shown in Figure 15.8, prompts the user with the text in the first set of brackets. Access substitutes the text the user types for the bracketed text. A second dialog box appears, prompting the user for whatever is in the second set of brackets. Access uses the user's responses as criteria for the query.

FIGURE 15.8

A dialog box that appears when a Parameter query is run.

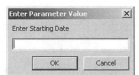

Task: Building a Parameter Query

▼ To Do

Let's take a look at the process of building a parameter query. In this task, you're going to add a parameter to the query `qryCustomerOrderSummary` so that you can view only `TotalPrice` summaries within a specific range.

1. Go to the criteria for `TotalPrice` and type **Between [Please Enter Starting Value] and [Please Enter Ending Value]**. This allows you to view all the

▼   records for which the total price is within a specific range. Access replaces the
         bracketed text with actual values when you run the query.

2. Click OK and run the query. Access prompts you to enter both a starting and an
   ending value.

To make sure Access understands what type of data the user should place in these para-
meters, you must define the parameters. You do this by selecting Query|Parameters to
open the Query Parameters dialog box. Another way to display the Query Parameters
dialog box is to right-click a gray area in the top half of the query grid and then select
Parameters from the context menu.

You must enter the text that appears within the brackets for each parameter in the
Parameter field of the Query Parameters dialog box. You must define the type of data in
the brackets in the Data Type column. Figure 15.9 shows an example of a completed
Query Parameters dialog box.

FIGURE 15.9

*A completed Query
Parameters dialog box
that declares two date
parameters.*

You can easily create parameters for as many fields as you want. You add additional
parameters just as you would add more criteria. For example, the query shown in Figure
15.10 contains parameters for the Title, HireDate, and City fields in the Employees
table from the Northwind database. Notice that all the criteria are on one line of the
query grid, which means that all the parameters entered must be satisfied in order for the
records to appear in the output. The criterion for the title is [Please Enter a Title].
This means that the records in the result must match the title the user enters when he or
she runs the query. The criterion for the HireDate field is >=[Please Enter a Hire
Date]. Only records with a hire date on or after the hire date the user enters when he or
she runs the query appear in the output. Finally, the criterion for the City field is
[Please Enter a City]. This means that only records with City containing the value
the user enters when he or she runs the query will appear in the output.

▼   The criteria for a query can also be the result of a function.

FIGURE 15.10

The Query Design window, showing a query with parameters for three fields.

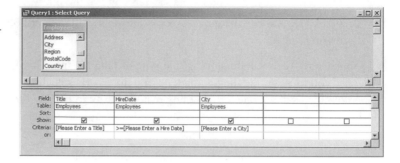

Parameter queries offer significant flexibility because they allow the user to enter specific criteria at runtime. What you type in the Query Parameters dialog box must exactly match what you type within the brackets; otherwise, Access prompts the user with additional dialog boxes.

You can add as many parameters as you like to a query, but the user might become bothered if Access presents too many dialog boxes. Instead, you should build a custom form that feeds the Parameter query.

Task: Building a Parameter Query That Groups by Client

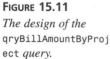

In this task, you build a query based on the `tblTimeCardHours` table, which is available in the `Chap15.mdb` sample database. This query gives you the total billing amount, by project, for a specific date range. Figure 15.11 shows the query's design. Notice that this query is a Totals query (also called an *aggregate function*) that groups results by project and totals the billable hours multiplied by the billing rate. Here's how it works:

FIGURE 15.11

The design of the `qryBillAmountByProject` *query.*

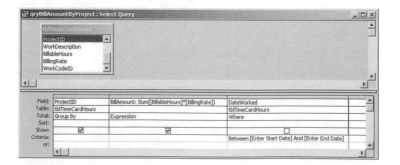

1. Enter the following expression:

   ```
   BillAmount: Sum([BillableHours]*[BillingRate])
   ```

2. Add the `Where` clause, using the `DateWorked` field as the `Where` clause for the query; here's the criterion for the `Where` clause:

   ```
   Between [Enter Start Date] And [Enter End Date]
   ```

   The example uses the Query Parameters dialog box to declare the two parameters of the criteria (see Figure 15.12).

FIGURE 15.12

The Parameters window for `qryBillAmountBy Project`.

3. Save this query as `qryBillAmountByProject`.

The second query is based on `tblClients`, `tblProjects`, and `tblTimeCardHours`. This query gives you the total billing amount, by client, for a specific date range. The query's design is shown in Figure 15.13. This query is an aggregate function that groups results by the company name from the `tblClients` table and totals by using the following expression:

```
BillAmount: Sum([BillableHours]*[BillingRate])
```

FIGURE 15.13

The design of the `qryBillAmountByClient` *query.*

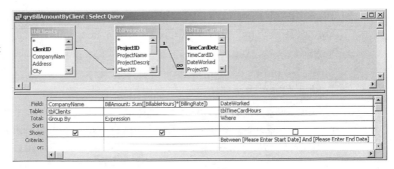

▼ As with the first query, `qryBillAmountByProject`, this query uses the `DateWorked` field
as the `Where` clause for the query, and it defines the parameters in the Query Parameters
▲ dialog box. Save this query as `qryBillAmountByClient`.

Creating and Running Action Queries

With Action queries, you can easily modify data without writing any code. In fact, using
Action queries is often a more efficient method of modifying data than using code. Four
types of Action queries are available: Update, Delete, Append, and Make Table. You use
Update queries to modify data in a table, Delete queries to remove records from a table,
Append queries to add records to an existing table, and Make Table queries to create an
entirely new table. The sections that follow explain these query types and their appropriate uses.

Creating and Running Update Queries

You use Update queries to modify all records or any records that meet specific criteria.
You can use an Update query to modify the data in one field or several fields (or even
tables) at one time. For example, you could create a query that increases the salary of
everyone in California by 10%. As mentioned previously, using Action queries, including
Update queries, is usually more efficient than performing the same task with Visual
Basic for Applications (VBA) code, so you can consider Update queries a respectable
way to modify table data.

To build an Update query, follow these steps:

1. In the Database window, Click Queries in the Objects list.

2. Double-click the Create Query in Design View icon. The Show Table dialog box
   appears.

3. In the Show Table dialog box, select the tables or queries that will participate in the
   Update query and click Add. Click Close when you're ready to continue.

4. To let Access know you're building an Update query, open the Query Type drop-
   down list on the toolbar and select Update Query. You can also choose Query|
   Update Query.

5. Add to the query fields that you will use for criteria or that Access will update as a
   result of the query. In Figure 15.14, `StateProvince` is included on the query grid
   because we will use it as a criterion for the update. `DefaultRate` is included
   because it's the field that Access will update.

FIGURE 15.14

An Update query that increases DefaultRate *for all clients in California.*

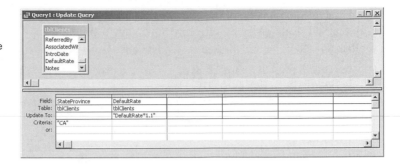

6. Add any further criteria, if you want. In Figure 15.14, the criterion for StateProvince is CA.

7. Add the appropriate Update expression. The example illustrated in Figure 15.14 increases DefaultRate by 10%.

8. Click Run on the toolbar. The message box shown in Figure 15.15 appears. Click Yes to continue. Access updates all records that meet the selected criteria.

FIGURE 15.15

The confirmation message you see when you run an Update query.

You should name Access Update queries with the prefix qupd. In fact, you should give each type of Action query a prefix indicating what type of query it is. This makes your application easier to maintain, makes your code more readable, and renders your code self-documenting. Table 15.1 lists all the commonly accepted prefixes for Action queries.

TABLE 15.1 Naming Prefixes for Action Queries

Type of Query	Prefix	Example
Update	qupd	qupdDefaultRate
Delete	qdel	qdelOldTimeCards
Append	qapp	qappArchiveTimeCards
Make Table	qmak	qmakTempSales

Access displays each type of Action query in the Database window with a distinctive icon.

Access stores all queries as Structured Query Language (SQL) statements. You can display the SQL for a query by selecting SQL View from the View drop-down list on the toolbar. The SQL behind an Access Update query looks like this:

```
UPDATE tblClients SET tblClients._
    DefaultRate = [DefaultRate]*1.1
     WHERE (((tblClients.StateProvince)="CA"));
```

You cannot reverse the actions taken by an Update query or by any Action queries. You must therefore exercise extreme caution when running any Action query.

It's important to remember that if you have turned on the Cascade Update Related Fields Referential Integrity setting and the Update query tries to modify a primary key field, Access updates the foreign key of each corresponding record in related tables. If you have not turned on the Cascade Update Related Fields setting and you have enforced referential integrity, the Update query doesn't allow you to modify the offending records.

Creating and Running Delete Queries

Rather than simply modify table data, Delete queries permanently remove from a table any records that meet specific criteria; they're often used to remove old records. You might want to use a Delete query to delete all orders from the previous year, for example.

To build a Delete query, follow these steps:

1. While in a query's Design view, select Delete Query from the Query Type drop-down list on the toolbar. Or, you can choose Query|Delete Query.

2. Add to the query grid the criteria you want. The query shown in Figure 15.16 deletes all time cards that are more than 365 days old.

3. Click Run on the toolbar. The message box shown in Figure 15.17 appears.

4. Click Yes to permanently remove the records from the table.

The SQL behind a Delete query looks like this:

```
DELETE tblTimeCards.DateEntered
    FROM tblTimeCards
    WHERE (((tblTimeCards.DateEntered)<Date()-365));
```

FIGURE 15.16

A Delete query that is used to delete all time cards entered more than a year ago.

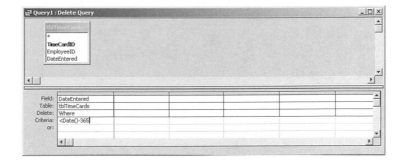

FIGURE 15.17

The Delete query confirmation message box.

Microsoft Access Enterprise Edition

⚠ **You are about to delete 7 row(s) from the specified table.**

Once you click Yes, you can't use the Undo command to reverse the changes.
Are you sure you want to delete the selected records?

[Yes]   [No]

It's often useful to view the results of an Action query before you actually affect the records included in the criteria. To view the records affected by an Action query, you click the Query View button on the toolbar before you select Run. All records that will be affected by the Action query appear in Datasheet view. If necessary, you can temporarily add key fields to the query to get more information about the records that are about to be affected.

Remember that if you turn on the Cascade Delete Related Records Referential Integrity setting, Access deletes all corresponding records in related tables. If you do not turn on the Cascade Delete Related Records setting and you do enforce referential integrity, the Delete query doesn't allow you to delete the offending records. If you want to delete the records on the "one" side of the relationship, first you need to delete all the related records on the "many" side.

Creating and Running Append Queries

You can use Append queries to add records to existing tables. You often perform this function during an archive process. First, you append to the history table the records that need to be archived by using an Append query. Next, you remove the records from the master table by using a Delete query.

To build an Append query, follow these steps:

1. While in Design view of a query, select Append Query from the Query Type drop-down list on the toolbar or choose Query|Append Query. The dialog box shown in Figure 15.18 appears.

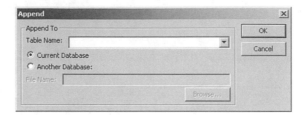

2. Select the table to which you want Access to append the data.

3. Drag all the fields whose data you want included in the second table to the query grid. If the field names in the two tables match, Access automatically matches the field names in the source table to the corresponding field names in the destination table. (See Figure 15.19.) If the field names in the two tables don't match, you need to explicitly designate which fields in the source table match which fields in the destination table.

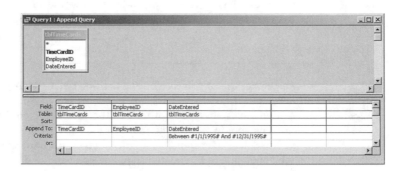

4. Enter any criteria in the query grid. Notice in Figure 15.19 that the example appends to the destination table all records with DateEntered in 1995.

5. To run the query, click Run on the toolbar. The message box shown in Figure 15.20 appears.

6. Click Yes to finish the process.

FIGURE 15.20

The Append Query confirmation message box.

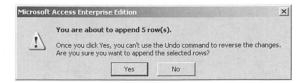

The SQL behind an Append query looks like this:

```
INSERT INTO tblTimeCardsArchive ( TimeCardID, EmployeeID, DateEntered )
    SELECT tblTimeCards.TimeCardID, tblTimeCards.EmployeeID,
    tblTimeCards.DateEntered
    FROM tblTimeCards
    WHERE (((tblTimeCards.DateEntered) Between #1/1/95# And #12/31/95#));
```

Append queries don't allow you to introduce any primary key violations. If you're appending any records that duplicate a primary key value, the message box shown in Figure 15.21 appears. If you go ahead with the append process, Access appends to the destination table only records without primary key violations.

FIGURE 15.21

The warning message you see when an Append query and conversion, primary key, lock, or validation rule violation occurs.

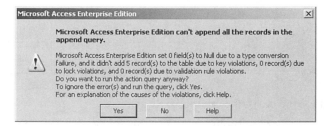

Creating and Running Make Table Queries

Whereas an Append query adds records to an existing table, a Make Table query creates a new table, which is often a temporary table used for intermediary processing. You might want to create a temporary table, for example, to freeze data while you are running a report. By building temporary tables and running a report from those tables, you make sure users can't modify the data underlying the report during the reporting process. Another common use of a Make Table query is to supply a subset of fields or records to another user.

To build a Make Table query, follow these steps:

1. While in the query's Design view, select Make Table Query from the Query Type drop-down list on the toolbar or choose Query|Make Table Query. The dialog box shown in Figure 15.22 appears.

FIGURE 15.22

The dialog box in which you enter a name for a new table and select which database to place it in.

2. Enter the name of the new table and click OK.

3. Move all the fields you want included in the new table to the query grid (see Figure 15.23). You will often include the result of an expression in the new table.

FIGURE 15.23

Adding an expression to a Make Table query.

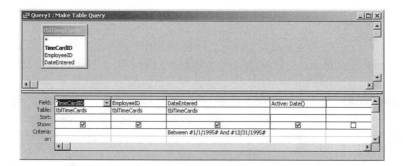

4. Add to the query the criteria you want.

5. Click Run on the toolbar to run the query. The message shown in Figure 15.24 appears.

FIGURE 15.24

The Make Table query confirmation message box.

6. Click Yes to finish the process.

If you try to run the same Make Table query more than one time, Access permanently deletes the table with the same name as the table you're creating. (See the warning message in Figure 15.25.)

FIGURE 15.25

The Make Table query warning message that is displayed when an existing table already has the same name as the table to be created.

The SQL for a Make Table query looks like this:

```
SELECT tblTimeCards.TimeCardID, tblTimeCards.EmployeeID,
    tblTimeCards.DateEntered, [DateEntered]+365 AS ArchiveDate
    INTO tblOldTimeCards
    FROM tblTimeCards
    WHERE (((tblTimeCards.TimeCardID) Between 1 And 10));
```

Using Aggregate Functions to Summarize Numeric Data

By using aggregate functions, you can easily summarize numeric data. You can use aggregate functions to calculate the sum, average, count, minimum, maximum, and other types of summary calculations for the data in a query result. These functions let you calculate one value for all the records in a query result or group the calculations as desired. For example, you could determine the total sales for every record in the query result, as shown in Figure 15.26, or you could output the total sales by country and city, as shown in Figure 15.27. You could also calculate the total, average, minimum, and maximum sales amounts for all customers in the United States. The possibilities are endless.

FIGURE 15.26

Total sales for every record in a query result.

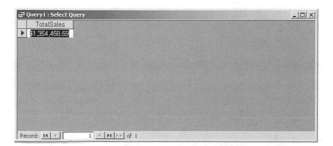

To create an aggregate function, follow these steps:

1. Add to the query grid the fields or expressions you want to summarize. It's important that you add the fields in the order in which you want them grouped. For example, Figure 15.28 shows a query grouped by country and then by city.

FIGURE **15.27**

Total sales by country and city.

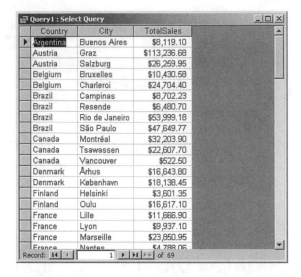

FIGURE **15.28**

Selecting from a drop-down list the type of calculation for the Total row.

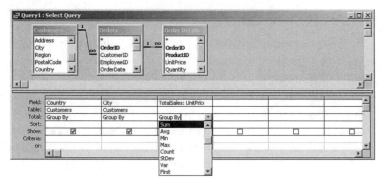

2. Click Totals on the toolbar or select View|Totals to add a Total row to the query. By default, each field in the query has Group By in the Total row.

3. Click the Total row on the design grid.

4. Open the combo box and choose the calculation you want, as shown in Figure 15.28.

5. Leave Group By in the Total row for any field you want to group by, as shown in Figure 15.28. Remember to place the fields in the order in which you want them grouped. For example, if you want the records grouped by country and then by contact title, you must place the Country field to the left of the ContactTitle field on the query grid. On the other hand, if you want records grouped by contact title

and then by country, you must place the ContactTitle field to the left of the Country field on the query grid.

6. Add to the query the criteria you want.

Figure 15.29 shows the design of a query that finds the total, minimum, maximum, and average sales by country and city; Figure 15.30 shows the results of running the query. As you can see, aggregate functions can give you valuable information.

FIGURE 15.29

A query that finds the total, minimum, maximum, and average sales by country and city.

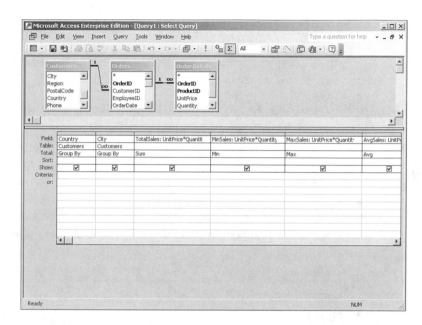

FIGURE 15.30

The result of running a query that has many aggregate functions.

Country	City	TotalSales	MinSales	MaxSales	AvgSales
Argentina	Buenos Aires	$8,119.10	$12.50	$1,215.00	$238.80
Austria	Graz	$113,236.68	$40.00	$6,360.00	$1,110.16
Austria	Salzburg	$26,259.95	$100.00	$10,540.00	$1,141.74
Belgium	Bruxelles	$10,430.58	$108.00	$2,200.00	$613.56
Belgium	Charleroi	$24,704.40	$14.00	$2,750.00	$633.45
Brazil	Campinas	$8,702.23	$38.60	$1,600.00	$458.01
Brazil	Resende	$6,480.70	$9.60	$1,552.00	$341.09
Brazil	Rio de Janeiro	$53,999.18	$29.20	$15,810.00	$650.59
Brazil	São Paulo	$47,649.77	$28.00	$8,432.00	$567.26
Canada	Montréal	$32,203.90	$112.00	$10,329.20	$1,006.37
Canada	Tsawassen	$22,607.70	$37.50	$2,958.00	$645.93
Canada	Vancouver	$522.50	$22.50	$154.00	$65.31
Denmark	Århus	$16,643.80	$65.00	$2,736.00	$536.90
Denmark	København	$18,138.45	$16.00	$10,540.00	$1,209.23
Finland	Helsinki	$3,601.35	$36.00	$550.00	$180.07
Finland	Oulu	$16,617.10	$22.35	$1,375.00	$449.11
France	Lille	$11,666.90	$15.50	$3,125.00	$729.18
France	Lyon	$9,937.10	$10.00	$1,972.00	$397.48
France	Marseille	$23,850.95	$37.50	$1,500.00	$542.07
France	Nantes	$4,788.06	$54.00	$1,733.06	$319.20
France	Paris	$2,423.35	$52.35	$1,317.50	$403.89

Record: 1 of 69

If you save this query and reopen it, you should see that Access has made some changes to its design. Access changes the Total cell for Sum to Expression, and it changes the Field cell to the following:

TotalSales: Sum([UnitPrice]*[Quantity])

If you look at the Total cell for Avg, you should see that Access changes it to Expression. Access changes the Field cell to the following:

AverageSales: Avg([UnitPrice]*[Quantity])

Access modifies the query in this way when it determines that you're using an aggregate function on an expression that has more than one field. You can enter the expression either way. Access stores and resolves the expression as noted.

Task: Building a Query to Summarize and Total Data

Modify the query used in the last task to show the total sales by country, city, and order date. Before you continue, save the query as qryCustomerOrderInfo and then close it. On the Query tab of the Database window, click qryCustomerOrderInfo. Choose Copy|Paste from the toolbar. Access should prompt you for the name of the new query. Type **qryCustomerOrderSummary** and click OK. With qryCustomerOrderSummary selected, click the Design command button. Delete both the UnitPrice and Quantity fields from the query output. To turn the query into an aggregate function, follow these steps:

1. Click Totals on the toolbar. Notice that Access adds an extra line, called the Total row, to the query grid; this line says Group By for all fields.

2. Group by country, city, and order date, but total by the total price (the calculated field). Click the Total row for the TotalPrice field and use the drop-down list to select Sum. (Refer to Figure 15.28.)

3. Run the query. Access should group and sort the result by country, city, and order date, with a total for each unique combination of the three fields.

4. Return to the query's design and remove the order date from the query grid.

5. Rerun the query. Notice that now you're summarizing the query by country and city.

6. Change the Total row to Avg. Now you're seeing the average price multiplied by quantity for each combination of country and city. Change the row to Sum, and save the query.

As you can see, aggregate functions are both powerful and flexible. You cannot edit their output, but you can use them to view the sum, minimum, maximum, average, and count

▼ of the total price, all at the same time. You can easily modify whether you're viewing this
▲ information by country, country and city, and so on, all at the click of a mouse.

Working with Outer Joins

NEW TERM *Outer joins* are used when you want the records on the "one" side of a one-to-many relationship to be included in the query result, regardless of whether there are matching records in the table on the "many" side. With a `Customers` table and an `Orders` table, for example, users often want to include only customers with orders in the query output. An *inner join* (the default join type) does this. In other situations, users want all customers to be included in the query result, regardless of whether they have orders. This is when an outer join is necessary.

> There are two types of outer joins: left outer joins and right outer joins. A left outer join occurs when all records on the "one" side of a one-to-many relationship are included in the query result, regardless of whether any records exist on the "many" side. A right outer join means all records on the "many" side of a one-to-many relationship are included in the query result, regardless of whether there are any records on the "one" side. A right outer join should never occur if referential integrity is being enforced because all orders should have associated customers.

To establish an outer join, you must modify the join between the tables included in the query:

1. Double-click the line joining the tables in the query grid.
2. The Join Properties window appears (see Figure 15.31). Select the type of join you want to create. To create a left outer join between the tables, select Option 2. Select Option 3 if you want to create a right outer join. Notice in Figure 15.31 that the description is Include ALL Records from Customers and Only Those Records from Orders Where the Joined Fields Are Equal.
3. Click OK to accept the join. An outer join should be established between the tables. Notice that the line joining the two tables now has an arrow pointing to the "many" side of the join.

The SQL statement produced when a left outer join is established looks like this:

```
SELECT Customers.CustomerID, Customers.CompanyName
FROM Customers
LEFT JOIN Orders ON Customers.CustomerID = Orders.CustomerID;
```

FIGURE 15.31

Establishing a left outer join.

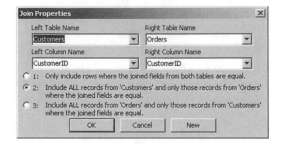

You can use a right outer join to identify all the records on the "one" side of a join that don't have any corresponding records on the "many" side. To do this, you simply enter Is Null as the criterion for any required field on the "many" side of the join. A common solution is to place the criterion on the foreign key field. In the query shown in Figure 15.32, only customers without orders are displayed in the query result.

FIGURE 15.32

A query showing customers without orders.

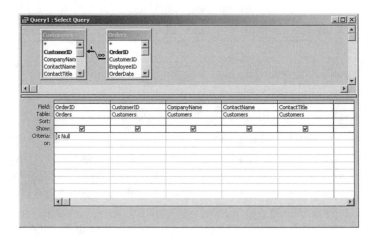

Refining Queries with Field, Field List, and Query Properties

You can use field and query properties to refine and control the behavior and appearance of the columns in a query and of the query itself. Here's how:

1. Click a field to select the field, click a field list to select the field list, or click the Query Design window anywhere outside a field or the field list to select the query.
2. Select Properties on the toolbar.
3. Modify the desired property.

If you click a field within the query design grid that has its Show check box cleared, Access displays only the query properties, not the field properties, when you bring up the Properties window for that field. If you select the Show check box with the Properties window open, Access displays the field properties.

Field Properties: Changing the Behavior of a Field

The properties of a field in a query include the Description, Format, Input Mask, and Caption properties of the column. The Description property documents the use of the field and controls what appears on the status bar when the user is in that column in the query result. The Format property is the same as the Format property in a table's field: It controls the display of the field in the query result. The Input Mask property, like its table counterpart, actually controls how the user enters the data and modifies it in the query result. The Caption property in the query does the same thing as a Caption property of a field: It sets the caption for the column in Datasheet view and the default label for forms and reports.

You might be wondering how the properties of the fields in a query interact with the same properties of a table. For example, how does the Caption property of a table's field interact with the Caption property of the same field in a query? All properties of a table's field are automatically inherited in queries. Properties you explicitly modify in a query override those same properties of a table's fields. Any objects based on the query inherit the properties of the query, not those of the original table.

In sthe case of the Input Mask property, it is important that the Input Mask property in the query not be in conflict with the Input Mask property of the table. You can use the Input Mask property of the query to further restrict the Input Mask property of the table, but not to override it. If the query's Input Mask property conflicts with the table's Input Mask property, the user will not be able to enter data into the table.

Field List Properties: Changing the Properties of the Field List

Field list properties specify attributes of each table participating in a query. The two field list properties are Alias and Source. You most often use the Alias property when you use the same table more than once in the same query. You do this in self-joins. The Source property specifies a connection string or database name when you're dealing with external tables that aren't linked to the current database.

Query Properties: Changing the Behavior of the Overall Query

Microsoft offers many properties, shown in Figure 15.33, that allow you to affect the behavior of a query.

FIGURE 15.33

Query properties that affect the behavior of a given query.

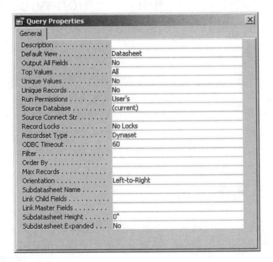

The Description property documents what the query does. Access 2002 introduced the Default View property. This property determines which view displays by default whenever the user runs the query. Datasheet is the default setting; PivotTable and PivotChart are the other two Default View property settings that are available. Output All Fields shows all the fields in the query results, regardless of the contents of the Show check box in each field. Top Values lets you specify the top x number or x percentage of values in the query result. You use the Unique Values and Unique Records properties to determine whether Access displays only unique values or unique records in the query's output. The following sections cover the Top Values, Unique Values, and Unique Records properties in more detail.

Several other more advanced properties exist. The Run Permissions property has to do with security. Source Database, Source Connect Str, ODBC Timeout, and Max Records all have to do with client/server issues. The Record Locks property is concerned with multiuser issues. The Recordset Type property determines whether you can make updates to the query output. By default, Access sets this property to the Dynaset type, allowing updates to the underlying data. Filter displays a subset that you determine, rather than the full result of the query. Order By determines the sort order of a query. The Orientation property determines whether the visual layout of the fields is left-to-right or right-to-left. The Subdatasheet Name property allows you to specify the name of the table or query that will appear as a subdatasheet within the current query. After you set the Subdatasheet Name property, the Link Child Fields and Link Master Fields properties designate the fields from the child and parent tables or queries that Access uses to link the current query to its subdatasheet. Finally, the Subdatasheet Height property sets the maximum height for a subdatasheet, and the Subdatasheet Expanded property determines whether the subdatasheet automatically appears in an expanded state.

The Top Values Property

The Top Values property enables you to specify a certain percentage or a specific number of records that the user wants to view in the query result. For example, you can build a query that outputs the country/city combinations with the top 10 sales amounts. You can also build a query that shows the country/city combinations whose sales rank in the top 50%. You can specify the Top Values property in a few different ways. Here are two examples:

- Click the Top Values combo box on the toolbar and choose from the predefined list of choices. (Note that this combo box is not available for certain field types.)

- Type a number or a number with a percent sign directly into the Top Values property in the Query Properties window, or select one of the predefined entries from the drop-down list for the property.

Figure 15.34 illustrates the design of a query showing the companies with the top 25% of sales. This aggregate function summarizes the result of BillableHours multiplied by BillingRate for each company. Notice that the Top Values property is set to 25%. Access has sorted the output of the query in descending order by the result of the TotalAmount calculation (see Figure 15.35). If the SaleAmount field were sorted in ascending order, Access would display the bottom 10% of the sales amount in the query result. Remember that the field(s) Access uses to determine the top values must appear as the left-most field(s) in the query's sort order.

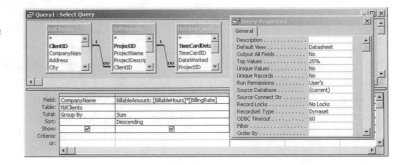

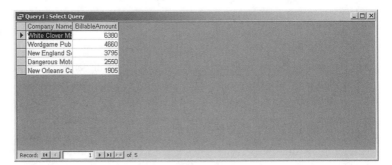

You might be surprised to discover that the Top Values property doesn't always seem to accurately display the correct number of records in the query result. All records with values that match the value in the last record are returned as part of the query result. In a table with 100 records, for example, the query asks for the top 10 values. Twelve records appear in the query result if the 10th, 11th, and 12th records all have the same value in the field being used to determine the top value.

The Unique Values Property

When it is set to Yes, the Unique Values property causes the query output to contain no duplicates for the combination of fields included in it. Figure 15.36, for example, shows a query that includes the Country and City fields from tblClients. The Unique Values property in this example is set to No, its default value. Notice that many combinations of countries and cities appear more than once. This happens whenever more than one client is found in a particular country and city. Compare this with Figure 15.37, in which the Unique Values property is set to Yes. Each combination of country and city appears only once.

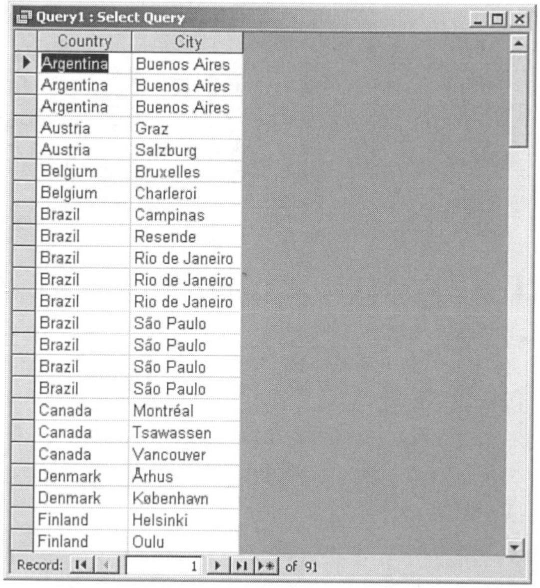

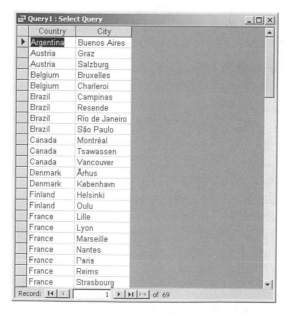

FIGURE 15.36

A query with the Unique Values *property set to* No.

FIGURE 15.37

A query with the Unique Values *property set to* Yes, *showing unique country/city combinations.*

The Unique Records Property

In Access 2000 and above, the default value for the Unique Records property is No. Setting it to Yes causes Access to include the DISTINCTROW statement in the SQL statement underlying the query. When set to Yes, the Unique Records property denotes that Access includes only unique rows in the recordset underlying the query in the query result—and not just unique rows based on the fields in the query result. The Unique Records property applies only to multitable queries; Access ignores it for any query that includes only one table.

Summary

As you can see, Microsoft provides a sophisticated query builder for constructing complex and powerful queries. In this hour you have learned how to work with calculated fields and advanced filters. You have also learned how you can use parameters to supply variable criteria to Parameter queries at runtime. Action queries let you modify table data without writing code; you can use these queries to add, edit, or delete table data. Finally, you have learned how to incorporate aggregate functions into queries and how to refine queries with field, field list, and query properties.

Q&A

Q Define *Parameter query*.

A A Parameter query allows you to supply criteria at runtime.

Q Define *Action query*.

A An Action query modifies table data.

Q Define *aggregate function*.

A An aggregate function summarizes numeric data.

Workshop

The Workshop includes quiz questions that are designed to help you test your understanding of the material covered and activities to help put what you've learned to practice. You can find the answers to the questions in the section immediately following the quiz.

Quiz

1. Name the four types of Action queries.
2. Name some aggregate expressions.
3. What database rules do calculated fields help you to enforce?

15

4. Access stores the results of a query in a database (True/False).

5. Action queries allow you to override referential integrity rules (True/False).

Quiz Answers

1. Insert, Update, Delete, and Make Table.

2. `Sum`, `Max`, `Min`, `Count`, and `Average`.

3. Calculated fields help you to enforce normalization rules.

4. False. Access stores all queries as SQL.

5. False. When running Action queries, Access enforces all referential integrity rules.

Activities

Practice building each type of Action query: Insert, Update, Delete, and Make Table queries. Use parameters to determine the criteria for Action queries.

Hour 16

Power Form Techniques

In Hour 11, "Creating Forms," you learned the basics of building your own forms. During this hour you will learn power techniques that will help you to build more complex forms than those you built in Hour 11. In this hour you'll learn the following:

- More about form properties
- Quite a bit about control properties
- How to work with bound, unbound, and calculated controls
- How to use expressions to enhance forms
- How to build forms based on data from more than one table

The Other Properties of a Form

As described in Hour 11, Format properties affect the appearance of a form and Data properties affect the data underlying a form. This hour focuses on the Other properties of a form. As you'll see, although these properties don't fit neatly into the Format and Data categories, they are extremely robust and powerful properties. To access these properties, you use the form selector (the intersection between the horizontal and vertical rulers) to select the form, open the Properties window, and click the Other tab of the Properties window (see Figure 16.1). The following sections describe the Other properties.

FIGURE 16.1
The Other properties of a form.

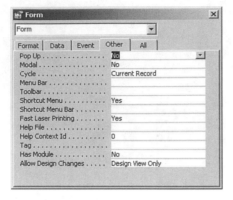

Pop Up

The Pop Up property indicates whether a form always remains on top of other windows. You will often set this property, along with the Modal property (discussed next), to Yes when creating custom dialog boxes.

Modal

The Modal property indicates whether the user can remove focus from a form while it's open. When the Modal property is set to Yes, the user must close the form before he or she can continue working with the application. As mentioned earlier, this property is used with the Pop Up property to create custom dialog boxes.

Cycle

The Cycle property controls the behavior of the Tab key in a form. The settings are All Records, Current Record, and Current Page. When you set the Cycle property to All Records, the user moves to the next record on a form when he or she presses Tab from the last control on the previous record. When the property is set to Current Record, the user is moved from the last control on a form to the first control on the same record. The Current Page option refers only to multipage forms; when you set the Cycle property to Current Page, the user tabs from the last control on the page to the first control on the same page. All three options are affected by the tab order of the objects on the form.

Menu Bar

The Menu Bar property specifies a menu bar associated with a form. The menu bar, sometimes referred to as a *command bar* in Access 2002 and Access 2003, is created by using the Customize dialog box. You reach this dialog box by choosing View|Toolbars| Customize. Hour 24, "Finishing Touches," covers the process of creating menus.

Toolbar

The Toolbar property designates a toolbar associated with a form. The toolbar, sometimes referred to as a *command bar* in Access 2002 and Access 2003, is created by using the Customize dialog box. The toolbar you select is displayed whenever the form has the focus. Hour 24 covers toolbars.

Shortcut Menu and Shortcut Menu Bar

The Shortcut Menu property indicates whether a shortcut menu displays when the user clicks with the right mouse button over an object on a form. The Shortcut Menu Bar property lets you associate a custom menu with a control on the form or with the form itself. As with a standard menu bar, you create a shortcut menu bar by choosing View| Toolbars|Customize. Hour 24 covers shortcut menus.

Fast Laser Printing

The Fast Laser Printing property determines whether lines and rectangles print along with a form. When you set this property to Yes, you see a definite improvement when printing the form on a laser printer.

Help File and Help Context ID

The Help File and Help Context ID properties are used to associate a specific Help file and topic with a form.

Tag

The Tag property is used to store miscellaneous information about a form. This property is often set and monitored at runtime to store necessary information about a form. You could use the Tag property to add a tag to each of several forms that should be unloaded as a group.

Has Module

The Has Module property determines whether a form has a class module. If no code is associated with a form, setting this property to No can noticeably decrease load time and improve the form's performance while decreasing the database's size.

Allow Design Changes

The Allow Design Changes property determines whether changes can be made to the design of a form while you're viewing form data. If this property is set to All Views, the Properties window is available in Form view, and changes made to form properties while you're in Form view are permanent if the form is saved.

16

Control Properties and Why to Use Them

Available control properties vary quite a bit, depending on the type of control. The following sections cover the most common properties. To view the properties of a control, you select the control and then open the Properties window.

The Format Properties of a Control

The Format properties of a control affect the appearance of the control. You use these properties to change the color, size, font, and other physical attributes of the control. To view the Format properties of a control, with the control already selected and the Properties window open, you click the Format tab (see Figure 16.2). The following sections discuss each of these properties and their uses.

FIGURE 16.2

*The Format properties
of a control.*

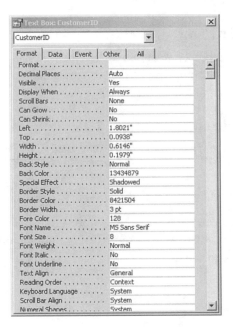

The TextBox control in Figure 16.3 uses many of the Format properties. It has the Scroll Bars property set to Vertical so that the control appears with a vertical scrollbar. The Back Color property has been modified, and the Border Style property is set to Solid, its color has been modified, and it is *very* wide. The font has been enlarged and made bold and italic. Finally, the text is aligned so that it is centered within the control. Notice that you can see all these changes graphically, as well as the properties that affect the control.

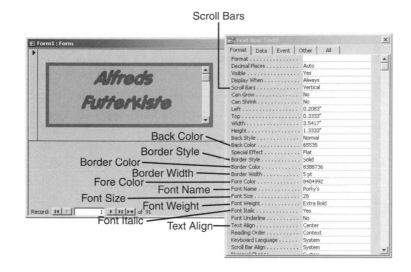

FIGURE **16.3**
*A TextBox control
using many of the
Format properties.*

Format

The Format property of a control determines how Access displays the data in the control.
A control's format is automatically inherited from its underlying data source. Access lets
you use this property in three situations: when the Format property is not set for the
underlying field, when you want to override the existing Format setting for the field, and
when you want to apply a format to an unbound control. You can select from a multitude
of predefined values for a control's format, or you can create a custom format. I often
modify the Format property at runtime to vary the format of a control, depending on a
certain condition. For example, the format for a Visa card number is different from the
format for an ATM card number.

Decimal Places

The Decimal Places property specifies how many decimal places you want to appear in
the control. This property is used with the Format property to determine the control's
appearance.

Caption

You use the Caption property to specify information that is helpful to the user. It's available for labels, command buttons, and toggle buttons.

Hyperlink Address

The Hyperlink Address property is available only for command buttons, images, and
unattached labels. It contains a string that is used to specify a UNC (path to a file) or a

URL (Web page address) associated with a control. When a form is active and the cursor is placed over the control, clicking the control displays the specified object or Web page.

Hyperlink SubAddress

Like the Hyperlink Address property, the Hyperlink SubAddress property is available only for command buttons, images, and unattached labels. The Hyperlink SubAddress property is a string that represents a location in the document specified in the Hyperlink Address property.

Visible

The Visible property indicates whether a control is visible. This property can be toggled at runtime, depending on specific circumstances. For example, a question on the form might apply only to records in which the gender is set to Female; if the gender is set to Male, the question isn't visible.

Display When

The Display When property is used when you want certain controls on a form to be sent only to the screen or only to the printer. The three settings for this property are Always, Print Only, and Screen Only. An example of the use of the Display When property is for a label containing instructions. You can use the Display When property to have the instructions appear onscreen but not on the printout.

Scroll Bars

The Scroll Bars property determines whether scrollbars appear when the data in a control doesn't fit within the control's size. The options are None and Vertical. I often set the Scroll Bars property to Vertical when the control is used to display data from a memo field. The scrollbar makes it easier for the user to work with a potentially large volume of data in the memo field.

Can Grow and Can Shrink

The Can Grow and Can Shrink properties apply only to a form's printed version. When the Can Grow property is set to Yes, the control expands when the form is being printed so that all the data in the control fits on the printout. When the Can Shrink property is set to Yes and the user has not entered any data, the control shrinks so that blank lines aren't printed.

Left, Top, Width, and Height

You use the Left, Top, Width, and Height properties to set a control's position and size.

Back Style and Back Color

You can set the Back Style property to Normal or Transparent. When this property is set to Transparent, the form's background color shows through the control. This is often the preferred setting for an option group. The control's Back Color property specifies the background color (as opposed to text color) for the control.

 If the Back Style property of a control is set to Transparent, the control's Back Color property is ignored.

Special Effect

The Special Effect property adds 3D effects to a control. The settings for this property are Flat, Raised, Sunken, Etched, Shadowed, and Chiseled. Each of these effects gives a control a different look.

Border Style, Border Color, and Border Width

The Border Style, Border Color, and Border Width properties affect the look, color, and thickness of a control's border. The settings for the Border Style property are Transparent, Solid, Dashes, Short Dashes, Dots, Sparse Dots, Dash Dot, and Dash Dot Dot. The Border Color property specifies the color of the border; you can select from a variety of colors. The Border Width property can be set to one of several point sizes.

 If the Border Style property of a control is set to Transparent, Access ignores the control's Border Color and Border Width properties.

Fore Color, Font Name, Font Size, Font Weight, Font Italic, and Font Underline

The Fore Color, Font Name, Font Size, Font Weight, Font Italic, and Font Underline properties control the appearance of the text in a control. As their names imply, they let you select a color, font, size, and thickness of the text and determine whether the text is italicized or underlined. You can modify these properties in response to a runtime event. For example, you can modify a control's text color if the value in that control exceeds a certain amount. The Font Weight property settings generally exceed what is actually available for a particular font and printer—normally, you have a choice of only Regular and Bold in whatever value you select for this property.

Text Align

The Text Align property is often confused with the ability to align controls, but the Text Align property affects how the data is aligned *within* a control.

Reading Order

The Reading Order property was introduced with Access 2002. As its name implies, the Reading Order property allows you to specify the reading order for text in a control. This feature is available only if you are using a version of Microsoft Office that supports right-to-left features.

Keyboard Language

The Keyboard Language property, which was introduced with Access 2002, allows you to override the keyboard language currently in use. This means that when a specific control receives the focus, the language specified in this property becomes the keyboard language in effect while you're typing data into the control.

Scroll Bar Align

The Scroll Bar Align property is a language-related property that was introduced with Access 2002. You use this property to place the vertical scrollbar in the appropriate left-to-right or right-to-left position. If this property is set to System, the position of the scrollbar is based on the selected user interface language. The scrollbar is placed on the right for left-to-right languages and on the left for right-to-left languages. If this property is set to Left or Right, the scrollbar is placed on the left or right side of the control, respectively.

Numerical Shape

The Numerical Shape property, which was introduced with Access 2002, allows you to designate whether numeric shapes are displayed in the Arabic or Hindi style. The available choices for this property are System, Arabic, National, and Context. System bases the numeric shape on the operating system. Arabic and National use the Arabic and Hindi styles, respectively. Context bases the numeric shape on the text adjacent to the control.

Left Margin, Top Margin, Right Margin, and Bottom Margin

The Left Margin, Top Margin, Right Margin, and Bottom Margin properties determine how far the text appears from the left, top, right, and bottom of the control. They are particularly useful with controls such as text boxes based on memo fields, which are generally large controls.

Line Spacing

The `Line Spacing` property is used to determine the spacing between lines of text in a multiline control. This property is most commonly used with text boxes based on memo fields.

Is Hyperlink

When the `Is Hyperlink` property is set to `Yes`, the data in the control is formatted as a hyperlink. If the data in the control is a relevant link (for example, `http:\\microsoft.com`), the data functions as a hyperlink.

The Data Properties of a Control

Whereas Format properties affect the appearance of a control, Data properties affect the data that displays in a control. The following sections explore the various Data properties. You'll learn about everything from the `Control Source` property, which determines what data displays in a control, to the `Input Mask` property, which determines what data the user can enter into each character of the control. As you'll see, there's a very rich list of Data properties for a control. They appear in Figure 16.4 and are described in the following sections. To access the Data properties of a control, you select the control, open the properties sheet, and click to select the Data tab.

FIGURE 16.4

The Data properties of a control.

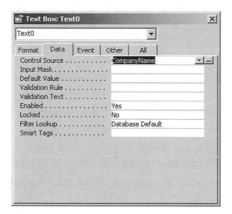

Take a look at the example in Figure 16.5. Notice that the `TextBox` control has its `Control Source` property set to `Region`, indicating that it is bound to the `Region` field in the underlying data source. Its `Default Value` property is set to `CA`. This means that when the user adds a new record, the `Region` field defaults to `CA`. The `Validation Rule` property connotes that the region must be `CA`, `UT`, `AZ`, `NJ`, or `NY`. The `Validation Text` property provides the error message the user will receive if the user violates the validation rule.

Default Value

Control Source

FIGURE 16.5

The Display Control property, on the Lookup tab of the Table Design window.

Text Box: Text4					✕

Text4 ▾

Format	Data	Event	Other	All

Control Source	Region
Input Mask	
Default Value	"CA"
Validation Rule	In ("CA","UT","AZ","NJ","NY")
Validation Text	State Must Be CA, UT, AZ, NJ, or NY
Enabled	Yes
Locked	No
Filter Lookup	Database Default
Smart Tags	

Validation Rule

Validation Text

Control Source

The `Control Source` property specifies the field from the record source that's associated with a particular control. The `Control Source` property can also be set to any valid Access expression.

Input Mask

Whereas the `Format` and `Decimal Places` properties affect the appearance of a control, the `Input Mask` property affects what data the user can enter into the control. The input mask of the field underlying the control is automatically inherited into the control. If no input mask is entered as a field property, the input mask can be entered directly in the form. If you entered the input mask for the field, you can use the input mask of the associated control on a form to further restrict what the user enters into that field via the form. If you select the `Input Mask` property and click the Build button, the Input Mask Wizard appears (see Figure 16.6). This wizard is covered in Hour 14, "Power Table Techniques."

> If a control's `Format` property and `Input Mask` property are set to different values, the `Format` property affects the display of the data in the control until the control gets the focus. When the control gets the focus, the `Input Mask` property prevails.

FIGURE 16.6
*The Input Mask
Wizard.*

16

Default Value

The Default Value property of a control determines the value assigned to new records entered in a form. You can set this property within the field properties of the underlying table. A default value set at the field level of the table is automatically inherited into the form. The default value set for the control overrides the default value set at the field level of the table.

Validation Rule and Validation Text

The Validation Rule and Validation Text properties of a control perform the same functions as they do for a field. This means that the Validation Rule allows you to validate the data that the user enters into the control and the Validation text allows you to supply the user with the error message that appears when he enters a value that violates the Validation Rule.

> Because a validation rule is enforced at the database engine level, the validation rule set for a control can't be in conflict with the validation rule set for the field to which the control is bound. If the two rules conflict, the user can't enter data into the control.

Enabled

The Enabled property determines whether you allow a control to get the focus. If this property is set to No, the control appears dimmed.

Locked

The Locked property determines whether the user can modify the data in a control. When the Locked property is set to Yes, the control can get the focus but can't be edited. The Enabled and Locked properties of a control interact with one another. Table 16.1 summarizes their interactions. Where you see the Enabled column equal to Yes in the table, that means that the Enabled property is set to Yes. Where you see the Locked property equal to Yes in the table, that means that the Locked property is set to Yes. The third column shows the effect of the combination of those two property settings. For example, if you set Enabled to Yes and Locked to Yes, the control can get the focus and its data can be copied but not modified.

TABLE 16.1   How Enabled and Locked Properties Interact

Enabled	Locked	*Effect*
Yes	Yes	The control can get the focus; its data can be copied but not modified.
Yes	No	The control can get the focus, and its data can be edited.
No	Yes	The control can't get the focus.
No	No	The control can't get the focus; its data appears dimmed.

Filter Lookup

The Filter Lookup property indicates whether you want the values associated with a bound text box to appear in the Filter by Form window (covered in Hour 4, "Forms Introduced").

The Other Properties of a Control

The Other properties of a control are properties that do not fit neatly into any of the other categories. This does not mean that they are unimportant. In fact, you can find some of the most important and useful control properties under the Other properties of a control. To access these properties, you select a control, invoke the Properties window, and then click the Other tab of the Properties window (see Figure 16.7). The following sections describe the Other properties of a control.

Name

The Name property allows you to name a control. You use the name that is set in this property when you refer to the control in code, and this name is also displayed in various drop-down lists that show all the controls on a form. It's important to name controls because named controls improve the readability of code and make working with Access forms and other objects easier.

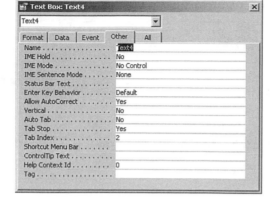

FIGURE 16.7
The Other properties of a control.

IME Hold, IME Mode, and IME Sentence Mode

The Input Method Editor (IME) is a program that converts keystrokes into East Asian character sets. The IME Hold, IME Mode, and IME Sentence Mode properties, which were introduced with Access 2002, are used to designate the settings in effect when an IME is used.

Status Bar Text

The Status Bar Text property specifies the text that appears in the status bar when a control gets focus. The setting of this property overrides the Description property that you can set in a table's design.

Enter Key Behavior

The Enter Key Behavior property determines whether the Enter key causes the cursor to move to the next control or to add a new line in the current control. You are likely to change the setting of this property for text boxes that you use to display the contents of memo fields.

Allow AutoCorrect

The Allow AutoCorrect property specifies whether the AutoCorrect feature is available in a control. The AutoCorrect feature automatically corrects common spelling errors and typos.

Vertical

The Vertical property is used to control whether the text in a control is displayed horizontally or vertically. The default setting is No, or horizontal. When you select Yes (vertical display), Access rotates the text in the control 90 degrees (see Figure 16.8).

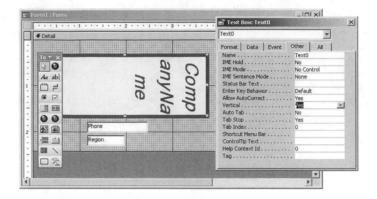

FIGURE 16.8

The CompanyName *text box with the* Vertical *property set to* Yes.

Auto Tab

When the Auto Tab property is set to Yes, the cursor automatically advances to the next control when the user enters the last character of an input mask. Some users like this option, and others find it annoying, especially if they must tab out of some fields but not others.

Default

The Default property applies to a command button or to an ActiveX control and specifies whether the control is the default button on a form.

Cancel

The Cancel property applies to a command button or to an ActiveX control. It indicates that you want the control's code to execute when the user presses the Esc key while the form is active.

Auto Repeat

The Auto Repeat property specifies whether you want an event procedure or a macro to execute repeatedly while the user is pressing its command button.

Status Bar Text

The Status Bar Text property specifies the message that appears in the status bar when a control has the focus.

Tab Stop

The Tab Stop property determines whether the user can use the Tab key to enter a control. It's appropriate to set this property to No for controls whose values rarely get modified. The user can opt to click in the control when necessary.

Tab Index

The `Tab Index` property sets the tab order for a control. I generally set the `Tab Index` property by using View|Tab Order rather than by setting the value directly in the control's `Tab Index` property. This allows me to set the tab order graphically, which is more intuitive, easier, and saves me a lot of time.

Shortcut Menu Bar

The `Shortcut Menu Bar` property attaches a specific menu to a control. The menu bar appears when the user right-clicks the control.

ControlTip Text

The `ControlTip Text` property specifies the ToolTip associated with a control. The ToolTip automatically appears when the user places the mouse pointer over the control and leaves it there for a moment.

Help Context ID

The `Help Context ID` property designates the Help topic associated with a control.

Tag

The `Tag` property is used to store information about a control. Your imagination determines how you use this property. The `Tag` property can be read and modified at runtime.

Bound, Unbound, and Calculated Controls

NEW TERM   There are important differences between bound and unbound controls. *Unbound controls* display information to the user or gather from the user information that's not going to be stored in the database. Here are some examples of unbound controls:

- A label providing instructions to the user
- A logo placed on a form
- A combo box or text box placed on a form in which the user can enter report criteria
- A rectangle placed on the form to logically group several controls

NEW TERM   *Bound controls* are used to display and modify information stored in a database table. A bound control automatically appears with the control type specified in its `Display Control` property; the control automatically inherits many of the attributes assigned to the field that the control is bound to.

16

You set the Display Control property in the design of the underlying table. Located on the Lookup tab of the Table Design window (see Figure 16.9), the Display Control property determines the default control type that Access uses when you add a control to a form or report.

FIGURE 16.9

The Display Control *property, on the Lookup tab of the Table Design window.*

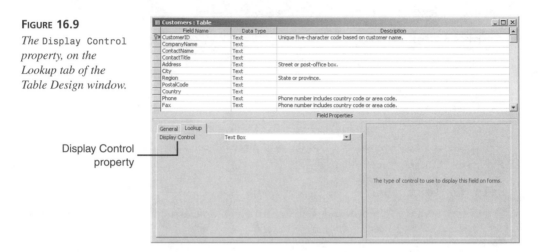

Display Control property

NEW TERM   A *calculated control* is a special type of control that displays the results of an expression. The user cannot modify the data in a calculated control. The control's value automatically changes as the user changes the values in its expression. For example, a sales total may change as the price or quantity is changed.

Using Expressions to Enhance Forms

A control can contain any valid expression as its control source. When you enter an expression as a control source, the expression must be preceded by an equal sign. You can manually type the control source, or you can use the Expression Builder to make the process easier.

To add an expression to a control source, you start by adding an unbound control to a form. To use the Expression Builder, you click the control's Control Source property and then click the ellipsis (...). The Expression Builder appears (see Figure 16.10). In the list box on the left, you select the type of object you want to include in the expression. The middle and right list boxes let you select the specific element you want to paste into the expression. The Expression Builder is useful when you're not familiar with the syntax required for the expression. You can also enter an expression directly into the text box for the Control Source property. To view the expression more easily, you can use the Zoom feature (Shift+F2). The Zoom dialog box for the control source is pictured in Figure 16.11; the expression shown in the figure multiplies UnitPrice by Quantity.

FIGURE 16.10

The Expression Builder, where you can add an expression as a control's control source.

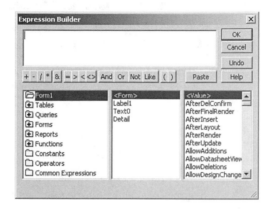

FIGURE 16.11

The Zoom dialog box for a control source.

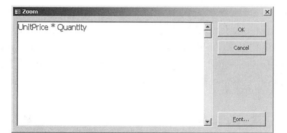

The Command Button Wizard: Programming Without Typing

With the Command Button Wizard, you can quickly and easily add functionality to forms. The wizard writes the code to perform more than 30 commonly required tasks that are separated into record navigation, record operations, form operations, report operations, application operations, and other miscellaneous tasks. The Command Button Wizard is automatically invoked when you add a command button with the Control Wizards tool selected. The first step of the Command Button Wizard is shown in Figure 16.12; in this dialog box you specify the category of activity and specific action you want the command button to perform. The subsequent wizard steps vary, depending on the category and action you select.

FIGURE 16.12

The first step of the
Command Button
Wizard.

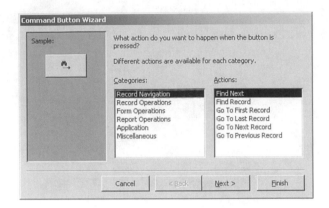

Figure 16.13 shows the second step of the Command Button Wizard when you select the Form Operations category and the Open Form action in the first step. This step asks which form you want to open. After you select a form and click Next, you're asked whether you want Access to open the form and find specific data to display or whether you want Access to open the form and display all the records. If you indicate that you want to display only specific records, the dialog box shown in Figure 16.14 appears. This dialog box asks you to select fields related to the two forms. You must select the related fields and then click the double-arrow (<>) button to notify Access of the relationship. In the next step of the wizard, you select text or a picture for the button. The final step of the wizard asks you to name the button. When you're done, you click Finish.

FIGURE 16.13

The Command Button
Wizard, requesting the
name of a form to
open.

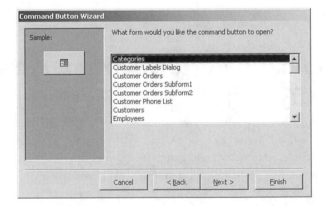

What's surprising about the Command Button Wizard is how much it varies depending on the features you select. It allows you to add somewhat sophisticated functionality to an application without writing a single line of code. Figure 16.15 shows the code gener- ated by the example just outlined. This code will make a lot more sense to you after you've read Hour 23, "VBA Introduced." After you have the Command Button Wizard generate code for you, you can modify it; this means that you can have Access do some of the dirty work for you and then customize the work to your liking.

FIGURE 16.14

The Command Button Wizard, asking for the fields that relate to each form.

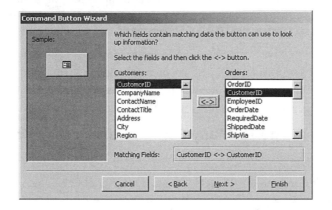

16

FIGURE 16.15

Code generated by the Command Button Wizard.

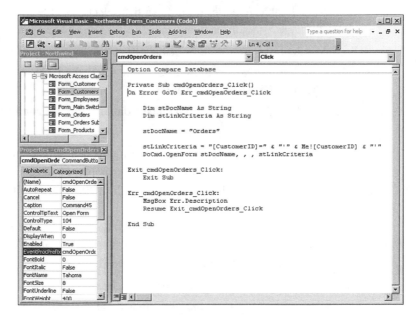

Building Forms Based on More Than One Table

NEW TERM Many forms are based on more than one table; such forms are called *one-to-many forms*. For example, a form that shows a customer at the top and the orders associated with that customer at the bottom is considered a one-to-many form. Forms can also be based on a query that joins more than one table. Rather than see a one-to-many relationship in such a form, you see the two tables displayed as one, with each record on the "many" side of the relationship appearing with its parent's data.

Creating One-to-Many Forms

There are several ways to create one-to-many forms. As with many other types of forms, you can use a wizard to help you or you can build the form from scratch. Because all the methods for creating a form are helpful to users and developers alike, the available options are covered in the following sections.

Building a One-to-Many Form by Using the Form Wizard

Building a one-to-many form by using the Form Wizard is a simple 10-step process:

1. Click Forms in the Objects list and double-click the Create Form by Using Wizard icon.

2. From the Tables/Queries drop-down list, select the table or query that will appear on the "one" side of the relationship.

3. Select the fields you want to include from the "one" side of the relationship.

4. Use the Tables/Queries drop-down list to select the table or query that will appear on the "many" side of the relationship.

5. Select the fields you want to include from the "many" side of the relationship.

6. Click Next.

7. Select whether you want the parent form to appear with subforms or the child forms to appear as linked forms. In this example, I want the parent form to appear with subforms, so I clicked the Form with Subform(s) option (see Figure 16.16). Click Next.

8. Indicate whether you want the subform to appear in a tabular format, as a datasheet, as a PivotTable, or as a PivotChart. (This option is not available if you selected Linked Forms in step 7.) Click Next.

9. Select a style for the form and then click Next.

10. Name both the form and the subform and then click Finish.

The result of this process is a main form that contains a subform. Figure 16.17 shows an example.

FIGURE 16.16

The Form Wizard, creating a parent form with subforms.

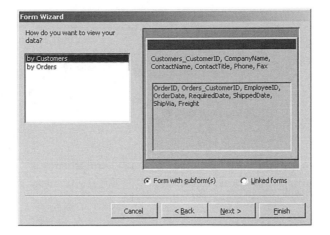

16

FIGURE 16.17

The result of creating a one-to-many form by using the Form Wizard.

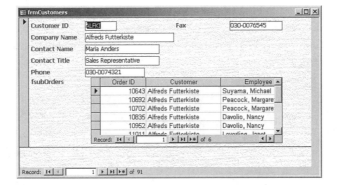

Building a One-to-Many Form by Using the SubForm Wizard

You can create a one-to-many form by building the parent form and then adding a Subform/Subreport control from the toolbox. If you want to use the SubForm Wizard, you need to make sure that you select the Control Wizards tool before you add the Subform/Subreport control to the main form. Then you follow these steps:

1. Click to select the Subform/Subreport control.
2. Click and drag to place the Subform/Subreport control on the main form. The SubForm Wizard appears.
3. Indicate whether you want to use an existing form as the subform or build a new subform from an existing table or query.
4. If you select Use Existing Tables and Queries, the next step of the SubForm Wizard prompts you to select a table or query and which fields you want to include (see Figure 16.18). Select the fields and then click Next.

FIGURE 16.18
Selecting fields to include in a subform.

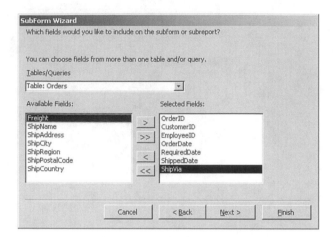

5. The next step of the SubForm Wizard allows you to define which fields in the main form link to which fields in the subform. You can select from the suggested relationships or define your own (see Figure 16.19). Select the appropriate relationship and click Next.

FIGURE 16.19
Defining the relationship between the main form and the subform.

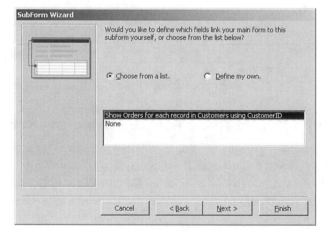

6. Name the subform and click Finish.

The resulting form should look similar to the form created with the Form Wizard. Creating a one-to-many form this way is simply an alternative to using the Form Wizard.

> Another way to add a subform to a main form is to click and drag a form
> from the Database window onto the main form. Access then tries to identify
> the relationship between the two forms.

Working with Subforms

After you have added a subform to a form, you need to understand how to work with it.
To begin, you need to familiarize yourself with a few properties of a Subform control:

- **Source Object**—Specifies the name of the form that's being displayed in the control.

- **Link Child Fields**—Specifies the fields from the child form that link the child form to the master form.

- **Link Master Fields**—Specifies the fields from the master form that link the child form to the master form.

You should also understand how to make changes to a subform. One option is to open a
subform in a separate window (as you would open any other form). After you close and
save the form, all the changes automatically appear in the parent form. The other choice
is to modify a subform from within the main form. With the main form open, the subform is visible. Any changes made to the design of the subform from within the main
form are permanent.

The default view of the subform is Datasheet or Continuous Forms, depending on how
you added the subform and what options you selected. If you want to modify the default
view, you simply change the subform's Default View property.

> When the subform is displayed in Datasheet view, the order of the fields in
> the subform has no bearing on the datasheet that appears in the main
> form. The order of the columns in the datasheet depends on the tab order
> of the fields in the subform. You must therefore modify the tab order of the
> fields in the subform to change the order of the fields in the resulting
> datasheet.

> Access 2002 and Access 2003 make it easier than ever before to work with
> subforms and subreports in Design view. Scrolling has been improved so that
> it's easier to design subforms and subreports. In addition, you can now open

16

a subform in its own separate Design view window by right-clicking the subform and selecting Subform in New Window. Or, instead of right-clicking the
subform, you can select the subform and then select View | Subform in New
Window from the menu bar.

Basing Forms on Queries: The Why and How

One strategy when building forms is to base them on queries. By doing this, you generally get optimal performance and flexibility. Rather than bring all fields and all records
over the network, you bring only the fields and records you need. The benefits of doing
this are especially pronounced in a client/server environment where the query is run on
the server. Even in an environment where data is stored in the proprietary Access file format (.mdb) on a file server, a form based on a stored query can take better advantage of
Access's indexing and paging features than a form based on a table. By basing a form on
a query rather than a table, you also have more control over which records are included
in the form and in what order they appear. Finally, you can base a form on a query that
contains a one-to-many join and view parent and child information as if it were one
record. Notice in Figure 16.20 that the customer and order information appear on one
form as if they were one record.

FIGURE 16.20

*A form based on a
one-to-many query.*

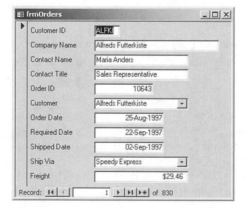

Embedding SQL Statements Versus Stored Queries

NEW TERM   In versions of Access prior to Access 2000, stored queries offer better performance than embedded SQL statements. This is because when you save a
query, Access compiles the query and creates a *query plan*, which has information on the
best way to execute the query based on available indexes and the volume of data. In ver-

sions of Access prior to Access 2000, if a form is based on an embedded SQL statement, the SQL statement is compiled and optimized each time the form is opened. With Access 2000 and above, embedded SQL statements are compiled the same way as stored queries. You might ask whether with Access 2003 it is better to base a query on a stored query or on a SQL statement. This is my personal preference: If I plan to use the same or a similar query with multiple forms and reports, I build a query and base multiple forms and reports on that query. This keeps me from having to duplicate my efforts in building the query. If I have a query that is unique to the form, I build it as an embedded SQL statement. This eliminates the extra clutter of the query in the database container.

A query plan can sometimes be inaccurate because a query plan optimizes the query based on the amount of data in the underlying tables. If the amount of data in the tables underlying a form changes significantly, it is necessary to rebuild the query plan. You can do this by opening, running, and saving the query or by compacting the database.

Summary

In this hour you have learned quite a bit about the intricacies of working with forms. You have learned about important form and control properties and about the differences between bound, unbound, and calculated controls. You have learned how to use expressions to enhance forms and how to build forms that are based on data from more than one table. These are all important techniques for building complex data entry forms.

Q&A

Q Describe the `Pop Up` property of a form and how it relates to the `Modal` property.

A The `Pop Up` property indicates whether the form always remains on top of other windows. The `Modal` property indicates whether the user can remove focus from the form while it is open. By setting both of these properties to `Yes`, you can create custom dialog boxes.

Q Describe some uses of unbound controls.

A You could use an unbound control to create a label providing instructions to the user, a logo placed on a form, a combo or text box placed on a form so that the user can enter report criteria, or a rectangle placed on a form to logically group several controls.

Q What is the purpose of the Command Button Wizard?

A The purpose of the Command Button Wizard is to quickly and easily add functionality to forms. It accomplishes this by writing the code necessary to perform more than 30 commonly required tasks.

Q Describe a query plan.

A A query plan has information on the best way to execute a query based on available indexes and the volume of data.

Workshop

The Workshop includes quiz questions that are designed to help you test your understanding of the material covered and activities to help put what you've learned to practice. You can find the answers to the questions in the section immediately following the quiz.

Quiz

1. Name the property that determines the behavior of the Tab key on a form.

2. The Display When property applies only when printing (True/False).

3. The Can Grow and Can Shrink properties apply only when you're printing (True/False).

4. Name the property that specifies the field from the record source that is associated with a particular control.

5. The Validation Rule property for a form control can override the Validation Rule property set for the field that is bound to the control (True/False).

Quiz Answers

1. The Cycle property.

2. False. You can use the Display When property to indicate that the control displays always, only when printing, or only onscreen.

3. True.

4. The Control Source property specifies the field from the record source that is associated with a particular control.

5. False. Because the validation rule is enforced at the database engine level, the Validation Rule property set for a control can't be in conflict with the Validation Rule property set for the field to which the control is bound. If the two properties conflict, the user can't enter data into the control.

Activities

Practice changing the form and control properties that you have learned about in this hour. Practice adding bound, unbound, and calculated controls to a form. Build a few forms that display data from more than one table.

16

HOUR 17

Power Report Techniques

In Hour 12, "Creating Reports," you learned quite a bit about the process of building reports. During this hour you'll go a step further and learn about the power techniques that help the experts build more complex reports than those you built in Hour 12. In this hour you'll learn the following:

- How to use report and control properties
- How to insert page breaks
- The differences between bound, unbound, and calculated controls
- How to use expressions to enhance reports
- How to base reports on data from more than one table
- How to work with sorting and grouping

Other Properties of a Report

A report has 12 Other properties (see Figure 17.1); these miscellaneous properties, described in the following text, allow you to control other important aspects of a report:

Record Locks

The Record Locks property determines whether Access locks the tables used in producing a report while it runs the report. The two values for this property are No Locks and All Records. No Locks is the default value; it means that no records in the tables underlying the report are locked while the report is being run. Users can modify the underlying data as the report is run; this can be disastrous when running sophisticated reports. If users can change the data in a report as the report is being run, figures for totals and percentages of totals are invalid. Although using the `All Records` option for this property locks all records in all tables included in the report (thereby preventing data entry while the report is being run), it might be a necessary evil for producing an accurate report.

FIGURE 17.1

The Other properties of a Report.

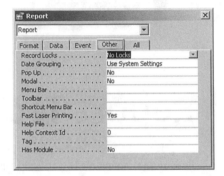

Date Grouping

The `Date Grouping` property determines how grouping of dates occurs in a report. The `US Defaults` setting means that Access uses U.S. defaults for report groupings; therefore, Sunday is the first day of the week, the first week begins January 1, and so on. The `Use System Settings` setting means that date groupings are based on the locale set in the Control Panel's Regional Settings, rather than on U.S. defaults.

Pop Up

The `Pop Up` property determines whether a report's Print Preview window opens as a pop-up window. In Microsoft Access, pop-up windows always remain on top of other open windows.

Modal

The `Modal` property instructs Access to open the Report window in a modal or modeless state. The default is `No`, meaning that the window will not be opened as modal. A modal window retains the application program's focus until the window receives the user input that it requires.

Menu Bar

The Menu Bar property allows you to associate a custom menu bar with the report that's visible when the user is previewing the report. Adding a custom menu to a report lets you control what the user can do while the report is active.

Toolbar

The Toolbar property lets you associate a custom toolbar with the report that's visible when the user is previewing the report.

Shortcut Menu Bar

The Shortcut Menu Bar property determines what shortcut menu is associated with the report while the user is previewing the report. The shortcut menu bar appears when the user clicks the right mouse button over the Print Preview window.

Fast Laser Printing

The Fast Laser Printing property determines whether lines and rectangles are replaced with text character lines when you print a report by using a laser printer. If fast printing is an objective and you're using a laser printer, you should set this property to Yes.

Help File and Help Context ID

The Help File and Help Context ID properties let you associate a help file and a help topic with a report.

Tag

The Tag property stores information defined by the user at either design time or runtime. It is Microsoft Access's way of giving you an extra property. Access makes no use of this property; if you don't take advantage of it, it will never be used.

Has Module

The Has Module property determines whether a report contains an associated class module. If no code will be included in the report, eliminating the class module can reduce the size of the application database, thereby improving performance. A report that does not have a class module is considered a "lightweight object," which loads and displays faster than an object with an associated class module.

A couple of the Has Module property's behaviors deserve special attention. When a report is created, the default value for the Has Module property is No. Access automatically sets the Has Module property to Yes as soon as you try to view a report's module. If you set the Has Module property of an existing report to No, Access asks you whether you wish to proceed. If you confirm the change, Access deletes the object's class module and all the code it contains.

Control Properties and Why to Use Them

Just as reports have properties, so do controls. You can change most control properties at design time or at runtime; this allows you to easily build flexibility into reports. For example, certain controls are visible only when specific conditions are true. The following sections discuss the Format properties of a control and the Data and Other properties of a control.

The Format Properties of a Control

The Format properties of a control allow you to customize the appearance of the control. By using the Format properties, you can modify control attributes such as the back color, font, special effect, and text alignment of the control. You can modify many of the Format properties of selected objects by using the Formatting toolbar (see Figure 17.2). If you prefer, you can set the Format properties in the Properties window (see Figure 17.3). The following sections discuss the Format properties that are available.

FIGURE 17.2

The Formatting toolbar.

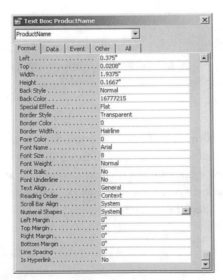

The Formatting toolbar

FIGURE 17.3
The Format properties of a control.

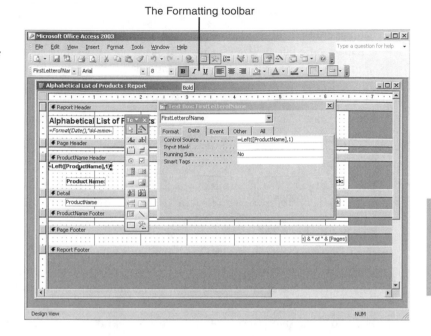

Format

The Format property determines how Access displays the data in a control. This property is automatically inherited from the underlying field. If you want the control's format on the report to differ from the underlying field's format, you must set the Format property of the control. It's important to note that the Format options available vary based on the field type of the underlying field. In other words, the Formatting options vary if the underlying field is a Text field versus a Number field.

Caption

The Caption property specifies the text displayed for labels and command buttons. A caption is a string that contains up to 2,048 characters.

Hyperlink Address

The Hyperlink Address property is a string representing the path to a UNC (network path) or URL (Web page). Command buttons, image controls, and labels all contain the Hyperlink Address property. Therefore, if you attach a hyperlink for your company's Web page on a command button, the user can click the button to be taken to that Web page.

Hyperlink SubAddress

The Hyperlink SubAddress property is a string that represents a location within the document specified in the Hyperlink Address property. Command buttons, image controls, and labels all contain the Hyperlink SubAddress property.

Decimal Places

The Decimal Places property defines the number of decimal places displayed for numeric values.

Visible

The Visible property determines whether a control is visible. You can use this property to toggle the visibility of a control in response to different situations.

Hide Duplicates

The Hide Duplicates property hides duplicate data values in a report's Detail section. Duplicate data values occur when one or more consecutive records in a report contain the same value in one or more fields. Figure 17.4 shows a report with the Hide Duplicates property set to its default value, False. Notice the duplicate sales person values. Figure 17.5 shows the same report with the Hide Duplicates property set to True. Notice that the duplicate sales person values no longer appear.

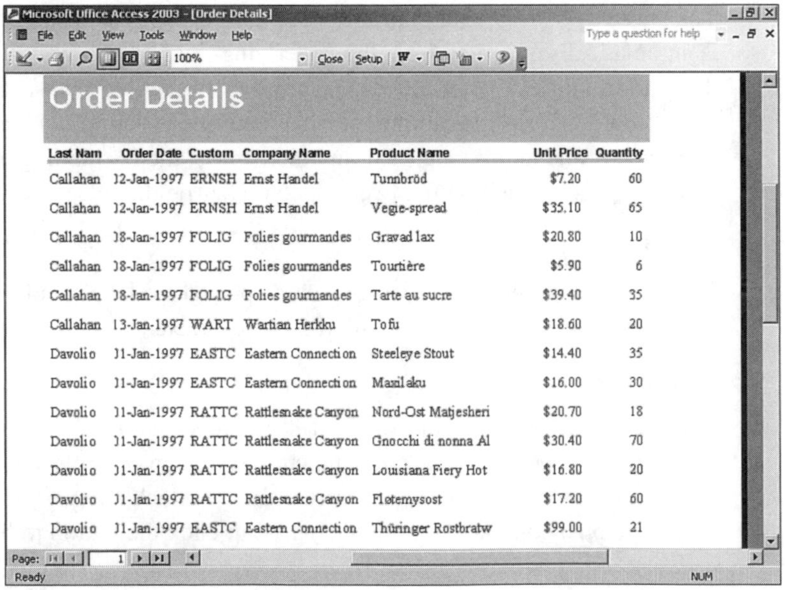

FIGURE 17.4

The Hide Duplicates *property set to* False.

FIGURE 17.5

The Hide Duplicates *property set to* True.

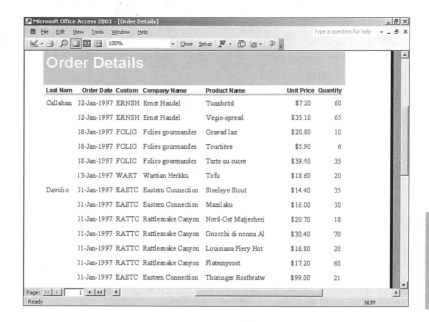

Can Grow and Can Shrink

When the Can Grow property is set to Yes in a control, the control can expand vertically to accommodate all the data in it. The Can Shrink property eliminates blank lines when no data exists in a field for a particular record. For example, if you have a second address line on a mailing label, but there's no data in the Address2 field, you don't want a blank line to appear on the mailing label (see Figure 17.6). You must therefore set the Can Shrink property for the Address2 control to Yes (see the results in Figure 17.7). Likewise, if you have a memo that sometimes has only one line of data but at other times has multiple lines of data, you might want to set the Can Grow property to Yes so that the control grows as necessary.

Left, Top, Width, and Height

The Left, Top, Width, and Height properties set the size and position of the controls on a report.

Back Style and Back Color

You can set the Back Style property to Normal or Transparent. When this property is set to Transparent, the color of control. When it is set to Normal, the control's Back Color property determines the object's color.

FIGURE 17.6

The Can Shrink *property set to* False.

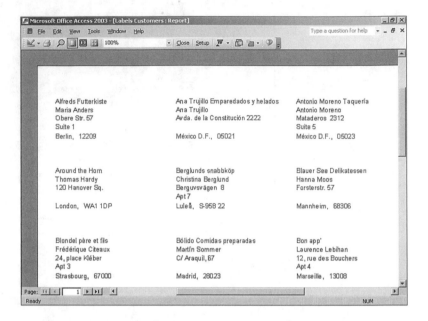

FIGURE 17.6

The Can Shrink *property set to* False.

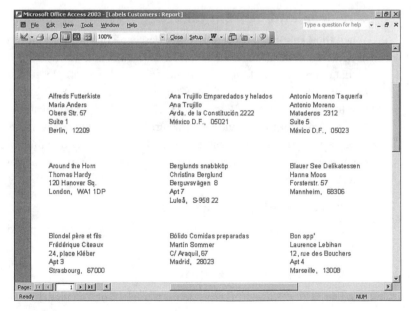

FIGURE 17.7

The Can Shrink *property set to* True.

Special Effect

The Special Effect property adds 3D effects to a control.

Border Style, Border Color, and Border Width

The Border Style, Border Color, and Border Width properties set the physical attributes of a control's border.

Fore Color

The Fore Color property sets the color of the text within a control.

Font Color, Font Name, Font Size, Font Weight, Font Italic, and Font Underline

The Font Color, Font Name, Font Size, Font Weight, Font Italic, and Font Underline properties affect the appearance of the text within a control.

Text Align

The Text Align property sets the alignment of the text within a control. You can set this property to Left, Center, Right, or Distribute. When it is set to Distribute, text is justified (see the Product Name column in Figure 17.8).

FIGURE 17.8

The Text Align property of a control.

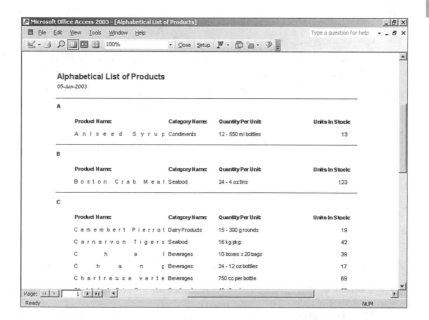

Reading Order

The Reading Order property determines the visual order in which characters, words, and groups of words are displayed. This property is often used with language-specific editions of Microsoft Access for which the reading order needs to be changed. The default setting is Context; Left-to-Right and Right-to-Left are the other available settings.

Scroll Bar Align

The Scroll Bar Align property specifies the visual placement of the control's vertical scrollbars and buttons. This property works in conjunction with language-specific versions of Access to determine scrollbar placement in either the right-to-left or left-to-right directions. The default setting is System, which lets the operating system determine the scrollbar alignment.

Numeral Shapes

The Numeral Shapes property determines the format for displaying numeric characters. This property works in conjunction with language-specific versions of Access to determine the type of numeric character to display. The default setting is System, which lets the operating system determine the numeric character display format. The other settings are Arabic, National, and Context.

Left Margin, Top Margin, Right Margin, and Bottom Margin

The Left Margin, Top Margin, Right Margin, and Bottom Margin properties are used to determine how far the text within a control prints from the left, top, right, and bottom of the control, respectively. These properties are particularly useful for large controls that contain a lot of text, such as memo on invoices.

Line Spacing

The Line Spacing property is used to control the spacing between lines of text within a control. The Line Spacing property is designated in inches.

Is Hyperlink

The Is Hyperlink property is used to determine whether Access displays the text within a control as a hyperlink. If you set the Is Hyperlink property to Yes and the text within the control is a relevant link, the text serves as a hyperlink. (This is useful only if you save the report in Hypertext Markup Language [HTML] format.)

The Data Properties of a Control

The Data properties of a control (see Figure 17.9), described in the following section, specify information about the data underlying a particular report control. By using the Data properties, you can designate everything from what data displays in a control to whether the data sums as it displays.

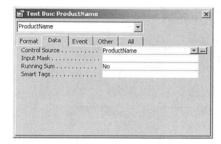

FIGURE 17.9

A control's Data properties.

Control Source

The Control Source property specifies the field in the report's record source that's used to populate the control. An example would be FirstName. A control source can also be a valid expression.

Input Mask

The Input Mask property assigns specific formatting to any data that is entered into a particular control. For example, you could use the input mask (999) 000-0000 to format data entered as a phone number.

Running Sum

The Running Sum property (which is unique to reports) is powerful. You can use it to calculate a record-by-record or group-by-group total. You can set it to No, Over Group, or Over All. When it is set to No, no running sum is calculated. When it is set to Over Group, the value of the text box accumulates from record to record within the group but is reset each time the group value changes. An example is a report that shows deposit amounts for each state, with a running sum for the amount deposited within the state. Each time the state changes, the amount deposited is set to zero. When this property is set to Over All, the sum continues to accumulate over the entire report.

The Other Properties of a Control

The Other properties of a control include properties, such as those described in the following sections, that don't fit into any other category (see Figure 17.10).

Name

The Name property provides an easy and self-documenting way to refer to a control in Visual Basic for Applications (VBA) code and in many other situations. You should name every control so that you can easily identify them in queries, code, and so on.

FIGURE 17.10
*The Other properties
of a control.*

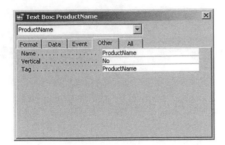

Vertical

The Vertical property is used to determine whether the text within a control is displayed vertically. The default value for this property is No.

Tag

Like the Tag property of a report, the Tag property of a control provides a user-defined slot for the control. You can place extra information in the Tag property.

A common mistake many Access developers and users make is to give controls names that conflict with Access names. This type of error is very difficult to track down. You need to make sure you use distinctive names for both fields and controls. Furthermore, you should not give a control the same name as a field within its expression. For example, the expression =ContactName & ContactTitle shouldn't have the name "ContactName"; that would cause an #error# message when you run the report. Finally, you shouldn't give a control the same name as its control source. Access gives a bound control the same name as its field, and you need to change this name to avoid problems. Following these simple warnings will spare you a lot of grief!

Inserting Page Breaks

You can set page breaks to occur before, within, or at the end of a section. Different types of page breaks are set in different ways. To set a page break within a section, you must use the Page Break tool in the toolbox. You click the Page Break tool in the toolbox (see Figure 17.11) and then click the report where you want the page break to occur. To set a page break before or after a section, you set the Force New Page property of the section to Before Section, After Section, or Before & After. The Force New Page property applies to group headers, group footers, and the report's Detail section.

FIGURE 17.11
The Page Break tool.

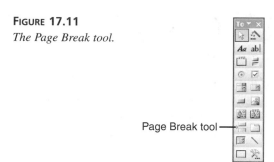

Page Break tool ——

You need to be careful not to place a page break within a control on a report. If you do, the page break occurs in the middle of the control's data.

Bound, Unbound, and Calculated Controls

You can place three types of controls on a report: bound, unbound, and calculated. Bound controls are tied to data within a field of the table or query underlying the report. Unbound controls, such as logos placed on reports, aren't tied to data. Calculated controls contain valid expressions; they can hold anything from a page number to a sophisticated financial calculation. Most complex reports have a rich combination of bound, unbound, and calculated controls.

Using Expressions to Enhance Reports

Calculated controls use expressions as their control sources. To create a calculated control, you must first add an unbound control to a report. An expression must be preceded by an equal sign (=); an example of a report expression is =Sum([Freight]). This expression, if placed in the report footer, totals the contents of the Freight control for all detail records in the report. You can build an expression by typing it directly into the control source or by using the Expression Builder, covered in Hour 16, "Power Form Techniques."

Building Reports Based on More Than One Table

The majority of reports you create will probably be based on data from more than one table. This is because a properly normalized database usually requires that you bring table data back together to give users valuable information. For example, a report that combines data from a Customers table, an Orders table, an Order Details table, and a Product table can supply the following information:

- Customer information, such as company name and address
- Order information, such as order date and shipping method
- Order detail information, such as quantity ordered and price
- A product table, including a product description

You can base a multitable report directly on the tables whose data it displays, or you can base it on a query that has already joined the tables, providing a flat table structure.

Creating One-to-Many Reports

You can create a one-to-many report by using the Report Wizard, or you can build a report from scratch. Different situations require different techniques, some of which are covered in the following sections.

Building a One-to-Many Report by Using the Report Wizard

Building a one-to-many report with the Report Wizard is quite easy. You just follow these steps:

1. Click Reports in the Objects list and double-click Create Report by Using Wizard.
2. From the Tables/Queries drop-down list box, select the first table or query whose data will appear on the report.
3. Select the fields you want to include from that table.
4. Select each additional table or query you want to include on the report, selecting the fields you need from each (see Figure 17.12). Click Next.
5. The next step of the Report Wizard asks you how you want to view the data (see Figure 17.13). You can accept Access's suggestion (By Orders), or you can choose from any of the available options (By Customers, By Orders, By Order Details, or By Products). Click Next.
6. The next step of the Report Wizard asks whether you want to add any grouping levels. You can use grouping levels to visually separate data and to provide

subtotals. In the example in Figure 17.14, the report is grouped by country and city. After you select grouping levels, click Next.

FIGURE 17.12

The first step of the Report Wizard: selecting the fields you want on a report.

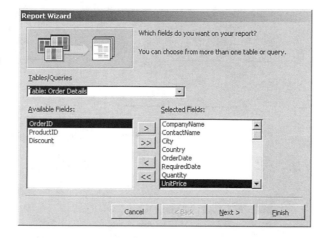

FIGURE 17.13

The second step of the Report Wizard: designating how you want to view the data.

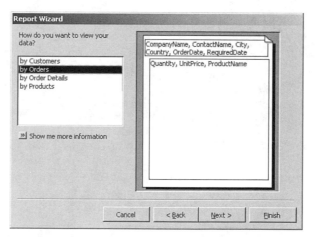

7. The next step of the Report Wizard lets you select how you want the records in the report's Detail section to be sorted (see Figure 17.15). This step of the wizard also allows you to specify any summary calculations you want to perform on the data (see Figure 17.16). Click the Summary Options button to specify the summary calculations. By clicking the Summary Options button, you can even opt to include the percentage of total calculations. Click OK when you're done adding the summary options.

FIGURE **17.14**

The third step of the Report Wizard: selecting groupings.

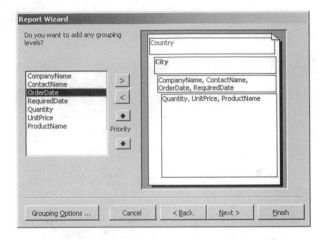

FIGURE **17.15**

The fourth step of the Report Wizard: selecting a sort order.

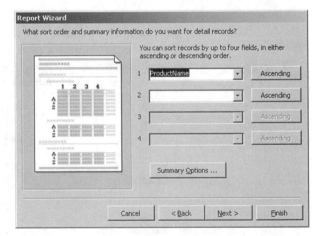

FIGURE **17.16**

Adding summary calculations.

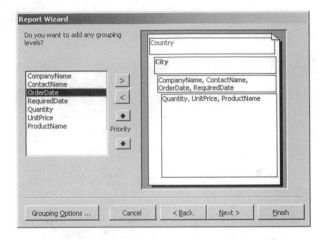

8. In the next step of the Report Wizard, you select the layout and orientation of the report. Layout options include Stepped, Blocked, Outline 1, Outline 2, Align Left 1, and Align Left 2. You can click the different option buttons to preview how each of the reports will look.

9. The next step of the Report Wizard lets you select from predefined styles for a report, including Bold, Casual, Compact, Corporate, Formal, and Soft Gray. You can preview each style to see what it looks like.

10. In the next step of the Report Wizard, you select a title for the report. The title also becomes the name of the report. I like to select an appropriate name and change the title after the wizard is finished. The final step also allows you to determine whether you want to immediately preview the report or see the report's design first. Click Finish when you are ready to complete the process.

The report created in this example is shown in Figure 17.17. Notice that the report is sorted and grouped by `Country`, `City`, and `OrderID`. The report's data is in order by `ProductName` within an `OrderID` grouping.

FIGURE 17.17

A completed one-to-many report.

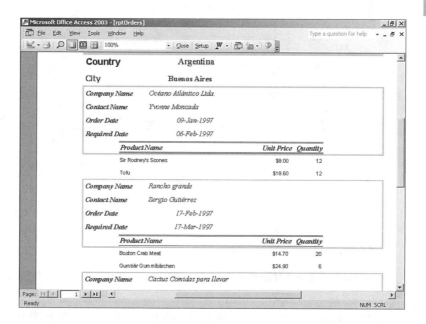

This method of creating a one-to-many report is by far the easiest. In fact, the "background join" technology that the wizards use when they allow you to pick fields from multiple tables—figuring out how to build the complex queries needed for the report or form—is one of the major benefits of using Access as a database tool. It's a huge timesaver and helps hide unnecessary complexity from you as you build a report. Although you should take advantage of this feature, it's important that you know what's happening under the covers. The following two sections give you this necessary knowledge.

Building a Report Based on a One-to-Many Query

A popular method of building a one-to-many report is from a one-to-many query. A one-to-many report built in this way is constructed as though it were based on the data within a single table. First, you build the query that will underlie the report (see Figure 17.18).

FIGURE 17.18

An example of a query underlying a one-to-many report.

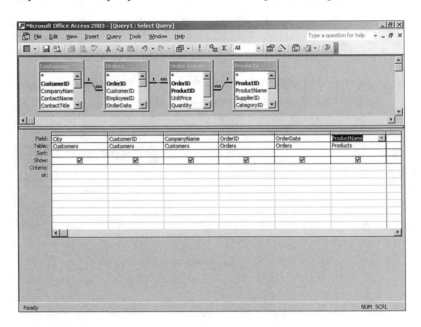

When you have finished the query, you can select it rather than select each individual table (as done in the previous section). After you select the query, you follow the same process to create the report as described in the preceding section.

Building a One-to-Many Report with the SubReport Wizard

You can build a one-to-many report by building the parent report and then adding a SubReport control. This is often the method used to create reports such as invoices that show the report's data in a one-to-many relationship rather than in a denormalized format. If you want to use the SubReport Wizard, you must make sure that you select the

Control Wizards tool before you add the SubReport control to the main report. Here is the process:

1. Click to select the SubForm/SubReport control tool.

2. Click and drag to place the SubForm/SubReport control on the main report. You usually place the SubForm/SubReport control in the report's Detail section. When you place the SubForm/SubReport control on the report, the SubReport Wizard is invoked (see Figure 17.19).

SubForm/SubReport control   SubReport Wizard

FIGURE 17.19

Adding a SubForm/SubReport control to invoke the SubReport Wizard.

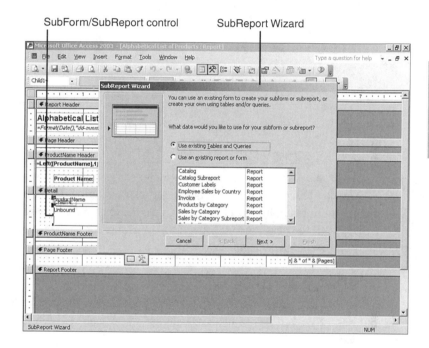

17

3. Indicate whether you want to base the subreport on an existing form or report or whether you want to build a new subreport based on a query or table. Click Next.

4. If you select Table or Query, you have to select the table or query on which you will base the subreport. You can then select the fields you want to include on the subreport. You can even select fields from more than one table or query. When you're finished making selections, click Next.

5. The next step of the SubReport Wizard suggests a relationship between the main report and the subreport (see Figure 17.20). You can accept the selected relationship, or you can define your own. When you're finished, click Next.

6. The final step of the SubReport Wizard asks you to name the subreport. Click Finish when you're finished.

FIGURE 17.20

The SubReport Wizard: identifying the relationship.

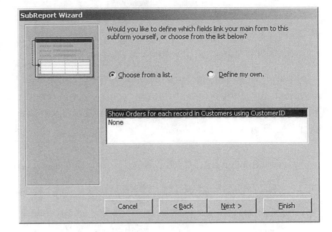

To follow standards, a subreport name should begin with the prefix rsub.

As you can see in Figure 17.21, the one-to-many relationship between two tables is clearly highlighted by this type of report. In the example in Figure 17.21, each customer is listed. All the detail records reflecting the orders for each customer are listed immediately following each customer's data.

Working with Subreports

When you add a subreport to a report, it's important to understand what properties the SubReport Wizard sets so that you can modify the SubForm/SubReport control, if needed.

Subreport Properties

You should become familiar with the properties of a SubForm/SubReport control, which are described in the following sections (see Figure 17.22).

Source Object

The Source Object control specifies the name of the report or other object that's being displayed within the control.

Link Child Fields

The Link Child Fields control specifies the fields from the child report that link the child report to the master report.

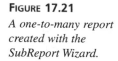

FIGURE 17.21

A one-to-many report created with the SubReport Wizard.

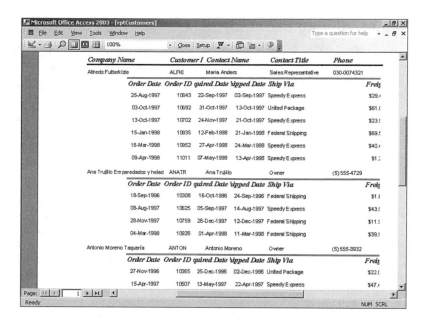

FIGURE 17.22

Properties of the SubForm/SubReport control.

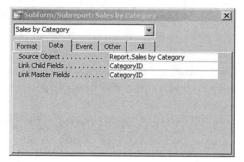

Link Master Fields

The Link Master Fields control specifies the fields from the master report that link the master report to the child report.

Modifying Subreports

Not only should you know how to work with the properties of a SubForm/SubReport object, but you should also be able to easily modify the subreport from within the main report. You can always modify the subreport by selecting it from the list of reports in the Database window. To do this, you select the report you want to modify and then click Design. You can also modify a subreport by selecting its objects directly within the parent report.

> Access 2002 and Access 2003 make it easier than earlier versions of Access to work with subforms and subreports in Design view. Scrolling has been improved so that it's easier than ever to design subforms and subreports. In addition, you can now open a subreport in its own separate Design view window by right-clicking the subreport and selecting Subreport in New Window. Or, instead of right-clicking the subreport, you can select the subreport and then click View | Subreport in New Window from the menu bar.

Working with Sorting and Grouping

Unlike sorting data within a form, sorting data within a report isn't determined by the underlying query. In fact, the underlying query affects the report's sort order only when you have not specified a sort order for the report. Any sort order specified in the query is completely overwritten by the report's sort order, which is determined in the report's Sorting and Grouping window (see Figure 17.23). The sorting and grouping of a report is affected by what options you select when you run the Report Wizard. You can use the Sorting and Grouping window to add, remove, or modify sorting and grouping options for a report. Sorting simply affects the order of the records in the report. Grouping adds group headers and footers to the report.

Adding Sorting and Grouping to a Report

Often, you want to add sorting and grouping to a report. Grouping allows you to add group headers and group footers to a report, and sorting allows you to designate the sort order within your groups. To add grouping and sorting, follow these four steps:

1. Click Sorting and Grouping on the Report Design toolbar to open the Sorting and Grouping window.

2. Click the selector of the line above where you want to insert the sorting and grouping level. In Figure 17.24, a sorting and grouping level is being added above the City grouping. Press the Insert key on the keyboard to insert a blank line in the Sorting and Grouping window.

FIGURE 17.23

The Sorting and Grouping window, showing grouping by Country, City, *and* OrderID *and sorting by product name.*

Report grouping

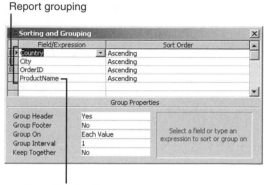

Report sort order

FIGURE 17.24

Inserting a sorting and grouping level.

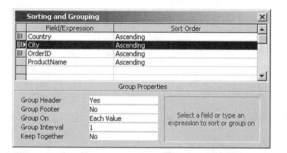

3. Click in the Field/Expression column and use the drop-down list to select the field on which you want to sort and group.

4. Set the properties to determine the nature of the sorting and grouping (see the next section, "Sorting and Grouping Properties"). Close the Sorting and Grouping window, if desired.

 To remove a sorting or grouping that you have added, you click the selector on the line of the field in the Sorting and Grouping window that you want to delete; then you press the Delete key. Access warns you that any controls in the group header or footer will be lost.

Sorting and Grouping Properties

Each grouping in a report has properties that define the group's attributes. Each group has five properties that determine whether the field or expression is used for sorting, grouping, or both (see Figure 17.25). They are also used to specify details about the grouping options. The following sections describe the sorting and grouping properties.

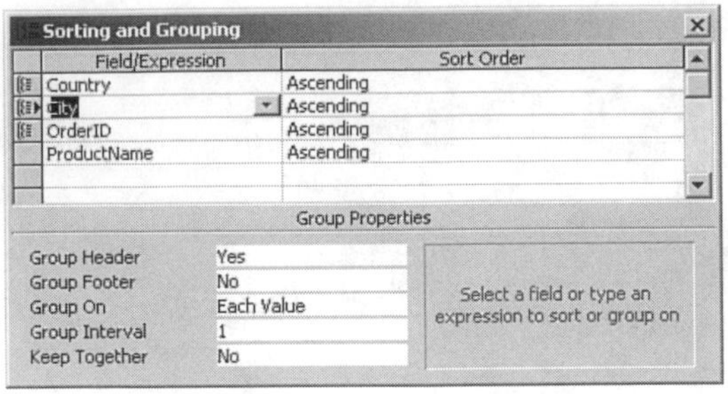

FIGURE 17.25

The Sorting and Grouping window, showing the five sorting and grouping properties.

Group Header

The Group Header property specifies whether the selected group contains a header band. When you set the Group Header property to Yes, an additional band appears in the report that you can use to display information about the group. For example, if you're grouping by country, you can use the Group Header property to display the name of the country you're about to print. If the Group Header and Group Footer properties are both set to No, the field is used only to determine the sort order of the records in the report.

Group Footer

The Group Footer property specifies whether the selected group contains a footer band. When you set the Group Footer property to Yes, an additional band appears in the report. You can use this band to display summary information about the group; it's often used to display subtotals for a group.

Group On

The Group On property specifies what constitutes a new group. It is often used for situations such as departmental roll-ups where you roll several subdepartments into a summary department. Rather than group on the entire department number, you might want to group on the first three digits, for example.

The Group On settings for Text fields are Each Value and Prefix Characters. For Date fields, the settings are much more complex. They include Each Value, Year, Qtr, Month, Week, Day, Hour, and Minute. This means you could group by a Date field and have Access subtotal and begin a new group each time the week changes in the field. For AutoNumber, Currency, and Number fields, the settings are Each Value and Interval.

Group Interval

You use the Group Interval property with the Group On property to specify an interval value by which data is grouped. If, for example, the Group On property for a Text field is set to Prefix Characters, and the Group Interval property is set to 3, the field's data is grouped on the first three characters.

Keep Together

The Keep Together property determines whether Access tries to keep an entire group together on one page. The three settings for the property are No, Whole Group, and With First Detail. Setting this property to Whole Group causes Access to try to keep the entire group together on one page. This includes the group header, the group footer, and the Detail section. Setting this property to With First Detail causes Access to print the group header on a page only if it can also print the first detail record on the same page.

> If you have set the Keep Together property to Whole Group and the group is too large to fit on a page, Access ignores the property setting. Furthermore, if you set Keep Together to With First Detail and either the group header or the detail record is too large to fit on one page, that setting is ignored, too.

Group Header and Footer Properties and Why to Use Them

Each group header and footer has its own properties that determine the behavior of the group header or footer (see Figure 17.26). The following sections describe these properties.

FIGURE 17.26
Group header and footer properties.

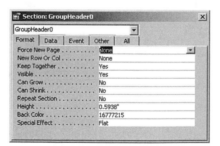

Force New Page

You can set the Force New Page property to None, Before Section, After Section, or Before & After. If it is set to None, no page break occurs either before or after the report section. If it is set to Before Section, a page break occurs before the report section prints; if it is set to `After Section`, a page break occurs after the report section prints. If it is set to `Before & After`, a page break occurs before the report section prints as well as after it prints.

New Row or Col

The `New Row or Col` property determines whether a column break occurs whenever the report section prints. This property applies only to multicolumn reports. The settings are `None`, `Before Section`, `After Section`, and `Before & After`. Like the `Force New Page` property, this property determines whether the column break occurs before the report section prints, after it prints, or before and after, or whether it's affected by the report section break at all.

Keep Together

The `Keep Together` property specifies whether you want Access to try to keep an entire report section together on one page. If this property is set to `Yes`, Access starts printing the section at the top of the next page if it can't print the entire section on the current page. When this property is set to `No`, Access prints as much of the section as possible on the current page, inserting page breaks as necessary. If a section exceeds the page length, Access starts printing the section on a new page and continues printing it on the following page.

Visible

The `Visible` property indicates whether the section is visible. It's common to hide the visibility of a particular report section at runtime in response to different situations. You can easily accomplish this by changing the value of the report section's `Visible` property with a macro or VBA code, usually on the `Format` event.

Can Grow and Can Shrink

The `Can Grow` property determines whether you want the section to stretch vertically to accommodate the data in it. The `Can Shrink` property specifies whether you want the section to shrink vertically, eliminating blank lines.

Repeat Section

The `Repeat Section` property is a valuable property that lets you specify whether Access repeats the group header on subsequent pages if a report section needs to print on more than one page.

Basing Reports on Stored Queries or Embedded SQL Statements

Basing Access reports on stored queries offers two major benefits:

- The query underlying the report can be used by other forms and reports.
- Sophisticated calculations need to be built only once—they don't need to be re-created for each report (or form).

With versions of Access prior to Access 2000, reports based on stored queries open faster than reports based on embedded SQL statements. This is because when you build and save a query, Access compiles and creates a query plan. This query plan is a plan of execution that's based on the amount of data in the query's tables as well as all the indexes available in each table. In versions of Access prior to Access 2000, if you run a report based on an embedded SQL statement, the query is compiled, and the query plan is built at runtime, slowing the query's execution. With Access 2000, query plans are built for embedded SQL statements when a form or report is saved. Query plans are stored with the associated form or report.

So what are the benefits of basing a report on a stored query instead of an embedded SQL statement? You may want to build several reports and forms, all based on the same information. An embedded SQL statement can't be shared by multiple database objects. At the very least, you must copy the embedded SQL statement for each form and report you build. Basing reports and forms on stored queries eliminates this problem. You build the query once and then modify it if changes need to be made to it. Many forms and reports can all use the same query (including its criteria, expressions, and so on).

Reports often contain complex expressions. If a particular expression is used in only one report, nothing is lost by building the expression into an embedded SQL statement. On the other hand, many complex expressions are used in multiple reports and forms. If you build these expressions into queries on which the reports and forms are based, you have to create each expression only one time.

It's easy to save an embedded SQL statement as a query, and doing so allows you to use the Report Wizard to build a report using several tables. You can then save the resulting SQL statement as a query. With the report open in Design view, you bring up the Properties window. After you select the Data tab, click in the Record Source property and click the ellipsis (...). The embedded SQL statement appears as a query. You need to select File|Save As, enter a name for the query, and click OK. Then you close the Query win-

17

> dow, indicating that you want to update the Record Source property. The
> query is then based on a stored query instead of an embedded SQL state-
> ment.

Although basing reports on stored queries offers several benefits, it has downside as well.
For example, if a database contains numerous reports, the database container becomes
cluttered with a large number of queries that underlie those reports. Furthermore, queries
and the expressions within them are often very specific to a particular report. If that is
the case, you should opt to use embedded SQL statements rather than stored queries. As
a general rule, if several reports are based on the same data and the same complex calculations, you should base them on a stored query. If a report is based on a unique query
with a unique set of data and unique calculations, you should base it on an embedded
SQL statement.

Summary

In this hour you have learned numerous advanced report techniques that will help you
quite a bit in building and maintaining complex reports. You have learned about several
report and control properties. You have also learned how to insert page breaks as well as
how to include bound, unbound, and calculated controls on the reports you build. You
have also learned how to build reports based on data stored in more than one table, as
well as how to modify sorting and grouping options.

Q&A

Q **Describe the problem associated with setting the Record Locks property to No
Locks.**

A With No Locks, Access does not lock any data while it runs the report. Users can
modify the data while the report is running, rendering subtotals and percentages of
total calculations incorrect.

Q **Explain the main reason you may see #error# in a control on a report when
you run it.**

A Access does not allow you to give a control the same name as any field in the
expression on which it is based. In other words, if you have a control named qty,
you cannot base it on the expression =qty*price.

Q Explain the concept of the `Link Child` and `Link Master` properties.

A The `Link Child` fields are the fields from the child report that link the child report to the master report. The `Link Master` fields are the fields from the master report that link the master report to the child report.

Q Explain what differentiates a sorting from a grouping.

A When you designate a group header or a group footer in the Sorting and Grouping window, you create a grouping. Without the group header or group footer, Access uses the field or expression for sorting only.

Workshop

The Workshop includes quiz questions that are designed to help you test your understanding of the material covered and activities to help put what you've learned to practice. You can find the answers to the questions in the section immediately following the quiz.

Quiz

1. If you have the `Keep Together` property set to `Whole Group` and the group is too large to fit on a page, Access ignores the property setting (True/False).

2. It's always best to base a report on a stored query (True/False).

3. Name the property that allows a control to expand vertically to accommodate all the data in it.

4. What property allows you to easily accumulate a value from record to record within a group or overall?

5. Where does the `Source Object` property apply?

Quiz Answers

1. True.

2. False. The *only* advantage of basing a report on a stored query is that you can share the query with multiple reports.

3. The `Can Grow` property.

4. The `Running Sum` property.

5. The `Source Object` property applies when you are working with subreports.

Activities

Practice working with the report and control properties that you have learned about in this hour. Practice inserting page breaks and working with bound, unbound, and calculated controls. Finally, build a couple reports based on data stored in more than one table. Modify the sorting and grouping options that the wizard sets for you.

PART V

Advanced Topics

Hour 18

Sharing Data with Other Applications

Microsoft Access is very capable of interfacing with data from other sources. It can use data from any OLE DB or Open Database Connectivity (ODBC) data source, as well as data from FoxPro, dBASE, Paradox, Lotus, Excel, and many other sources. In this hour, you will learn how to interface with external data sources other than OLE DB and ODBC data sources.

NEW TERM *External data* is data that is stored outside the current database. External data may be data that you store in another Microsoft Access database, or it might be data that you store in a multitude of other file formats—including Indexed Sequential Access Method (ISAM), spreadsheet, ASCII, and more. This hour focuses on accessing data sources other than ODBC and OLEDB data sources. Other, more advanced, books, including *Alison Balter's Mastering Access 2002 Enterprise Development* (Sams Publishing), cover the process of accessing data stored in these data sources.

NEW TERM Access is an excellent *front-end* product, which means that it provides a powerful and effective means of presenting data— even data from external sources. You might opt to store data in places other than Access for many reasons. You can most effectively manage large databases, for example, on a back-end database server such as Microsoft SQL Server. You might store data in a FoxPro, dBASE, or Paradox file format because a legacy application written in one of those environments is using the data. You might download text data from a mainframe or midrange computer. Regardless of the reason the data is stored in another format, it is necessary that you understand how to manipulate this external data in Access applications. With the capability to access data from other sources, you can create queries, forms, and reports.

When you're accessing external data, you have two choices: You can import the data into an Access database or you can access the data by linking to it from an Access database. Importing the data is the optimum route (except with ODBC data sources), but it is not always possible. If you can't import external data, you should link to external files because Microsoft Access maintains a lot of information about these linked files. This optimizes performance when manipulating the external files.

In this hour you will accomplish the following tasks:

- Gain an understanding of importing versus linking
- Learn how to export to various file formats
- Learn how to import from various file formats
- Learn how to link to various file formats
- Learn how to work with the Linked Table Manager

Importing, Linking, and Opening Files: When and Why

When you import data into an Access table, Access makes a copy of the data and places it in the Access table. After Access imports the data, it treats the data like the data in any other native Access table. In fact, neither you nor Access has any way of knowing from where the data came. As a result, imported data offers the same performance and flexibility as any other Access table data.

Linking to external data is quite different from importing data. Linked data remains in its native format. By establishing a link to the external data, you can build queries, forms, and reports that present the data. After you create a link to external data, the link remains permanently established unless you explicitly remove it. The linked table appears in the Database window just like any other Access table, except that its icon is different. In fact, if the data source permits multiuser access, the users of an application can modify the data as can the users of the applications written in the data source's native database format (such as FoxPro, dBASE, or Paradox). The main difference between a linked table and a native table is that you cannot modify a linked table's structure from within Access.

Determining Whether to Import or Link

It is important that you understand when to import external data and when to link to external data. You should import external data in either of these circumstances:

- If you are migrating an existing system into Access.
- If you want to use external data to run a large volume of queries and reports, and you will not update the data. In this case, you want the added performance that native Access data provides.

When you are migrating an existing system to Access and you are ready to permanently migrate test or production data into an application, you import the tables into Access. You might also want to import external data if you convert the data into ASCII format on a regular basis and you want to use the data for reports. Instead of attempting to link to the data and suffering the performance hits associated with such a link, you can import the data each time you download it from the mainframe or midrange computer.

You should link to external data in any of the following circumstances:

- The data is used by a legacy application that requires the native file format.
- The data resides on an ODBC-compliant database server.
- You will access the data on a regular basis, making it prohibitive to keep the data up-to-date if you do not link to it.

Often, you won't have the time or resources to rewrite an application written in FoxPro, Paradox, or some other language. You might be developing additional applications that will share data with the legacy application, or you might want to use the strong querying and reporting capabilities of Access instead of develop queries and reports in the native environment.

If you link to the external data, users of existing applications can continue to work with the applications and their data. Access applications can retrieve and modify data without concern for corrupting, or in any other way harming, the data.

If the data resides in an ODBC database such as Microsoft SQL Server, you want to reap the data-retrieval benefits provided by a database server. By linking to the ODBC data source, you can take advantage of Access's ease of use as a front-end tool and also take advantage of client/server technology.

Finally, if you intend to access data on a regular basis, linking to the external table provides you with ease of use and performance benefits. After you create a link, in most cases, Access treats the table just like any other Access table.

18

Although this hour covers the process of importing external data, this is essentially a one-time process and doesn't require a lot of discussion. It is important to note, however, that after you import data into an Access table, you can no longer use the application in its native format to access the data.

Looking at Supported File Formats

Microsoft Access enables you to import and link to files in these formats:

- Microsoft Jet databases (including versions of Jet prior to version 4.0)
- Access projects (.ADP and .ADE files)
- ODBC databases
- Hypertext Markup Language (HTML) documents
- Extensible Markup Language (XML) documents (import and open only)
- Microsoft Exchange and Outlook
- dBASE III, dBASE IV, and dBASE 5.0
- Paradox 3.x, 4.x, and 5.x
- Microsoft Excel spreadsheets, versions 3.0, 4.0, 5.0, and 8.0
- Lotus WKS, WK1, WK3, and WK4 spreadsheets (import and open only)
- ASCII text files stored in a tabular format

Exporting to Another Access Database

You can easily export Access tables and queries to another Access database. The following is the required process:

1. Right-click the object you want to export and select Export from the context menu. The Export Table dialog box appears.

2. Select the Access database to which you want to export the object and then select Export. The Export dialog box appears (see Figure 18.1).

3. In the Export dialog box, select Definition and Data or Definition Only, depending on whether you want to export just the structure or the structure and the data. Click OK.

When you export an object to another database, Access exports a copy of the object. When you choose Definition Only, Access copies just the object's structure (no data) to the receiving database.

FIGURE 18.1

The Export dialog box, which allows you to designate the destination table.

FIGURE 18.1

The Export dialog box, which allows you to designate the destination table.

Exporting to an Excel Spreadsheet

You might want to export table data or query results to an Excel spreadsheet so that you can utilize Excel's analytical features. You can accomplish this in many ways. You can export an object by right-clicking it, by using drag and drop, or by using OfficeLinks.

Exporting to an Excel Spreadsheet

To export table data or query results to an Excel spreadsheet, follow these steps:

1. Right-click the object you want to export and select Export from the context menu. The Export dialog box appears.
2. From the Save As Type drop-down, select the appropriate version of Microsoft Excel.
3. Click Export.

18

Exporting to an Excel Spreadsheet Using Drag and Drop

You can export a table or query to Microsoft Excel by dragging and dropping it directly onto an Excel spreadsheet. This whizbang technology makes the integration between these two powerful products virtually seamless. Here are the steps involved:

1. Arrange the Access and Excel application windows so that both are visible.
2. Drag the object (that is, the table or query) from the Access Database window onto the Excel spreadsheet. The results of dragging and dropping the Customers table from the Access Database window to Microsoft Excel appear in Figure 18.2.

Exporting to an Excel Spreadsheet by Using OfficeLinks

You can use the OfficeLinks feature to export an Access table or query to Microsoft Excel. The process works like this:

1. Select the object you want to export.

2. Click the drop-down arrow in the OfficeLinks button.

3. Choose Analyze It with Microsoft Excel to export the data to Excel (see Figure 18.3).

FIGURE 18.2

Dragging and dropping an object directly from the Access Database window onto an Excel spreadsheet.

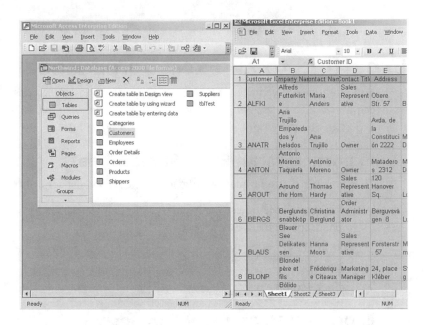

FIGURE 18.3

Selecting Analyze It with Microsoft Excel from the OfficeLinks button.

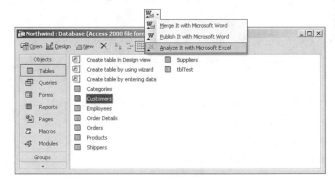

It's important to note the following facts concerning the process of exporting by using OfficeLinks:

• The face of the OfficeLinks button changes, depending on the most recent choice.

- You can open the exported object within Excel.
- If you export a query to Excel, Access runs the query and exports the results of the query to the Excel spreadsheet.

Exporting to ASCII

ASCII is a standard file format that many programs can work with. Exporting to the ASCII format allows you to make the data in an Access database available to other applications.

It is easy to export Access tables and queries to the ASCII file format. Here's how it works:

1. Right-click the object you want to export and select Export from the context menu. The Export dialog box appears.
2. Select Text Files from the Save As Type drop-down box.
3. Select the destination folder for the database.
4. Click Export. The Export Text Wizard appears (see Figure 18.4). This step allows you to select the export format you want to use. You must select between Delimited and Fixed Width. These are two different text file formats that you can output to. The dialog box provides examples of the output to help you to make a selection.
5. Select Delimited and then click Advanced. The Text Export Specification dialog box appears (see Figure 18.5). Here you can designate the field delimiter, text qualifier, language, date order, and other specifics about the file you are exporting. You can modify these options to meet the specifications of the consumer of the file you are creating.

18

FIGURE 18.4

The Export Text Wizard dialog box.

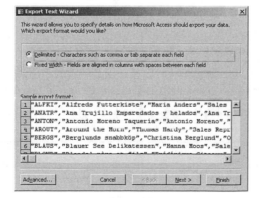

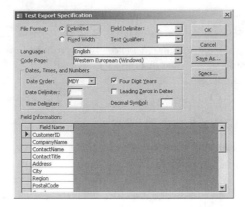

6. Select the desired settings, and click OK.

7. Click Next.

8. Select Comma for the delimiter so that the output file will contain commas between the fields.

9. Select Include Field Names on First Row so that the output file will include all the field names in the first row. Figure 18.6 provides an example of an output file. Click Next. The final step of the Export Text Wizard appears.

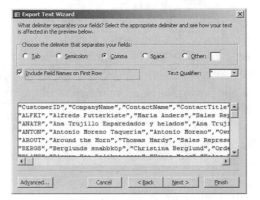

10. Type the *appropriate* destination in the Export to File text box.

11. Click Finish to complete the process and click OK to acknowledge completion.

If you are exporting the file to a location other than the location that Access indicates in the Export to File text box, you need to change the location. For example, `C:\My Documents\Interests.txt` provides the entire path and file-name for the file.

Importing from Another Access Database

You can import objects (for example, tables, queries, reports) from one Access database into another. When you import an object, you are making a copy of the object. Any changes you make to the imported object do not affect the original object.

To see how to import an Access table object, follow these steps:

1. Open the database into which you want to import the table.
2. Right-click anywhere in the Database window and select Import from the context menu. The Import dialog box appears.
3. Select the folder where the Microsoft Access database you want to import is located.
4. Double-click the database file that contains the object you want to import.
5. Select the Table tab from the Object window.
6. Select the table from the list of tables.
7. Click the Options button.
8. Select the desired options. Options include whether to import relationships, menus, and toolbars, as well as import and export specifications. You can also designate whether to import just the table definitions or the table definitions and the data. Finally, you can opt to import the queries as either queries or as tables (the result of executing the queries). Generally, you will leave all these options at their default values, although you might want to modify them for specific applications.
9. Click OK.

18

Importing Spreadsheet Data

You can easily import an Excel spreadsheet into an Access database. To do so, follow these steps:

1. Open the database into which you want to import the spreadsheet.
2. Right-click anywhere in the Database window and choose Import from the context menu. The Import dialog box appears.
3. Select the folder where the spreadsheet file you want to import is located.

4. From the Files of Type drop-down list box, select Microsoft Excel.

5. Double-click the spreadsheet you want to import.

6. Select Show Worksheets or Show Named Ranges (Access does not display this step of the wizard if the spreadsheet contains only one worksheet) and then click Next. The Import Spreadsheet Wizard appears.

> If you plan to import spreadsheet data on a regular basis, it is helpful to define in the Excel spreadsheet a named range that contains the data you want to import. You can then easily opt to import the named range in step 6 each time you execute the import process.

7. Select First Row Contains Column Headings, if appropriate (see Figure 18.7). Notice in Figure 18.7 that the first row appears as column headings rather than data. Click Next.

8. Select In a New Table, and then click Next (see Figure 18.8). This means that Access will place the data you are importing into a new table rather than into an existing table.

Does the first row of data contain column names?

FIGURE 18.7

Designating whether the first row of the spreadsheet contains column headings.

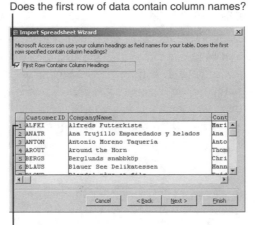

The first row of data

9. Type the field name in the Field Name text box, if necessary.

10. Select whether you want Access to index the field.

11. Indicate whether to import a field by selecting the Do Not Import option for that field, if desired.

Whether field is indexed
Field name

FIGURE **18.8**
*The Import
Spreadsheet Wizard.*

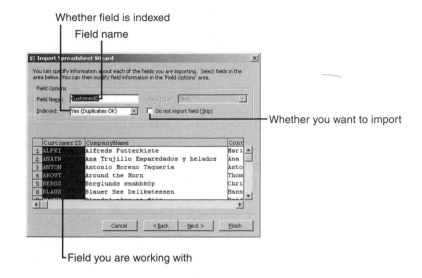

Whether you want to import

Field you are working with

12. Click in the field list to select the next field.

13. Repeat steps 9–12 as appropriate for each field and then click Next.

14. If your data has a column that is appropriate for the primary key, select Choose My Own Primary Key. Otherwise, select Let Access Add Primary Key.

15. If you opted to choose your own primary key, select from the drop-down box the field that you want Access to use as the primary key, and then click Next.

16. Type the table name in the Import to Table text box.

17. Click Finish.

18. Click OK.

Importing ASCII Data

Mainframes and minicomputers often export data in the ASCII file format. When you import ASCII data, you often need to make some changes for Access to handle the data properly.

To import ASCII data into Access, follow these steps:

1. Open the database into which you want to import a table.

2. Right-click anywhere in the Database window and select Import from the context menu. The Import dialog box appears.

3. Select the folder where the ASCII file you want to import is located.

18

4. Select Text Files from the Files of Type drop-down list box.

5. Double-click the file you want to import. This launches the Import Text Wizard.

6. Select Delimited or Fixed Width, to designate the format of the file you want to import. Click Next.

Xx'x , ᵧᵧ ᵧ = Delimited
| xᵪᵪ | ᵧᵧ ᵧ | = Fixed width

7. Select or deselect First Row Contains Field Names, as appropriate, and then click Next.

8. Select In a New Table or In an Existing Table, as appropriate, and then click Next.

9. Type the field name in the Field Name text box.

10. Select whether you want Access to create an index for the field.

11. Repeat steps 10 and 11, as appropriate, and then click Next.

12. If your data has a column that is appropriate for the primary key, select Choose My Own Primary Key. Otherwise, select Let Access Add Primary Key.

13. If you opted to choose your own primary key, select from the drop-down box the field that you want Access to use as the primary key, and then click Next.

14. Type the table name in the Import to Table text box.

15. Click Finish and then click OK.

> There are some important thing that you should be aware of when working with ASCII data. These notes can save you lots of time and effort in working with the imported data:
>
> - After you import a table, you should open it and view its data. You might want to modify some of the field types to make them the appropriate Access data types. For example, the table you imported from might not have had a currency type.
>
> - You can click the Advanced button anytime in the Import Text Wizard to change the import specifications for each field.

Linking to Tables in Another Access Database

When you link to data in another database, the data remains in its source location. Access simply creates a pointer to the data. To practice linking to data in different types of databases, follow these steps:

1. Open the database that will contain the link.

2. Right-click within the Database window and choose Link Tables from the context menu.

3. Navigate to the folder that contains the source database.

4. Double-click the source database. The Link Tables dialog box appears (see Figure 18.9).

5. Select the table(s) you want to link to.

6. Click OK. Figure 18.10 shows the results of such an operation.

FIGURE **18.9**

The Link Tables dialog box.

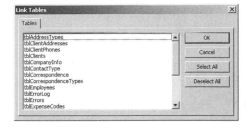

FIGURE **18.10**

The linked tables with an arrow that indicates that they are linked.

18

There are some very important things that you must remember when working with linked tables in another Access database:

- When you link a table to the source, there are some properties that you cannot change in the linked table. The descriptions of these properties appear in red when you're in Design view of the table.

- If you make a change to any data in a linked table, the change will be reflected in the underlying table.

- Any relationships established between tables in the source are reflected in the linked tables.

- When working with data that needs to be kept on a file server, you should keep the data (that is, the tables) in one database and the other objects (for example, forms, reports) in another database. You then link from the application database to the data database.

Linking to Another Type of Database

Even if you're not ready to actually import data from a database management system (such as FoxPro), you still might want to make changes to it by using Access. You can link to other types of databases and to Excel spreadsheets.

Linking to Excel Spreadsheets

Linking to Excel spreadsheets involves the following steps:

1. Open the database that will contain the link.
2. Right-click in the Database window and select Link Tables from the context menu.
3. Select Microsoft Excel from the Files of Type drop-down list box.
4. Navigate to the folder that contains the source database.
5. Double-click the source spreadsheet.
6. Select Show Worksheets or Show Named Ranges, as appropriate, and then click Next.
7. Click to select First Row Contains Column Headings, if appropriate.
8. Click Next.
9. Type a name for the linked table.
10. Click Finish and then click OK. An icon that is associated with the linked table appears (see Figure 18.11).

FIGURE 18.11

Access associating an Excel icon with a link.

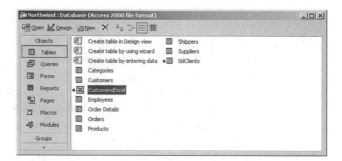

Linking to Other Databases

In addition to linking to Access tables and Excel spreadsheets, you might want to link to dBASE, FoxPro, Paradox, and other database files. Here are the required steps:

1. Open the database that will contain the links.
2. Right-click in the Database window and select Link Tables from the context menu.

3. Select the type of database you will link to from the Files of Type drop-down list box.

4. Change to the folder that contains the source database.

5. Double-click the source database and then click Link.

6. Click Yes to create a new information file in Access.

7. Click to add any necessary index files and then click Close.

8. Select a unique record identifier from the list of fields and then click OK. This step is required by certain programs, such as FoxPro, so that Access can properly update the data in the source database.

9. Click OK and then click Close.

There are some very important things that you must remember when working with linked tables in other databases:

- When you link a table to the source, there are some properties that you cannot change in the linked table. The descriptions of these properties appear in red when you're in Design view of the table.

- Any data you change in a linked table changes in the source table as well.

The Linked Table Manager

The Linked Table Manager is an important tool for working with linked tables. It allows you to move tables to another folder or another drive and then update the link to that table.

To move and update table links, follow these steps:

1. Choose Tools|Database Utilities|Linked Table Manager. The Linked Table Manager appears (see Figure 18.12).

FIGURE 18.12

The Linked Table Manager.

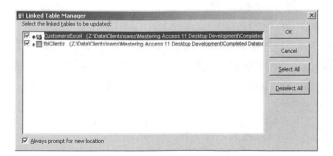

2. Select the linked table(s) you want to update.

3. Select the Always Prompt for New Location check box.

4. Click OK.

5. Select the folder or drive to which you have moved the table.

6. Select the table and then click Open.

7. Click OK.

You might at some time have a link that you no longer need. For example, you might import data because it is no longer necessary to utilize the legacy system that you have in place. The following are the steps necessary to remove such a link:

1. Select the link you want to remove.

2. Press the Delete key. The dialog box shown in Figure 18.13 appears.

FIGURE 18.13

*Access prompting you
to remove a link.*

3. Click Yes to remove the link. The link is removed.

> It is important to note that this process does not remove the linked object. It simply removes the link.

Task: Linking Tables from One Database to Another and Exporting Data to Other Databases

Follow these steps to practice the skills that you have learned in this hour:

1. Open the Northwind database that ships with Access.

2. Export the Orders table as an Excel spreadsheet.

3. Export the Products table as a text file.

4. Import the Orders spreadsheet into the Northwind database and name it Orders2. Base the primary key on the OrderID field.

5. Import the Products text file into the Northwind database and name it ProductsBackup. The ProductId field is the primary key.

6. Create a new database called Northwind2003.

▼ 7. Import the Orders table from Northwind into Northwind2003.

8. Link the Customers table from the Northwind2003 database to the Northwind database.

9. Add the records shown in Table 18.1 to the Customers table in the Northwind2003 database.

TABLE 18.1 Records to Add to the Customers Table

CustomerID	CompanyName	ContactName	ContactTitle	City
ALEXI	Alexis' Flowers	Alexis Balter	President	Oak Park
BREND	Brendan's Trucking	Brendan Balter	CEO	Westlake

10. Add the records shown in Table 18.2 to the Orders table in the Northwind2003 database.

TABLE 18.2 Records to Add to the Orders Table

ClientID	EmployeeID	OrderDate	Freight
ALFKI	1	6/2/2001	100
QUICK	4	7/4/2001	300

11. Close the Northwind2003 database and open the Northwind database.

12. Open the Orders table and notice that the records you added to this table in the Northwind2003 database do not appear in this table.

13. Close the table.

14. Open the Customers table and notice that the records you added to this table in the Northwind2003 database appear in this table.

▲ 15. Close the table and the database.

Summary

In this hour you have learned how to import and link to external data. You have learned the differences between importing and linking and when it is appropriate to use each technique. You have also learned how to export to various file formats, as well as how to import from various file formats into Microsoft Access. Finally, you have learned how to link to different file formats and how to work with an important tool called the Linked Table Manager.

Q&A

Q Explain the difference between importing and linking.

A Importing makes a copy of the data, whereas linking causes data to remain in its source location and format.

Q What is the purpose of the Linked Table Manager?

A The Linked Table Manager allows you to update broken links.

Q Name some uses of importing.

A You might use importing when you are migrating a system to Access or when you want to run a series of reports on data that is stored in another format.

Q Name some uses of linking.

A You might use linking if the data for a system is used by a legacy application, it resides on a database server (for example, SQL Server), or you will access the data on a regular basis.

Workshop

The Workshop includes quiz questions that are designed to help you test your understanding of the material covered and activities to help put what you've learned to practice. You can find the answers to the questions in the section immediately following the quiz.

Quiz

1. Name two file formats that you can export to.

2. Name two file formats that you can import from.

3. When you remove a link, Access deletes the associated data (True/False).

4. When you update data in a linked table, the process affects the data in the source table (True/False).

5. When you update data in an imported table, the process affects the data in the source table (True/False).

Quiz Answers

1. You can export to ASCII, HTML, XML, and many other formats.

2. You can import from spreadsheets, ASCII, HTML, XML, and many other formats.

3. False. When you remove a link, Access deletes the link, not the underlying data store.

4. True.

5. False. When you update data in an imported table, you are updating a copy of the data and therefore do not affect the data in the source table.

Activities

Practice exporting the Northwind database Categories table (available in the Northwind sample database that ships with Microsoft Access) to Excel, ASCII, and FoxPro. Then try linking to the files that the export process created. Delete the links and then import the exported data.

18

HOUR 19

Access and the Internet

The Internet is part of our everyday lives, and the Internet has penetrated into the life of Access developers. You can save almost every Access 2003 object as an Hypertext Markup Language (HTML) or Extensible Markup Language (XML) document. Furthermore, Access 2000 introduced a new object type called *data access pages*. Using data access pages, you can quickly and easily create a Web view of data. Data access pages are extremely flexible and scalable. You can create the simplest data access page as easily as you can create any Access form. On the other hand, by using the Microsoft Script Editor (MSE), you can turn data access pages into powerful Web pages. Probably the biggest downside of data access pages is that you must view them on a machine that has Internet Explorer 5 or above and that has Microsoft Office installed. This makes data access pages an excellent candidate for intranet applications but not for Internet applications.

This hour covers several topics that relate to Access and its tight integration with the Internet:

- Exporting to and importing from HTML
- Exporting to and importing from XML
- Working with data access pages

Saving Database Objects as HTML

Probably one of the most basic but powerful features in Access is the capability to save database objects as HTML documents. You can publish table data, query results, form datasheets, forms, and reports as HTML. Each of these objects is covered in the sections that follow.

Saving Table Data as HTML

When saving table data, you can store it in the HTML file format so that you can easily publish it on the Web. To save table data as HTML, just follow these steps:

1. Click Tables in the Objects list of the Database window.
2. Select the table whose data you want to save as HTML.
3. Choose File|Export to open the Export Table dialog box.
4. From the Save As Type drop-down list, select HTML Documents.
5. Select a filename and a location for the HTML document.
6. Click Export to finish the process.

Access exports the file to HTML so that you can view it from any Web browser (see Figure 19.1). You can also view the HTML source, as shown in Figure 19.2. To view the HTML file in a browser, you simply locate the file on your hard disk in Explorer or My Computer and double-click the file. The file then launches in Internet Explorer (or your default browser). To view the source, you select View|Source while in Internet Explorer.

Saving Query Results as HTML

The capability to save query results as HTML means you don't need to save all fields and all records to an HTML file. In fact, you can even save the results of Totals queries and other complex queries as HTML. Saving the result of a query as HTML is similar to saving a table as HTML. It involves these steps:

1. Click Queries in the Objects list of the Database window.
2. Select the query whose results you want to save as HTML.
3. Choose File|Export to open the Export Query dialog box.
4. From the Save As Type drop-down list, select HTML Documents.
5. Select a filename and a location for the HTML document.
6. Click Export to finish the process. Access exports the file to HTML so that you can view it from any Web browser.

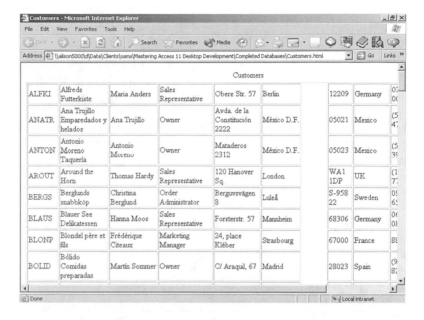

FIGURE 19.1

The Northwind *data-base* Customers *table saved as HTML.*

FIGURE 19.2

The source of the Northwind *database* Customers *table's HMTL file.*

Saving Forms as HTML

You can't save an entire form as HTML, but you can save a form's datasheet as HTML because an HTML file is a static file. It doesn't change as the data in the database changes, nor can you modify the data in an HTML file. To save a form's datasheet as HTML, follow these steps:

1. Click Forms in the Objects list of the Database window.

2. Select the form whose results you want to save as HTML.

3. Choose File|Export to open the Export Form dialog box.

4. From the Save As Type drop-down list, select HTML Documents.

5. Select a filename and a location for the HTML document.

6. Click Export. The HTML Output Options dialog box, shown in Figure 19.3, appears.

The HTML Output Options dialog box, which allows you to select an HTML template and the encoding you want Access to apply when exporting the form.

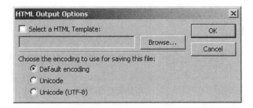

7. Select an optional HTML template for Access to apply to the HTML document. By selecting an HTML template, you can easily maintain a consistent look for your Web publications. Select the type of encoding that you want to use. Depending on the language you are using, you might need to select Unicode or Unicode (UTF-8) encoding. Click OK. Access exports the form's datasheet to HTML. If you selected the Autostart option, the browser launches. Otherwise, you are returned to the Database window.

Saving Reports as HTML

You can save reports and their formatting as HTML, and this is an elegant way to publish data on an Internet or intranet site. To publish a report as HTML, just follow these steps:

1. Click Reports in the Objects list of the Database window.

2. Select the report whose results you want to save as HTML.

3. Choose File|Export to open the Save As dialog box.

4. From the Save As Type drop-down list, select HTML Documents.

5. Select a filename and a location for the HTML document.

6. Click Export. The HTML Output Options dialog box appears.

7. Select an optional HTML template for Access to apply to the HTML document. Select the type of encoding you want to use and click OK. Access exports the report to HTML. If you selected the Autostart option, the browser launches. Otherwise, you are returned to the Database window.

Figure 19.4 shows a report published as HTML. Because the report is a multipage report, Access generates several HTML files. The generated HTML links each page of the report, and the user can easily navigate from page to page by using the First, Previous, Next, and Last hyperlinks that are automatically generated during the Save process.

FIGURE 19.4

Viewing the Northwind *database Alphabetical List of Products report as HTML.*

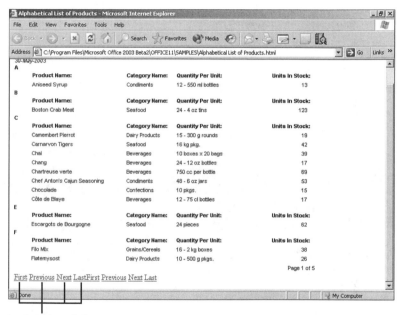

Navigation Hyperlinks

Linking to HTML Files

Just as you can link to dBase tables, Paradox tables, or Open Database Connectivity (ODBC) data sources in Access, you can also link to HTML files. Just follow these steps:

1. Right-click in the Database window and select Link Tables from the context menu. The Link dialog box appears.

2. From the Files of Type drop-down list, select HTML Documents.

3. Select the HTML file you want to link to and click Link. The Link HTML Wizard appears (see Figure 19.5).

4. In the wizard's first window, indicate whether the first row of data contains column headings. You can also see Access's proposed layout for the linked table.

FIGURE 19.5

The first step of the Link HTML Wizard.

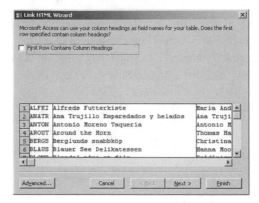

5. Click Advanced to designate specifics about the linked table. The Customers Link Specification dialog box opens (see Figure 19.6). Here you can select which fields you want to include in the linked table, date delimiters, and other specifics of the linked file. Make the appropriate selections and then click OK.

FIGURE 19.6

Using the Customers Link Specification dialog box to designate specifics about the linked table.

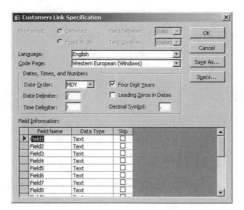

6. Click Next to proceed with the Link HTML Wizard.

7. In the next window of the wizard, select a field name and a data type for each field in the HTML file. Make the appropriate selections and then click Next.

8. In the wizard's last window, supply a table name for the linked table. Make the appropriate selection and then click Finish. A message appears, saying that the table linked successfully. The table appears in the Database window, with a special icon indicating that it's an HTML file (see Figure 19.7).

FIGURE 19.7
The Database window with a linked HTML document.

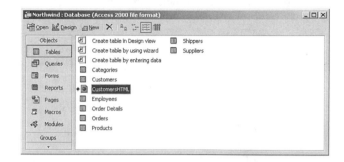

You can browse, query, and report on the linked HTML table just as you would on any other table. However, you cannot modify any of the data in the linked file.

Importing HTML Files

You can import the data from an HTML file so that it becomes exactly like any other Access table. Follow these steps to import an HTML file:

1. Right-click in the Database window and select Import from the context menu. The Import dialog box appears.

2. From the Files of Type drop-down list, select HTML Documents.

3. Select the HTML file you want to import and click Import to open the Import HTML Wizard. This wizard is almost identical to the Link HTML Wizard.

4. In the wizard's first window, indicate whether the first row of data contains column headings. You can also see Access's proposed layout for the imported table.

5. Click Advanced to designate specifics about the imported table. The Import Specification dialog box opens. Here you can select which fields you want to include in the imported table, date delimiters, and other specifics of the imported file. Make the appropriate selections and then click OK.

6. Click Next to go to the next window of the wizard. Here, you have the choice of importing the data into a new table or adding it to an existing table. Make the appropriate selection and then click Next.

7. In the next window of the wizard, select a field name and a data type for each field in the HTML file. You can also designate whether you want Access to create an

19

index for the field and even whether you want to exclude the field entirely. Make the appropriate selections and then click Next.

8. In the next window of the wizard, designate a primary key for the imported table (see Figure 19.8). If you prefer, you can have Access supply the primary key. Make the appropriate selection and then click Next.

FIGURE **19.8**

Designating a primary key for a new table.

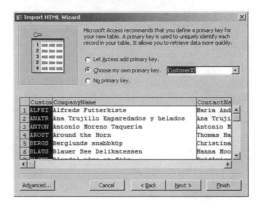

9. In the wizard's last window, supply a table name for the linked table. If you're concerned about whether the imported table is normalized, you can have Access launch the Table Analyzer after it completes the import process. Make the appropriate selections and then click Finish. A message appears, stating that Access imported the table successfully. The table then appears in the Database window just as any other Access table does.

Exporting Data to XML

HTML has one major limitation: It in no way separates data from the presentation of data. XML's main objective is to separate data and its structure from the presentation of the data. Furthermore, it provides a universal data format that can be read by a multitude of machines on a multitude of operating systems and platforms. It bridges the gap between the variety of systems that store data in a variety of disparate formats. Access makes it easy for you to export data to XML. To export an object to an XML file, follow these steps:

1. Right-click the object you want to export and select Export from the context menu. The Export dialog box appears.

2. From the Save As Type drop-down box, select XML.

3. Select the folder where you want Access to save the XML file and click Export. The Export XML dialog box appears (see Figure 19.9).

FIGURE 19.9

Designating what XML-related documents to create.

4. Select what to export: the data, the schema of the data, the presentation of the data, or any combination of the three.

5. Click the More Options button to designate additional options.

6. Click OK to create the XML document. If you selected the Presentation of Your Data option in step 4 and you view the XML document in a browser, it looks as shown in Figure 19.10.

FIGURE 19.10

An XML document viewed in a browser after the Presentation of Your Data option is selected.

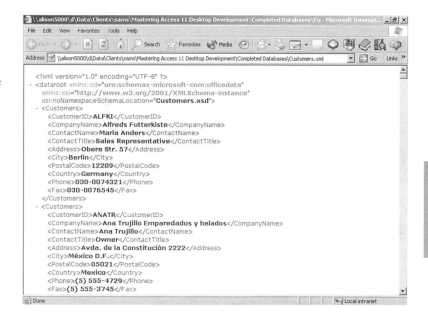

19

Importing XML Data into Access

You can import an XML file into Access. The process is very simple but is also somewhat limited in that it does not provide you with very many import options. To import an XML file, follow these steps:

1. Open the database that is to contain the XML file.

2. Right-click in the Database window and choose Import from the context menu. The Import dialog box appears.

3. From the Files of Type drop-down box, select XML.

4. Select the folder where the XML file is located.

5. Select the XML file.

6. Click Import. The Import XML dialog box appears (see Figure 19.11).

FIGURE 19.11

The Import XML dialog box, which allows you to specify the details of the import process.

7. Select the table whose data you want to import and then click OK. Access imports the XML file.

There are several problems and limitations associated with the process of importing XML data:

- The only type of Schema Definition (XSD) files that Access can read are Access-generated XSD files. This means that unless an Access-generated XSD file is available to you to use during the import process, you have little control over the structure of the imported table.

- If the XML file is not syntactically correct, the import process fails. In that case, Access generates an `ImportErrors` table.

- Access can only read an element-centric rather than an attribute-centric XML file.

- If the table name in the XML file is `dataroot`, `root`, or `schema`, the export process fails, resulting in the generation of an `ImportErrors` table.

Despite all these limitations, the ability to import XML files into Access is a valuable aspect of Access 2003. If the XML file is properly formatted, the import process should go rather smoothly.

Creating and Modifying Data Access Pages

Data access pages are similar to forms. Access stores them as dynamic HTML files with the `.HTM` extension. Users can view and update data access pages in Internet Explorer 5.0 and above. You create data access pages in one of the following four ways:

- Using AutoPage
- Using a wizard
- From an existing Web page
- From scratch

Creating a Data Access Page by Using the AutoPage Feature

To create a data access page using AutoPage, follow these steps:

1. Click Pages in the list of objects in the Database window.
2. Click the New button in the Database window. The New Data Access Page dialog box appears.
3. Choose the table or query on which you want to base the data access page.
4. Select AutoPage: Columnar from the list of options for creating a data access page (see Figure 19.12).

FIGURE 19.12

The New Data Access Page dialog box, which allows you to select the type of data access page to create.

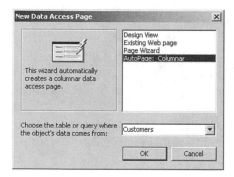

5. Click OK. Access creates the data access page (see Figure 19.13).

Creating a Data Access Page Using a Wizard

To create a data access page using a wizard, follow these steps:

1. Click Pages in the list of objects in the Database window.
2. Double-click the Create Data Access Page By Using Wizard option. The Page Wizard appears (see Figure 19.14).
3. Select the table or query on which you want to base the data access page. In Figure 19.15, the Customers table is selected.

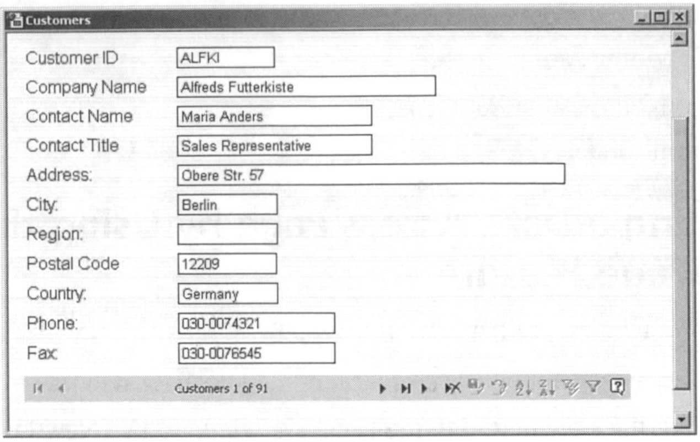

FIGURE 19.13
A data access page based on the Northwind *database* Customers *table, using the AutoPage feature.*

FIGURE 19.14
The Page Wizard.

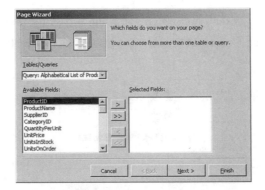

FIGURE 19.15
Selecting the table or query on which you want to base a data access page.

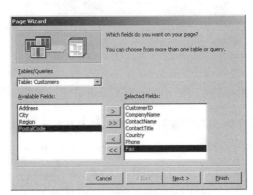

4. Select the fields that you want to appear on the data access page. In Figure 19.15 the CustomerID, CompanyName, ContactName, ContactTitle, Country, Phone, and Fax fields are selected. Click Next to continue.

5. In the next window of the wizard (see Figure 19.16), add any desired grouping levels to the page. In Access 2000 the created page is rendered not editable when you apply grouping. Fortunately, that is not the case in Access 2002 and 2003! Click Next to continue.

FIGURE **19.16**

Adding grouping levels to a data access page.

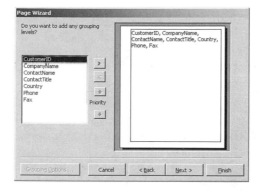

6. In the next page of the wizard (see Figure 19.17), select a sort order for the records included on the page. You can select either ascending or descending order. In Figure 19.17, the page is sorted by the ContactTitle field combined with the ContactName field. Click Next to continue.

FIGURE **19.17**

Selecting a sort order for the records on a page.

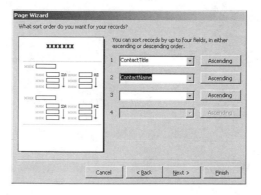

19

7. The last page of the wizard asks you for a title for the page. You can also opt to apply a theme to the page. Enter the title, select whether to apply a theme, and then designate whether to open the page or modify the page's design. Click Finish to complete the process. If you elected to apply a theme to the page, the Theme dialog box appears (see Figure 19.18). Select a theme and click OK. Figure 19.19 shows the completed page in Design view. Figure 19.20 shows the completed page in Page view.

FIGURE 19.18

The Theme dialog box, which allows you to apply a theme to a page.

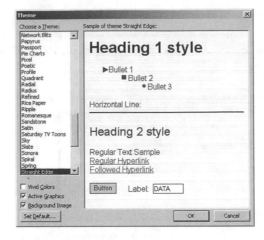

FIGURE 19.19

A completed data access page in Design view.

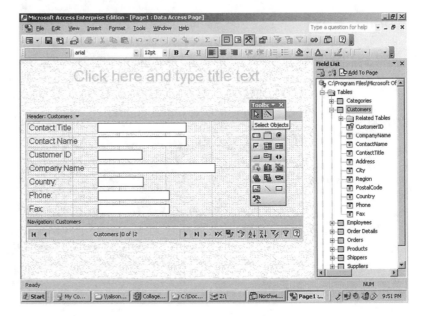

Access does not store data access pages in a database file or project. Instead, it saves data access pages as HTML files. To save a data access page, follow these steps:

1. Click Save on the toolbar. The Save As Data Access Page dialog box appears (see Figure 19.21).

2. Enter the name of the HTML document. The figure shows the name `Customers.htm`. Click Save.

FIGURE 19.20

A completed data access page in Page view.

FIGURE 19.21

The Save As Data Access Page dialog box.

3. A dialog box appears, suggesting that the connection string should point to a universal naming convention (UNC) path. Pointing the connection string to a UNC path helps ensure that the data behind the page will be available over the network.

Although Access saves the data access page as a separate document, the page appears in the Database window (see Figure 19.22). Notice in the figure that a ToolTip appears, indicating the name and location of the saved HTML document. When you open the data access page from within Microsoft Access, it appears as a window in the Access environment. To view the page as it will appear in a browser, you right-click the page in the Database window and select Web Page Preview from the context menu.

19

FIGURE 19.22

A completed data access page that appears as an object.

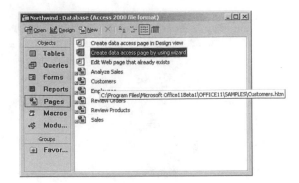

Creating a Data Access Page from Scratch

Although the Page Wizard is very powerful, there may be times when you want to build a data access page from scratch. To do this, follow these steps:

1. Click Pages in the list of objects in the Database window.

2. Double-click the Create Data Access Page in Design View option. Access presents a dialog box, indicating that you cannot open in Access 2000 or Access 2002 a data access page that you create in Access 2003 in Design view. Click OK, and a blank data access page appears (see Figure 19.23).

FIGURE 19.23

A blank data access page.

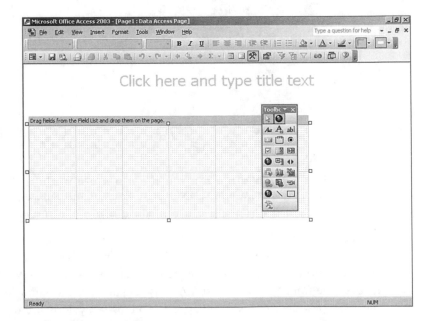

3. Add controls to the data access page and set their properties.

You might wonder how to associate a table from a database with a data access page that you build from scratch. The process differs somewhat from the process of associating a form with data. The process is as follows:

1. Click the Field List tool on the toolbar. The Field List window appears (see Figure 19.24). Notice that the Field List window shows two expandable lists: one with the tables in the database and one with the queries in the database (see Figure 19.25).

FIGURE 19.24

Adding table and query fields from the Field List window.

19

2. To add all fields from an existing table or query to the data access page, drag an entire table or query from the field list to the data access page.

3. To add specific fields from a table or query to the data access page, expand the field list to display the desired table or query and then drag and drop individual fields to the data access page. Figure 19.26 shows selected fields from the Employees table added to the data access page.

FIGURE 19.25

The expanded Field List window.

FIGURE 19.26

A data access page that contains selected fields from the Employees table.

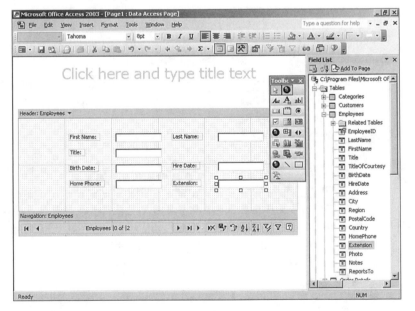

Saving PivotTables and PivotCharts to Data Access Pages

Access allows you to easily add PivotTables and PivotCharts to the data access pages that you create. Here's the process:

1. From the Database window, click Pages in the list of objects.
2. Double-click the Create Data Access Page in Design View item.
3. Activate the field list.
4. Click and drag a table or query to the data access page. The Layout Wizard appears (see Figure 19.27).

FIGURE 19.27

The Layout Wizard, where you can add a PivotTable or PivotChart.

5. Select PivotTable and click OK. If you based the data access page on a query and the query required parameters, the Enter Parameters dialog box appears (see Figure 19.28).

19

FIGURE 19.28

The Enter Parameters dialog box, which allows you to specify parameter values.

6. Click OK. Access adds the PivotTable to the data access page (see Figure 19.29). The PivotTable appears as a control on the data access page.

FIGURE **19.29**

A PivotTable appearing as a control.

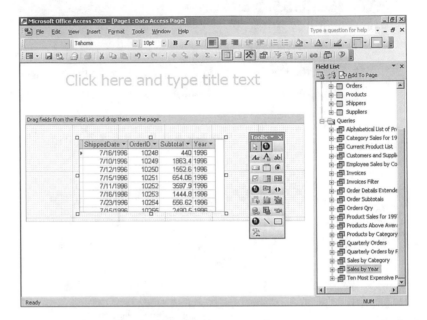

7. Right-click the control and select Commands and Options from the context menu. The Commands and Options dialog box appears (see Figure 19.30). Click the Behavior tab.

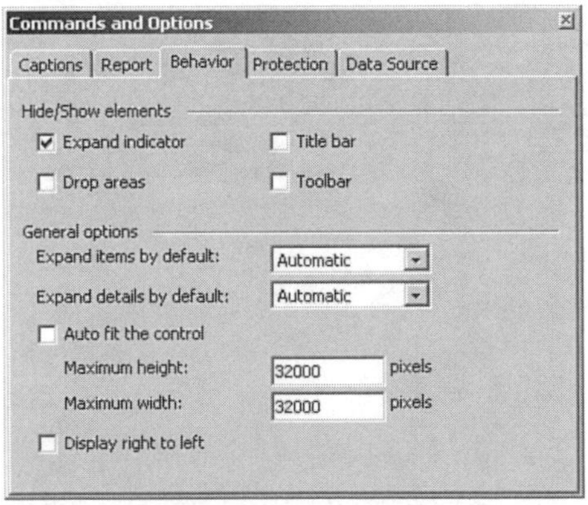

FIGURE **19.30**

The Commands and Options dialog box.

8. Select the Drop Areas and Toolbar check boxes. The resulting PivotTable appears as shown in Figure 19.31.

FIGURE 19.31

A PivotTable that contains drop areas.

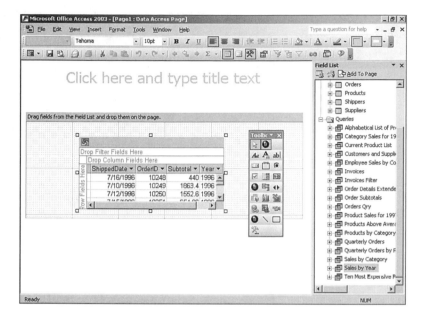

9. Switch to Form view and enter any necessary parameters.

10. Drag and drop row and column headings to the Drop Filter Fields Here and Drop Column Fields Here drop zones, as desired.

11. Use the filter drop-downs to apply desired filters.

12. Save your work.

To add a PivotChart to a data access page, follow these steps:

1. From the Database window, click Pages in the list of objects.

2. Double-click the Create Data Access Page in Design View item.

3. Activate the field list.

4. Right-click and drag the appropriate query to the data access page. (This is an alternative to using the Layout Wizard.)

5. Select PivotChart from the pop-up menu.

6. Move and size the PivotChart as appropriate (see Figure 19.32).

7. Drag and drop the appropriate fields to the Drop Series Fields Here and Drop Filter Fields Here regions of the data access page. Figure 19.33 shows a PivotChart that results after the `CategoryName` field is dropped from the `Northwind` database `Category Sales for 1997` query on the Drop Filter Fields Here region and the `ProductSales` field is dropped on the Drop Series Fields Here region.

FIGURE **19.32**
A PivotChart control.

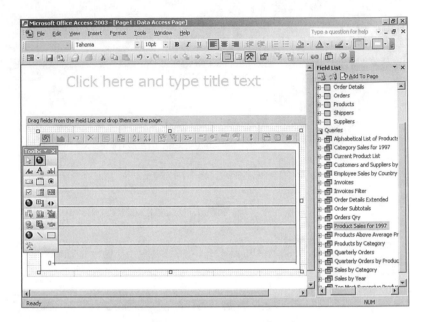

FIGURE **19.33**
*A PivotChart based on
the* CategoryName *and*
ProductSales *fields
from the* Northwind
database Category
Sales for 1997 *query.*

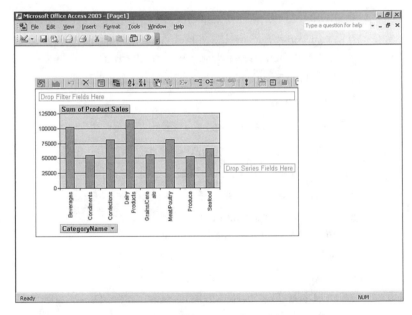

Summary

It's easy to integrate Access with the Internet or with an intranet. Access enables you to easily publish database objects to the Web and import HTML data from the Web. In fact, you can even create dynamic Web pages! By using data access pages, which is covered in the Hour 20, "Database Administration," you can even build forms that display and update live data directly from a browser. Access 2003 helps bring data to the continually evolving information superhighway, and the possibilities are endless.

Q&A

Q Name three ways you can build a data access page.

A You can use AutoPage, use a wizard, create a data access page from scratch, or create a data access page from an existing page.

Q What database objects can you publish as HTML?

A You can publish table data, query results, form datasheets, forms, and reports as HTML.

Q Name some limitations you face when importing XML files in Access.

A The only type of XSD file that Access can read is an Access-generated XSD files. If the appropriate XSD file is not available, you have little control over the structure of the imported file. Furthermore, if the XML file is not syntactically correct, the import process fails.

Workshop

19

The Workshop includes quiz questions that are designed to help you test your understanding of the material covered and activities to help put what you've learned to practice. You can find the answers to the questions in the section immediately following the quiz.

Quiz

1. You can save the Form view of a form as HTML (True/False).

2. You can save the results of a query as HTML (True/False).

3. When you save a multipage report as HTML, Access generates multiple HTML pages (True/False).

4. Just as you can modify data in a linked FoxPro file, you can modify data in a linked HTML document.

5. Data access pages are the perfect Internet solution (True/False).

Quiz Answers

1. False. You can only save the Datasheet view of a form as HTML.

2. True.

3. True.

4. False. Data in a linked HTML file is read-only.

5. False. Data access pages require Internet Explorer 5.0 and above and Microsoft Office, making them more of an intranet solution than an Internet solution.

Activities

Export a table to HTML. Export another table to XML. Practice importing both of those tables into another database. Build data access pages from each of the imported tables.

HOUR 20

Database Administration

NEW TERM Although you don't need to do too much to maintain an Access database, you must know about a few important techniques that ensure that you maintain databases as effectively as possible. The first technique you should be familiar with is compacting. *Compacting* a database means removing unused space from a database (that is, an .MDB file). The second technique involves backing up databases. Without a proper backup procedure in place, you are like a circus performer without a safety net. Another useful technique to have at your disposal is the ability to convert Access databases between the various file formats. Finally, it is important that you be able to detect broken references within a database. This hour covers these maintenance techniques, including the following:

- How to back up and restore a database
- How to compact and repair a database
- How to encrypt and decrypt a database
- How to convert a database to another version
- How to create an MDE file
- How to use the Database Splitter

Backing Up a Database

 New to Access 2003 is the ability to back up a database right from within Microsoft Access. Here's the process:

1. Open the database that you want to back up.

2. Select Tools|Database Utilities|Back Up Database. The Save Backup As dialog box appears (see Figure 20.1).

FIGURE 20.1

The Save Backup As dialog box.

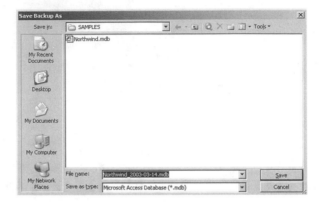

3. Supply a filename and location for the database that you are backing up.

4. Click Save. Access creates a backup that has the name and location you designated.

Because the backup process simply creates a copy of the open database with a name and in a location that you specify, restoring the database involves moving and/or renaming the backup database file to the production location and with the original name. You can then simply open the backup database and continue working as usual.

Compacting and Repairing a Database

As you and the users of an application work with a database, the database grows in size. In order to maintain a high state of performance, Access defers the removal of discarded pages from the database until you explicitly compact the database file. This means that as you add data and other objects to a database and remove data and objects from the database, Access does not reclaim the disk space that the deleted objects occupied. This not only results in a very large database file, but it also ultimately degrades performance as the physical file becomes fragmented on disk. Compacting a database accomplishes these tasks:

- It reclaims all the space occupied by deleted data and database objects.
- It reorganizes the database file so that the pages of each table in the database are contiguous. This improves performance because as the user works with the table, the data in the table is located contiguously on the disk.

- It resets counter fields so that the next value will be one more than the last *undeleted* counter value. If, while testing, you add many records that you delete just prior to placing the application in production, compacting the database resets all the counter values back to 1.

- It re-creates the table statistics used by the Jet Engine when it executes queries, and it marks all queries so that Jet recompiles them the next time they are run. These are two very important related benefits of the compacting process. If you have added indexes to a table or if the volume of data in the table has changed dramatically, the query won't execute efficiently. This is because Jet bases the stored query plan it uses to execute the query on inaccurate information. When you compact the database, Jet updates all table statistics and the plan for each query to reflect the current state of the tables in the database.

It is a good idea to defragment the hard drive that a database is stored on before performing the compacting process. The disk defragmentation process ensures that as much contiguous disk space as possible is available for the compacted database. The compaction process is a defragmentation of the database. By defragmenting the disk drive and then the database, you increase the database performance, as well as the performance of the entire computer system.

In versions of Access prior to Access 2000, the repair process is a separate utility from the compacting process. With Access 2000, Access 2002, and Access 2003, there is no longer a separate repair process. The compact and repair processes both occur when you compact a database. When you open a database that is in need of repair, Access prompts you to compact it.

To compact a database, you can use one of three techniques:

- Use commands provided in the user interface.
- Click an icon you set up.
- Set up the database so that Access compacts it whenever you close it.

Regardless of which method you select for the compacting procedure, the following conditions must be true:

20

- The user performing the procedure must have the rights to open the database exclusively.

- The user performing the procedure must have Modify Design permission for all tables in the database.

- The database must be available so that you or the user can open it for exclusive use. This means that no other users can be using the database.

- The drive or network share that the database is located on cannot be read-only.

- You cannot set the file attribute of the database to read-only.

- Enough disk space must be available for both the original database and the compacted version of the database. This is true even if you compact the database to a database with the same name as the original.

It is a good idea to back up a database before you attempt to compact it. It is possible for the compacting process to damage the database, such as when a power failure occurs during the compaction process. Also, you should not use the compacting process as a substitute for carefully following backup procedures. The compacting process is not always successful. Nothing is as foolproof as a fastidiously executed routine backup process.

If, at any time, Access detects that something has damaged a database, it prompts you to repair the database. This occurs when you attempt to open, compact, encrypt, or decrypt a damaged database. At other times, Access might not detect the damage. Instead, you might suspect that damage has occurred because the database behaves unpredictably. If you suspect damage, you should first back up and then perform the compacting process, using one of the methods covered in this hour.

Using the User Interface to Compact a Database

Access provides a fairly straightforward user interface for the compacting operation. To compact a currently open database, choose Tools|Database Utilities|Compact and Repair Database. Access closes the database, compacts it, and then reopens it.

To compact a database other than the currently open database, follow these steps:

1. Close the open database.

2. Choose Tools|Database Utilities|Compact and Repair Database. The Database to Compact From dialog box appears, as shown in Figure 20.2.

FIGURE 20.2

The Database to Compact From dialog box.

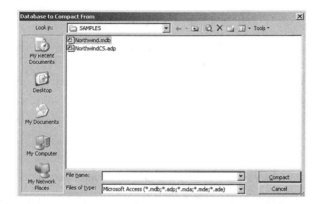

3. Select the database you want to compact and click Compact. The Compact Database Into dialog box appears, as shown in Figure 20.3.

FIGURE 20.3

The Compact Database Into dialog box.

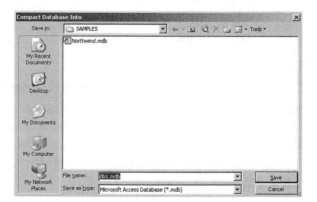

4. Select a name for the compacted database. You can make it the same name as the original database name, or you can create a new name. (If you are compacting a database to the same name, make sure that it is backed up.) Click Save.

5. If you select the same name for the compacted database as for the original, Access prompts you to replace the existing file. Click Yes.

20

Using a Shortcut to Compact a Database

To give users a very simple way to compact a database, you can create an icon that performs the compacting process. You accomplish this by using the /Compact command-line option, which compacts the database without ever opening it. The shortcut looks like this:

```
c:\MSOffice\Access\Msaccess.EXE c:\Databases\TimeAndBilling.MDB /Compact
```

This command compacts a database named TimeAndBilling in a folder called c:\Databases. You can follow this command with a space and the name of a destination database if you do not want Access to overwrite the current database with the compacted version. If you do not include a path for the destination database, Access places it in the My Documents folder by default. You can have Access automatically create the shortcut for you, using the Setup Wizard that ships with Office 2003 Developer. To create a shortcut, follow these steps:

1. Open the folder where you have installed an application.
2. Right-click the application (MDB) icon for a database and choose Create Shortcut from the context menu. A shortcut appears on the desktop.
3. Right-click the shortcut and choose Properties from the context menu. The Properties dialog box appears.
4. Click the Shortcut tab.
5. Modify the shortcut so that it has the following syntax:
   ```
   MSACCESS.EXE filename /Compact
   ```

Compacting Whenever a Database Closes

Using the environmental setting Compact on Close, you can designate that Access should compact specific databases whenever the user closes them. Access compacts a database upon close only if it determines that the compacting process will reduce the size by at least 256KB. To set the Compact on Close environmental setting, follow these steps:

1. Open the database that you want to affect and select Tools|Options.
2. Click the General tab of the Options dialog box.
3. Select the Compact on Close check box.

Although you set the Compact on Close setting by selecting Tools|Options, this setting applies only to the database that is open when you select the option. This allows you to selectively designate which databases Access compacts when the user closes them.

Remember that when you use the Compact on Close option, the database must meet all the conditions ordinarily required for Access to compact a database. For example, if other users are in the database when someone tries to close it, the user trying to close the database receives an error.

Encrypting and Decrypting a Database

Before we move on to the more sophisticated methods of securing a database, it is important that you understand what any method of security does and does not provide for you. No matter how well you learn about and implement the techniques in this section, you will not be protected against someone attempting to read the data contained in a database. Even after you secure a database, someone with a disk editor can view the contents of the file. Although the data in the file will not appear in an easy-to-read format, the data is there and available for unauthorized individuals to see.

You might be feeling discouraged and asking why you should bother with security. Do not despair! Access enables you to encrypt a database, rendering the data in the database indecipherable in word processors, disk utilities, and other products that are capable of reading text. When a database is encrypted, it is difficult to decipher any of its data.

The database you are encrypting cannot be open. To encrypt a database using Access's standard menus, follow these steps:

1. Choose Tools | Security | Encrypt/Decrypt Database. The Encrypt/Decrypt Database dialog box appears.

2. In the Encrypt/Decrypt Database dialog box, select the file you want to encrypt and then click OK. Access prompts you for the name of the encrypted database.

3. If you select the same name as the existing file, Access deletes the original decrypted file after it determines that the encryption process is successful.

20

You cannot encrypt a database to itself if it is open. You must first close the database and then select Tools | Security | Encrypt/Decrypt Database.

It is always a good idea to back up the original database before you begin the encryption process. This ensures that if something goes awry during the encryption process, you won't lose data.

When you encrypt a database, Access encrypts the entire database—not just the data. As you access the data and the objects in the database, Access needs to decrypt the objects so that users can use them. When users are finished accessing the objects, Access encrypts them again. Regardless of the method of encryption you use, the encrypted database degrades performance by about 15%. Furthermore, encrypted databases usually cannot be compressed by most disk-compression software utilities because compression software usually relies on repeated patterns of data. The encryption process is so effective at removing any patterns that it renders most compression utilities ineffective. You need to decide whether this decrease in performance and the inability to compress the database file is worth the extra security that encryption provides.

Converting a Database to Another Version

Access 2002 and 2003 make it easy to interact with other versions of Access. Access 2002 and 2003 allow you to open, read, and update Access databases stored in the Access 2000 file format without converting the files to the Access 2002-2003 file format. Furthermore, Access 2002 and 2003 allow you to easily convert files stored in the Access 2002-2003 file format to either the Access 97 or the Access 2000 file format.

To convert an Access 2002 or 2003 database to a format that is compatible with an earlier version of Access, select Tools|Database Utilities|Convert Database|To Access 2000 File Format or select Tools|Database Utilities|Convert Database|To Access 97 File Format.

As mentioned earlier, you can use Access 2000 files in Access 2002 and Access 2003. If you want to convert an open database stored in the Access 2000 file format to the Access 2002-2003 file format, select Tools|Database Utilities|Convert Database|To Access 2002-2003 File Format.

In versions of Access prior to Access 2002, when problems occur during the conversion process, users are left wondering exactly what has gone awry. Access 2002 and Access 2003 address this problem. If errors occur while converting from earlier versions of Access to the Access 2002-2003 file format, Access creates a table that lists each error. You can easily use the data in that table to handle the conversion problem gracefully.

Task: Compacting, Repairing, and Converting a Database into Another Version

To practice compacting, repairing, and converting a database to another version, let's start by compacting and repairing a database and then convert the database to Access 97:

1. Open the Northwind sample database.

▼ To Do

▼ 2. Compact and repair the database.

▲ 3. Convert the database to Access 97. Call the converted database Northwind97.

Creating an MDE File

NEW TERM Access 2003 offers an additional level of security through the creation of MDE files. An *MDE (compiled database) file* is a database file that has all editable source code removed. This means that Access eliminates all the source code behind the forms, reports, and modules contained in the database. An MDE file offers additional security because the forms, reports, and modules in an MDE file cannot be modified. Other benefits of an MDE file include reduced size and optimized memory usage. To create an MDE file, follow these steps:

1. Open the database on which you will base the MDE file.

2. Choose Tools|Database Utilities|Make MDE File. The Save MDE As dialog box appears.

3. Select a name for the MDE file and click OK.

Before you begin creating and using MDE files, you need to be aware of the restrictions they impose. If you plan ahead, these restrictions probably will not cause you too many problems. On the other hand, if you enter the world of MDE files unaware, they can cause you much grief. You should consider these restrictions:

- No one can view or modify the design of the forms, reports, and modules in an MDE file. In fact, no one can add new forms, reports, and modules to an MDE file. It is therefore important that you keep the original database when you create an MDE file: That is where you will make changes to existing forms, reports, and modules and add new forms, reports, and modules. When you are finished making changes to the database, you simply rebuild the MDE file.

- Because you must rebuild the MDE file every time you make changes to the application, the front-end/back-end approach is a good approach to take: You place the tables in a standard Access database and store the other objects in the MDE file. You can therefore rebuild the MDE file without worrying about the reconciliation of data.

- You cannot import or export forms, reports, or modules to or from an MDE file.

- You cannot convert an MDE file to later versions of Access. It is necessary to convert the original database and then rebuild the MDE file with the new version.

- You cannot add or remove references to object libraries and databases from an MDE file. Also, you cannot change references to object libraries and databases.

20

- Every library database that an MDE references also must be an MDE file. This means that if Database1 references Database2, which references Database3, all three databases must be stored as MDE files. You first must save Database3 as an MDE file, reference it from Database2, and then save Database2 as an MDE file. You can then reference Database2 from Database1, and finally, you can save Database1 as an MDE file.

- A replicated database cannot be saved as an MDE file. The replication must first be removed from the database. You accomplish this by removing the replication system tables and properties from the database. The database can then be saved as an MDE file, and the MDE file can be replicated and distributed as a replica set. Any time changes must be made to the database, they must be made to the original database, resaved as an MDE file, and then redistributed as a new replica set.

- Any security that applies to a database follows through to an MDE file that is created from it. To create an MDE file from a database that is already secured, you must first join the workgroup information file associated with the database. You must have Open/Run and Open Exclusive permissions to the database. You must also have Modify Design and Administer permissions to all tables in the database, or you must own all tables in the database. Finally, you must have Read Design permissions on all objects contained in the database. These permissions are all covered in Hour 22, "Security Introduced."

- If you want to remove security from the database, you must remove the security from the original database and rebuild the MDE file.

As long as you are aware of the restrictions associated with MDE files, they can offer many benefits. In addition to the natural security they provide, the size and performance benefits MDE files offer are significant.

A great use for MDE files is for demo versions of applications. Performance of MDE files is excellent, but more importantly, if you use Visual Basic for Applications (VBA) code, MDE files can easily be rendered both time- and data-limited.

Other programmatic limitations exist regarding MDE files that are beyond the scope of this book. To learn more about these restrictions, please consult a programming text such as *Alison Balter's Mastering Access 2003 Desktop Development* (Sams Publishing).

Using the Database Splitter

When you're designing an application, you should split the application objects into two separate .MDB files. One .MDB file should contain the tables, and the other should contain the application queries, forms, reports, data access pages, macros, and modules. This allows you and others to enter data while you continue to refine the other application objects. When you need to make changes to the application, you simply copy the application database. When you have made the appropriate changes, you can copy the application database over the production copy without overwriting the data in the data database.

To split the objects in a database into two separate .MDB files, follow these steps:

1. Open the database whose objects you want to split.

2. Choose Tools|Database Utilities|Database Splitter to open the Database Splitter Wizard, shown in Figure 20.4.

FIGURE 20.4

The Database Splitter Wizard.

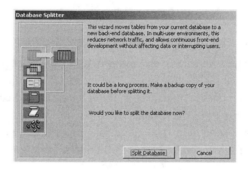

3. Click Split Database. The Create Back-end Database dialog box appears (see Figure 20.5). Enter a name for the database that will contain all the tables.

FIGURE 20.5

Entering a name for a new shared database.

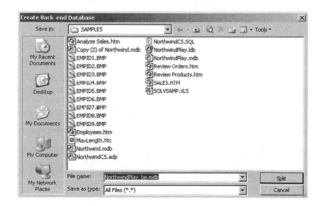

20

4. Click Split. The Database Splitter Wizard creates a new database that holds all the tables. It creates links between the current database and the database that contains the tables. (See Figure 20.6.)

Figure 20.6

A database that has been split.

Summary

You should perform the compacting process regularly—especially on databases that contain application data. The compacting process provides major benefits in terms of both performance and conservation of disk space. The more activity that occurs on a database, the more frequently you should compact it. Although you should consider the compacting process an important part of the database maintenance process, you also need to remember that there is absolutely no substitute for proper backup techniques. This hour shows you a new feature included in Access 2003 that allows you to back up an open database.

You also need to understand the database conversion options that are available in Access 2003. You can convert databases from one version of Access to another by using the user interface. Using all the techniques covered in this hour should save you a lot of time and effort in maintaining and working with databases.

Q&A

Q Explain what the process of compacting a database does.

A It reclaims unused space, improves performance, resets counter fields, and re-creates table statistics.

Q Name three techniques you can use to compact a database.

A You can use commands via the user interface, a shortcut that you set up, and the Compact on Close option.

Q **Explain why encrypting a database is a good idea.**

A Encrypting a database prevents a user from being able to read table data in a text editor.

Q **Explain the downsides of encrypting a database.**

A An encrypted database functions more slowly than a database that is not encrypted because it constantly encrypts and decrypts objects. Access also places several restrictions on encrypted databases. For example, encryption renders most disk-compression utilities useless because compression software usually relies on repeated patterns of data.

Workshop

The Workshop includes quiz questions that are designed to help you test your understanding of the material covered and activities to help put what you've learned to practice. You can find the answers to the questions in the section immediately following the quiz.

Quiz

1. Databases can automatically be compacted when they are closed (True/False).
2. You can convert Access 2002 databases to what other Access database formats?
3. The backup feature was added to what version of Microsoft Access?
4. The compact and repair utilities in Access 2003 are two separate features (True/False).
5. What is the major use of an MDE file?

Quiz Answers

1. True.
2. Access 2000 and Access 97.
3. Access 2003.
4. False. In Access 2003, the compact and repair utilities are combined.
5. It provides an additional means of security.

Activities

Practice backing up, compacting, and splitting a database file.

20

HOUR 21

Database Documentation

Back in the days of mainframes and very formal, centralized management information systems (MIS) departments, documentation was a mandatory requirement for the completion of an application. Today, it seems as though all types of people are developing applications: administrative assistants, CEOs, sales managers, MIS professionals, and so on. Furthermore, even those of us who consider ourselves MIS professionals never received any formal systems training. Finally, the demand to get an application up and running and then to move on to the next application is more prevalent than ever. As a result of all these factors, it seems that documentation has gone by the wayside.

Despite all the reasons documentation doesn't seem to happen, it is even more important in today's complex world to properly document an application than it was in the mainframe days. The proper time to document is as you develop an application. Documentation provides you and everyone else who uses your application with these benefits:

- It makes the system easy for you and others to maintain.
- It helps state the purpose and function of each object in the application.

This hour covers the various ways in which you can document application objects and code. It includes the following topics:

- Preparing an application to be self-documenting
- Documenting tables, queries, forms, reports, macros, and modules

- Using database properties to document the overall database
- Using the Documenter
- Exploring the object dependency feature

Preparing an Application to Be Self-Documenting

Access ships with an excellent tool to assist with the process of documenting a database: the Documenter. Although you can use this tool without any special preparation on your part, a little bit of work as you build the components of a database can go a long way toward enhancing the value of the Documenter's output.

Documenting Tables

The Documenter prints all field and table descriptions that you enter in the design of a table. Figure 21.1 shows a table in Design view. Notice the descriptions for the ClientID and StateProvince fields. These descriptions provide additional information that is not readily obvious from looking at the field names. The Table Properties window also contains a Description property. The Documenter includes this property when you print a table's documentation.

FIGURE 21.1

Documenting a table by including descriptions of each field and using the Table Properties dialog box.

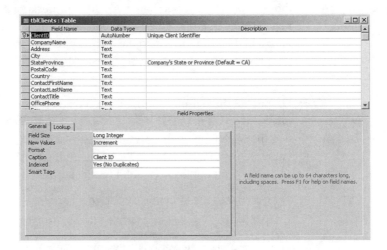

Entering a table description also assists you and the users of your database work with the tables in the database. Figure 21.2 shows the Database window after table descriptions have been entered. The description of each table then appears in the Database window.

Table descriptions appear only if you select Details as the format for the objects in the Database window.

FIGURE 21.2

The Database window, with table descriptions.

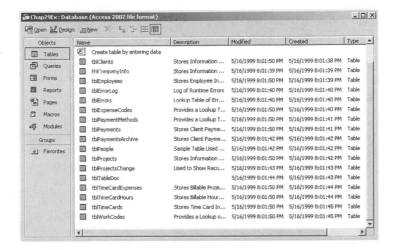

Documenting Queries

Just as you can enhance the output that the Documenter provides for tables, you can enhance the output the Documenter provides for queries. Figure 21.3 shows the Query Properties, in which the Description property has a detailed description of the purpose of the query. Figure 21.4 shows the description of an individual column in a query. Access includes both the query and field descriptions in the output provided by the Documenter.

FIGURE 21.3

Documenting a query by using the Description *property.*

21

FIGURE 21.4

Documenting a column in a query.

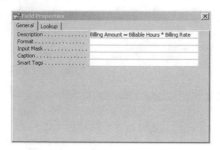

Documenting Forms

Documentation is not limited to table and query objects. A form also has a Description property. You cannot access it from the Design view of the form, though. To view or modify the Description property of a form, follow these steps:

1. Make the Database window the active window.

2. Right-click the form for which you want to add a description and choose Properties from the context menu. The frmClients Properties dialog box appears, as shown in Figure 21.5.

FIGURE 21.5

Using the Object Properties dialog box to document each object in a database.

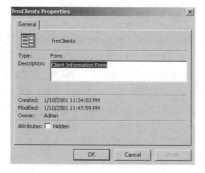

3. Enter a description in the Description text box.

4. Click OK. The description you entered appears in the Database window, as shown in Figure 21.6, and it also appears in the output from the Documenter.

Documenting Reports

You document reports in exactly the same way you document forms. Reports have a Description property that you must enter in the Properties dialog box. Remember that to access this dialog box, you right-click the object in the Database window and choose Properties from the context menu.

FIGURE 21.6

The Database window, with a description of a form.

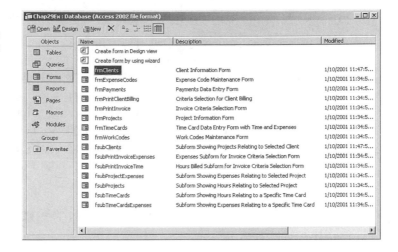

FIGURE 21.6

The Database window, with a description of a form.

Documenting Macros

You can document macros in significantly more detail than you can document forms and reports. You can document each individual line of a macro, as shown in Figure 21.7. Not only does this provide documentation in the Documenter, but also, macro comments become code comments when you convert a macro to a VBA module. In addition to documenting each line of a macro, you can add a description to the macro. As with forms and reports, to accomplish this, you right-click the macro in the Database window and choose Properties from the context menu.

FIGURE 21.7

Documenting a macro by including a description of what each line of the macro does.

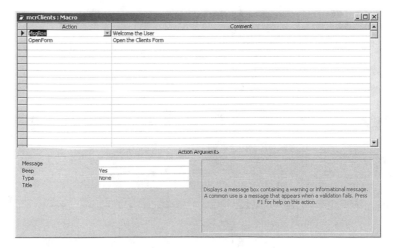

21

Documenting Modules

I cannot emphasize enough how important it is to document modules with comments. Of course, you do not need to document every line of code. I document all areas of my code that I feel are not self-explanatory. Comments help me when I revisit the code to make modifications and enhancements. They also assist anyone who is responsible for maintaining my code. Finally, they provide the user with documentation about what the application is doing. Comments print with code modules, as shown later in this hour in the section "Using the Documenter." As with the other objects, you can right-click a module in the Database window and choose Properties from the context menu to assign a description to it.

Using Database Properties to Document an Overall Database

In addition to enabling you to assign descriptions to the objects in the database, Microsoft Access enables you to document the database as a whole. You do this by filling in the information included in the Database Properties window. To access a database's properties, you choose File|Database Properties or right-click the title bar of the Database window and choose Database Properties from the context menu. The Database Properties dialog box appears, as shown in Figure 21.8. As you can see, this dialog box has five tabs: General, Summary, Statistics, Contents, and Custom.

FIGURE 21.8

The General tab of the Database Properties window.

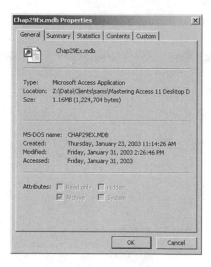

The tabs in the Database Properties dialog box do the following:

- **General**—The General tab displays general information about a database. This includes the date the database was created, when it was last modified, when it was last accessed, its location, its size, its MS-DOS name, and its file attributes. You cannot modify any of the information on the General tab.

- **Summary**—The Summary tab, shown in Figure 21.9, contains modifiable information that describes the database and what it does. This tab includes the database title, its subject, and comments about the database. It also includes the *hyperlink base*—a base address that is used for all relative hyperlinks inserted in the database. This can be an Internet address (URL) or a filename path (UNC).

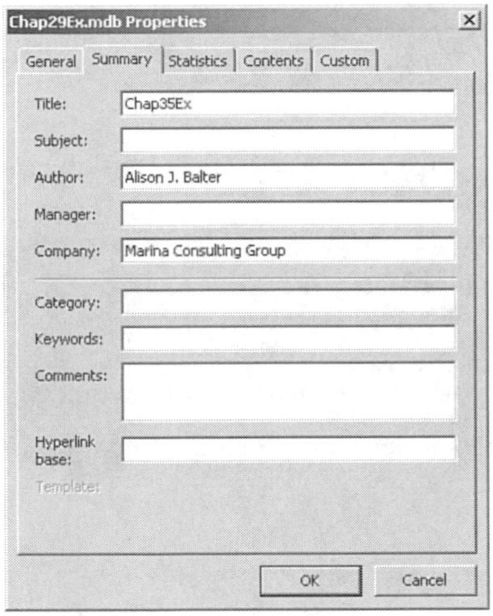

FIGURE 21.9

The Summary tab of the Database Properties window.

- **Statistics**—The Statistics tab contains statistics of the database, such as when it was created, last modified, and last accessed.

- **Contents**—The Contents tab, shown in Figure 21.10, includes a list of all the objects contained in the database.

- **Custom**—The Custom tab enables you to define custom properties associated with the database. This is useful when you are dealing with a large organization with numerous databases and you want to be able to search for all the databases that contain certain properties.

21

FIGURE 21.10

The Contents tab of the Database Properties window.

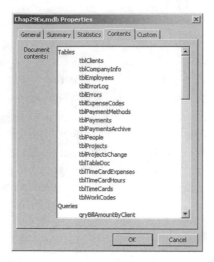

Using the Documenter

The Documenter is an elegant Access tool. It enables you to selectively produce varying levels of documentation for each object in a database. To use the Documenter, follow these steps:

1. Make sure that the Database window is the active window.

2. Choose Tools|Analyze|Documenter. The Documenter dialog box appears, as shown in Figure 21.11.

FIGURE 21.11

Using the Documenter dialog box to designate which objects you want to document.

3. Select the appropriate tab to select the type of object you want to document. To document a table, for example, you click the Tables tab.

4. Enable the check box to the left of each object that you want to document. You can click the Select All button to select all objects shown on a tab.

5. Click the Options button to refine the level of detail provided for each object. Depending on which object type you selected, the Documenter displays different

options. (The next section of this hour, "Using the Documenter Options," covers Documenter options.)

6. Repeat steps 3–5 to select all the database objects you want to document.

7. Click OK when you are ready to produce the documentation.

> To document all objects in a database, you click the All Object Types tab and then click Select All.

> Access can take quite a bit of time to produce the requested documentation, particularly if you select numerous objects. For this reason, you should not begin the documentation process if you will soon need your computer to accomplish other tasks. While Access is processing this task, switching to another application becomes difficult, if not impossible. How difficult it is depends on the amount of RAM installed on your system as well as the type of processor (CPU) installed on your computer and its speed.

> To document the properties of a database or the relationships between the tables in a database, you can click the Current Database tab and select Properties or Relationships.

After you select all the desired objects and options and click OK, the Object Definition window appears. You can use this window to view the documentation output for the objects you selected (see Figure 21.12). This window is just like any other Print Preview window; you can use it to view each page of the documentation and send the documentation to the printer.

Using the Documenter Options

By default, the Documenter outputs a huge volume of information for each selected object. For example, the Documenter documents each control on a form, including every property of a control. It is easy to produce 50 pages of documentation for a couple database objects. Besides being a tremendous waste of paper, this volume of information is overwhelming to review. Fortunately, you can refine the level of detail provided by the Documenter for each category of object you are documenting. To do so, you just click the Options button in the Documenter dialog box.

21

FIGURE 21.12
*The Object Definition
Print Preview window.*

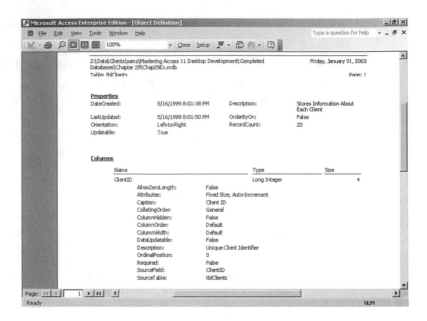

Figure 21.13 shows the table definition options. Notice that you can specify whether you want to print table properties, relationships, and permissions by user and group. You also can indicate the level of detail you want to display for each field: Nothing; Names, Data Types, and Sizes; or Names, Data Types, Sizes, and Properties. For table indexes, you can opt to include the following: Nothing; Names and Fields; or Names, Fields, and Properties.

FIGURE 21.13

*Using the Print Table
Definition dialog box
to designate which
aspects of a table's
definition Access
should document.*

If you select the Queries tab in the Documenter dialog box and then click Options, the Print Query Definition dialog box appears, as shown in Figure 21.14. Here, you can select the level of detail the Documenter will output for the selected queries. You can choose whether to include properties, SQL, parameters, relationships, and permissions by user and group for the query. You also can select the level of detail for each column of the query and for the indexes involved in the query.

Using the Print Query Definition dialog box to designate which aspects of a query's definition the Documenter should include in the output.

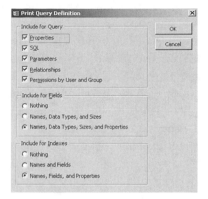

The form and report options are similar to one another. Figure 21.15 shows the Print Form Definition dialog box. Here, you can specify whether you want to print properties, code, and permissions by user and group for a form. For each control on a form, you can choose to print nothing, the names of the controls, or the names and properties of the controls. The Print Report Definition dialog box offers the same options. Both dialog boxes offer a Properties button, which you use to designate the categories of properties that the Documenter prints. You can opt to print other properties, event properties, data properties, or format properties.

FIGURE 21.15

Using the Print Form Definition dialog box to designate which aspects of a form's definition the Documenter should include in the output.

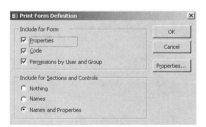

For macros, you can choose whether you want to print macro properties, actions and arguments, or permissions by user and group. For modules, you can choose to view properties, code, and permissions by user and group.

As you can see, the Documenter gives you great flexibility in choosing the level of detail it should provide. Of course, if you haven't filled in the properties of an object (for example, the Description property), it does you no good to ask the Documenter to print those properties.

21

Producing Documentation in Other Formats

 After you produce documentation and it appears in the Object Definition Print Preview window, you can output that documentation to other formats. From the Print Preview window for a report, you choose File|Export. The Export Report dialog box appears, as shown in Figure 21.16. You can output the documentation to Microsoft Excel, HTML, text files, Rich Text Format (.RTF) files, snapshot format, or XML. You need to enter the filename, select Save As Type, and then click Export. If you select the Autostart check box, the Documenter creates the file and then launches the appropriate application, depending on the computer's registry entries. If Microsoft Internet Explorer is the application associated with the file extension .HTML, for example, Autostart launches Internet Explorer with the Documenter output loaded when you output to an HTML file. Similarly, if you choose a Microsoft Excel file format and Excel is associated through the registry with the .XLS file extension, Autostart launches Excel with the output loaded in Excel when the process is complete. The same holds true for the other file types—.RTF and .TXT and their respective registry associations, which are usually Word and Notepad.

FIGURE 21.16

Using the Export Report dialog box to designate the type of file to which the object definition should be output.

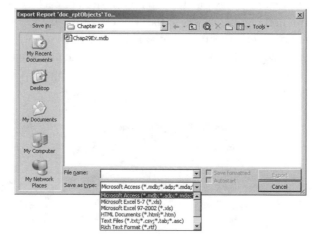

The Object Dependencies Feature

 Microsoft added a wonderful feature to Access 2003: Access 2003 provides the ability to view information about object dependencies. Here's how you use this feature:

1. To invoke the Object Dependencies feature, right-click the object whose dependencies you want to view and select Object Dependencies from the context menu. The

first time you perform this task for a database, a dialog box appears, prompting you to update object dependency information for the database (see Figure 21.17). After you click OK, Access updates the dependency information for the database and displays the Object Dependencies window on the right-hand side of the Access desktop (see Figure 21.18).

FIGURE 21.17

Access prompting you to update dependency information for the database.

FIGURE 21.18

The Object Dependencies window.

2. By default, the Object Dependencies window shows you the objects that depend on the selected object. You can click the Objects that I depend on option to view the objects that the selected object depends on.

3. Click the node of an item to drill down to additional dependencies. For example, in Figure 21.19 the qryClientListing and qryClients nodes are expanded. The qryClientListing query depends on the tblClients table (the table whose dependencies we are viewing). The report called rptClientListing depends on the qryClientListing query, which ultimately depends on the tblClients table. The qryClients query depends on the tblClients table. The frmClients form uses the

21

qryClients query. The qryPayments and qryProjects queries and the frmPayments, frmProjects, and fsubClients forms *all* depend on the frmClients form. Using the Object Dependencies window, you can drill even further down the chain to the objects that depend on those objects.

FIGURE 21.19
Drilling down to see the chain of dependencies for an object.

4. Close the Object Dependencies window when you are finished viewing and working with object dependencies.

Summary

Documentation is a necessary part of the application development process, and fortunately, Microsoft Access makes it very easy. This hour covers the object Description properties Access provides, as well as the extremely powerful Documenter. It also covers a new feature related to documentation, called the Object Dependencies feature. Using any combination of the techniques covered in this hour, you can produce very complete documentation for all aspects of an application.

Q&A

Q Name some benefits of documentation.

A Documentation makes a system easy for you and others to maintain. It also helps state the purpose and function of each object in an application.

Q How do you document an overall database?

A You use the Database Properties window to document the database as a whole.

Q How do you document macros and modules?

A You add comments to macros and modules to document them.

Workshop

The Workshop includes quiz questions that are designed to help you test your understanding of the material covered and activities to help put what you've learned to practice. You can find the answers to the questions in the section immediately following the quiz.

Quiz

1. Name the Access tool that assists you with the documentation process.
2. Name the tabs of the Database Properties dialog box.
3. You can modify the Documenter options (True/False).
4. Name alternative output formats for the Documenter.
5. What Access 2003 feature helps you learn about the objects that a particular object depends on?

Quiz Answers

1. The Documenter.
2. General, Summary, Statistics, Contents, and Custom.
3. True.
4. You can output the Documenter to Excel, HTML, text, rich text (.RTF), snapshot (.SNP), and XML.
5. The Object Dependencies feature.

Activities

Practice using various options for your own applications in the Documenter. As you change the options for each object type, view the differences in the output.

21

HOUR 22

Security Introduced

After you design and develop a sophisticated application, you should ensure that the users of the application cannot violate its integrity and the data it maintains. Microsoft Access gives you several options for securing databases. These options range from a very simple method of applying a password to the entire database to applying varying levels of security to each and every object in the database. The more intricate the security solution, the more difficult it is to implement. Fortunately, you can tailor the complexity of the security you implement to the level of security required by each particular application. This hour covers the following concepts:

- Implementing share-level security
- Implementing user-level security

This hour delves into these topics so that you can grasp all the basics of Access security.

Implementing Share-Level Security: Assigning a Database Password

NEW TERM   The simplest, yet least sophisticated, method of implementing security is to assign a password to the overall database. This means that every person who wants to gain access to the database must enter the same password. After a user gains access to the database, Access renders all of the database's objects available to that user. This type of security is called *share-level security*.

Share-level security is the simplest and quickest method of security to set up. With almost no effort, you can secure a database and its objects. This method of security is quite adequate for a small business in which the administrators of the database want to ensure that no unauthorized people can access the data but that each authorized person has full access to all the objects in the database.

To assign a database password to a database, follow these steps:

1. Open the database to which you want to assign a password by opening the Open dialog box and selecting Open Exclusive from the Open drop-down list box. You cannot assign a password to a database unless you open it exclusively.

2. Choose Tools|Security|Set Database Password. The Set Database Password dialog box appears, as shown in Figure 22.1.

FIGURE 22.1

The Set Database Password dialog box.

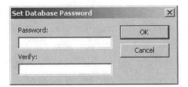

3. Type the password and verify it and then click OK. Keep in mind that the password is case-sensitive.

After you assign a password to a database, Access prompts users for the password each time they open the database. The Password Required dialog box (see Figure 22.2) appears each time a user opens the database.

FIGURE 22.2

The Password Required dialog box.

After a user enters a valid password, he or she gains access to the database and all its objects. In fact, the user can even remove the password by choosing Tools|Security|Unset Database Password. The Unset Database Password dialog box only requires that users know the original password (see Figure 22.3).

Although share-level security is extremely easy to understand and implement, they also are extremely unsophisticated. As you can see, users either have or do not have access to the database, and it is very easy for any user who has access to the database to modify or unset its password.

FIGURE 22.3

The Unset Database Password dialog box.

If you forget the password associated with a database, it is not easy to gain access to the database and its objects. It is therefore extremely important that you carefully maintain a list of the passwords associated with each database. On the other hand, it is not impossible to break security that is set on an Access database. In fact, there are Web sites that offer to remove Access database security for a fee! This means that, if security is of the utmost importance to you or your users, Access database security might not be the appropriate solution for you. To ensure that your data is secure, you can store it in a Microsoft SQL Server database. A client/server database such as Microsoft SQL Server offers a much more robust security model than what is available with the .MDB file format.

If you want to assign a password to a database, users must be able to open the database exclusively. You can grant or deny users the right to open a database exclusively by using the User and Group Permissions dialog box. Assigning rights that permit or deny users or groups exclusive open rights is covered in the section "Step 11: Assigning Rights to Users and Groups," later in this hour.

Establishing User-Level Security

NEW TERM   For most business environments, share-level security is not sufficient. Therefore, it is necessary to take a more sophisticated approach toward securing the objects in a database. *User-level security* enables you to grant specific rights to users and groups in a workgroup. This means that each user or group can have different permissions on the same object. With this method of security, each user begins by entering his or her username and password. The Jet Engine validates the username and password and determines the permissions associated with the user. Each user maintains his or her own password, which is unrelated to the passwords of the other users.

In this method of security, users belong to groups. You can assign rights at the group level, the user level, or both. Users inherit the rights of their least restrictive group. This is highlighted by the fact that security is always on. By default, Access grants the Users group all rights to all objects. Every user is a member of the group called Users and therefore implicitly gets all rights to all objects. If you have not implemented security, Access logs all users in as the Admin user, who is a member of the Users group and the all-powerful Admins group. The Jet Engine determines that the Admin user has no password and therefore does not display an opening logon screen. Because members of the Users and Admins groups get rights to all objects by default, it appears as though no security is in place.

With user-level security, you can easily customize and refine the rights to different objects. One set of users might be able to view, modify, add, and remove employee records, for example. Another set of users might be able to only view employee information. The last group of users might be denied access to the employee information, or it might be allowed access only to specific fields (such as fields for name and address). The Access security model easily accommodates these types of scenarios.

These are the major steps to implementing user-level security:

1. Use the Workgroup Administrator to establish a new system database.
2. Start Access and change the Admin user's password to a non-null password.
3. Create a new user who will be the administrator of the database.
4. Make the user a member of the Admins group.
5. Exit and restart Access, logging on as the new system administrator.
6. Remove the Admin user from the Admins group.
7. Assign a password to the new system administrator.
8. Open the database you want to secure.
9. Run the Security Wizard.
10. Create users and groups consisting of members of the workgroup defined by the system database.
11. Assign rights to users and groups for individual objects.

Each of these steps is described in detail throughout the remainder of this hour.

You can accomplish many of these steps by using the User-Level Security Wizard. Although the Security Wizard is a powerful tool, it does not provide the same level of flexibility afforded to you when you perform the steps

22

yourself. The next several sections therefore focus on performing the steps without the Security Wizard. The Security Wizard is covered in detail in the section "Step 9: Running the Security Wizard," later in this hour. Throughout this hour, I designate which steps the Security Wizard performs.

Step 1: Creating a Workgroup

The first step in establishing user level security involves setting up a workgroup. Then you can define groups and users who belong to that workgroup and assign rights to those groups and users. You define groups and users only in the context of a specific workgroup. You can think of a workgroup as a group of users in a multiuser environment who share data and applications.

NEW TERM When you establish a new workgroup, Access creates a *workgroup information file*. The workgroup information file contains tables that keep track of the following:

- The name of each user and group
- The list of users who make up each group
- The encrypted logon password for each user who is defined as part of the workgroup
- Each user's and group's unique security identifiers (SIDs)

NEW TERM A *SID* is a machine-generated binary string that uniquely identifies each user or group. The system database contains the names and SIDs of the groups and users who are members of that particular workgroup and, therefore, share a system database.

All application databases can share the same workgroup file, or you can maintain separate workgroup files for different application databases.

Understanding Workgroups: The `System.mdw` File

The default name for the workgroup information file is `System.mdw`. Access associates each application database with a specific workgroup information file. This combination of the information stored in the workgroup information file and the information stored in the database grants or denies individual users access to the database or to the objects in it. Multiple databases can share the same workgroup information file.

You can create many workgroup information files. Access stores the name of the workgroup information file currently being used in the Windows registry. You can view it under `HKEY_CURRENT_USER` in the key `Software\Microsoft\Office\11.0\Access\Jet\4.0\Engines`. (See Figure 22.4.)

Value name   Workgroup information file

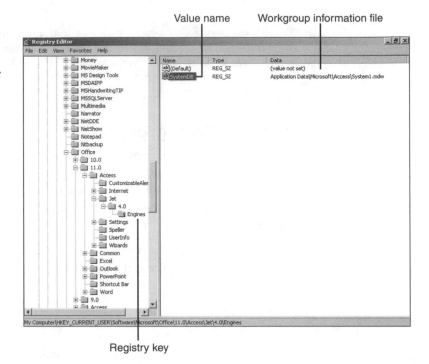

FIGURE 22.4
Viewing the current system information file in the Windows registry.

Registry key

Because the machine used for the screen shots in this book contains multiple versions of Access, the name of the system file in Figure 22.4 is System1.mdw. Microsoft changes the name of the file like this so that the versions of Access I have running will not conflict with one another.

You can access the Windows registry by using the RegEdit utility. To run this utility, you select Start|Run and then type **RegEdit**.

Establishing a Workgroup

One way to establish a new workgroup is to use the Workgroup Administrator. Prior to Access 2002, the Workgroup Administrator was a separate program that you executed outside Microsoft Access. With Access 2002 and Access 2003, the Workgroup Administrator is integrated into Access. To launch the Workgroup Administrator, with the Database window active, you select Tools|Security|Workgroup Administrator.

Figure 22.5 shows the Workgroup Administrator dialog box.

FIGURE 22.5

The Workgroup Administrator dialog box.

From the Workgroup Administrator dialog box, you can create a new workgroup or you can join one of the existing workgroups. If you click Create, you see the Workgroup Owner Information dialog box, which is shown in Figure 22.6.

FIGURE 22.6

The Workgroup Owner Information dialog box.

In the Workgroup Owner Information dialog box, you can enter a name, an organization, and a case-sensitive workgroup ID to uniquely identify the workgroup to the system. If you do not establish a unique workgroup ID, the database is not secure. As you will see, anyone can find out your name and organization. If you do not establish a workgroup ID, anyone can create a new system information file with your name and company, rendering any security that you implement totally futile.

It is important that you record and store all workgroup information in a very safe place so that you can re-create it in an emergency.

After you enter the workgroup owner information, click OK. The Workgroup Information File dialog box appears, prompting you for the name and location of the workgroup information file, as shown in Figure 22.7.

FIGURE 22.7

*The Workgroup
Information File
dialog box.*

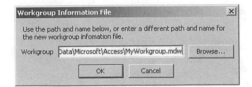

After you type the name of a new workgroup file and click OK, Access gives you one
final opportunity to change any information: It prompts you to confirm the information,
as shown in Figure 22.8. Click OK to confirm the information. Next, Access notifies you
that it has successfully created the workgroup. You can then click OK to close the
Workgroup Administrator.

FIGURE 22.8

*The Confirm
Workgroup
Information
dialog box.*

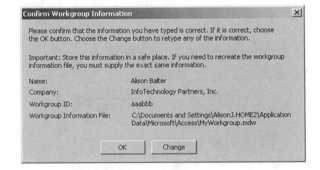

You can use the Security Wizard, covered later in this chapter, in the section "Step 9:
Running the Security Wizard," to create a new workgroup information file. The Security
Wizard prompts you for the information that is necessary to create the workgroup information file. It doesn't matter whether you opt to create a workgroup information file
using the Workgroup Administrator or the Security Wizard: The results will be the same.

Joining a Different Workgroup

If different groups of users in an organization work with entirely different applications, it
might be appropriate to create multiple workgroup information files. To access a database that you have properly secured with a specific workgroup information file, you must
access the database while the user is a member of that workgroup. If the same user
requires access to more than one database, each associated with a different workgroup
information file, it might be necessary for the user to join a different workgroup. You can
accomplish this by using the Workgroup Administrator or by using a desktop shortcut
that associates a specific database with a workgroup file.

To join a different workgroup using the Workgroup Administrator, follow these steps:

1. Launch the Workgroup Administrator.
2. Click the Join button. The Workgroup Information File dialog box appears.
3. Locate the name of the workgroup file you want to join. You can click the Browse button to help locate the workgroup file.
4. Click OK. Access notifies you that you successfully joined the workgroup, as Figure 22.9 shows.
5. Click OK to close the Workgroup Administrator.

FIGURE 22.9

Confirmation that a workgroup was joined successfully.

Step 2: Changing the Password for the Admin User

After you create a new workgroup, you can change the logon for the workgroup by adding a password for the Admin user. This is necessary so that Access will prompt you with a logon dialog box when you launch the product. If the Admin user has no password, the logon dialog box never appears when you log on, and you will never be able to log on as yourself.

To change the password for the Admin user, you launch Access and select Tools| Security|User and Group Accounts. The User and Group Accounts dialog box appears. It does not matter what database you are in when you do this. In fact, you do not need to have any database open because the password that you create applies to the workgroup information file rather than to a database.

The User and Group Accounts dialog box enables you to create and delete users and assign their group memberships. It also enables you to create and delete groups and invoke a logon password for Microsoft Access.

It is important to understand that even if you access the User and Group Accounts dialog box from a specific database, you are setting up users and groups for the entire workgroup. This means that if you assign a password while you are a member of the standard SYSTEM.MDW workgroup and others on your network share the same system workgroup file, each user on the network is prompted with a logon dialog box when he or she attempts to launch Microsoft Access. If you do not want this to occur, you must create a new system workgroup file before you establish security.

When you are sure that you are a member of the correct workgroup and are viewing the User and Group Accounts dialog box, you are ready to assign a password to the Admin user. You click the Change Logon Password tab of the User and Group Accounts dialog box to select it, as shown in Figure 22.10.

FIGURE 22.10

The Change Logon Password tab of the User and Group Accounts dialog box.

You assign a new password and verify it. (There is no old password unless you think of the old password as blank.) Then you click Apply to establish a password for the Admin user. You are now ready to create a new user who will administer the database.

If you choose to use the Security Wizard to secure a database, it changes the password for the Admin user. This ensures that the logon dialog appears when you use the workgroup file created by the Security Wizard.

Step 3: Creating an Administrative User

After you assign a password to Admin, you are ready to create a new administrative user. The administrative user is someone who will manage your database for you. You accomplish this from within the User and Group Accounts dialog box. Access comes with two predefined groups: the Admins group and the Users group. The Admins group is the system administrator's group account. This group automatically contains a member called Admin. Members of the Admins group have the irrevocable power to modify user and group memberships and clear user passwords, so anyone who is a member of the Admins group is all-powerful within a system. The Admins group must contain at least one member at all times.

It is extremely important to create a unique workgroup ID when you create a new workgroup. The workgroup administrator uses this workgroup ID to create a unique identifier for the workgroup. If you do not create a unique workgroup ID, people using other copies of Microsoft Access or Visual Studio can create their own workgroup files and grant themselves permissions to a database's objects. Furthermore, it is important to ensure that the Admin user does not own any objects and that you do not give the Admin user any explicit permissions. Because the Admin user is the same across all workgroups, all objects that Admin owns or has permissions to are available to anyone using another copy of Microsoft Access or Visual Basic.

The predefined Users group in Access is the default group composed of all user accounts. Access automatically adds all users to the Users group, and you cannot remove them from this group. Access automatically grants the Users group all permissions to all objects. As with the Admin user, the Users group is the same across all workgroups. It is therefore extremely important that you take steps to remove all rights from the Users group, thereby ensuring that you properly secure the objects in the database. Fortunately, the Security Wizard, covered in the section "Step 9: Running the Security Wizard," accomplishes the task of removing all rights from the Users group. Because you cannot remove rights from the Admins group and the Admin user is the same across all workgroups, you must create another user. This new user will be responsible for administrating the database.

To create a new user to administrate a database, you select the Users tab of the User and Group Accounts dialog box. (If you closed the dialog box after the last step, choose Tools|Security|User and Group Accounts to open the dialog box again.) Just as when you assign a password for the Admin user, it does not matter which database you are in when you do this; it is only important that you are a member of the proper workgroup. Remember that you are defining a user for the workgroup—not for the database. Figure 22.11 shows the Users tab of the User and Group Accounts dialog box.

FIGURE 22.11

The Users tab of the User and Group Accounts dialog box.

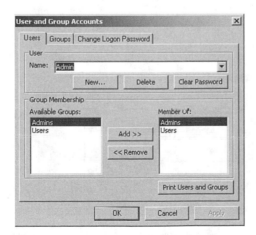

To establish a new administrative user, click New. The New User/Group dialog box appears, as shown in Figure 22.12.

FIGURE 22.12
The New User/Group dialog box.

The New User/Group dialog box enables you to enter the username and a unique personal ID. This personal ID is not a password. The username and personal ID combine to become the encrypted SID that uniquely identifies the user to the system. Users create their own passwords when they log on to the system.

The Security Wizard allows you to create one or more administrative user for a database. In fact, the Security Wizard automatically creates a user called Administrator, and this user becomes the owner of the database.

Step 4: Making the Administrative User a Member of the Admins Group

To make the new user a member of the Admins group, you open the User and Group Accounts dialog box, select the Admins group from the Available Groups list box, and then click Add with the new user selected in the Name drop-down list box. The new user should appear as a member of the Admins group, as shown in Figure 22.13.

FIGURE 22.13
Adding the new user to the Admins group.

New user

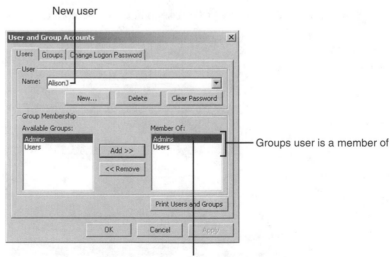

Groups user is a member of

New user as a member of Admins group

If you use the Security Wizard, Access automatically adds the user called Administrator to the Admins group. Of course, you can also add other users to the Admins group.

Step 5: Exiting Access and Logging On as the System Administrator

You are now ready to close the User and Group Accounts dialog box and exit Access. After you exit Access, attempt to run it again. After you attempt to open any database (or if you created a new database), Access prompts you with the Access Logon dialog box, as shown in Figure 22.14.

FIGURE 22.14

The Access Logon dialog box.

Log on as the new system administrator. You do not have a password at this point; only the Admin user has a password. It still does not matter which database you open.

Step 6: Removing the Admin User from the Admins Group

At this point you should remove the Admin user from the Admins group. Remember that the Admin user is the same in every workgroup. Because the Admins group has all rights to all objects in the database (including the right to assign permissions to and remove permissions from other users and objects), if you do not remove Admin from the Admins group, the database will not be secure. To remove the Admin user from the Admins group, follow these steps:

1. With the Database window active, select Tools|Security|User and Group Accounts.
2. Make sure you select the Users tab.
3. Select the Admin user from the Name drop-down list box.
4. Select Admins from the Member Of list box.
5. Click Remove. The User and Group Accounts dialog box appears, as shown in Figure 22.15.

If you use the Security Wizard to secure a database, Access automatically removes the Admin user from the Admins group. In fact, the Security Wizard does not make the Admin user a member of any group besides Users (the group of which all users must be members).

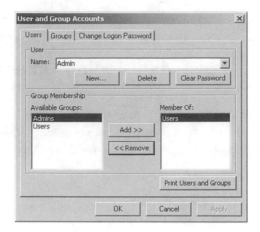

FIGURE 22.15

The User and Group Accounts dialog box.

Step 7: Assigning a Password to the System Administrator

Now that you have logged on as the new Administrator user, you should modify your password. If you have closed the User and Group Accounts dialog box, choose Tools| Security|User and Group Accounts to open the dialog box. Click the Change Logon Password tab. Remember that you can assign a password only for the user who is logged on.

One of the really cool aspects of the Security Wizard is that it allows you to assign passwords for all users who are members of a workgroup. This saves you a lot of time and effort when establishing a large number of users.

Step 8: Opening the Database You Want to Secure

You are finally ready to actually secure the database. Up to this point, it has not mattered which database is open. Everything you have done so far has applied to the workgroup rather than to a particular database. At this point, you need to open the database you want to secure. At the moment, the Admin user owns the database, and members of the Users group have rights to all objects in the database.

Step 9: Running the Security Wizard

Unless you are creating a brand-new database after you perform all the preceding steps, the first thing you should do to secure an existing database is to use the Security Wizard. The Security Wizard allows you to perform the following tasks:

- Join an existing workgroup or create a new workgroup information file
- Designate the database objects you want to secure

- Assign a password for the Visual Basic project
- Select from predefined groups that the wizard creates
- Assign desired rights to the Users group
- Create users
- Assign users to groups
- Create an unsecured backup copy of a database

To run the Security Wizard, you choose Tools | Security | User Level Security Wizard. You cannot have the database open exclusively when you attempt to do this. The first step of the Security Wizard dialog box appears, as shown in Figure 22.16.

You cannot run the Security Wizard if you have set a Visual Basic Environment (VBE) password for the project. You must unlock the VBE project before you run the wizard. This book does not cover VBE passwords. Refer to *Alison Balter's Mastering Office Access 2003 Desktop Development*, published by Sams, for more information on this topic.

FIGURE 22.16

The first step of the Security Wizard, which prompts you to select an existing workgroup file or create a new workgroup information file.

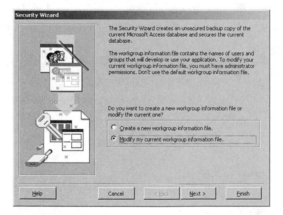

The first window of the Security Wizard prompts you to select an existing workgroup information file or create a new workgroup information file. You need to select Create a New Workgroup Information File and click Next to proceed to the second window of the Security Wizard (pictured in Figure 22.17). If you opt to create a new workgroup information file, the second window of the wizard prompts you to provide required information about the workgroup information file that you are creating. The wizard asks you to enter a filename, a workgroup identifier (WID), your name, and your company name.

You can designate the new workgroup file as the default workgroup file on your computer, or you can have Access create a shortcut to the secured database, including the name and path to the workgroup file.

FIGURE 22.17
The second step of the Security Wizard, where you enter required information about the workgroup file.

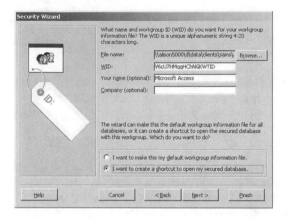

The third window of the Security Wizard, shown in Figure 22.18, allows you to select the objects you want to secure. Notice that you can secure all objects or you can opt to secure specific tables, queries, forms, reports, or macros. Modules, including the code behind forms and reports, are secured separately (that is, not as part of this wizard).

FIGURE 22.18
The third step of the Security Wizard, where you select the objects you want to secure.

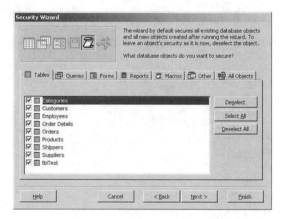

The fourth window of the Security Wizard, pictured in Figure 22.19, allows you to easily create group accounts. If your security needs match those predefined by one of the default groups, you can save yourself a significant amount of time by allowing the Security Wizard to create the necessary groups for you. An example of a predefined group is read-only users who can read all data but cannot modify data or the design of database objects. Another predefined group is for project designers who can edit all data and the design of application objects but cannot modify the structure of tables or relationships.

FIGURE 22.19

The fourth step of the Security Wizard, where you create groups from a list of predefined group accounts.

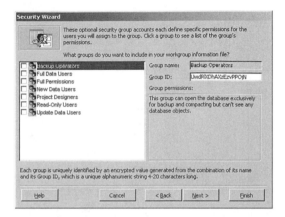

In the fifth window of the Security Wizard, shown in Figure 22.20, you designate what permissions, if any, you want to grant to the Users group. It is important to remember that *all* users are members of the Users group. Therefore, any permissions that you grant to the Users group Access grants to all the users of the application. As a general rule, I recommend not granting any rights to the Users group. It is better to assign rights to other groups and then make specific users members of those groups.

FIGURE 22.20

The fifth step of the Security Wizard, where you grant specific rights to the Users group.

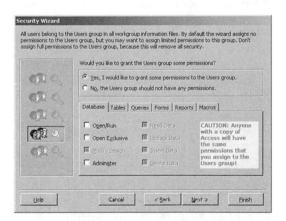

The sixth window of the Security Wizard allows you to define the users who will use your database. In this step of the wizard, you supply each user's name, a password, and a

unique personal identifier (PID), and then you click the Add This User to the List button
(see Figure 22.21). To delete a user, you select that user and then click the Delete User
from the List button. You click Next when you are finished defining all users.

Adding a new user

FIGURE 22.21

*The sixth step of the
Security Wizard, where
you define the users of
your database.*

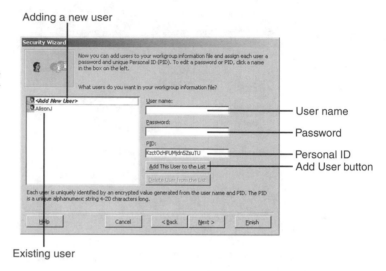

User name

Password

Personal ID

Add User button

Existing user

In the next window of the Security Wizard, you assign the users created in the sixth window to the groups designated in the fourth window. To assign a user to a group, you
click Select a User and Assign the User to Groups. Next, you select a user from the
Group or User Name drop-down list box. Then you click to add the selected user to any
of the predefined groups (see Figure 22.22).

FIGURE 22.22

*The seventh step of the
Security Wizard, where
you assign users to
groups.*

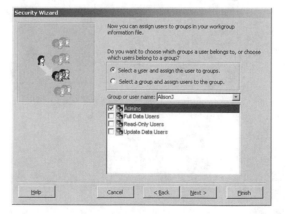

22

The final window of the Security Wizard prompts you to enter the name of the backup copy of the unsecured database. After you click Finish, Access secures the existing database, and it gives the original unsecured database the name designated for the backup.

You cannot change the owner of a database, and the owner of a database always has rights to everything in the database. Because Admin is the owner of the database and is the same in all workgroups, Access must copy all the database objects to a new, secure database that is owned by the new user. The wizard is intelligent enough to create a new secure database with the original database name and create a backup with the name that you designate. Access in no way modifies the existing, unsecured database. When the process is complete, the security report shown in Figure 22.23 appears.

FIGURE 22.23

The One-step Security Wizard Report.

The One-step Security Wizard Report contains detailed information about the workgroup the wizard created, the objects it secured, and the groups and users it created. The new system administrator owns the new copy of the database. The Security Wizard revokes all rights from the Users group.

When you close this report, Access prompts you to save it as a snapshot so that you can view it again later. Because the report contains valuable information about the workgroup and the secured database, I strongly suggest that you save it in a very safe place. Armed with the information contained in the report, a savvy user could violate the security of the database.

Step 10: Creating Users and Groups

Any time after you establish and join a workgroup, you can establish the users and groups who will be members of the workgroup. Users represent individual people who will access your database files. Users are members of groups, and groups are categories of users who share the same rights. You can assign rights at the user level or at the group level. Administratively, it is easier to assign all rights at the group level. However, this involves categorizing access rights into logical groups and then assigning users to those groups.

Establishing groups properly greatly facilitates the administration of a system. If you need to change the rights of a category of users, you can modify those rights at a group level. If a user is promoted and needs additional rights, you can make that user a member of a new group. This is much easier than trying to maintain separate rights for each user.

You generally create groups and then assign users to the appropriate groups. It is important to evaluate the structure of the organization as well as the application before you begin the mechanical process of adding groups and users.

Adding Groups

To add new groups, follow these steps:

1. Make sure you are a member of the correct workgroup. With or without a database open, select Tools|Security|User and Group Accounts.
2. Select the Groups tab of the User and Group Accounts dialog box.
3. Click New. The New User/Group dialog box appears.
4. Type the name of the group and enter a PID that uniquely identifies the group.
5. Click OK.
6. Repeat steps 3 through 5 for each group you want to add.

The PID is a case-sensitive, alphanumeric string that can be from 4 to 20 characters in length. In combination with the user or group name, the PID uniquely identifies the user or group in a workgroup. You should store PIDs in a very safe place. In the hands of the wrong person, access to PIDs can lead to a breach of security. On the other hand, if the database is damaged and an important PID is not available, the data and objects in the database will not be accessible, even to legitimate users.

Adding Users

To add users through the user interface, follow these steps:

1. Choose Tools|Security|User and Group Accounts. (You do not need to have a database open to complete this step.)
2. Select the Users tab if it is not already selected.
3. Click New. The New User/Group dialog box appears.
4. Enter the name of the user and the PID associated with the user. Remember that the PID is not a password; instead, it combines with the username to create a unique identifier for the user.
5. Click OK.
6. Repeat steps 3 through 5 for each user you want to define.

Assigning Users to the Appropriate Groups

Before you assign rights to users and groups, you should make each user a member of the appropriate group. A user can be a member of as many groups as you choose, but you need to remember that each user gets the rights of his or her most forgiving group. In other words, if a user is a member of both the Admins group and a group with read-only access to objects, the rights of the Admins group prevail for that user in all cases. To assign users to the appropriate groups, follow these steps:

1. Choose Tools|Security|User and Group Accounts. (You do not need to have a database open to complete this step.)
2. Select the Users tab if it is not already selected.
3. From the Name drop-down list box, select the user for whom you want to create group membership(s).
4. Double-click the name of the group to which you want to add the user, or single-click the group and then click the Add button.
5. Repeat steps 3 and 4 for each user to whom you want to assign a group membership.

Figure 22.24 shows a user named DanB who has been added to the Full Data Users group.

Remember that the users and groups you create are for the workgroup as a whole—not just for a specific database.

FIGURE 22.24

Assigning a user to the appropriate group.

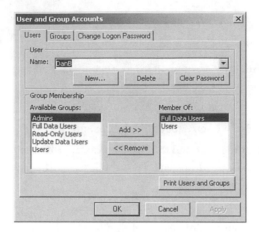

Step 11: Assigning Rights to Users and Groups

So far, you have created groups and users, but you haven't given any of your groups or users rights to objects in the database. The key is to assign specific rights to each group and then to make sure that all users are members of the appropriate groups. After that, you can assign each group specific permissions to the objects in the database. Access maintains user and group information in the system database; it stores permissions for objects in system tables in the application database file (that is, the .MDB file). After you establish a workgroup of users and groups, you must assign rights to specific objects in the database by following these steps:

1. Open the database that contains the objects you want to secure.

2. Choose Tools|Security|User and Group Permissions. The dialog box shown in Figure 22.25 appears. Notice that as you click each user in the User/Group Name box, as indicated by the check boxes in the Permissions section of the dialog box, you see that only the Administrator has rights to any objects. The Security Wizard automatically removed all permissions from the user named Admin. If you select the Groups option button, you see that only the Admins group has any rights. (If you have previously run the Security Wizard and added other users and groups, they have rights as well.)

3. To assign rights to a group, select the Groups option button. All the available groups appear in the User/Group Name box.

4. From the Object Type drop-down list box, select the type of object you want to secure.

5. From the Object Name list box, select the names of the objects to which you want to assign rights. You can select multiple objects by pressing the Ctrl and Shift keys.

FIGURE 22.25

The User and Group Permissions dialog box.

22

6. Enable the appropriate check boxes in the Permission section of the dialog box to select permissions for the objects. The text that follows discusses the types of available permissions.

7. Repeat steps 4 through 6 for all objects to which you want to assign rights.

I recommend that you assign groups the rights to objects and then simply make users members of the appropriate groups. Notice that you can use the Object Type drop-down list box in the User and Group Permissions dialog box to view the various types of objects that make up the database.

To assign permissions appropriately, it is important that you understand the types of permissions available and what each type of permission allows a user to do. Table 22.1 lists the types of permissions that are available.

TABLE 22.1   Access Permissions

Permission	Allows User To
Open/Run	Open a database, form, or report, or run a macro.
Open Exclusive	Open a database with exclusive access.
Read Design	View tables, queries, forms, reports, macros, and modules in Design view.
Modify Design	View and change the design of tables, queries, forms, reports, macros, and modules.

continues

TABLE 22.1   continued

Permission	Allows User To
Administer	Set the database password, replicate the database, and change startup properties (when the user has Administer permission of a database). Have full access to the object and its data (when the user has Administer permission of a database object—such as a table, query, form, report, macro, or module). Assign permissions for that object to other users (when the user has Administer permissions for an object).
Read Data	View the data in a table or query.
Update Data	View and modify table or query data. A user with this permission cannot insert and delete records, however.
Insert Data	Add records to a table or query.
Delete Data	Delete records from a table or query.

Some of these permissions implicitly include associated permissions. A user must first have the rights to read the data and the design of a table before he or she can update data in the table, for example.

Summary

The security system in Access 2003 is quite robust but also somewhat complex. By using Access security, you can fully secure a database and all its objects. As a developer, you might want to prevent people from modifying the objects in a database. Furthermore, you might want to restrict certain users from viewing certain data, using specific forms, or running certain reports.

This hour walks through all the steps required to properly secure a database. It begins by showing you how to set up a database password and how to encrypt a database. It also covers all the details of implementing user-level security.

Invoking user-level security first involves using the Workgroup Administrator to set up a workgroup. You then must create an administrative user and make that user a member of the Admins group. Next, you change the password for the Admin user and remove the Admin user from the Admins group. You then exit Access, log on as the system administrator, and assign yourself a password. All these steps are covered in detail in this hour. In addition, this hour walks you through using the Security Wizard to perform many necessary tasks, such as changing the owner of the database from Admin to the new Administrator user and revoking all permissions from the Users group. This ensures that

22

the database is truly secure. As described in this hour, the final step is to assign permissions to groups and/or users for the objects that reside in the newly secured database.

Q&A

Q **Describe the main difference between share-level and user-level security.**

A Share-level security involves assigning a password to the overall database, whereas user-level security involves assigning different security levels to various users and groups.

Q **Explain the concept of a workgroup.**

A A workgroup is a database of users and groups who have access to various databases.

Q **Name some uses of the Security Wizard.**

A You can use the Security Wizard to establish workgroup files, create users, create groups, assign users to groups, and more.

Workshop

The Workshop includes quiz questions that are designed to help you test your understanding of the material covered and activities to help put what you've learned to practice. You can find the answers to the questions in the section immediately following the quiz.

Quiz

1. What is the name of the default workgroup file?
2. How do you activate the logon dialog box?
3. User-level security is easier to implement than share-level security (True/False).
4. There are Web sites that can help a person remove Access security (True/False).
5. What is a SID?

Quiz Answers

1. `System.mdw`.
2. Supply a password for the Admin user.
3. False. Share-level security is much easier to implement than user-level security.
4. True.
5. A SID is a user's or group's machine-generated unique security identifier.

Activities

Back up a database that you use and then practice running the Security Wizard on that database.

Hour **23**

VBA Introduced

The Visual Basic for Applications (VBA) language is at the heart of every Access application you write. VBA is the key to taking Access beyond the world of wizards into a world where anything is possible. This hour introduces you to the VBA language, which serves as a foundation for any programming code that you write. After following along with the text in the hour, you will be familiar with the development environment. In this hour you'll learn the following:

- What VBA is
- How to declare and work with variables
- How to utilize control structures
- How to pass parameters and return values
- How to execute commands with the DoCmd object
- How to work with built-in functions

VBA Explained

VBA is the development language for Microsoft Access 2003. It offers a consistent language for application development in the Microsoft Office suite. The core language, its constructs, and the environment are the same in Microsoft Access 2003, Microsoft Visual Basic 6.0, Microsoft Excel, Microsoft Word, Microsoft Outlook (for applicationwide programming), and

Microsoft Project. What differs among these environments are the built-in objects specific to each application. For example, Access has a `CurrentProject` object, but Excel has a `Workbook` object. Each application's objects have appropriate properties (attributes) and methods (actions)—and, in some cases, events—associated with them. This hour gives you an overview of the VBA language and its constructs.

Unlike macros in Word or Excel, an Access macro is not a subprocedure in a module; instead, it is a different type of database object, with its own interface. Because of this, you can't use Access macros to learn to program in VBA, as you can by recording a Word or Excel macro and then examining its VBA code. You can write simple Access applications by using macros, but although macros are okay for quick prototyping and very basic application development, you will perform most serious Access development by using the VBA language. Unlike macros, VBA gives you the ability to perform tasks that are not available with macros. (See Hour 13, "Creating Macros," for more information.)

Access Class Modules, Standard Modules, Form Modules, and Report Modules

NEW TERM You write VBA code in units called *subroutines* and *functions* that you store in modules. Microsoft Access modules are either Standard modules or Class modules. You create *Standard modules* by selecting the Modules icon in the Database window and then clicking New. Standard modules contain libraries of subroutines and functions. *Class modules* can be standalone objects, or they can be associated with a form or report. To create a standalone Class module, you choose Insert|Class Module. Whenever you add code behind a form or report, Microsoft Access creates a Class module associated with that form or report that contains the code you create.

NEW TERM Modules specific to a form or report are generally called *Form* and *Report Class modules*, and their code is often referred to as *Code Behind Forms* (CBFs). Access creates and stores CBF in that form or report and triggers the code within it from events occurring within the form or report.

NEW TERM A *subroutine* (or *subprocedure*) is a routine that responds to an event or performs some action. An *event procedure* is a special type of subroutine that automatically executes in response to an event such as a mouse click on a command button or the loading of a form. A *function* is a special type of routine because it can return a value; a subroutine can't return a value. As with a subroutine, you can trigger a function from an event.

Where Do You Write VBA Code?

You write all VBA code in the Visual Basic Editor (VBE). Access places you in the VBE any time you attempt to access the code in a Standard or Class module. Figure 23.1 shows the VBE. The VBE environment in Microsoft Access is now consistent with the editor interfaces in other Microsoft Office products. The VBE is a separate window from that of Microsoft Access, and it consists of a menu bar, toolbar, Project window, Properties window, Immediate window, Locals window, Watch window, Object Browser, and Code windows.

23

FIGURE 23.1
The VBE.

Project Explorer window   Object Drop-down   Code window   Procedure Drop-down

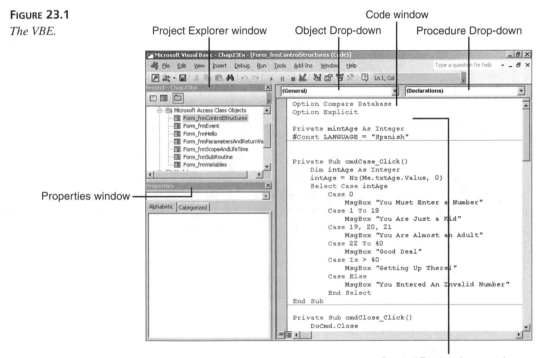

Properties window

General Declarations section

The Anatomy of a Module

NEW TERM Whether you're dealing with a Standard module or a Class module, every module contains a General Declarations section (see Figure 23.2). As the name implies, this is where you can declare variables and constants that you want to be visible to all the functions and subroutines in the module. We refer to these variables as *module-level* or *Private variables*. You can also declare Public variables in the General Declarations section of a module, and you can set options there, too. Any function or procedure in any module in the database can see and modify *Public variables*.

FIGURE 23.2

*The General
Declarations section of
a module, where you
declare Private and
Public variables.*

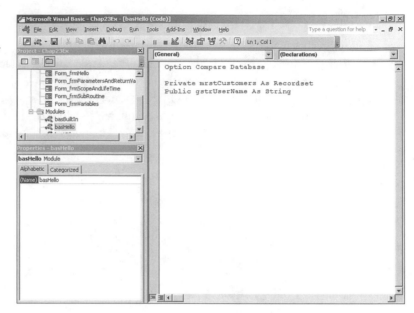

Public variables in Access 97, 2000, 2002, and 2003 replace Access 2.0's
Global variables. Although Access still supports Global variables, today most
people use Public variables rather than Global variables.

A module is also made up of user-defined subroutines and functions. Figure 23.3 shows
a subroutine called SayHello. Notice the drop-down list in the upper-right portion of the
window with SayHello selected. This is the Procedure drop-down list. You might want to
associate subroutines and functions with a specific object, such as a form or a control
within a form. The Procedure drop-down list is where Access notes such an association.
In the example shown in Figure 23.3, the subroutine named SayHello is not associated
with any object, so the Object drop-down list contains (General).

Using the Option Explicit Statement

Option Explicit is a statement that you can include in the General Declarations section
of any module, including the Class module of a form or report. When you use Option
Explicit, you must declare all variables in that module before you use them, or an error
message saying that a variable is undefined appears when you compile the module. If the
VBA compiler encounters an undeclared variable when compiling a module without
Option Explicit, it simply treats it as a new variable and continues without issuing a

warning. It might appear at first glance that because `Option Explicit` can cause compiler errors that would otherwise not occur, it might be better to avoid the use of this option. However, just the opposite is true. You should use `Option Explicit` in every module, without exception. For example, look at the following code:

```
intAmount = 2
intTotal = intAmont * 2
```

FIGURE 23.3

An example of a user-defined subroutine called SayHello.

Clearly, the intent of this code is to multiply the value contained in the variable `intAmount`, in this case 2, by 2. Notice, however, that the variable name is misspelled on the second line. If `Option Explicit` is not set, VBA views `intAmont` as a new variable and simply continues processing. The code sets the variable `intTotal` to 0 instead of 4, and the VBA compiler provides no error indication at all. You can completely eliminate this kind of result by using `Option Explicit`.

In Access 2.0, you have to manually enter the `Option Explicit` statement into each module, form, and report. Since Access 97, developers have had the option of globally instructing Access to insert the `Option Explicit` statement in all new modules. To do this in Access 2003, with the VBE active, you choose Tools|Options. On the Editor tab, click Require Variable Declaration. It's important that you place the `Option Explicit` statement in all modules, so you need to make sure you set this option to `True`. The default when you install Microsoft Access 2003 is `False`. `Option Explicit` can save you hours of debugging and prevent your beeper from going off after you distribute an application to users.

In addition to a General Declarations section and user-defined procedures, forms, and reports, Class modules also contain event procedures that Access associates with a particular object on a form. Notice in Figure 23.4 that the Object drop-down list says `cmdHello`. This is the name of the object whose event routines you are viewing. The drop-down list on the right shows all the events that you can code for a command button; each of these events creates a separate event routine. You will have the opportunity to write many event routines in this hour.

23

FIGURE 23.4

An event procedure for the Click *event of the* cmdHello *command button.*

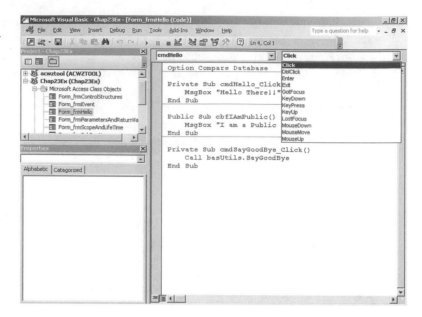

Creating Event Procedures

Access automatically creates event procedures when you write event code for an object. For example, it automatically creates the routine Private Sub cmdHello_Click when you place code in the Click event of the cmdHello command button shown in Figure 23.4. To get to the event code of an object, follow these steps:

1. Click the object in Design view and click the Properties button on the toolbar or right-click the object and choose Properties from the context menu.

2. Click the Event Properties tab.

3. Select the property you want to write code for (for example, the On Click event).

4. Select [Event Procedure] from the drop-down list.

5. Click the ellipsis (…) button, and you are taken to the VBE and placed in the event code for that object.

As discussed at the beginning of this hour, the VBE opens in a separate window from Access. It provides a programming environment that is consistent with that of all the other Microsoft Office applications. Modules you add in the VBE do not appear in the database container until you save them within the VBE.

Creating Functions and Subroutines

You can create your own procedures that aren't tied to a particular object or event. Depending on how and where you declare them, you can call them from anywhere in an application or from a particular Code module, Form module, or Report module.

Creating a User-Defined Routine in a Code Module

There are several different methods that you can use to create a user-defined routine in a Code module. They are all quite simple. The text that follows defines one process:

1. Select Modules from the Objects list in the Database window.

2. Click New to create a new module or select an existing module and click Design. The VBE appears.

3. Select Procedure from the Insert drop-down list box on the toolbar (the second icon from the left) or choose Insert|Procedure. The Add Procedure dialog box, shown in Figure 23.5, appears.

FIGURE 23.5

The Add Procedure dialog box, where you specify the name, type, and scope of the procedure you're creating.

4. Type the name of the procedure.

5. Select Sub, Function, or Property as the type of procedure.

6. To make the procedure available to an entire application, select Public as the scope; to make the procedure private to this module, select Private.

7. Click OK.

Creating a User-Defined Routine in a Form or Report Class Module

The process of creating a user-defined routine in a Form or Report class module is almost identical to that of creating a subroutine or function in a Standard module. Here's the process:

1. While in Design view of a form or report, select the View menu. Notice the icon beside the Code submenu. This same icon is also available on the toolbar. You can view the code behind the form or report by clicking this icon on the toolbar or by selecting View|Code. Access places you in the VBE.

2. Select Procedure from the Insert drop-down list box on the toolbar (the second icon from the left) or choose Insert|Procedure to open the Insert Procedure dialog box.

3. Type the name of the procedure.

4. Select Sub, Function, or Property as the type of procedure.

5. To make the procedure available to an entire application, select Public as the scope; to make the procedure private to this module, select Private.

6. Click OK.

> Whether you're creating a procedure in a Standard module or a Class module, you're now ready to enter the code for a procedure. A great shortcut for creating a procedure is to type directly in the code window the name of the new procedure, preceded by its designation as either a Sub or a Function—for example, Sub *Whatever* or Function *Whatever*. As soon as you press Enter, the new subroutine or function is created.

> You'll learn about the concept of Public versus Private procedures and the concept of scope later in this hour, in the section "The Scope and Lifetime of Procedures."

Calling Event and User-Defined Procedures

Access automatically calls Event procedures when an event occurs for an object. For example, when a user clicks a command button, the Click event code for that command button executes.

The standard method for calling user-defined procedures is to use the Call keyword—for example, Call SayHello. You can also call the same procedure without using the Call keyword—for example, SayHello.

Although not required, using the `Call` keyword makes the statement self-documenting and easier to read. You can call a user-defined procedure from an event routine or from another user-defined procedure or function. Here's an example:

```
SayHello
Call SayHello
```

Both of these lines of code accomplish the same task: calling the `SayHello` routine. The only difference is that the second is more self-documenting due to the `Call` statement.

The Scope and Lifetime of Procedures

You can declare the scope of a procedure as Public or Private. A procedure's scope determines how widely you can call it from other procedures. In addition to a procedure's scope, the placement of a procedure can noticeably affect an application's functionality and performance.

Public Procedures

You can call a Public procedure that you place in a code module from anywhere in the application. Procedures you declare in a module are automatically Public. This means that unless you specify otherwise, you can call procedures you place in any code module from anywhere within an application.

You might think that two Public procedures can't have the same name. Although this is the case in earlier versions of Access, it isn't true in Access 2000, Access 2002, and Access 2003. If two Public procedures share a name, the procedure that calls them must explicitly state which of the two routines it's calling. You can find the following code snippet, in `frmHello`'s `Class` module in the sample database, `Chap23Ex.mdb`, at www.samspublishing.com:

```
Private Sub cmdSayGoodBye_Click()
    Call basUtils.SayGoodBye
End Sub
```

This code calls the `SayGoodBye` routine in the `basUtils` module.

> You can find this code, and all the sample code in this chapter, in
> `Chap23Ex.mdb` at www.samspublishing.com.

You will find the `SayGoodBye` routine in two Access code modules; however, the prefix `basUtils` indicates that the routine you want to execute is in the Standard module named `basUtils`.

Procedures declared in Form or Report Class modules are also automatically Public, so you can call them from anywhere within the application. You can find the procedure called cbfIAmPublic, shown in Figure 23.6, in the form called frmHello. In order to call this procedure from outside the form, the only requirement is that the form containing the procedure must be open in Form view. You can call the cbfIAmPublic procedure from anywhere within the application by using the following syntax (found in the Standard module basHello):

```
Sub CallPublicFormProc()
    Call Forms.frmHello.cbfIAmPublic
End Sub
```

FIGURE 23.6

A Public form procedure.

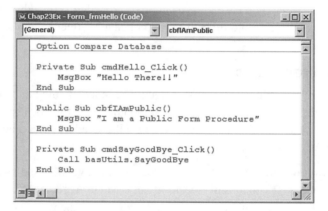

```
Chap23Ex - Form_frmHello (Code)
(General)                              cbfIAmPublic

Option Compare Database

Private Sub cmdHello_Click()
    MsgBox "Hello There!!"
End Sub

Public Sub cbfIAmPublic()
    MsgBox "I am a Public Form Procedure"
End Sub

Private Sub cmdSayGoodBye_Click()
    Call basUtils.SayGoodBye
End Sub
```

Although all procedures (except event procedures) are by default Public, you should use the Public keyword to show that the procedure is visible to any subroutine or function in the database.

Private Procedures

As mentioned previously, all user-defined procedures are automatically Public. If you want a procedure declared in a module to have the scope of that module only, meaning that you can call it only from another routine within the module, you must explicitly declare it as Private (see Figure 23.7).

The procedure shown in Figure 23.7, called IAmPrivate, is Private. You can call it only from other procedures in the Standard basUtils module.

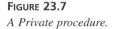

FIGURE 23.7

A Private procedure.

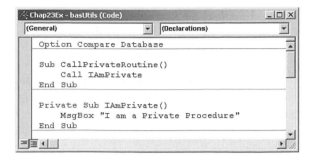

Scope Precedence

Private procedures always take precedence over Public procedures. If a Private procedure in one module has the same name as a Public procedure declared in *another* module, the Private procedure's code executes if you call it from any routine in the module where it was declared. Naming conflicts don't occur between Public and Private procedures (unless you declare a Public variable and a Private variable with the same name in the same module).

Working with Variables

You must consider many issues when creating VBA variables. The way you declare a variable determines its scope, its lifetime, and more. The following sections will help you better understand how to declare and work with variables in VBA.

Declaring Variables

There are several ways to declare variables in VBA. For example, you could simply declare x=10. With this method of variable declaration, you really aren't declaring variables at all; you're essentially declaring variables as you use them. This method is quite dangerous. It lends itself to typos and other problems. If you follow the practice recommended previously—of always using the Option Explicit statement—Access will not allow you to declare variables in this manner.

You can also type Dim intCounter to declare the variable intCounter because the Dim statement declares a variable. The only problem with this method is that you haven't declared the type of the variable to the compiler, so you have declared a variant variable. Variant variables are slow and are also dangerous in that the compiler cannot do type checking to try to ensure that you store valid data within them (for example, a number in an integer variable).

Another common mistake is declaring multiple variables on the same line, as in this example:

```
Dim intCounter, intAge, intWeight As Integer.
```

In this line, you've only explicitly declared the last variable as an integer variable. You've implicitly declared the other variables as variants. If you're going to declare multiple variables on one line, you need to make sure you specifically declare each variable, as in the following example:

```
Dim intCounter As Integer, intAge As Integer, intWeight As Integer
```

The most efficient and bug-proof way to declare variables is to strongly type them to the compiler and declare only one variable per line of code, as in this example:

```
Dim intCounter As Integer
Dim strName As String
```

As you can see, strongly typing declares the name of the variable as well as the type of data it can contain. This enables the compiler to catch errors, such as storing a string in an integer variable, before a program runs. If implemented properly, this method can also reduce the resources needed to run programs by selecting the smallest practical data type for each variable.

> You should try to avoid using variants whenever possible. Besides requiring a significant amount of storage space, variants are also slow because the compiler must resolve them at runtime. However, certain situations warrant using variants. One example is when you want a variable to contain different types of data at different times. Another case is when you want to be able to differentiate between an empty variable (one that hasn't been initialized) and a variable that contains a zero or has a zero-length string. Also, variant variables are the only type of variable that can hold the special value `Null`.

VBA Data Types

VBA offers several data types for variables. Table 23.1 lists the available data types, the standards for naming them, the amount of storage space they require, the data they can store, and their default values.

TABLE 23.1 VBA Data Types

Data Type	Naming Conv Default Example	Storage of Data	Range	*Default* Value
Byte	bytValue	1 byte	0 to 255	0
Boolean	boolAnswer	2 bytes	True or False	False
Integer	intCounter	2 bytes	−32768 to 32767	0
Long Integer	lngAmount	4 bytes	−2,147,483,648 to 2,147,483,647	0
Single	sngAmount	4 bytes	−3.402823E38 to −1.401298E-45 for negative values; from 1.401298E-45 to 3.402823E38 for positive values	0
Double	dblValue	8 bytes	−1.79769313486231E308 to −4.94065645841247E-324 for negative values; from 4.94065645841247E-324 to 1.79769313486232E308 for positive values	0
Currency	curSalary	8 bytes	−922,337,203,685,477.5808 to 922,337,203,685,477.5807	0
Date	dtmStartDate	8 bytes	1/1/100 to 12/31/9999	12/30/1899
Object Reference	objExcel	4 bytes	Any object	N/A
Fixed String	strName	varies	Up to 65,526 characters	" "
Variable String	strName	varies	Up to approximately 2 billion characters	" "
Variant	varData	varies	Can contain any of the other data types except Fixed String	Empty
User-Defined Data Type	typEmp	varies	Based on Elements	N/A
Decimal	decTaxAmount	12 bytes	+/−79,228,162,514,264, 337,593,543,950,335 with 0 decimal places to ±7.9228162514264337593543950335 with 28 decimal places	0

23

Scope and Lifetime of Variables: Exposing Variables as Little as Possible

In this hour you have read about the different types of variables available in VBA. Like procedures, variables also have scope. You can declare a variable as Local, Private (Module), or Public in scope. You should try to use Local variables in code because they're shielded from being accidentally modified by other routines.

NEW TERM　Variables have an attribute that is referred to as their *lifetime*. The lifetime of a variable reflects the time during which the variable actually exists and, therefore, the time during which the compiler retains the value of the variable. The following sections take a closer look at how you can set the scope and lifetime of variables.

Local Variables

Local variables are available only in the procedure where they are declared. Consider this example (not included in Chap23Ex.mdb):

```
Private Sub cmdOkay_Click
  Dim strAnimal As String
  strAnimal = "Dog"
  Call ChangeAnimal
  Debug.Print strAnimal 'Still Dog
End Sub

Private Sub ChangeAnimal
  strAnimal = "Cat"
End Sub
```

This code can behave in one of two ways. If Option Explicit were in effect, meaning that you must declare all variables before you use them, this code would generate a compiler error. If you don't use the Option Explicit statement, the code would change strAnimal to Cat only within the context of the subroutine ChangeAnimal.

> Apostrophes are used to denote comments in VBA. Comments are covered later in this hour.

Notice the Debug.Print statement in the cmdOkay_Click event routine shown previously (see Figure 23.8). The code prints the expression that follows the Debug.Print statement in the Immediate window. The Immediate window is a tool that helps you to troubleshoot applications. You can invoke the Immediate window from almost anywhere within an application. The easiest way to activate the Immediate window is by using the Ctrl+G key combination. Access then places you in the VBE within the Immediate window, where you can view the expressions that the compiler printed.

FIGURE 23.8

The Immediate window, which helps you to troubleshoot applications.

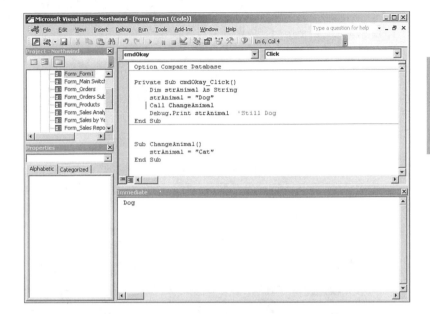

Static Variables

Static variables are a special type of Local variables. The following examples illustrate the difference between Local and Static variables. The compiler reinitializes Local variables each time you call the code.

You can run the following procedure by opening the form named frmScopeAndLifeTime and clicking the Local Age button. Notice that each time you run the procedure, the code displays the numeral 1 in the txtNewAge text box.

```
Private Sub cmdLocalAge_Click()
  Dim intAge As Integer
  intAge = intAge + 1
  Me.txtNewAge.Value = intAge
End Sub
```

Me refers to the current form or report. For example, Me.txtNewAge.Value refers to the Value property of the txtNewAge text box on the current form.

Each time this code runs, the Dim statement reinitializes intAge to zero. This is quite different from the following code, which illustrates the use of a Static variable:

```
Private Sub cmdStaticAge_Click()
  Static sintAge As Integer
  sintAge = sintAge + 1
  Me.txtNewAge.Value = sintAge
End Sub
```

Each time this code executes, it increments the variable called sintAge and retains its value. You can test this by opening the form named frmScopeAndLifeTime and clicking the Static Age button.

Private Variables

So far, this discussion has been limited to variables that have scope within a single procedure. You can see Private (Module) variables in any routine in the module you declared them in, but not from other modules. Thus, they are private to the module. You declare Private variables by placing a Private statement, such as the following, in the General Declarations section of a form, report, or Access module:

```
[General Declarations]
Option Explicit
Private mintAge As Integer
```

The code can change the value of a variable declared as Private by any subroutine or function within that module. For example, the following subroutine increments the value of the Private variable mintAge by 1:

```
Private Sub cmdModuleAge_Click()
  mintAge = mintAge + 1
  Me.txtNewAge.Value = mintAge
End Sub
```

You can run this code by opening the form frmScopeAndLifeTime and clicking the Module Age button.

Notice the naming convention of using the letter m to prefix the name of the variable. This denotes the variable as a Private module-level variable. You should use Private declarations only for variables that need to be seen by multiple procedures in the same module. You should aim to make most of your variables Local variables in order to make your code modular and more bugproof.

Public Variables

You can access Public variables from any VBA code in an application. They're usually limited to things such as login IDs, environment settings, and other variables that an entire application must see. You can place declarations of Public variables in the General Declarations section of a module. The declaration of a Public variable looks like this:

```
Option Explicit
Public gintAge As Integer
```

Notice the prefix g (a relic of the old Global variables), which is the proper prefix for a Public variable declared in a Standard module. You should use this standard because Public variables declared in a Standard module are visible not only to the module they were declared in but also to other modules. The following code, placed in the Click event of the cmdPublic command button, increments the Public variable gintAge by 1:

```
Private Sub cmdPublicAge_Click()
  gintAge = gintAge + 1
  Me.txtNewAge.Value = gintAge
End Sub
```

You can run this code by opening the form frmScopeAndLifeTime and clicking the Public Age button.

Adding Comments to Code

You add comments, which have been color-coded in versions of Access since Access 97, to modules by using an apostrophe ('). You can place the apostrophe at the beginning of the line of code or anywhere within it. The compiler considers anything following the apostrophe a comment. Figure 23.9 shows code that contains comments.

FIGURE 23.9

Code containing comments that clarify what the subroutine is doing.

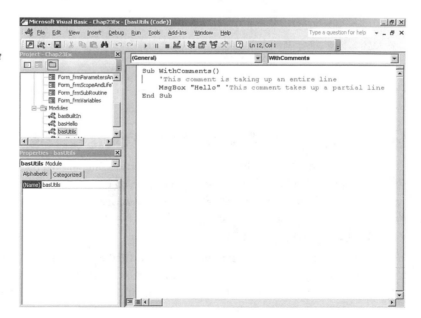

23

Many people ask if it is possible to comment several lines of code at once. Although not easily discoverable, the process is quite simple. Within the VBE, you right-click any toolbar or menu bar and display the Edit toolbar. You select the text you want to comment, and then you click the Comment Block tool on the Edit toolbar. To uncomment the block of code, you select the text you want to uncomment and then you click the Uncomment Block tool.

Using the Line Continuation Character

The line continuation character, which allows you to break up a long line of code, is an underscore (_). Figure 23.10 illustrates the use of this character.

FIGURE 23.10

The line continuation character.

Using the VBA Control Structures

VBA provides several different constructs for looping and decision processing. The sections that follow cover the most commonly used constructs. You can find the examples in the form called frmControlStructures at www.samspublishing.com.

If...Then...Else

The If...Then...Else construct evaluates whether a condition is true. In the following example, anything between If and Else occurs if the statement evaluates to True, and any code between Else and End If execute if the statement evaluates to False:

```
Private Sub cmdIfThenElse_Click()
  If IsNull(Me.txtName.Value) or IsNull(Me.txtAge.Value) Then
     MsgBox "Name or Age is Blank"
  Else
     MsgBox "Your Name Is " & Me.txtName.Value _
          & " And Your Age Is " & Me.txtAge.Value
  End If
End Sub
```

The `Else` in this code is optional. This code tests whether the text boxes called `txtName` and `txtAge` contain a `Null` (absence of a value). The code displays a different message, depending on whether one of the text boxes contains a `Null` value.

VBA also permits one-line `If` statements; they look like this:

```
If IsNull(Me.txtvalue.Value) Then MsgBox "You must Enter a Value"
```

However, I don't recommend this format for an `If` statement because it reduces readability.

Another useful form of an `If` statement is `ElseIf`, which enables you to evaluate an unlimited number of conditions in one `If` statement. The following code is an example (not included in `Chap23Ex.mdb`):

```
Sub MultipleIfs(intNumber As Integer)
    If intNumber = 1 Then
       MsgBox "You entered a One"
    ElseIf intNumber = 2 Then
       MsgBox "You entered a Two"
    ElseIf intNumber >= 3 And intNumber <= 10 Then
       MsgBox "You entered a Number Between 3 and 10"
    Else
       MsgBox "You Entered Some Other Number"
    End If
End Sub
```

The compiler evaluates the conditions in an `If` statement in the order in which they appear. For this reason, it's best to place the most common conditions first. After a condition is met, execution continues immediately after the `End If`. If no conditions are met and there's no `Else` statement, execution also continues immediately after the `End If`.

> If multiple conditions exist, it's almost always preferable to use a `Select Case` statement, described later in this hour, rather than an `If` statement. `Case` statements generally make code easier to read and maintain than `If...Then...Else` statements.

23

Immediate If (IIf)

An `Immediate If` (`IIf`) is a variation of an `If` statement. It's actually a built-in function that returns one of two values, depending on whether the condition you are testing for is true or false. Here's an example (not included in `Chap23Ex.mdb`):

```
Function EvalSales(curSales As Currency) As String
   EvalSales = IIf(curSales >= 100000, "Great Job", "Keep Plugging")
End Function
```

This function evaluates the `curSales` parameter to see whether its value is greater than or equal to $100,000. If the value is greater than or equal to $100,000, the code returns the string `"Great Job"` from the function; otherwise, the code returns the string `"Keep Plugging"`.

> The code evaluates both the true and false portions of the `IIf`, so if there's a problem with either part of the expression (for example, a divide-by-zero condition), an error occurs.

You most often use the `IIf` function in a calculated control on a form or report, or to create a new field in a query. Probably the most common example is an `IIf` expression that determines whether the value of a control is `Null`. If it is, you can have the expression return a zero or an empty string; otherwise, you can have the expression return the value in the control. The following expression, for example, evaluates the value of a control on a form:

```
=IIf(IsNull(Forms!frmOrders.txtFreight.Value),0, _
   Forms!frmOrders.txtFreight.Value)
```

This expression displays either a zero or the value for freight in the control called `txtFreight`.

> Although you can use the `IIf` function to handle `Null` values, the built-in `Nz` function is a more efficient solution to this problem and avoids the inherent pitfalls of `IIf`. The section that follows shows you how to use the `Nz` function.

> The IIf function executes slowly. It is best to avoid using it whenever possible.

Select Case

Rather than use multiple If...Then...Else statements, it's often much clearer to use a Select Case statement, as shown here and found under the Select Case command button of the frmControlStructures form:

```
Private Sub cmdCase_Click()
    Dim intAge As Integer
    intAge = Nz(Me.txtAge.Value, 0)    Select Case intAge
      Case 0
        MsgBox "You Must Enter a Number"
      Case 1 to 18
        MsgBox "You Are Just a Kid"
      Case 19, 20, 21
        MsgBox "You are Almost an Adult"
      Case 22 to 40
        MsgBox "Good Deal"
      Case Is > 40
        MsgBox "Getting Up There!"
      Case Else
        MsgBox "You Entered an Invalid Number"
    End Select
End Sub
```

This subroutine first uses the Nz function to convert a Null or empty value in the txtAge control to 0; otherwise, the code stores the value in txtAge in the intAge variable. The Select Case statement then evaluates intAge. If the value is 0, the code displays a message box that says You Must Enter a Number. If the value is between 1 and 18 inclusive, the code displays a message box that says You Are Just a Kid. If the user enters 19, 20, or 21, the code displays the message You are Almost an Adult. If the user enters a value between 22 and 40 inclusive, the code displays the message Good Deal. If the user enters a value greater than 40, the code displays a message Getting Up There!. If the user enters any other number, he or she gets a message indicating that it is an invalid number.

Looping

Several looping structures are available in VBA; this section discusses most of them. Take a look at the following example of a looping structure (found under the Do While...Loop command button of the frmControlStructures form):

```
Sub cmdDoWhileLoop_Click()

    Do While Nz(Me.txtAge.Value)< 35

        Me.txtAge.Value = Nz(Me.txtAge.Value) + 1
    Loop
End Sub
```

In this structure, if the value in the txtAge text box is greater than or equal to 35, the code in the loop is not executed. If you want the code to execute unconditionally at least one time, you need to use the following construct (found under the Do...Loop While command button of the frmControlStructures form):

```
Sub cmdDoLoopWhile_Click()

    Do

        Me.txtAge = Nz(Me.txtAge.Value) + 1
    Loop While Nz(Me.txtAge.Value) < 35
End Sub
```

This code executes one time, even if the value in the txtAge text box is set to 35. Do While...Loop in the previous example evaluates before the code executes, so it doesn't ensure code execution. The code evaluates Do...Loop While at the end of the loop and it therefore guarantees execution.

Alternatives to Do While...Loop and the Do...Loop While are Do Until...Loop and Do...Loop Until. Do Until...Loop (found under the Do Until...Loop command button of the frmControlStructures form) works like this:

```
Sub cmdDoUntil_Click()

    Do Until Nz(Me.txtAge.Value) = 35

        Me.txtAge.Value = Nz(Me.txtAge.Value) + 1
    Loop
End Sub
```

This loop continues to execute until the value in the txtAge text box becomes equal to 35. The Do...Loop Until construct (found under the Do...Loop Until command button of the frmControlStructures form) is another variation:

```
Sub cmdLoopUntil_Click()

    Do

        Me.txtAge.Value = Nz(Me.txtAge.Value) + 1
    Loop Until Nz(Me.txtAge.Value) = 35
End Sub
```

As with the Do...Loop While construct, the Do...Loop Until construct doesn't evaluate the condition until the end of the loop, so the code in the loop is guaranteed to execute at least once.

It is not a good idea to reference a control over and over again in a loop. Notice that the code in the looping examples references the txtAge control each time through the loop. I did this to keep the examples simple. To eliminate the performance problem associated with this technique, you should use the code that follows (found under the cmdEfficient command button on the frmControlStructures form):

```
Private Sub cmdEfficient_Click()
    Dim intCounter As Integer
    intCounter = Nz(Me.txtAge.Value)
    Do While intCounter < 35
        intCounter = intCounter + 1
    Loop
    Me.txtAge.Value = intCounter
End Sub
```

With *any* of the looping constructs, it's easy to unintentionally cause a loop to execute endlessly. This can also be illustrated with the code samples shown previously and the following example, which shows an endless loop (not included in Chap23Ex.mdb):

```
Sub EndlessLoop()
    Dim intCounter As Integer
    intCounter = 5
    Do
        Debug.Print intCounter
        intCounter = intCounter + 1
    Loop Until intCounter = 5
End Sub
```

This code snippet sets intCounter equal to 5. The code in the loop increments intCounter and then tests to see whether intCounter equals 5. If it doesn't, the code in the loop executes another time. Because intCounter will never become equal to 5 (it starts at 6 within the Do loop), the loop executes endlessly. You need to use Ctrl+Break to exit the loop; however, Ctrl+Break doesn't work in Access's runtime version. The user must instead use the Task Manager to end the task.

For...Next

You use the For...Next construct when you have an exact number of iterations you want
to perform. It looks like this and is found under the For...Next command button of the
frmControlStructures form:

```
Sub cmdForNext_Click()
    Dim intCounter As Integer
    For intCounter = 1 To 5
        Me.txtAge.Value = Nz(Me.txtAge.Value) + 1
    Next intCounter
End Sub
```

Note that intCounter is self-incrementing. The start value and the stop value can both be
variables. You can give a For...Next construct a step value, as shown in the following
example, in which the code increments the counter by the value of Step each time it
processes the loop:

```
Sub ForNextStep()
' Note that this code is not in database Chap23Ex.mdb
    Dim intCounter As Integer
    For intCounter = 1 To 5 Step 2
        Me.txtAge.Value = Nz(Me.txtAge.Value) + 1
    Next intCounter
End Sub
```

With...End With

The With...End With statement executes a series of statements on a single object or
user-defined type. Here's an example (found under the With...End With command button of the frmControlStructures form):

```
Private Sub cmdWithEndWith_Click()
   With Me.txtAge
      .BackColor = 16777088
      .ForeColor = 16711680
      .Value = "40"
      .FontName = "Arial"
   End With
End Sub
```

This code performs four operations on the txtAge text box, found on the form it's run
on. The code modifies the BackColor, ForeColor, Value, and FontName properties of the
txtAge text box.

The With...End With statement offers two main benefits. The first is simply less typing: You don't need to repeat the object name for each action you want to perform on the object. The more important benefit involves performance. Because code refers to the object once rather than multiple times, this code runs much more efficiently than code without the With...End With construct. The benefits are even more pronounced when the With...End With construct is found in a loop.

23

Passing Parameters and Returning Values

Both subroutines and functions can receive arguments (parameters), but only functions can return values. The following subroutine (found under the Pass Parameters command button of the frmParametersAndReturnValues form) receives two parameters, txtFirst and txtLast. It then displays a message box with the first character of each of the parameters passed to it:

```
Private Sub cmdPassParameters_Click()
  Call Initials(Nz(Me.txtFirstName.Value), Nz(Me.txtLastName.Value))
End Sub

Sub Initials(strFirst As String, strLast As String)
' This procedure can be found by selecting General in
' the Object drop-down list in the VBE window
  MsgBox "Your Initials Are: " & Left$(strFirst, 1) _
    & Left$(strLast, 1)
End Sub
```

Notice that the values in the controls txtFirstName and txtLastName from the current form (represented by the Me keyword) are passed to the subroutine called Initials. That subroutine receives the parameters as strFirst and strLast and displays the first character of each parameter in the message box.

The preceding code simply passes values and then operates on those values. This next example (found under the Return Values command button of the frmParametersAndReturnValues form) uses a function to return a value:

```
Private Sub cmdReturnValues_Click()
    Dim strInitials As String
    strInitials = ReturnInit(Nz(Me.txtFirstName.Value), _
        Nz(Me.txtLastName.Value))
    MsgBox "Your initials are: " & strInitials
End Sub
```

```
Function ReturnInit(strFName As String, strLName As String) As String
' This procedure can be found by selecting General in
' the Object drop-down list in the VBE window
    ReturnInit = Left$(strFName, 1) & Left(strLName, 1)
End Function
```

Notice that this example calls the function ReturnInit, sending values contained in the two text boxes as parameters. The function sets the ReturnInit function equal to the first two characters of the strings. This returns the value to the calling routine (cmdReturnValues _Click) and sets strInitials equal to the return value.

> Notice that the function ReturnInit is set to receive two string parameters. You know this because of the As String keywords that follow each parameter. The function is also set to return a string. You know this because the keyword As String follows the list of the parameters, outside the parentheses. If you don't explicitly state that the function should return a particular type of data, it returns a variant.

The DoCmd Object: Performing Macro Actions

The Access environment is rich with objects that have built-in properties and methods. By using VBA code, you can modify properties and execute methods. One of the objects available in Access is the DoCmd object, which is used to execute macro actions in Visual Basic procedures. You execute the macro actions as methods of the DoCmd object. The syntax looks like this:

```
DoCmd.ActionName [arguments]
```

Here's a practical example:

```
DoCmd.OpenReport strReportName, acPreview
```

The OpenReport method is a method of the DoCmd object that runs a report. The first two parameters that the OpenReport method receives are the name of the report you want to run and the view in which you want the report to appear (Preview, Normal, or Design). The name of the report and the view are both arguments of the OpenReport method.

Most macro actions have corresponding DoCmd methods, but some don't. The macro actions that don't have corresponding DoCmd methods are AddMenu, MsgBox, RunApp, RunCode, SendKeys, SetValue, StopAllMacros, and StopMacro. The SendKeys method is the only one of these methods that has any significance to you as a VBA programmer. The remaining macro actions either have no application to VBA code, or you can perform them more efficiently by using VBA functions and commands. The VBA language includes a MsgBox function, for example, that's far more robust than its macro action counterpart.

Many of the DoCmd methods have optional parameters. If you don't supply an argument, the compiler assumes the argument's default value. You can use commas as place markers to designate the position of missing arguments, as shown here:

```
DoCmd.OpenForm "frmOrders", , ,"[OrderAmount] > 1000"
```

The OpenForm method of the DoCmd object receives seven parameters; the last six parameters are optional. In the example, I have explicitly specified two parameters. The first is the name of the form ("frmOrders"), a required parameter. I have omitted the second and third parameters, meaning that I'm accepting their default values. The commas, used as place markers for the second and third parameters, are necessary because I am explicitly designating one of the parameters following them. The fourth parameter is the Where condition for the form, which I am designating as the record in which OrderAmount is greater than 1,000. I have not designated the remaining parameters, so Access uses the default values for these parameters.

If you prefer, you can use named parameters to designate the parameters that you are passing. Named parameters can greatly simplify the preceding syntax. With named parameters, you don't need to place the arguments in a particular order, nor do you need to worry about counting commas. You can modify the preceding syntax to the following:

```
DoCmd.OpenForm FormName:="frmOrders", WhereCondition:=
"[OrderAmount] > 1000"
```

Working with Built-in Functions

VBA has a rich and comprehensive function library as well as tools to assist in their use. The subsections that follow introduce you to many of the commonly used functions. You will see examples of how they are used. Be aware that this is just a sampling of the functions available and provides you with just a few ideas of how you can use these functions. The potential use of the VBA function library is limited only by your needs and your imagination.

Built-in Functions

The following sections describe some of the most commonly used functions and provide examples. On some rainy day, you should go through the online Help to become familiar with the rest of VBA's built-in functions.

You can find the following examples in `basBuiltIn` in the `Chap23Ex.mdb` database.

The `Format` Function

The `Format` function formats expressions in the style specified. The first parameter is the expression you want to format; the second is the type of format you want to apply. Here's an example of using the `Format` function:

```
Sub FormatData()
    Debug.Print Format$(50, "Currency")
    'Prints $50.00
    Debug.Print Format$(Now, "Short Date")
    'Prints the current date
    Debug.Print Format$(Now, "DDDD")
    'Displays the word for the day
    Debug.Print Format$(Now, "DDD")
    'Displays 3 - CHAR Day
    Debug.Print Format$(Now, "YYYY")
    'Displays 4 - digit Year
    Debug.Print Format$(Now, "WW")
    'Displays the Week Number
End Sub
```

The result of using this function appears in Figure 23.11.

FIGURE 23.11

The Format *function, which formats expressions in the specified style.*

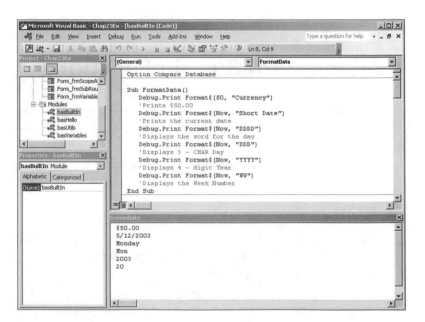

The Instr Function

The Instr function returns the position where one string begins within another string:

```
Sub InstrExample()
  Debug.Print InStr("Alison Balter", "Balter") 'Returns 8
  Debug.Print InStr("Hello", "l") 'Returns 3
  Debug.Print InStr("c:\my documents\my file.txt", "\") 'Returns 3
End Sub
```

The InStrRev Function

InStrRev begins searching at the end of a string and returns the position where the compiler finds one string within another string:

```
Sub InstrRevExample()
    Debug.Print InStrRev("c:\my documents\my file.txt", "\") 'Returns 16
End Sub
```

Notice that the InStr function returns 3 as the starting position for the backslash character within "c:\my documents\my file.txt", whereas the InStrRev function returns 16 as the starting position for the backslash character in the same string. This is because InStr starts searching at the beginning of the string, continuing until it finds a match, whereas InStrRev begins searching at the end of the string, continuing until it finds a match.

The Left Function

Left returns the left-most number of characters in a string:

```
Sub LeftExample()
  Debug.Print Left$("Hello World", 7) 'Prints Hello W
End Sub
```

The Right Function

Right returns the right-most number of characters in a string:

```
Sub RightExample()
 Debug.Print Right$("Hello World", 7) 'Prints o World
End Sub
```

The Mid Function

Mid returns a substring of a specified number of characters in a string. This example starts at the fourth character and returns five characters:

```
Sub MidExample()
    Debug.Print Mid$("Hello World", 4, 5) ''Prints lo Wo
End Sub
```

23

The `UCase` Function

UCase returns a string that is all uppercase:

```
Sub UCaseExample()
    Debug.Print UCase$("Hello World") 'Prints HELLO WORLD
End Sub
```

The `DatePart` Function

DatePart returns the specified part of a date:

```
Sub DatePartExample()
    Debug.Print DatePart("YYYY", Now)
    'Prints the Year
    Debug.Print DatePart("M", Now)
    'Prints the Month Number
    Debug.Print DatePart("Q", Now)
    'Prints the Quarter Number
    Debug.Print DatePart("Y", Now)
    'Prints the Day of the Year
    Debug.Print DatePart("WW", Now)
    'Prints the Week of the Year
End Sub
```

The `DateDiff` Function

DateDiff returns the interval of time between two dates:

```
Sub DateDiffExample()
  Debug.Print DateDiff("d", Now, "12/31/99")
  ''Days until 12/31/99
  Debug.Print DateDiff("m", Now, "12/31/99")
  ''Months until 12/31/99
  Debug.Print DateDiff("yyyy", Now, "12/31/99")
  ''Years until 12/31/99
  Debug.Print DateDiff("q", Now, "12/31/99")
  ''Quarters until 12/31/99
End Sub
```

The `DateAdd` Function

DateAdd returns the result of adding or subtracting a specified period of time to or from a date:

```
Sub DateAddExample()
    Debug.Print DateAdd("d", 3, Now)
    'Today plus 3 days
    Debug.Print DateAdd("m", 3, Now)
    'Today plus 3 months
    Debug.Print DateAdd("yyyy", 3, Now)
    'Today plus 3 years
    Debug.Print DateAdd("q", 3, Now)
```

```
    'Today plus 3 quarters
    Debug.Print DateAdd("ww", 3, Now)
    'Today plus 3 weeks
End Sub
```

The `Replace` Function

`Replace` replaces one string with another:

```
Sub ReplaceExample()
    Debug.Print Replace("Say Hello if you want to", "hello", "bye")
    'Returns Say Bye if you want to
    Debug.Print Replace("This gets rid of all of the spaces", " ", "")
    'Returns Thisgetsridofallofthespaces
End Sub
```

The `StrRev` Function

`StrRev` reverses the order of text in a string:

```
Sub StrReverseExample()
    Debug.Print StrReverse("This string looks very funny when reversed!")
    'Returns !desrever nehw ynnuf yrev skool gnirts sihT
End Sub
```

The `MonthName` Function

`MonthName` returns the text string associated with a month number:

```
Sub MonthNameExample()
    Debug.Print MonthName(7)
    'Returns July
    Debug.Print MonthName(11)
    'Returns November
```

Functions Made Easy with the Object Browser

With the Object Browser, you can view members of an ActiveX component's type library. In plain English, the Object Browser enables you to easily browse through a component's methods, properties, and constants. You can also use it to copy information and add it to your code. The Object Browser even adds a method's parameters for you.

The following steps let you browse among the available methods, copy the method you want, and paste it into your code:

1. With the VBE active, select View|Object Browser (note that the Object Browser submenu also shows an icon that you can use from the toolbar) or press F2 to open the Object Browser window (see Figure 23.12).

2. The Object Browser window is divided into an upper part and a lower part. You use the drop-down list at the upper-left of the window to filter the items you want to

display in the lower part of the window. Use this drop-down list to select the project or library whose classes and members you want to view in the lower part of the window.

FIGURE 23.12

The Object Browser, showing all the classes in the Chap23ex.mdb *database and all the members in the* basUtils *module.*

Copy to Clipboard

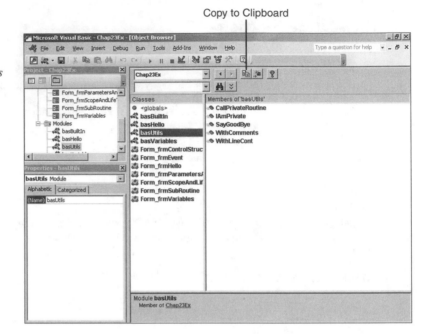

3. In the lower portion of the window, select the class from the left list box, which lists Class modules, templates for new objects, Standard modules, and modules containing subroutines and functions.

4. Select a related property, method, event, constant, function, or statement from the Members Of list box. In Figure 23.12, the basUtils module is selected from the list box on the left. Notice that the subroutines and functions included in basUtils appear in the list box on the right.

5. Click the Copy to Clipboard button to copy the function name and its parameters to the Clipboard so that you can easily paste it into your code.

The example in Figure 23.12 shows choosing a user-defined function selected from a module in a database, but you can select any built-in function. Figure 23.13 shows an example in which the DatePart function is selected from the VBA library.

FIGURE 23.13
The Object Browser with the VBA library selected.

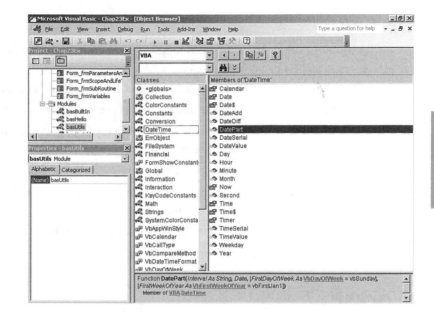

23

Summary

A strong knowledge of the VBA language is imperative for an Access developer. This hour covers all the basics of the VBA language. You have learned the differences between Code, Form, and Report modules and how to effectively use each. You have also learned the difference between event procedures and user-defined subroutines and functions. So that you can get the most mileage out of subroutines and functions, you have learned how to pass parameters to and receive return values from procedures.

You use variables throughout application code. Declaring each variable with the proper scope and lifetime helps make an application bugproof and easy to maintain. Furthermore, selecting an appropriate variable type ensures that the variable consumes the minimal amount of memory and that an application's code protects itself. Effectively using control structures and built-in functions gives you the power, flexibility, and functionality required by even the most complex applications.

For more information about the VBA language and programming in Microsoft Access, consult *Alison Balter's Mastering Access 2003 Desktop Development* and *Alison Balter's Mastering Access 2002 Enterprise Development*, both published by Sams Publishing.

Q&A

Q **Explain the purpose of the General Declarations section of a module.**

A The General Declarations section is where you declare variables and constants that you want to be visible to all functions and subroutines in a module.

Q **Explain the purpose of the `Option Explicit` statement.**

A The `Option Explicit` statement requires that you declare all variables before you use them. This reduces the number of errors in programming code.

Q **Explain the difference between the scope and the lifetime of a variable.**

A Scope refers to where the compiler can see a variable, whereas lifetime refers to how long the variable remains in memory.

Q **Explain the difference between a subroutine and a function.**

A A subroutine does not return a value, whereas a function does return a value.

Workshop

The Workshop includes quiz questions that are designed to help you test your understanding of the material covered and activities to help put what you've learned to practice. You can find the answers to the questions in the section immediately following the quiz.

Quiz

1. What does VBA stand for?
2. Name the two units in VBA code.
3. Standard modules are associated with a form or report (True/False).
4. Name three variable scopes.
5. What character do you use to add a comment to code?

Quiz Answers

1. Visual Basic for Applications.
2. Subroutine and function.
3. False. Class modules are associated with a form or report.
4. Local, Private, and Public.
5. An apostrophe.

Activities

Practice creating a standard module. Add a subroutine to that module. Create a new form. Add a command button to the form. Use the Click event behind the command button to execute the subroutine that you added to the module.

23

HOUR 24

Finishing Touches

Finishing touches can add polish and professionalism to an application. Finishing touches include things like menu bars, toolbars, and switchboard forms that allow the user to easily navigate from form to form within an application. In this hour you'll learn the following:

- How to add menu bars, toolbars, and shortcut menus to forms and reports
- How to build application switchboards
- How to set startup properties

Adding Custom Menu Bars, Toolbars, and Shortcut Menus

You can create custom menus, toolbars, and shortcut menus to display with forms and reports. There's no limit to how many custom menu bars, toolbars, and shortcut menus you can use. You can attach each menu bar, toolbar, and shortcut menu to one or more forms or reports. Quite often, you need to restrict what users can do while they're working with a form or report. By creating a custom menu, toolbar, or shortcut menu, you can restrict and customize what users are allowed to do.

Designing a Menu Bar, Toolbar, or Shortcut Menu

NEW TERM   Prior to Access 97, Access users could create a custom menu bar by setting
the MenuBar property to the name of a menu bar macro. This function is
supported in Access 2003 for backward compatibility only. In Access 97 and above, custom menu bars, toolbars, and pop-up menus are called *command bars*. To create any of
these three objects, you choose View|Toolbars and then select Customize. After you have
created a custom command bar, you can easily associate it with forms and reports by
using the MenuBar, Toolbar, and Shortcut MenuBar properties.

Follow these steps to create a custom command bar:

1. Choose View|Toolbars and click Customize or right-click any command bar and
   select Customize.

2. When the Customize dialog box opens, click the Toolbars tab and then click New.
   The New Toolbar dialog box appears (see Figure 24.1).

FIGURE 24.1

*Using the New Toolbar
dialog box to create a
new command bar.*

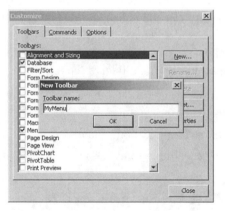

3. Assign a name to the new menu bar, toolbar, or pop-up menu. The new command
   bar then appears.

4. Click the Properties button on the Customize dialog box to view the properties for
   the newly created command bar. In the Toolbar Properties dialog box that appears,
   you name the toolbar, select the toolbar type, indicate the type of docking that's
   allowed, and set other options for the command bar. The Type drop-down list box
   allows you to select Menu Bar, Toolbar, or Pop-up. The options in the Docking
   drop-down list box are Allow Any, Can't Change, No Vertical, and No Horizontal.
   You can also choose whether you will allow the user to customize or move the
   command bar.

5. After you select the options you want, click Close.

Menu bars, toolbars, and pop-up menus are all referred to generically as *command bars*. The process you use to create each of these objects is very similar. You use the Type property of the command bar to designate the type of object you want to create.

Now you're ready to add items to the new command bar. The process you use depends on whether you are working with a toolbar, menu bar, or pop-up menu. To add items to a command bar, you click the Commands tab of the Customize dialog box, shown in Figure 24.2, and drag and drop command icons onto the new command bar.

FIGURE 24.2

Using the Commands tab to add items to a command bar.

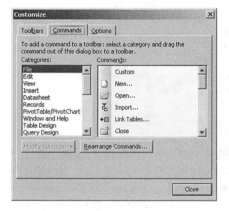

24

Here are some tips to help you to create custom menu bars, toolbars, and pop-up menus:

- To add an entire built-in menu to a menu bar, select Built-in Menus from the Categories list box on the Commands tab of the Customize dialog box. Click and drag a menu pad from the Commands list box over to the menu bar to add the entire built-in menu pad to the custom menu.

- To create a custom menu pad, select New Menu from the Categories list box. Click and drag the New Menu option to the menu bar. To modify the text on the menu pad, right-click the menu pad and type a new value in the Name text box.

- To add a built-in command to the menu, select a category from the Categories list box and then click and drag the appropriate command to the menu pad. The new item appears underneath the menu pad.

- To add a separator bar to a menu, right-click the menu item that will follow the separator bar and select Begin a Group. To remove the separator bar, again select Begin a Group.

- Menu items can contain text only or images and text. To select one of these options, right-click a menu item and select Default Style, Text Only (Always), Text Only (in Menus), or Image and Text. To customize an image, right-click a menu item and select Change Button Image and choose one of the available images. To modify the button image, right-click a menu item and select Edit Button Image; the Button Editor dialog box appears (see Figure 24.3). If you want to reset the button to its original image, right-click the menu item and select Reset Button Image.

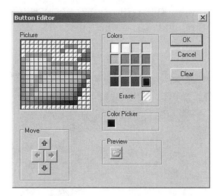

- If you want to modify several properties of a menu item at once, you can right-click the menu item and select Properties (while viewing the design of the menu) to open the file Control Properties dialog box (see Figure 24.4). In this dialog box you can select properties for the menu item, such as `Caption`, `Screen Tip`, `Style`, `Help File`, and `Help ContextID`. You can also associate an action with a custom menu item (which you'll learn about in the next section, "Associating a Command with a Menu Item").

Associating a Command with a Menu Item

In Access, it's easy to customize menus with both built-in commands and macros that you've written. For built-in commands, you can simply drag and drop commands onto command bars. To have a command bar item run a macro, follow these steps:

1. Right-click any toolbar or menu bar and select Customize to open the Customize dialog box. Select the Commands tab.

2. Select All Macros from the Categories list box (see Figure 24.5).

FIGURE 24.5

Selecting All Macros from the Categories list box.

24

3. Click and drag the macro from the Commands list box directly onto the command bar.

4. Right-click the menu item to change the name, button image, style, or properties.

Deleting and Renaming Menus

You can use the Customize dialog box to delete and rename menus by following these steps:

1. Right-click any command bar and select Customize. The Customize dialog box appears.

2. Click in the Toolbars list box to select the command bar you want to delete or rename (see Figure 24.6).

3. Click Delete to delete the command bar or click Rename to rename it.

FIGURE 24.6
Deleting and renaming a menu.

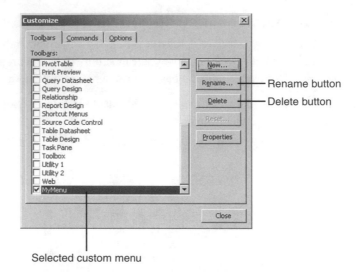

Rename button

Delete button

Selected custom menu

Creating an Application Switchboard

When you're creating an application with distribution to users in mind, you need to build the application around forms. This means that everything in the application needs to be forms driven. The application generally should begin by displaying a Main switchboard. The Main switchboard can then navigate the user to additional switchboards, such as a Data Entry switchboard, Reports switchboard, Maintenance switchboard, and so on. The easiest way to create such a switchboard is by using the Switchboard Wizard. Here's how it works:

1. Choose Tools | Database Utilities | Switchboard Manager. If you have not yet created a switchboard for the application, the Switchboard Manager message box appears, asking if you would like to create one, as shown in Figure 24.7.

FIGURE 24.7
The Switchboard Manager message box.

2. Click Yes. The Switchboard Manager dialog box appears, as shown in Figure 24.8. Notice that Access automatically creates a Main Switchboard.

3. Add additional switchboard pages. To do this, click New. The Create New dialog box appears, as shown in Figure 24.9.

FIGURE 24.8

Creating a new switch-board.

FIGURE 24.9

The Create New dialog box.

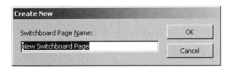

24

4. Type a name for the new switchboard page and click OK.

5. Repeat steps 3 and 4 for each switchboard page you want to add.

6. When you are done adding pages, the Switchboard Manager dialog box should look something like the one in Figure 24.10. You now are ready to add items to each switchboard page. To add items to the Main Switchboard, click the Main Switchboard entry and click Edit. The Edit Switchboard Page dialog box appears, as shown in Figure 24.11.

FIGURE 24.10

The Switchboard Manager dialog box after you add pages.

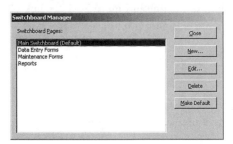

FIGURE 24.11

The Edit Switchboard Page dialog box.

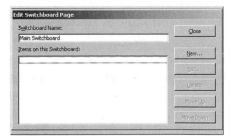

7. Click New to add a new item to the Main Switchboard. The Edit Switchboard Item dialog box appears, as shown in Figure 24.12.

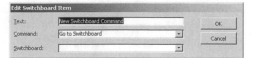

8. In the Text text box, enter the text for the new switchboard item.

9. Select an appropriate command from the Command drop-down list box. The commands that are available in this list box control the capability to go to another switchboard, open a form, and open a report.

10. The third item in the Edit Switchboard Item dialog box varies, depending on which command you select from the Command drop-down list box. If you select Go to Switchboard from the Command drop-down list box, for example, the third option enables you to select from available switchboards. If you select Open Form in Edit Mode, the third option enables you to select from available forms. If you select Open Report, the third option enables you to select from available reports. Select an appropriate value for the third option and click OK.

11. Repeat steps 6 through 10 to add each item to the Main Switchboard.

12. After you add entries to the Main Switchboard, the Edit Switchboard Page dialog box should look similar to the one in Figure 24.13. Click Close to return to the main Switchboard Manager dialog box.

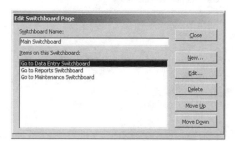

13. Repeat steps 6 through 12 for each switchboard page.

14. When you are ready to generate the switchboard, click Close on the main Switchboard Manager dialog box. Access generates the switchboard.

Follow these steps to add, remove, or edit items from an existing switchboard:

1. Choose Tools|Add-ins|Switchboard Manager. The Switchboard Manager dialog box appears.

2. Select the switchboard page you want to affect. Click Delete to delete the page, click Edit to make changes to the page, or click Add to add a new page.

3. If you click Edit, the Edit Switchboard Page dialog box appears. You can click the Move Up and Move Down buttons to move items up and down on the switchboard page. You also can add, edit, and delete items from the page.

4. When you are finished, click OK. The changes take effect immediately.

Figure 24.14 shows a completed switchboard.

FIGURE 24.14
A completed switch-board.

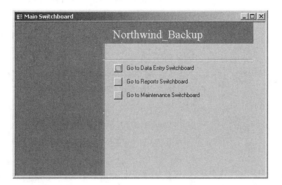

Setting Startup Options

Access provides several startup options that enable you to control what happens to an application when it is loaded. Figure 24.15 shows the Startup dialog box, and Table 24.1 lists each option in the Startup dialog box.

FIGURE 24.15
The Startup dia-log box.

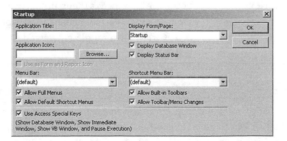

24

TABLE 24.1   Startup Dialog Box Options

Option	Function
Application Title	Sets the `AppTitle` property, which displays a custom title in the application title bar.
Application Icon	Sets the `AppIcon` property, which displays a custom icon in the application title bar.
Menu Bar	Sets the `StartupMenuBar` property, which specifies the custom menu bar displayed by default when the application is loaded.
Allow Full Menus	Sets the `AllowFullMenus` property, which allows or restricts the use of Access menus.
Allow Default Shortcut Menus	Sets the `AllowShortcutMenus` property, which allows or restricts the use of standard Access shortcut menus (that is, menus accessed with a right-click).
Display Form/Page	Sets the `StartupForm` property, which specifies the form displayed when the application is loaded.
Display Database Window	Sets the `StartupShowDBWindow` property, which determines whether the Database window is visible when the application is opened.
Display Status Bar	Sets the `StartupShowStatusBar` property, which determines whether the status bar is visible when the application is opened.
Shortcut Menu Bar	Sets the `StartupShortcutMenuBar` property, which specifies that a menu bar should be displayed by default as the shortcut (that is, right-click) menu bar.
Allow Built-in Toolbars	Sets the `AllowBuiltInToolbars` property, which indicates whether built-in toolbars are available to users.
Allow Toolbar/Menu Changes	Sets the `AllowToolbarChanges` property, which determines whether users can customize toolbars in the application.
Use Access Special Keys	Sets the `AllowSpecialKeys` property, which determines whether users can use keys such as F11 to display the Database window, Ctrl+F11 to toggle between custom and built-in toolbars, and so on.

Notice that the Use as Form and Report Icon option that is grayed out in Figure 24.15 is available when you designate an application icon (see Figure 24.16). When you check this option, Access uses the icon you designate as the application icon as the icon for forms and reports.

Use as the Form and Report Icon property

FIGURE 24.16

Using the application icon for forms and reports.

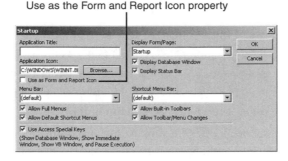

As you might have guessed, many of the options in the Startup dialog box apply only when you are running the application under the full version of Access (as opposed to the runtime version). You do not need to set the Display Database Window option, for example, if the application will be running only under the runtime version of Access. The Database window is never available under the runtime version of Access, so Access ignores this property when the application is run under the runtime version. Nevertheless, I like to set these properties to ensure that the application behaves as I want it to under *both* the retail and runtime versions of Access.

Only users with Administer permission for the database can modify the Startup dialog box options. If you want to ensure that certain users cannot modify these options of the database, you must make sure that they do not have Administer permission.

Summary

In this hour you have learned how to add finishing touches to applications. Finishing touches help to make applications look professional and appealing to users. You have learned how to add menu bars, toolbars, and shortcut menus to applications, as well as how to build switchboards that help users navigate around an application. You have also learned how to set startup properties.

Congratulations! You made it through 24 hours of Access training. You've not only learned the basics of working with Microsoft Access, but you've also explored many advanced techniques. Armed with the information that you've learned, you can fully harness the power of this very robust member of the Microsoft Office suite.

Q&A

Q **Explain the use of the Application Icon startup option.**

A Access uses the application icon specified in the Application Icon option of the Startup dialog box as the custom icon in the title bar of the application. This icon also appears on the taskbar when the user minimizes the application.

Q **Explain the use of the Menu Bar startup option.**

A Access uses the menu designated in the Menu Bar option of the Startup dialog box as the default menu that appears when the user first loads the application.

Q **Explain the use of the Display Form/Page startup option.**

A Access uses the Display Form/Page option of the Startup dialog box to determine the form that it displays when the user loads the application.

Q **Why would you want to display a custom menu bar or toolbar?**

A By using custom menu bars and toolbars, you can limit users to just the functionality that you want them to have. Furthermore, you can simplify the application by providing users with only the features they need.

Workshop

The Workshop includes quiz questions that are designed to help you test your understanding of the material covered and activities to help put what you've learned to practice. You can find the answers to the questions in the section immediately following the quiz.

Quiz

1. What term is used to describe menu bars, toolbars, and shortcut menus?

2. What property is used to differentiate between a menu bar, a toolbar, and a shortcut menu?

3. You can customize the image associated with a menu item (True/False).

4. What tool allows you to easily create application switchboards?

5. What menu options do you select to find the tool that allows you to create application switchboards?

Quiz Answers

1. Command bars.

2. The Type property of the command bar.

3. True.

4. The Switchboard Manager.

5. Tools|Database Utilities|Switchboard Manager.

Activities

Practice adding menus, toolbars, and shortcut menus to forms and reports. Practice building an application switchboard that allows you to navigate among the forms and reports that make up an application. Set the various startup properties and watch the effect they have on the application.

24

INDEX

Symbols

& (ampersand), 288, 296
* (asterisk), 40, 62, 85, 180
@ (at sign), 288
\ (backslash), 297
: (colon), 288
, (comma), 288
$ (dollar sign), 288
= (equality) operator, 185
> (greater than) operator, 64, 185, 288, 296
>= (greater than or equal to) operator, 185
<> (inequality) operator, 64, 185
<= (less than or equal to) operator, 64, 185
< (less than) operator, 64, 185, 288, 296

_ (line continuation character), 512
% (percent sign), 288
. (period), 288
(pound sign), 40, 85, 288, 296
? (question mark), 40, 62, 85, 296
; (semicolon), 297
/ (slash), 288
0 placeholder, 288, 296
3D control effects, 341
9 placeholder, 296

A

a placeholder, 296
Access file format, 142
Access Logon dialog box, 481

C

C placeholder, 296
calculated controls, 350, 375
calculated fields
creating, 195-197
queries, 305-307
Call statement, 502
calling event procedures, 502-503
Can Grow property
controls, 340, 369
reports, 388
Can Shrink property
controls, 340, 369
reports, 388
subreports, 383
Cancel property (controls), 348
candidate keys, 157
Caption property
controls, 339, 367
fields, 289, 327
forms, 225
reports, 248
captions, 367
fields, 289
labels, 214
Cascade Delete Related Fields option, 171-173
Cascade Update Related Fields option, 170, 173
case sensitivity of passwords, 470

CBFs (Code Behind Forms), 496
Change Logon Password tab (User and Group Accounts dialog box), 478, 482
changes, undoing, 34, 77-78
changing passwords, 477-478
characters, literals, 297
Chart Wizard, 92
charts
PivotCharts, 433-435
reports, 235
Check Box tool, 220
check boxes, 220
CheckBirthDate subroutine, 263, 268
CheckGender subroutine, 265, 269
checking spelling, 47
child tables, 37
Choose Builder dialog box, 203
class modules, 496-497
clearing fields, 33
client/server applications, 8-9
Close Button property
forms, 228
reports, 250
Close command (File menu), 24, 33, 90
CloseAnyForm subroutine, 262

closing
databases, 24
forms, 88
queries, 68-69
reports, 106
tables, 33
Codd, Dr. E. F., 156
Code Behind Forms (CBFs), 496
Code command (View menu), 502
code modules. See modules
Collapse All command (Subdatasheet menu), 46
colon (:), 288
colors
control background colors, 341
reports, 250
Column Count property (combo boxes), 219
Column Width property (combo boxes), 219
columns
defined, 134
freezing, 42-44
hiding/unhiding, 45
unfreezing, 44
widths, 42
Combo Box Wizard, 215-219
combo boxes, 215-219, 231
comma (,), 288

Else statement, 512-513

empty fields, 294-295

Enabled property (controls), 345-346

Encrypt/Decrypt Database command (Security menu), 445

Encrypt/Decrypt Database dialog box, 445

encrypting databases, 445-446

End key, 31

enforced referential integrity, 172, 192

Enter Key Behavior property (controls), 347

Enter Parameters dialog box, 433

entity integrity, 161

equal sign (=), 185

error checking, 46-47

event procedures

calling, 502-503

creating, 500

defined, 496

precedence, 505

private procedures, 504

public procedures, 503-504

events

associating macros with, 266-267

event procedures

calling, 502-503

creating, 500

defined, 496

precedence, 505

private procedures, 504

public procedures, 503-504

triggering macros from, 267

exact match queries, 59-60

Excel spreadsheets

exporting files to, 399-401

importing data from, 403-405

linking, 408

Expand All command (Subdatasheet menu), 46

Export command (File menu), 416-418, 464

Export dialog box, 398-399, 422

Export Form dialog box, 418

Export Query dialog box, 416

Export Report dialog box, 464

Export Table dialog box, 398, 416

Export Text Wizard, 401

Export XML dialog box, 422

exporting files

to another Access database, 398

to ASCII, 401-402

documentation, 464

example, 410-411

to Excel spreadsheets, 399-401

to HTML

forms, 417-418

query results, 416

reports, 418-419

tables, 416

to XML, 422-423

Expression Builder, 197-198, 260, 308, 350-351

expressions

adding to controls, 350-351

adding to macros, 260-261

calculated controls, 375

creating in queries, 197-198, 308

date expressions, 187-188

Expression Builder, 197-198, 260, 308, 350-351

Extensible Markup Language (XML), 9

exporting data to, 422-423

importing, 423-424

X-Z

Your Guide to Computer Technology

www.informit.com

Sams has partnered with **InformIT.com** to bring technical information to your desktop. Drawing on Sams authors and reviewers to provide additional information on topics you're interested in, **InformIT.com** has free, in-depth information you won't find anywhere else.

ARTICLES

Keep your edge with thousands of free articles, in-depth features, interviews, and information technology reference recommendations—all written by experts you know and trust.

POWERED BY
Safari

ONLINE BOOKS

Answers in an instant from **InformIT Online Books'** 600+ fully searchable online books. Sign up now and get your first 14 days **free**.

CATALOG

Review online sample chapters and author biographies to choose exactly the right book from a selection of more than 5,000 titles.

 SAMS www.samspublishing.com